Effective Meetings for Busy People

Effective Meetings for Busy People

Let's Decide It and Go Home

William T. Carnes

McGraw-Hill Book Company

New York   St. Louis   San Francisco   Auckland
Bogotá   São Paulo   Johannesburg   London
Madrid   Mexico   Montreal   New Delhi
Panama   Hamburg   Singapore
Sydney   Tokyo   Paris
Toronto

Library of Congress Cataloging in Publication Data

Carnes, William T
  Effective meetings for busy people.

  Includes Index.
  1. Corporate meetings. 2. Meetings. I. Title.
HD2743.C37   658.4'56   79-19770
ISBN 0-07-010117-5

34567890   DODO   89876543210

The editors for this book were Robert L. Davidson and
Beatrice E. Eckes, the designer was Mark E. Safran, and
the production supervisor was Sally Fliess. It was set in
Palatino by University Graphics, Inc.

Printed and bound by R. R. Donnelley & Sons Company.

Contents

v

Author's Preface

This book is about meetings, meetings that will not go away despite wishful thinking. I shall admit to their ineffectiveness, their inefficiency, their tedium, and the utter impossibility of doing much to improve some kinds of meetings. But *decision-making meetings* are the worst at their best, and at their worst they are the most awful meetings imaginable.

Yet decision-making meetings are the ones we must attend; these are the ones for which we cannot "let George do it." Fortunately, something *can* be done to improve decision-making meetings, and this book will describe, with details, the methodology for turning "command performance" nightmares into something alive and useful and desirable. If meetings are inevitable, should we not learn how to make the best of them? The answer is "Yes, of course," and we should get started. But this book will upset a few old theories; it will pull rugs from under old institutions and traditions; it will make you ponder what you have been doing and, I hope, teach you some new tricks while saving you money and time. It may even entertain you a bit, while showing you the way to get more use and fewer ulcers from your next decision-making meeting.

Inasmuch as this book may start a few small revolutions in the decision-making capitals of industry and government, it might be wise to begin with a few words of a general nature before tearing to bits all our most esteemed chairmen and their followers at the very beginning of Chapter 2. Therefore, a few urgent "whereases" have been squeezed into this Author's Preface, a few "necessities" are documented in Acknowledgments, and the introduction and background are poured out in Chapter 1.

First, I must state, firmly and without apology, that these principles of the Goldfish Bowl deliberative conference are drawn from real life as the practices and procedures of an important committee in a major industry; they are not creatures of academia, developed from scientific or logical deduction. These practices are the final result of five decades of tinkering with real-life decision processes in that industry rather than new ideas generated as a possible solution to old mistakes. These means of deciding complex matters have been utilized, essentially in their present form, for a quarter century, with only fine-tuning being applied to the process, rather than being an oscillatory reaction to some transient psychological upset. The industry is commercial air transportation. The activity is the standardization of the electronic devices and systems utilized by the world's airline aircraft. The entity is the Airlines Electronic Engineering Committee (AEEC). The organization is Aeronautical Radio, Incorporated (ARINC), the airline industry's own telecommunication company.

The necessity for expedited standardization caused that effort, but the usual methodology for standardization produced little benefit and proved much too ponderous and expensive. It was that evolutionary improvement in the standardization process for this major industry which produced a new methodology applicable to decision making that finally evolved into the Goldfish Bowl deliberative conference as the best possible environment for complex, large-scale decision making.

Second, this book is applicable to decision making for any purpose, not just for standardization. And although examples are given throughout the text to illustrate the application of the Goldfish Bowl deliberative conference and its methodology to product standardization, such "how to do it" is *not* a purpose of this text. Product standardization is a highly complex and very specialized field and must be the subject of a separate text. True, much industry and government decision making relates to some kind of standard, but product standardization is different from, for example, the standardizing of procedures, practices, regulations, policies, or just plain words.

Yet, because it was the product standardization effort that produced a better methodology for deliberative decision making than had been applied before, this text must give some background information on the need for airline standardization, the history of its evolution, and the benefits realized (Chapters 1 and 15 and Appendix 1). The application of this text is much broader than standardization: it pertains to the gamut of deliberative conferences in industry and government, in which there is strong motivation to develop a consensus where at first none seems to be possible. It is this motivation that generally pervades commerce (where industry is paying the bill) which makes simplification possible in traditional parliamentary procedures. This text will explain where and how to effect such simplification in the interest of speeding up a democratic process that traditionally is as lengthy as the 7-year itch in most pedigreed organizations and sometimes is equally ponderous in industry. It will concentrate, not on standardization, but on improving communication between and among a chairman and the meeting participants to expedite the decision making that is the foundation of commerce and industry. These processes have worked for one industry, resulting in a great economy of time, effort, and funds, and they will work for many industries in a broad spectrum of applications.

Third, not only has improved standardization sired the improved deliberative processes known as the Goldfish Bowl deliberative conference, but the latter has spawned innovations and improvements in other areas. One such improvement is in the field of conference room arrangement and hotel negotiation, with its subsets of meal planning, travel arrangements, social activities, and all the rest. This text will touch on these topics only to make the basic topic more understandable through the inclusion of such ancillary matters. Although this text will offer new angles, many other texts and magazines give more detailed coverage of that phase of conference management activity; however, I believe that the reader will profit from the new material on coffee breaks (Chapter 22), some mention of humorous happenings and how to make them work for you (Chapter 23), and some sacrilegious remarks about "that other type of conference" (Chapter 24) to achieve a better understanding of the Goldfish Bowl deliberative conference and its processes and procedures.

Fourth, the Goldfish Bowl is a form of deliberative conference, or the form of methodology utilized in such a conference, in which the process of large-scale decision making is parallel rather than serial and in which the procedures are informal, flexible, and thoroughly optimized for debate, deliberation, and decision, with all parties affected or involved present in the conference. It is a public meeting in which large-scale decision making occurs and is publicized.

The foregoing paragraph is intended as an explanation, rather than a lexicographic definition, of the term "Goldfish Bowl." Although the term implies a large affair subject to wide public scrutiny, it may be applied to a small meeting of, say, five people, if that meeting is publicized to and welcomes all the parties and groups and individuals likely to be concerned with the decisions. The distinction is that not just users are invited but that suppliers, regulators, administrators, inventors, and even "legal beagles" and "bean counters" are aware of the meeting and are adequately represented. A meeting held by an association, with only association members invited, could hardly be called a Goldfish Bowl deliberative conference. Neither could a corporate new-product meeting be called a Goldfish Bowl deliberative conference if the sales department were excluded.

Before the reader dismisses the Goldfish Bowl technique as just another group dynamics gimmick and probably a variant of the "fishbowl technique" known to psychologists, let me explain that the Goldfish Bowl and the fishbowl technique have nothing in common except the use of similar words. The fishbowl technique is a methodology used in group dynamics work and for group therapy in the field of psychology and social work. Although the term seems to be widely used in that field, I have found little in the available literature to define or explain it. Research at the Library of Congress turned up only three references, all in recent periodicals, none of which is suitable for a reference here. Thus, although the term "fishbowl technique" might seem to be related etymologically to our term "Goldfish Bowl," I must state categorically that the only relation is pseudoichthyological.

It may seem suprising that the name Goldfish Bowl as a description of the type of meeting, the environment of the meeting, and the processes of the meeting as it evolved was originated by a corporation legal counsel. The background of what happened and why it happened, more than a decade ago, is documented in Appendix 2.

Fifth, my use of the term "chairman" must be explained here. Not only do I avoid the term "chairperson" throughout the text, but I have used the words "he" and "man" when I mean "he or she" or "man or woman." I recognize the probable scorn of some feminists, but I believe that the clumsy nature of the acceptable alternatives for a text on conferences would produce even more objections.

Sixth, already in this Preface (and later in the Acknowledgments), the reader will have discovered warnings that this text will not be the usual conference manual. By the time that the reader gets through Chapter I he will have discovered that the author has assumed that considerable authority will have been delegated to the chairman and, in Chapter 4, will discover that considerable relaxation will be urged in the formal procedures established by the usual texts on parliamentary law. Furthermore, the reader may be shocked by the suggestion, in Chapter 5, that the chairman can expedite business by using first names in a very large conference.

How did the formalities of parliamentary procedure originate in the United States? Is there any historical basis for relaxing the pedantic rules as we approach the twenty-first century? How can we protect minorities? Can we keep order?

We gain an insight into the origin of formality when we observe that written parliamentary procedures began in the United States at about the time that the Constitution was written. Thomas Jefferson, in his *Manual of Parliamentary Practice* (ca. 1800), looked to the long experience of the House of Commons in encouraging strict and formal procedures as a means of protecting an important minority in the U.S. Congress. The traditions of his *Manual* were carried over into other writings, including the early works of Gen. Henry Robert in *Robert's Rules of Order*. The presumption seemed always to be that *all* deliberative bodies would forever have differences, differences that in the past had been so great that they "divided mankind into parties, inflamed them with mutual animosity, and rendered them much more disposed to vex and oppress each other, than to co-operate for their common good," in the words of James Madison, written in 1787 in his No. 10 in the series of *The Federalist Papers*. Several months later, in his No. 55, Madison applied this characteristic of political parties even more broadly: "In all very numerous assemblies, of whatever characters composed, passion never fails to wrest the scepter from reason."[1]

It was natural that when General Robert started writing *Robert's Rules of Order* in 1874 (first published by S. C. Griggs and Company in 1876), he would lean heavily on the traditional practices of Thomas Jefferson and others who followed him. Whether it was simply a continuation of a long tradition or a firm belief in Jefferson's dictum stated in the last sentence of his *Manual of Parliamentary Practice*, "It is very material that order, decency, and regularity be preserved in a dignified public body," or for whatever reason, Robert prescribed the same measures of protection for minorities in his *Rules of Order*, intended for use by clubs, societies, lodges, and other chartered organizations of members. The formal rules and procedures seem always to have been perceived as the best means of protection for minorities, whether political or nonpolitical.

Certainly we should not expect to change the established patterns of any organization today. If a body operates satisfactorily under formal rules, that system should probably be continued. If a body has a long record of success without such rules (or possibly *any* rules), why should we suggest change? The informal approach happens to be the author's preference, and this text will lean pretty heavily on a quarter-century successful application of that preference. The author suggests that many new organizations can probably profit by this experience.

Thus, because the *role* and *purpose* of today's deliberative bodies, particularly deliberative decision-making groups in business and government, are considerably different from the bodies envisaged by Thomas Jefferson at the birth of a new republic two centuries ago, this text will offer some suggestions that most certainly are at odds with the old ideas.

Perhaps General Robert envisaged a possible future relaxation in his own *Rules of Order* when he wrote this:

> A chairman will often find himself perplexed with the difficulties attending his position, and in such cases he will do well to heed the advice of a distinguished writer on parliamentary law, and recollect that "The great purpose of all rules and forms is to subserve the will

[1] *The Federalist Papers*, The New American Library of World Literature, Inc., New York, copyright © 1961.

of the assembly rather than to restrain it; to facilitate, and not to obstruct, the expression of their deliberate sense."

That was the way General Robert expressed it in *Robert's Rules of Order* (page 125 of the 1907 edition, as reprinted in 1978 by Bell Publishing Company, New York). At the same time, Robert offered additional advice in "Hints to Inexperienced Chairmen," which appeared on pages 160–162 in the Bell Publishing Company's reprint of the 1907 edition, carried forward essentially unchanged into the 1951 edition published by Scott, Foresman and Company, Glenview, Illinois, and then dropped in that form from the 1970 edition. Here is the last paragraph of that section:

> Know all about parliamentary law, but do not try to show off your knowledge. Never be technical, nor be any more strict than is absolutely necessary for the good of the meeting. Use your judgment; the assembly may be of such a nature through its ignorance of parliamentary usages and peaceable disposition, that a strict enforcement of the rules, instead of assisting, would greatly hinder business; but in large assemblies, where there is much work to be done, and especially where there is liability to trouble, the only safe course is to require a strict observance of the rules.

It is that advice from General Robert that this text will build upon and apply to today's business world of meetings and conferences.

WILLIAM T. CARNES

Acknowledgments

To the most wonderful industry in the world and to all those thousands of nice people in that industry—airline officials, avionics suppliers, government regulatory people, and the many others who have worked with the Airlines Electronic Engineering Committee (AEEC) or its predecessor entities—I respectfully and thankfully dedicate this book.

To my own technical and secretarial staff and top management in Aeronautical Radio, Incorporated (ARINC), I express my thanks for a collective 30 years of dedicated help and commitment to a goal: the best aviation electronics that can be bought, but at an affordable cost with the minimum expenditure of industry time and money.

To the stalwarts of the past in our industry; to those who are still alive and kicking and can read here about nostalgic happenings; and to those who have passed on to that land where standardization is easy but unnecessary, conferences continue all day as one long coffee break, no one ever argues with anyone else during a debate, and parliamentary procedure becomes whatever you wish it to be—I would like to say, "Thank you for helping get it all started."

To those in our industry who have contributed laws, precepts, or syndromes for this text or those who have prompted the use of anecdotes, personal experiences, or ideas, I extend my thanks. Though they are not always identified by name, the origins of your contributions will be known to you and me.

To the ARINC legal firm of Kirkland & Ellis and its many staff lawyers who have had some part in shaping the activities of AEEC, I express my thanks. I particularly appreciate the advice and counsel of Charles R. Cutler and Richard C. Lowery.

To Dr. James L. McLain, Professor of Music Emeritus of American University and Organist and Director of Music Emeritus of Metropolitan Memorial United Methodist Church, I extend my gratitude for his encouragement and help and for first performing so effectively the song "Let's Have a Meeting, and We'll All Be There," the theme song of this book, which resulted from the happenings described in Chapter 26.

And to the official members and all the many past members of the committee that caused it all, the Airlines Electronic Engineering Committee, I express my profound thanks for a job that was complex, time-consuming, and seemingly thankless at times. You are the individuals who have made up what has been the brainiest collection of knowledge and capability of any committee of any industry, anywhere, ever. What you have discovered, sometimes by accident I admit, has proved to be sound, proper, and permanent. You have developed the ability to think as a single individual might think but with a perspicacity and a combined intellect that have astounded those of us who have watched. You have pioneered in consensus development processes; you have found ways through the abysmal swamps of disillusionment over adversity; you have discovered routes to successful decision making when not even a path was visible to others. Your methods will be studied by many others and undoubtedly improved upon. You got it all started: the first major improvement in the efficiency and effectiveness of committees since the invention of the circulating fan for smoke-filled conference rooms.

And then I must extend personal thanks to several more individuals: first, to ARINC's Chief Engineer, Francis L. Moseley, who got the effort started at ARINC in 1939 and introduced the first airline industry specification-writing effort; second, to ARINC's postwar Chief Engineer, Charles R. Banks, who was the first Chairman of the Airlines Electronic Engineering Committee in 1949 and established the committee as we know it today; and third, to the new, third Chairman of AEEC, B. Richard Climie, who has succeeded me in that post and has already done a memorable job in continuing the effort started so many years ago.

And last, for Maxine, for 40 years a cheerful greeting each night after many a late meeting and often a ruined dinner on that account; and, on her behalf, for all the thousands of spouses everywhere who make a meetinggoer's life tolerable, with a laugh and a smile, whether waiting at home or waiting in a hotel room in Cedar Rapids, or possibly Munich, for some meeting that started before breakfast to finish; to these dedicated helpmates we should offer a toast—if we ever get out of the meetings long enough.

WILLIAM T. CARNES

Effective Meetings for Busy People

"Let's Have a Meeting, and We'll All Be There" is the continuing cry of government, commerce, and industry. Saying it another way, "If *you* call a meeting, I'll *have* to be there." Whether you or I like meetings or abhor them, we are both destined to spend much of our commercial or government life attending them. You will attend my meetings (for your own protection), and I will attend yours (to find out what you are up to); and we will both attend thousands of other people's meetings, conferences, seminars, symposia, task force sessions, working-group get-togethers, and committee meetings. You will complain, loudly, and I will object, noisily; but we will go.

Everybody Attends Meetings to Decide Things

You or I need not be an active member of industry or government to become caught up in the whirlwind of meetings. If it is not the Parent-Teachers Association, it is the Civic Association Committee on Billboards, a committee of the League of Women Voters, the Baptist Elderly Care Working Group, or the Main Street Litter Cleanup Executive Committee. You may have discovered that by yourself you could not get the Main Street litter cleaned up, but with a committee, possibly working through an association, you could begin to make some progress. Everybody laughed when you sat down on the piano bench (your neighbors had filled the other seats in your home) and suggested a committee to clean up the litter. A committee? Why does the mere mention of a committee cause everyone to snicker? (I, too, shall snicker over a committee when I get to Chapter 7.)

We think we need a meeting to decide what to do. So we ask a bunch of people to serve on a committee, and they decide that someone must call a meeting. The consequence is new motivation for a proliferation of entities and subentities to do something or decide something. Obvi-

1

The Goldfish Bowl for Decision Making: Deliberative Conferences in the Round

ously, all these tasks need doing, or do they? Inasmuch as we are never quite sure *who* should do the starting, what should be started or eventually decided, and what should be done about it, we never pay much attention to established rules, principles, or parliamentary procedures or even to any requirements of the law until somebody complains. Until something is actually decided or accomplished or we all are ready to act on something, we don't hear any complaints. Then it all starts. We now learn that we have violated all the established rules, precepts, practices, and traditions. Or so it seems from the complaints of our critics.

We Hate Meetings, but We Go Anyway

Does the foregoing sound like the dilemmas you have observed in your church group, your lodge, your civic association, your company, your trade association, your government, your world, your life? Do your groups then revert to a ponderous procedure of parliamentary discipline with a careful following of all written-down charter requirements, bylaws, established rules, and precepts? Or, even worse, do you find your group caught up in a wild oscillatory frenzy, in which at one minute you are following the rhetoric of rules and at the next you are breaking the same rules, never quite sure what you should be doing or why? If either this mad roller coaster or a dogmatic arbitrariness describes your organization, I say, "Welcome to the club." If you ponder the seemingly inconsistent behavior patterns of the organizations with which you must deal every day as a part of your important decision making, I say, "This book is for you."

Decision making by a meeting can be effective and sensible. The answer is not in increased authority for the decision makers. The solution is not one of eliminating meetings, of abolishing committees, boards, and panels, or of setting up new rules to replace the old ones. Some of these things may happen as a consequence of other direct improvements, but by themselves such changes are inconsequential help.

If you hate meetings with a purple hate, as many who must attend meetings do, you have already cut from your calendar almost all that are unnecessary. The ones left are those that have a chance of *deciding* something or *doing* something. You have already scuttled the ones at which nothing except talk is likely. Action, or decision-making, meetings are the only ones you have left.

And If You Don't Yet Go, You Will

But perhaps you are not one of those lucky people who have savored many meetings as part of the activity of their organizations. Your time, too, will come; you, too, will get promoted into that mad world of meetings, boards, and conferences in which you can enjoy that 2-hour, three-martini business luncheon, sandwiched (perhaps literally) into the middle of that "standard" 6-hour conference day. You, too, can enjoy the wit-sharpening byplay of that lively and enervating discourse of erudite, cosmopolitan contemporaries of the near great. You, too, can experience the ego-building elbow contacts in that hallowed hall. You will then be a part, an important part, of life. *That is the acme of perceptive participative parliamentarianism.* Yes, eventually, it shall come to you, too, and then you can join others who have gone before you in participatory hatred of meetings.

Isn't This Book Just for Chairmen?

But hold everything! Even if I should get promoted into the conference participation echelon in my organization, that doesn't mean that I would ever become a chairman of anything. Attendees can leave meetings whenever they get bored; why do *I* need any book on improving meetings? Only the chairmen and other officers are capable of fixing anything; such a book as this would be wasted on me. If this is your answer, the author may have to let you in on a little secret that, for other readers, he will keep to himself until Chapter 33. But if you really wonder about that question, the author may have to offer you special dispensation to read, right now, all of Chapter 33. But not the rest of the readers. You must take these chapters in their proper order, as you do not need this special cheering up at this point in the text.

Thus, I have established that this book is for you, whether or not you attend meetings now and whether or not you are the chairman of anything now. Even if you are an adolescent and your most complex committee decision making *now* is that of selecting the site for your next outing with the scout troop, this book can help you be prepared for that future day when you can join the adult world and go to big meetings.

Many have pondered the reason why we seem to want to decide everything by means of a committee, or by a meeting. And then, after a meeting has been decided upon as the means of solving some superproblem of a community, an industry, or other entity, no one seems to want to attend; everyone wants *others* to go. But everyone affected by the matter shows up anyway, necessitating a mammoth drive to "reduce the size of committees to make them manageable." We all vacillate between two extremes: we know that we must have committees and meetings to settle things; we also know that they turn out to be less effective than we had hoped; and this conflict of emotions produces chaos in the administration of committees and their meetings.

Why Do Americans Seem to Have More Meetings Than Other People?

It's probably true that Americans do have more meetings. Even if it were not true, the world believes it to be true, probably on the basis of what a widely quoted Frenchman wrote a century and a half ago. It seems that Alexis de Tocqueville, a French statesman and author, visited this country in 1831 and wrote about his visit after he returned to France. These writings were widely publicized in books by the International Association of Convention Bureaus and others. De Tocqueville made the point that Americans of all ages, all conditions, and all dispositions constantly formed associations. He proceeded to describe the wide variety and scope of such organizations, formal and informal, and observed that Americans wanted to do by means of an association what was done throughout Europe by the decrees of government people. Naturally, de Tocqueville attributed this associationitis (or what we would call committeeitis) to freedom from a paternalistic government and an official church. The freedoms of democracy cause the clumsy constraints of living with it, and yet we have become a nation of committees without much training in committee methodology.

We should not assume from all this that only Americans suffer from committeeitis. Europeans are fast learners; they can get just as bogged down in committees as we do, and just as quickly. We can't really see much difference today, although there was a notable difference a quarter century ago. Nor do we find very much difference when we look outside the Western world. Our Russian friends accept all the principles of committees just as we do. As best we can determine, totalitarianism does not seem to reduce the problems of decision making. While Russians are extremely curious about how we make decisions in our Goldfish Bowl deliberative conferences, they seem only to want to learn the technique; we have sensed no desire to change it. Although politics may change the appearance of debate in the political arena, we see little evidence of significant differences between East and West in the complex technical world. It seems that a common solution acceptable to all is far more important than any parochial interest in winning.

Thus, wherever you may travel, there can be no escape from committees, boards, and panels; they will follow you to the ends of the earth. Committees are your destiny.

Shouldn't Someone Write a Book?

But if everyone everywhere is in this same kettle of soup, both needing and abhorring meetings, why is there not a suitable and proper solution in the established literature on committees, boards, and panels?

Should there not be some simple how-to-do-it book in every bookstore and library to which the neophyte can turn to learn "one, two, three" steps in dealing with a new committee with a new and complex task?

The author will avoid a direct answer to that question for a moment to recount the experience of an acquaintance who was faced with that same question some years ago. This acquaintance, whom I shall call Harold, discovered recently that I was writing a book "on conference management." He felt that this book would be an extraordinary contribution to the literature and proceeded to explain his reason for such a claim. Harold is an anthropologist, the only real, live anthropologist I know, and some years ago he was working for a United States government agency in international aspects of anthropology. As a part of that work, he found himself with an assignment to organize and administer an international decision-making conference related to that scientific discipline, only to discover that there wasn't much of anything available to help him to do it. He related his experiences as he relentlessly searched the libraries and bookstores. He sweated and tortured himself with worry, as he explained it, because the subject just wasn't explained.

Insurance Company Sales Meetings Get Lots of Advice; What About My Meetings?

What should Harold *do?* How do you start planning for a multinational conference that must *decide* something of importance? Harold found the usual books on conference planning and management, but I can guess that they concentrated on how a major insurance company should set up and administer a sales convention which the company's top qualifying sales representatives and their spouses attend as guests of the company management. (This is a type of conference that I shall only touch on, in Chapter 24 of this book.) Of course, not all books on conference planning concentrate on insurance company sales meetings, but a number do, because a lot of convention business is financed by insurance companies, appliance firms, or other consumer product sales organizations wishing to reward their top sales representatives.

Company meetings and association meetings traditionally are aimed at some purpose far removed from decision making. They may emphasize problem solving as a major purpose or even suggest that developing a plan of action is the aim. But, by and large, the major how-to books stay a long way from the real problems of deliberative conferences. Thus, was it any wonder that my friend Harold became instantly aroused when he learned of this new book? He had heard of all the usual "cures" for sluggish deliberation, such as:

1.   Make the committee *smaller* so that there won't be the impossible task of finding out what people want done.

2.   First, get all the influential people together separately, and convince them that they shouldn't argue in public but should accept the only satisfactory solution (yours) when it is proposed. If these first two cures don't work, try the third one.

3.   Subdivide the committee or the problem into several pieces and have these subcommittees or working groups sort out their problems before coming to the parent committee for resolution of the total problem.

While there are occasions when possibility 3 may be a proper way of proceeding (see the discussion of Oscar's syndrome in Chapter 22, the proper use of subcommittees in Chapter 24, and an informal chat of the principals near the end of Chapter 25), this is usually an utter failure if employed as a substitute for proper deliberation.

The Methods of Democracy Are the Methods of Decision-Making Committees

Harold did report to me on one book that at first seemed to explore an unrelated subject, that of democracy. He told me that this one book gave him greater insight into the *processes* of deliberation and its application to the type of conference he had to administer than all the other books and articles. The book, *Practical Applications of Democracy*, published by Harper & Brothers, New York (copyright 1945), was written by George B. de Huszar of the Faculty of European and Asiatic Area Study of the University of Chicago. It is interesting to observe the motivation for such a book in the questioning retrospective period after World War II, when democracy seemed to demand some better explanation for its failure in Europe during the late 1930s.

De Huszar's book suggests that democracy is not something to be talked about; it is something you *do*. The book concentrates on democratic *methods* rather than on democratic principles. The first how-to topics in the preface are "How to translate into action the beautiful but vague words: co-operation and co-ordination" and "How to transform empty-shelled institutions into living organisms."

The book does more than that: while describing forms of government under a description of democracy, it also gives an important lesson on deliberation and how to apply the methods of democracy to improvement of the effectiveness of deliberation: "But democracy is much more than a form of government: it is a kind of society where the development of the human personality is the aim, and co-operation the method. . . ." The author substitutes "do-democracy" for "talk democracy" and adds it to what he says was there before, namely, "consent democracy," a passive, sleepy form of accepting what the "others" want because it is too much trouble to object or to substitute something better than the usual solution. He urges creative participation by intelligent human beings in the cooperative solving of problems *together*.

I mention this book, *Practical Applications of Democracy*, here because for three decades it has shown the way to cooperative, democratic deliberation and decision making. It is ironic that it was rediscovered by an anthropologist searching, in outlandish places and in an outlandish field, for help in organizing a deliberative conference in this day and age.

What Do We Learn from Books on Sales Meetings?

My retrospective enthusiasm for a 1945 book should not imply that this is the only conference book to suggest problem-oriented committees, rather than standing subject-related entities, for decision making. Many books have been written about the business of conventions and the operation of committees. Books describe the problems and experience of the extremely large and profitable industry that serves convention planners of every corporation and every government entity. What is probably the best of a great many general guidance books on the subject is Coleman Finkel's *Professional Guide to Successful Meetings*, published by *Successful Meetings Magazine* (copyright 1976), a division of Bill Communications, Inc., Philadelphia. From it the reader will learn the proper method of arranging meetings and conferences, administering them, and the cleaning up after them, with heavy emphasis on company meetings, association meetings, and the corollary functions and services that must be understood to make those meetings successful. Although Finkel has written about all kinds of meetings in his magazine columns and books, he emphasizes that this book is not about deliberative meetings or even about decision-making meetings.

With industry and government depending so heavily upon deliberative decision making for the conduct of their business and the country's business and with such a great cost penalty for any but the most effective practices, why do so many authors of books on meetings ignore or treat with ultimate shallowness this highly important topic? Now that I have asked this rhetorical question, I find myself with no sensible answer.

What Do We Learn from Books on Parliamentary Law?

Now that my batting average on answering my own questions has hit a new low, let me ask some more questions just as difficult: why is it that the several great treatises that do cover deliberative conferences in complete depth (such as *Robert's Rules*) seem to emphasize mostly the practices and methods that are the least used in real-life deliberative conferences other than legislative ones? The question becomes even more confusing when we read such treatises very thoroughly and carefully and discover that most of the practices and methods set forth in this book have a solid basis in the *precepts* and *basics* of parliamentary practice, even though not actually sanctioned in the current rules and procedures of parliamentary law. That last is a mouthful and a brainful, and it is the meat of what this book contains: more about that in Chapter 4.

Or Should I Write My Own Book?

Here in Chapter 1 I must give a general introduction to a very complex topic, one which, as I have said, seems to have been left alone by most writers other than the interpreters and compilers of parliamentary law. To write in a general sort of way about some "new" conference management principles may seem about as futile as writing a new interpretation of Holy Writ. But how do you feel when you discover that the practices which your group introduced many years ago and fine-tuned over several decades can keep right on working successfully as you and other officers and members retire, so that the practices and procedures, rather than any particular people, are the cause of success? And you find that you are continually besieged by others for information on how this practice originated and how it can be applied to other organizations and functions, to the extent that a textbook is seen to be necessary?

The Methodology Has Worked for One Industry; Why Not for Others?

Yes! That's how this book came to be written. Some of the forcing functions that started the Airlines Electronic Engineering Committee (AEEC) down its road of exploring the unknown are explained in the Author's Preface and in the Acknowledgments section at the front. The true historical basis for the activity is set forth in Appendix 1 and in several anecdotes about the AEEC scattered throughout the text. Yet the major part of the text treats the application of these "new" (or at least rediscovered) practices and procedures that will do wonders for your organization as it has for one major committee.

Having the motivation to write is not sufficient in itself for a lucid exposition of such a complex subject. Fortunately, not all the inquiries regarding AEEC came from supporters. Particularly in the government

I discovered much inertia against *any* change; the questions I received were real, probing questions from people and offices that did not take kindly to any upset of their established practices. But their bosses wanted them to take a look, and they did; even if what they saw was good, they weren't going to like it; even if they liked it, they weren't going to implement it. And on and on. But the questions gave me just the pressure I needed to find real reasons, rather than fictional reasons, for our past successes. It took some probing and some careful introspection; much of the background of this introspection is explained in Appendix 1, under the heading "Ruminative Epoch VIII of 1971 Onward."

Let's Study General Robert's Book Carefully

It is interesting to observe the ruminative writings contained in the introduction to certain other books relating to this same, or at least a similar, topic. In *Robert's Rules of Order Newly Revised,* by Gen. Henry M. Robert, U.S. Army (Scott, Foresman and Company, Glenview, Illinois, 1970), we find a most interesting and enlightening historical treatment of the principles of parliamentary law. Previous editions of *Robert's Rules* had shorter versions, but the expanded history of the 1970 edition is undoubtedly the result of extended ruminative evaluation of the evolutionary changes that had taken place through the 100-year history of *Robert's Rules,* with a careful melding of that history with the longer history of parliamentary practice going back to the fifth century. General Robert did not write the complete history or even evaluate his own *Robert's Rules;* this task was undertaken by his descendants for later editions, and particularly for the latest, the 1970 edition. A careful reading of this historical section of *Robert's Rules* gives us a keen insight into the factors that were deemed of greatest importance as the practices and law evolved (see Chapter 4).

Lowell Thomas's Story about Dale Carnegie

Sometimes the ruminative review is undertaken by an outsider, as was the case with the introduction to Dale Carnegie's famous book. In the late fall of 1978, Lowell Thomas was lecturing in Washington. As is his custom, he no longer prepares a speech but talks about his experiences and then answers questions from the audience. (As he repeatedly says, "At my age, everything I say reminds me of something else.") Somebody in that audience was the proud owner of an early edition of Dale Carnegie's book, and he asked Lowell Thomas for any comment about the book that he cared to make. That question triggered Lowell Thomas into an interesting account of the circumstances behind his writing the introduction to the book for his good friend Dale Carnegie. Thomas explained that he could never remember exactly how many books he himself had written but that the introduction had been read by more people than anything else he had written. He explained that no one had believed it possible for such a tremendous sale of a single book to have extended over such a long period.

Noting Lowell Thomas's highly complimentary reference in 1978 to Dale Carnegie's 1936 best seller, I decided to review the book again, particularly Thomas's introduction. The key message I now see is that Dale Carnegie had been successfully teaching public speaking in New York City for a *quarter of a century* before his best seller was published. Further, through the years he had had published a variety of books, most of which were related to his first courses, public speaking for adults. Lowell Thomas's introduction repeats an important theme: "The ability to speak is a short cut to distinction." He continues, "It puts a man in the limelight, raises him head and shoulders above the crowd, and the man who can speak acceptably is usually given credit for an ability out of all proportion to what he really possesses."[1]

Dale Carnegie's Message to Decision Makers

Yet, despite the acknowledged advantage to an individual of learning how to speak properly and effectively, this is not the whole answer, as Carnegie himself explains in his preface to that best-seller book: "But gradually, as the seasons passed, I realized that surely as these adults needed training in effective speaking, they needed still more training in the fine art of getting along with people in everyday business and social contacts. . . ." He continues, "I also gradually realized that I was sorely in need of such training myself," and then emphasizes the real problem: "Dealing with people is probably the biggest problem you face, especially if you are a business man. Yes, and that is also true if you are an accountant, housewife, architect, or engineer."[2] Dale Carnegie was rather modest about himself and the market for his new book, as we may conclude when we observe that his worldwide best seller, *How to Win Friends and Influence People,* sold approximately half a million copies the first year; yet it had to go through four editions before as many copies were published as this book you are now reading had in its first printing.

[1]Dale Carnegie, *How to Win Friends and Influence People,* Simon & Schuster, New York, copyright 1936 by Dale Carnegie, renewed 1964 by Dorothy Carnegie. Reprinted by permission of Simon & Schuster, a division of Gulf & Western Corporation.
[2]Ibid.

I feel it imperative to draw a parallel here between the friendly, personal treatment of *other people* that Carnegie's book urges and the usual business practice of impersonal, almost gruff treatment of others that had been the norm before that time. The key to Carnegie's success (his own story) was in building upon the natural desire of people to be nice to other people in their daily dealings with them. The public-speaking part was a necessary ingredient in order that "nice smart people" might *communicate* with other "nice smart people." Thus, Dale Carnegie has given us a start by suggesting exactly where to begin in improving decision-making meetings.

Bullwhips and Smiles: The Mellowing of the Chairman as the Participants Learn Professional Audiencemanship

And now, dear reader, we are coming to the crux of what this book on "How to tolerate and make more effective those meetings that other people call and I have to attend for business or other reasons" is all about:

CARNES' CONSTRUCTIVE COMMITTEE CHAIRMAN CANON

Never use a bullwhip when a smile will do it better.

Unfortunately, as the paraphrased old German cliché states, we really ought to get smarter sooner than older, but we don't even learn the cliché until it is too late. As Dale Carnegie lamented his inadequacy in his earlier years, we all know that we have that trouble, but sometimes we fail to recognize it. Recently, a business friend of long standing found himself back in an original activity after many years in a different field. He was attending a meeting of this author's Airlines Electronic Engineering Committee after years of absence. I asked him what differences he could see, and his answer was: "Only that the chairman has mellowed with the passing years."

Historically, I can now see that the mellowing process did not begin at an early date. The reason is that when I took over that committee in 1952, I instituted numerous changes (the recommended practices of this text, but in a rather clumsy manner). I employed a method of implementation very much like the questions to committee members suggested in Chapter 5, in which the *authority* of the chairman (to maintain order and accomplish certain other functions as set forth in that chapter) was vested in the chairman directly by the members themselves. Because the changes were significant, the members immediately noticed the increased effectiveness of meetings and thereafter wouldn't have it any other way. They laughingly referred to the new regime as the "chairman with the big bullwhip," and they encouraged more of the same methods. As they themselves learned the rudiments of self-discipline over a period of time, the bullwhip was put away, but that latent image was always there, as this chairman became smart too late. A chairman must enforce a certain minimum of rules inexorably, and he may have to use a bullwhip if the membership decrees it to be necessary for the common good of the organization. But the training of chairmen is not the only thing taught in this book; audiencemanship training is also a prime goal through which chairman training can sometimes best be done.

An Introduction to the Beginning of the Rest of This Book

Now that I have provided here, in the Author's Preface, and in the Acknowledgments an introduction to the broad premises upon which this book is based, I should be a little more explicit in describing those premises before I start the how-to-do-it chapters. Here are those basic premises:

Premise No. 1   Serial decision making is the slowest of all possible management processes and, therefore, the most expensive and the least effective. Therefore, parallel decision making (the Goldfish Bowl for decision making), with everyone who is likely to be involved urged to be present and to take part in the debate, is the most effective and economical and *the most likely to produce lasting and acceptable decisions*, if we can just figure out some way to make this crazy idea work.

> NOTE: On September 26, 1978, in addressing a Washington, D.C., engineering symposium on managing government and industry decision processes, Dr. Eberhardt Rechtin, president of Aerospace Corporation, who has served in high-level posts in government as well as in industry, stated the problem: "One theory of management is that time to get a decision doubles for every two levels of management; thus, parallel instead of series decisions are best solutions."

Premise No. 2   Strict parliamentary procedures and laws that are abundantly necessary for legislative and certain other organizations are overly ponderous and confusing for certain kinds of deliberative actions, and the strict formality prescribed in such rules works to the detriment of cooperative problem solving in some instances.

Premise No. 3   In almost all *commercial* endeavors in which some legitimate decision or common action is desired, there exists an *overpower-*

ing common motivation for a solution that transcends the natural individual urge to have it my way. Thus, in commercial decision making we are not saddled with many of the political and other extraneous pressures for procrastination or narrow-minded solutions that exist continuously in the legislative decision making which begot almost all parliamentary rules and procedures.

Premise No. 4   The principles of democracy itself and the precepts set forth by such practical teacher-philosophers as Dale Carnegie would suggest that a careful use of the golden rule in such *parallel* decision making would best optimize the environment to let the natural tendencies of nice people to be nice to other nice people show through, in accord with Premise No. 3. Encouraging this informality and friendliness can overcome the predicted impracticality of any such parallel decision-making exercise and make the Goldfish Bowl practicable.

Premise No. 5   Once we admit to Premises Nos. 1 through 4, we will have started the process of simplifying and informalizing all the usually stated precepts for deliberative meetings. Yet we must do this without losing sight of the major goal stated in Premise No. 1: that we intend to capitalize on the major benefits of *parallel* decision making over *serial* decision making. This means that we must ever be awake to keeping unnecessary serial decision making out of the activity; otherwise, we would simply be substituting a new long path of serial decision making for an existing one. Thus, this leads me to one more important admonition:

Premise No. 6   To meet our stated goal, we must pull out all stops to notify the decision makers and others with information or beliefs that can and should influence those decision makers and *get them to the church on time*. Otherwise, somebody will miss the important wedding.

This Book Is for ———

Whew! As I said in the beginning, this book is for you, whether you are a chairman of anything or not, whether you are a member of anything or not, and whether you ever expect to attend any meetings or not. Meetings are democracy in action, do-democracy, the study of people, the art of people watching, and the "people are funny" show of real life. Whether this book will make you *love* attending meetings, I can't say, but it certainly should make you much more tolerant of your fellow human beings as you learn to understand them better. And when you do attend meetings, I wager that even the seats will seem a little softer after reading this book.

A dmittedly, a deliberative meeting with some 200 to 500 participants is a lot different from a small committee meeting. It can be
somewhat like a town meeting or a state legislature session, but it is
really different. As in a town meeting, we must assume that participants have more than a cursory curiosity about what is happening; participants know that they may be affected by the outcome of the meeting. Perhaps the meeting is for standardizing something; now
participants will be assumed to be either potential customers for the
product to be standardized or potential suppliers of that product. Each
has a specific monetary interest in the product specification and wants
it written his way, either because he commands a large customer market and has his own ideas of what he wants the product to do for him
or because he is a large manufacturer and wants the specification to
match up with his capabilities for design and fabrication or perhaps
even to coincide with a design he has about ready for production. *The
outcome of the meeting is worth dollars to the participant.* He also wants a
product defined with the greatest possible total market (for minimum
cost and maximum availability to the customer and maximum market
potential for the supplier). But most of all, he wants expedited decisions, but not such quick decisions that the community will later
change the spec or, even worse, insist on buying something "outside
the spec" after he has developed a standard product supposedly to a
spec acceptable to the whole industry.

Furthermore, it must be clear that such Goldfish Bowl conferences
are not the least bit similar to the usual sales meeting or company conference in which the boss is the chairman of the meeting and everyone
present works for him and has no independent say on policy matters of
the company or organization (see Chapter 18). The Goldfish Bowl can
be an effective medium for standardization when utilized as a meeting
of a whole broad heterogeneous community, industry, or group of
organizations. It is a deliberative conference which, under United
States antitrust laws, cannot *and should not* apply any pressure, com-

2

*How to Manage a
Goldfish Bowl Conference*

mercial or otherwise, to restrain commerce. Instead, if it is to be successful, it should supplement the usual commercial marketing processes to provide a means of ascertaining what the customer collectively
wants, needs, and is willing to pay for. There are many trade-offs in
product development that some direct customer-to-supplier communication can identify. Features that only a single customer wants should
be chargeable to that customer, not generally to the whole customer
community. Features that everyone wants and is willing to pay for
should be developed and improved in a true competitive manner with
the costs spread over the community of customers who will utilize those
features. Avionics for the airline industry is a particularly good example
in which such standardization has repeatedly paid off handsomely.
When several airlines have decided that it is now time to buy a new
batch of jumbo jets, the avionics for that $1 billion batch is no small
sum. The customers have discovered they *can* find a commonality in
their needs, whether for a small United States regional airline or for the
largest of the international airlines.

With these assumptions that a Goldfish Bowl conference is a large,
heterogeneous community unrelated by management hierarchy, it
should be evident that procedures for handling such a conference will
be different from the usual annual convention of an organization (see
Chapter 24, "The Pseudodeliberative Conference"), in which a superficial business meeting opens a multiday seminar with speakers
mouthing motherhood sentiments on the health and wealth of "our
organization" in a not very controversial manner. Nope! It is not a simple meeting. Even the *idea* of a Goldfish Bowl *deliberative* conference
can scare the daylights out of the ordinary meeting planner.

So let's consider the rudimentary modes of deliberative meetings in
a parliamentary sense and see what differences we should look for in
the Goldfish Bowl, compared with the usual small deliberative meeting.
First, it is important to recognize that there is only one rule for the
meeting attendee (despite everything that you have read on parliamentary procedure): he may do anything (within the bounds of propriety
in good company) that the chairman allows him to get away with.
Remember that the meeting attendee has a dollar (or perhaps even a
megabuck) reason for participating in that meeting. It is worth money
to him to have the meeting *do what he wants it to do*. There are no fun
and games here, with participants practicing parliamentary procedure
for the fun or tutorial advantage of it. These meetings are for business
and for real. (We have often quoted a figure of $500 per minute as the
calculated cost to *our* industry for *our* typical 3-day meeting, including
travel and housing and entertainment costs but not salary.) Thus, if one
supplier can get away with interrupting another speaker to make his

point, all suppliers should also be allowed that privilege despite the fracas that will ensue before the embarrassed chairman discovers his very bad mistake. Thus, the *major problem* of the Goldfish Bowl will always be the chairman. Even the best chairmen have their limitations, but success or failure rests squarely on the chairman, not on a bunch of written-down rules of procedure to which no one pays any attention.

Now that I have explained why the chairman is the key to success or failure, we need some suggestions for such a chairman so that he can avoid the usual but, unfortunately, not very well-known pitfalls. But before dissecting the chairman, piece by piece, let us look at the several modes that may exist in the meeting, either on purpose or inadvertently.

I have chosen to describe four specific modes that are identifiable in well-run and badly run, large and small, deliberative conferences. Depending upon the attention given to the meeting by the chairman, the meeting may shift from one to another of these modes at various times, finally shifting into the fourth mode when his attention is poorest. When the meeting passes into this mode (and every meeting is likely to pass into it for at least a few seconds), the chairman suddenly becomes extremely evident as the *problem*. Then, he has to extricate the meeting from the morass. Here the modes are presented in increasing order of confusion and futility for the meeting attendees:

1. *Triggered Ping-Pong mode.* This is the proper parliamentary practice whereby a speaker must first be recognized by the chairman. It is an ideal practice that is seldom followed except in formal deliberative meetings, in practice sessions, or in erudite clubs and fraternities. It is ideal for the inexperienced chairman but is extremely slow and ponderous.

2. *Self-disciplined Ping-Pong mode.* This is the usual variation of mode 1 whereby the chairman, ordinarily tacitly rather than explicitly, allows speakers to engage in rapid-fire debate between and among protagonists when he believes that the meeting can benefit from an exchange by experts who have a stake in the outcome of the deliberations. But in this mode the chairman must follow some very explicit rules if he is to keep control of the meeting and avoid either losing the interest of others or letting the meeting wander off into mode 3 or mode 4. There are many things that a chairman must watch carefully if a meeting is to remain in mode 2 for very long. These will be covered in Chapters 12, 13, and 21.

3. *Precarious Ping-Pong mode.* A dangerous step beyond mode 2 that is still acceptable for short periods, this is a mode in which participants are engaging one at a time in rapid-fire comment and countercomment applicable to the subject at hand and still of high interest to all participants. Sometimes, in a well-disciplined group, this mode can be highly effective as long as the chairman is watching very carefully and everyone present is helping to ensure that the meeting *never* switches to mode 4.

4.   *Random-splatter mode.* This is the only one of the four modes that involves undisciplined (non-Ping-Pong) speaking by several people at once or speaking followed by nonlistening, which is just as bad and is discussed in Chapter 13 under "Duplexer Failure Syndrome." This mode ruins more meetings and frustrates more participants than just about anything that can be done to anatagonize people who are in a meeting for a *real* purpose (see Chapters 12 and 13).

To use the time available most effectively, a good chairman should be able to let a meeting shift back and forth between modes 1 and 2 as appropriate and as the meeting itself determines what is best. A disciplined chairman will have a disciplined meeting which knows what is acceptable to the chairman, and the meeting will automatically sense when to shift modes even without any announcement by the chairman. That meeting will also know that the chairman will pounce on anyone who takes the first step into mode 4. As long as the meeting knows this, it can manage itself up to a point without intervention by the chairman, provided the chairman follows scrupulously certain principles, mostly the golden rule, of treating everyone the same and doing what is in the best interest of the meeting itself. (More details and guidelines are given in Chapters 12, 13, and 21.)

But first let's take a look at the kinds of chairman to illustrate the pitfalls of typical meetings caused by a chairman's idiosyncrasies. Here are several classifications of offenders:

1.   *Indifferent Horace.* This chairman is a classic, known to all meeting attendees as the guy who can't keep his mind on the subject and keeps getting into side discussions with associates, reading notes, or dozing off (you name it; he does it), to the consternation of someone who is trying to make a proposal to the group for some action but finds there is no one to hear it. The meeting comes apart, but the chairman never notices.

2.   *Inept Algernon.* This type is also a classic. He tries but doesn't know enough about the subject to recognize a good proposal from a bad one. Since he doesn't know the simplest parliamentary procedures, the effect is about the same as with an indifferent Horace. At least, Algernon tries. He might learn.

3. *Vacillating Timothy.* This chairman is the kind that can never be understood because he is so unpredictable. He may lapse into indifference, leaving the meeting in a shambles; he becomes a dictator for a few minutes to get the meeting back in shape, but then he lapses into the passive, sleepy type of chairman. He condones the practice of one individual and then bawls out another for doing the same thing. This chairman is very, very frustrating to any meeting.

4. *Flagellating Freddy.* This type is the all-the-time dictator who cannot tolerate any slight infraction of *his* rules and who rules in an unfair, rough procedure that is not conducive to the best cooperation of *volunteer* helpers in a community attempt to aid each other. He gets the means to the end mixed up with the end itself and leaves the impression that accomplishment is secondary to doing the work in a proper, prescribed (by him) manner. He is exemplified by the chairman who insists upon absolute, exact usage of complex parliamentary procedures in an environment in which it is neither necessary nor productive. He leaves the impression that he is more interested in showing off his erudite knowledge than in getting a job completed.

Now that we have looked at the problems and the culprits, let us consider the constructive side and list some of the things that make a *good* chairman for a large Goldfish Bowl deliberative conference.

RESPONSIBILITIES OF THE CHAIRMAN OF A GOLDFISH BOWL DELIBERATIVE CONFERENCE

1. Always remember that the rules for the meeting attender give him great freedom and that he is looking to the chairman to set and *enforce* the meeting rules and to enforce them fairly with respect to *all* participants and in the best interest of the meeting itself.

2. *Decide* which acceptable meeting mode is proper at any one time and ensure that the meeting knows which one the chairman intends at that time. If any doubt over that intent is possible (as with a group not used to the particular chairman), announce the mode and repeat the announcement frequently until all the meeting attenders know how to gauge the chairman's intent without such an announcement.

3. Rigidly ensure that at no time (not even for an instant) does the meeting shift into mode 4. And ensure that the meeting knows that any acceptance by the chairman of mode 3 is made with the promise that he will pounce immediately upon anyone attempting to move into mode 4. Make absolutely certain that the meeting knows that mode 4 is unacceptable under any conditions and that the chairman will *immediately* react. And be prepared to back that rule up with quick action before the violator gets his first words out.

4. Scan the meeting room *continuously* for raised hands, troubled expressions, lack of interest, or inattention, and learn to read minds, anticipate problems developing, and notice anything else that may interrupt the flow of communication from everyone to everyone else. Particularly watch for signs of the following problems (ways of correcting them are detailed in Chapters 12, 13, and 21):

a. Someone unable to hear someone else because of poor speaking, poor acoustics, or interference from talking by others. Correct this situation immediately.

b. Someone not *comprehending* what is being said. Although this incomprehension may be caused by poor acoustics, it is more likely to be caused by poor rhetoric, poor explanation, or other errors by the speaker; it must be corrected immediately if time is to be saved.

c. Someone disagreeing with what is being said. This requires a knowledge of facial motions and expressions but is highly important as a means of expediting the search for a consensus; when a chairman can discover such disagreement, he has advanced the meeting immensely and has saved it countless hours of discussion; otherwise, the disagreement would be discovered only after lengthy debate. If only one person in the room *knows* that a basic premise is wrong but doesn't get a chance to explain matters for an hour, a lot of valuable time can be wasted. If a knowledgeable chairman is watching the audience during a presentation (usually by an amateur who pays no attention to his audience while he is talking), the chairman can compensate for a lot of inexperience among the meeting attenders.

d. Someone who is directly involved leaving the room for a few minutes. If the discussion continues without that person, the whole subject will be back in debate as soon as he returns. The best course is to stop that topic and not waste time on it until any important actors in the drama can get back from the telephone booth or the washroom.

e. This problem is probably most important of all: someone who has just expressed his opinion to the meeting fails to hear the following speaker explain why he disagrees (described under "Duplexer Failure Syndrome" in Chapter 13). My experience shows that the typical inexperienced meeting attendee will make a point in a meeting and immediately engage in a private debate with a neighbor, usually on the same topic; he now becomes impervious to any arguments, pro or con, on his proposal. No one else in the meeting will observe that he has turned off his listening except an experienced chairman. If the chairman *doesn't* see this happen, the meeting can go on debating the topic for another hour oblivious to the fact that two protagonists for opposite points of view don't even know they disagree with each other; each thinks he has convinced the other to his view. That misunderstanding can take hours to sort out and waste much valuable time of the meeting unless an experienced chairman calls attention to it.

f.   Someone who is too hot, too cold, or otherwise uncomfortable to the extent that the chairman should do something about the discomfort. An experienced chairman knows that certain people in a meeting are excellent weathervanes and can give a good indication on the environment. Watch them for easy communication on the state of comfort of the audience.

5.   When an experienced chairman scans the meeting room continuously for communication with the audience, he can learn a lot, but he must learn how to do this without taking his attention from the speaker. He must always focus on the speaker to ensure that the speaker knows that the chairman is following, and *comprehending*, everything he is saying and proposing. Thus the chairman must learn how to scan the audience, particularly in the far corner of the room opposite the speaker's location, without the speaker or the audience being aware of it. With some practice, it is quite practicable for a chairman to tell a speaker, after he has finished what he thinks is a very convincing story, that Joe Doaks, back in the corner of the room, has some problems with what the speaker has proposed. The chairman then calls on Joe to explain his problem or his objection. This *can* be done in a deliberative conference of 500 people. It is an excellent time-saver. Remember that the chairman is bound to be the most experienced person in the room on such matters of procedure and methodology of conference management. If *he* doesn't *use* that experience, he is wasting time for everyone. He should develop a sixth sense that allows him to anticipate problems in the audience before they grow into mammoth time-wasters.

6.   Ensure, at all times, that the *whole meeting* knows what item and what question under it are being debated. Explain this repeatedly.

7.   Ensure, at all times, that *whole meeting* knows what the issue is or what several issues exist just as soon as the chairman can determine them.

8.   Ensure that before an issue is beaten to death, the *whole meeting* is made aware of who is on which side and their reasons and of who is undecided and their reasons.

9.   Never allow a proposal or even a suggestion to be ignored by a meeting. If you defer consideration of it, explain this and obtain the concurrence of the meeting. If objections exist, *find them* and have them

explained to the meeting. Have the meeting *act* on the proposal or set a time or date for its consideration.

10.   Ensure that any action, even tentative action, of the meeting is clearly explained to, understood by, and concurred with by the meeting even if it requires a question by the chairman to the meeting. Don't *assume* concurrence.

11.   *Never* depend upon the meeting's knowing parliamentary procedure. For even rudimentary practices, explain the procedure if in doubt of the meeting's knowledge.

12.   Use friendly but persistent persuasion to get the meeting to allow opinion sampling. This is difficult on controversial matters, for the simple reason that no one wants to expose himself to possible defeat until he is sure that he has everyone on his side. (There is a whole bag of tricks and procedures that can be used by an experienced chairman to find out the view of the meeting on any question, but this chapter won't go into them. See Chapter 21.) The important point to aim for is to find out, as early in the discussion as possible, who is on which side of an issue and whether their view is a fixed position or a flexible position that can be changed with argument, facts, or persuasion by the meeting. Until the relative size of the armies and the extent of their battle arrays can be brought into the open, it is very difficult to gauge progress or the lack of it in a deliberative session. Remember that it serves no useful purpose to continue a debate when a large majority is either in favor of a course of action or against a course of action. Once a majority develops and *the meeting becomes aware of that majority*, progress can be rapid to get to a point at which the matter can be firmly settled. As long as the meeting itself and the combatants can keep others in the dark on what they are in favor of or against, the meeting can make little progress. It is the chairman's duty to get the combatants to take positions, to say whether they are "for" or "against," "don't know," or "refuse to express any opinion," so debaters will know with whom to debate which points. Otherwise, meetings have been known to debate a topic all day, only to learn that all but a small minority had been in favor of the proposal since the beginning. A noisy minority can obstruct the actions of a majority, thereby violating the basic premise of all parliamentary procedures, unless a wide-awake and perceptive chairman ferrets out that situation. Opinion sampling, frequent and nonfinal, is the most effective way of uncovering such problems. Start sampling on inconsequential matters, such as whether the meeting room is too warm or too cold, and get the group used to the idea of the chairman's taking an opinion poll informally from time to time. (These polls help to keep the meeting attendees awake, too.)

13. Remember, again, that the chairman is the most experienced person in the room (if not, you have the wrong chairman) on matters of procedure and methodology for finding a consensus when none appears to exist. Thus it is the chairman's bounden duty to keep awake and attentive to everything going on and to make the meeting aware that he is. His every action must be in support of finding a consensus, searching out problems with that consensus, and ensuring that all persons in the room are willing to accept it as the consensus of the majority. They need not agree with it, if they are a part of the minority, but they *must* admit that it is the consensus of the *majority* for it to stand the test of time.

14. There are many other responsibilities too numerous to tabulate in this chapter. The foregoing are the ones that we have selected for prime emphasis here as those we deem of most importance to the *effectiveness* of *any* deliberative conference and, most explicitly, of the Goldfish Bowl deliberative conference that is to be optimized for maximum effectiveness in decision making on a large scale.

As noted in the Author's Preface, we have selected for emphasis in these first few chapters certain basic thoughts rather than the usual how-to-do-it topics of the chapters of the ordinary handbook on meetings. The most important items of Chapters 1 and 2 need to be supplemented here by a few additional items related specifically to the Goldfish Bowl deliberative conference. They will only be mentioned here; expanded coverage must await later chapters.

1.   Appoint a representative body of responsible members and give them decision authority (see Chapter 15).

2.   Seat those official members in the central area near the head table so that the chairman can see each member and easily poll members for opinions (see Chapters 21 and 27).

3.   Urge others who expect to take an active part to select seats immediately behind members, with those wishing only to observe sitting in the back or at the sides.[1]

4.   Circulate beforehand an agenda and suitable working papers relating to proposals to be presented to the meeting (see Chapters 11 and 16).

5.   Maintain a current mailing list of members and all others who desire to participate in the activity, and keep this group informed on what is expected to happen through regular mailings (see Chapter 11).

6.   Use a full-time professional staff and, preferably, a professional chairman and secretary if the work is of importance.

7.   Provide accessible, suitable, and comfortable conference facilities

---

[1]The origin of the seating arrangement in points 1, 2, and 3 is explained in Appendix 1: "Awakening Epoch V of 1952–1954."

3

Basic Methodology for a Successful Goldfish Bowl Conference

with meetings publicized well in advance to accommodate members, participants, and visitors (see Chapter 27).

8. Ensure that all members, participants, and even casual visitors know the responsibility of the members on behalf of everyone and also that everyone is welcome to submit proposals and comments by mail before and after any meeting and to participate freely during the meeting in any discussion, debate, or opinion sampling. Emphasize that the meeting is a public meeting open to everyone (see Chapters 14 and 15).

9. A helpful feature is a short premeeting administrative session, publicized to everyone as a meeting of the "body of representatives" for the chairman and staff to familiarize them with the agenda and action items scheduled. Such a meeting can greatly expedite the public meeting by alerting the chairman and staff to last-minute problems that may affect the time needed for various agenda items (see Chapter 17).

10. Utilize working groups or subcommittees to develop the detailed proposals in order to avoid technical details in the large general sessions (see Chapters 21 and 25).

11. Do not allow speeches, "presentations," or anything similar as a part of the deliberative conference. Explain to those who expect to make such a presentation that they should put their thoughts into a working paper for advance distribution and study and that they should be prepared to comment, *extemporaneously only,* on any point about which others wish to ask questions. *Do not fall into the trap of letting the deliberative conference turn into a symposium, or seminar, or talkathon.* A presentation can be tutorially useful at the very beginning of a series of complex deliberative conference sessions before any specific proposals have been developed for deliberation. But as soon as proposals begin to emerge, the presentation becomes essentially useless as a deliberative conference tool. A presentation degrades the deliberative process by frustrating those who want to get directly to the issues and debate them out, one by one. A presentation contains extraneous material on a bunch of unrelated issues rather than a recommendation on a single issue. Once started, a presentation must continue to the bitter end, and then the deliberative debate must usually start all over again. A presentation is usually just a mammoth time-waster in a deliberative conference (see Chapters 12 and 24).

With the foregoing points tabulated here, we shall, in Chapters 4, 5, and 6, depart from the general coverage of conferences (particularly the Goldfish Bowl deliberative conference) and concentrate on a very specific and much narrower topic than the others.

Why include a chapter on parliamentary practices so early in a text on deliberative conferences? Doesn't everyone know that parliamentary procedures have been standardized for 100 years? Isn't it common practice for *all* deliberative assemblies to follow, explicitly, the rules of parliamentary procedure in the interest of expediting and legalizing their actions? Now, I shall mark myself a revolutionary by answering the second and third questions with an emphatic "No." The answer to the first question should be obvious. But before you, dear reader, trot this book back to the bookstore to get your money back, I suggest that you read on and discover what I am up to and why I make such a distinction between "rules" and "basic premises."

Premises versus Rules

Keeping in mind the historical basis for formality of proceedings as a means of protection for a political minority, as set forth in the sixth point of the Author's Preface, how can we balance the need for effectiveness and efficiency in our modern business world with a long tradition of prudence still urged by parliamentarians today? Perhaps the best advice is that which Gen. Henry Robert stated nearly a century ago when he urged use of judgment, particularly with respect to an assembly of peaceable disposition, for which strict enforcement of rules would hinder business. Inasmuch as peaceable assemblies are what this text assumes will already exist or what the chairman will be capable of encouraging, such advice seems appropriate if the guidelines in this text for solicitous chairmanship are scrupulously followed.

Probably the most important advice that can be given to a chairman of a Goldfish Bowl deliberative conference—or, in fact, to the chairman and all the participants in *any* meeting in this day and age—is to follow carefully the fundamental premises and precepts upon which all proper parliamentary procedures are based. We must never forget that not only

4

Practical Parliamentary Procedures for Use in the Goldfish Bowl

does the minority have rights but members of the majority owe it to themselves to hear what members of the minority have to say, what they *feel,* and *why* they have those feelings and views. Emotions and feelings are an important part of the total picture in the search for the best answer and the best ideas for the solution (a totally acceptable, long-lasting solution) of a major problem. While political considerations will always dictate different factions and different views on political questions, it does not follow that other questions, particularly those in industry, will be fraught with such differences. The climate is not necessarily better at the start of debate, but the chairman can do much to help that climate improve. With some care and concern and solicitous empathy for those with different opinions from what seems to be the popular view, a much better *understanding* of the real problem can emerge. Unfortunately, a favorable climate for that understanding does not always exist.

But if a favorable climate can be made to exist, either because of a technical commonality of opinion, or because of a common need for resolving all issues to allow commerce to proceed, or for whatever reason, the parliamentary procedures can be less complex with no eroding of rights. Thus, since elimination of complex parliamentary procedures can be quite a time-saver, it behooves every chairman to develop the best mood and climate of a conference to facilitate the search for a consensus. A careful and perceptive chairman, always fair with everyone and always searching for what will best accommodate the majority with minimum upset to the minority, can do much to convince the conference of his impartiality and evoke its trust, thereby improving the effectiveness of the deliberative process.

A Myth: The Right Decision

In this introductory look at parliamentary procedures and the underlying philosophy on which they are predicated, I must dispel a few myths if we are to get to the root of how to find a lasting consensus in a Goldfish Bowl deliberative conference that may involve hundreds of people and organizations, all wanting their own way at the start. Here, I shall upset one particularly bad myth:

Carnes' Canon of "Right"

A deliberative conference seldom is successful in finding the "right" solution to a problem; it seldom ends up doing what the majority "intended" to do; and, in fact, it usually ends up doing *what no one thought it would do.*

The reason, of course, is that the word "right" has a moral implication while the Western world's embracing of democracy as a political system redefines "right" as the decision of the majority. It is the latter that a deliberative conference, particularly a large *public* deliberative conference such as the Goldfish Bowl, will ordinarily try to decide. Thus, we must abandon the idea that a deliberative conference decides on the basis of right and wrong, and we must accept the unqualified principle of basic democracy, whereby the decision of such a conference should and *must* be whatever the majority chooses to decide. Until a chairman can understand that premise, he will find himself tripping over his own feet and thoroughly confusing the conference every time he exhorts it to make the right decision.

Another Myth: Getting What They "Want"

Also, the chairman must help a conference understand its own limitations in what it *can* do. Most groups start their deliberations convinced that they will do what they "all" *want* to do, only to be frustrated in their discovery that this usually isn't possible. "Want" is a hopeless wish; deliberative conferences are constrained by practical problems that limit the boundaries of what can be decided. Conference attendees usually have rather lofty ideals, thinking that a simple decision will put into effect any kind of action that they have a whim for; they often believe that perpetual motion will immediately start to function as soon as they make a decision. It is only after long pondering of the likely consequence of each proposed decision that a conference comes down to earth and determines which, if any, of its many whims is actually practical as a decision. The participants eventually discover that there is no magic elixir in a decision of the usual deliberative conference that can generate superhuman energy. The motivation for action from such a decision must come from the motivation of the people who made that decision and probably from the commercial pressure that will be generated after the decision has been widely publicized and accepted by the whole community or industry. It is a very mature deliberative conference that can see all this in advance and carefully choose a decision that has some likelihood of generating that subsequent consequential action of the community or industry. The conference, therefore, must be carefully guided by its experienced members, with a lot of help from the chairman, into putting aside its impractical whims and wishes and sorting out a list of *practicable decision possibilities* from which it will select the most suitable decision. An inordinate amount of time is wasted by deliberative conferences in debating what the attendees would "like" to do.

The Answer: A "Suitable" Consensus

Again, let us remember that we are not discussing civic or club meetings that like to endorse resolutions in favor of mothers, the flag,
democracy, homemade apple pie, and good social security; our emphasis here is on *nonpowered* (nonlegislative) Goldfish Bowl conferences
searching for a consensus on important decisions that can stand the test
of time. The "good" decision must have an explanation and depend
upon *voluntary* contributions or investments of time, energy, and capital in a venture, probably commercial, which will sink or swim on the
basis of its own worth. The venture cannot survive by nice words that
appear in the resolution, decision, or action of the deliberative body.
Again, remember that the chairman is the most experienced individual
in finding a *suitable* consensus (assuming that you have selected the
right chairman) and that the chairman can best advise the meeting on
the pitfalls of debating the wrong questions and the wrong answers for
far too long a time.

Wants versus Hates

And even when a deliberative conference has finally set down a list of
the possible decisions open to it, that conference can still flounder
interminably as it tries to vote its preference—even the preference of
the majority. Afterward, the attendees may discover that their eventual
action was *not* the preference of the majority, and they still may not
have understood the processes which finally engulfed them, causing
them to shift gradually to a far different action from the one that the
majority would have believed likely. How can it be that the majority
was unable to get, in the final decision, what all its adherents had
intended to get? The answer lies in approaching consensus finding not
only from the "want and wish" side but from the "can't tolerate" side.
Remembering the basic premise of parliamentary law, that the majority
must get its way with an adequate hearing for the minority, we find
that a deliberative conference, properly following the right concepts
and treating the minority properly, will undoubtedly discover that the
minority view is not all bad and that the *people* on that side are not
bad. The conference learns the word "accommodation" and starts tabulating the possible courses of action in terms of "Who wants what?"
and also of "Who hates what?"

This latter negative question brings out new information that the
majority didn't have before: why are some possible actions completely
unacceptable to the minority, and others, although not liked, are less
objectionable? It is when the meeting starts to tabulate possible actions

in terms of quantitative "wanting it" and "hating it" that it becomes a mature deliberative body, finally able to find a consensus that may not please the most people but certainly infuriates the fewest people. Remember that the end result of a deliberative conference must never be just to get a decision; a conference decision that will not stand up as an acceptable decision afterward isn't worth the time to write it down. A decision that still remains in dispute by a noisy minority which thinks it can reverse the decision can help no one. Commercial firms are usually unwilling to risk investment in a product which may have a limited market if the decision remains inactive despite all the noise that the majority can generate.

Does the Majority Rule?

Thus, the myth that a deliberative conference is a tool of a majority, to do what it *wants*, what is *right*, and what it *intends* doing, is nothing more than that—a myth. An experienced chairman can alert a conference to such pitfalls before it wastes an inordinate amount of time and possibly ruins its credibility. Although a conference can be given this advice by an experienced chairman, we also know that experience usually has to be learned the hard way, by experimenting and by making mistakes.

Credibility and Practicability

A conference must learn through experience what can and should be attempted by its own people; it must learn through experience what is best left alone by the conference. Credibility is a conference's greatest asset, but this, like any reputation, is built slowly and painfully upon the record of the past, good or bad. A conference that develops its own capability and stature and carefully avoids attempting useless decisions, unstable decisions, or even decisions that are unkind to the minority will find its stature and credibility growing with every "good" decision. How an experienced chairman can guide a conference into such good decisions and into a position of recognized stature is a lesson in perceptive, disciplined concentration on learning through experience, aided by preconference analysis of possible courses of action and determined, but not so obvious, guiding and direction toward those possible actions and away from flimsy and probably popular, impossible, or at least impracticable actions. Sometimes (perhaps often) an experienced Goldfish Bowl chairman may discover that despite his long list of nice actions that are possible on a particular question, there is only *one single* practicable decision open to the conference, and this one is obviously unliked, unwanted, unsound, and abhorred by everyone. It is so unlikely as a candidate action that no one would suggest it or even discuss it if the chairman were to offer it. In such a case, the experienced chairman knows what the eventual outcome is bound to be but can do little, if anything, about it except to provide a suitable climate for someone eventually to offer it as the *only ultimate solution*. It may take a while, but a deliberative conference is a remarkable contraption. Given enough time and freedom of debate, it will find a consensus and talk itself, majority and minority alike, into that one practicable consensus, with all the correct reasons for its action. It will develop its reasons so that even a decision that on the surface appears silly will become erudite and comprehensible, and that decision will collect staunch supporters from both the majority and the minority factions.

A Decision That Lasts

Is this adoption of an unwanted decision by a deliberative conference an isolated, impossible, unbelievable happening? Not impossible, not isolated, but perhaps unbelievable until you have seen it happen innumerable times. This chairman *has* seen it happen time and time again. It is surprising when it happens but is now quite commonplace.

Its Best Consensus

It is perhaps fortunate that commercially motivated deliberative conferences have such a common aim to see a consensus develop, because it makes the task of the conference and of the chairman much easier than it otherwise would be. Thus, a chairman of such a conference is advised to be on the watch for signs of such motivation developing at the very beginning. When those signs become evident, as they most probably will begin to be evident, he should be prepared to start the relaxing process whereby the conference is allowed (by the chairman) to move in the direction in which it naturally will tend to move. A conference, particularly a deliberative conference motivated by commercial pressures, will tend to move in a direction that will expedite its own business. Certainly, in the beginning that conference will need some encouragement and even some cautious pushing in the direction in which it will eventually tend to move in finding that consensus; here an experienced chairman can do a lot to get it pointed in the proper direction. This is the circumstance in which a chairman's sixth sense can predict what is the most likely and most practicable course of action. Again, he should not emphasize what *he wants* or what he thinks *the attenders want;* instead, he must analyze what is the most practicable course of action for a consensus and, quietly and politely, point the conference toward that end. It will take a long time for a chairman to develop the experience with a particular group, industry, or community to gain its trust and ensure that he really has no ax to grind other than finding *its best consensus*. The advantages are great: economy in time is important, and finding a decision that will survive after the conference has adjourned is a major reason for rejoicing.

The Synergism of Consensus

Once the chairman and the conference accept the important precept that whatever they can decide upon and will last is right, the parliamentary procedures that are needed will be simplified automatically. Remembering the basic premise of parliamentary law, that the majority rules with careful consideration for the minority, the absent, and the community at large that would be affected by the decisions, we suddenly discover that most of the folderol drops by the wayside and that we have very little parliamentary procedure left. What we have left will not show off the prowess of the chairman; it will not allow the meeting to spend long periods debating the legality or the propriety of certain procedures; the group will now have to make its decisions and its debates sensible, economical of time, and logically sound for those who must understand the wisdom of the decisions when they read about them later. Everyone in the meeting, not just a chosen few who can follow every legal shift in the parliamentary maneuvers, will now understand not only what happened but *why* it happened that way; everyone will be capable of explaining the action to others who were not present. This synergism of getting an entire deliberative conference involved in a deliberative action is the most important key to a *lasting decision* (this process is explained in greater depth in Chapters 13, 16, and 21).

How to Make a Decision Stick

While most inexperienced chairmen will go to great lengths to avoid explaining an action to a meeting after it has taken place, the experienced chairman knows that it is the conference itself that must sell the decision of the conference to others affected. If the people at the conference don't know exactly what happened, there will be nobody to sell it. The conference itself must first be sold on the course of action; members of the minority must understand that they have been given a fair chance to defend their views and have been thoroughly unsuccessful. But even more important, the minority members must concede that even if they were to go home and rally their forces, they would be unable to sell their view in a later conference. When the chairman has ascertained that the minority has come to the conclusion that further procrastination is costing its organization more than an eventual win would save it, he can be pretty certain that the decision of the majority will stand the test of time: even the minority will leave the conference expecting to publicize the decision as the best of all possible actions. Not all decisions need this high degree of assurance of certainty. But such assurance can often be obtained by only slight additional time taken after the action: the chairman gives the conference a reprise of the action with a little time to ponder that action before he declares it final. It is surprising how much firmer a decision can be made by this simple action of careful, considerate reprise and explanation by the chairman *after* the decision has been finally made (Chapter 13 gives some helpful suggestions, and Chapter 28 explains the procedures and benefits of publicity for decisions). Remember, again, that we are considering deliberative conferences of a commercially motivated industry or community, not practice parliamentary training sessions, civic meetings, or club sessions, in which motivation for consensus may be totally nonexistent.

How to Simplify Parliamentary Procedures

Let's take a look at the simplified parliamentary procedures that oftentimes are the only ones needed, even in a very large deliberative conference, and see what can be done by the chairman and the conference itself to simplify its own procedures:

1. *Formal motions, seconds, and so on.* These are for the purpose of letting the chairman know what the conference is planning to do. If the chairman is awake, listens carefully for any proposal, and *reacts* to such a proposal, formal motions are a pedantic waste of time. Formal motions can be useful after the group has pretty well made up its collective mind on an action and is ready to formalize that action for the record, but a member of the group should feel that he has a receptive chairman awaiting a legitimate proposal for some action that has a reasonable chance of being accepted. Discussion and debate can be quite informal, with no hint of folderol just for the sake of folderol.

2. *Amendments to motions.* Amendments are absolutely taboo, first, because even the simplest amendments can cause immense misunderstanding and confusion (except in civic groups, clubs, and tutorial sessions, which thrive on complex parliamentary procedures). One amendment engenders another amendment. The situation gets worse rather than better. A chairman is advised to stop the discussion before it gets to that point and to ask the originator of the motion whether he likes the trend of the discussion. The chairman *can* do this. He can also ask the group whether it likes the trend or prefers the original concept

of the motion or proposal. A well-organized large conference can give the chairman a very fast reaction to such a question; once he knows the feeling of the conference, he can then suggest either (a) that the originator of the motion withdraw it in favor of a more acceptable one or (b) that the maker of the amendment withdraw his proposal because it isn't what the group wants.

Remember that the chairman is the agent of the meeting; anything he does that the meeting wants will automatically be the proper thing to do. But he must be sure that he does the *meeting's* bidding rather than press his own desires. A conference can waste far too much time in debating with itself the proper parliamentary procedure for withdrawing a motion or an amendment; such time is taken from the time that could have been used in debating the *issues.*

3. *"Committee of the whole" and "discuss informally."* Such complexities are highly important for formal organizations such as Congress and state legislatures and even for some formally chartered organizations that must, under the law, operate in a highly structured manner for legal reasons. But that is not the kind of conference we are talking about. The people who attend the commercially motivated deliberative conferences we *are* talking about would seldom be sufficiently familiar with such complexities for them to be anything except a tutorial training exercise and not a decision-making aid. I need not mention that seldom does an individual taking part in a decision-making exercise understand the five (and only five) methods of making an amendment: that only *two* amendments can be pending at one time; that any number of amendments can be made to a motion; there is a proper way to transact two pending amendments; that primary and secondary amendments have different functions and different ranking; that an ungermane amendment can be acted upon and made legal despite procedural mispractice, and so on, ad infinitum. Yet, by not asking for a formal motion, an experienced chairman can bypass all this folderol with a *cooperative conference wanting a consensus,* and he can handle substitution of proposals, amendment of proposals, and fine-tuning of proposals and actions without any hint of trouble, need for explanation, or arguing over procedure. But again, don't forget that the chairman must be the ever-solicitous agent, father confessor, fairy godfather, and perceptive, always-listening parent, to his "brood," the conference. If the chairman ever forgets this, even for a moment, he incurs the wrath of a spiteful conference that will unfrock him as someone with his own ax to grind.

4. *Motions to recess, adjourn, raise a question of privilege, and so on.* Such motions are unnecessary if the chairman is awake. If the air conditioning suddenly stops or a wall of water comes through the conference

room door, it shouldn't require a motion to attract the chairman's attention; whoever observes the problem should (and most certainly will) yell it out in simple language regardless of what he is interrupting. The chairman will *immediately* determine what should be done, whether the person who has the floor should stop while "we attend to more important matters" or whether the occurrence need not interrupt the proceedings. But the chairman *must react* to such a notice. He is the agent for the conference and must be responsive and protective of its comfort. Similarly, a parliamentary inquiry becomes absurdly unnecessary when there is no parliamentary action; instead, the matter becomes a simple question from someone who wants an answer. If someone has a question which the experienced chairman has not already explained satisfactorily, the chairman *should* be interrupted when the problem is discovered. Remember that parliamentary procedure was established by mutual agreement hundreds of years ago to accommodate both friendly and hostile people and organizations in meetings. It accommodates the needs of individuals by mechanizing the language and the form and the priority of such interventions by the people attending. But when few if any hostile people or organizations are present (remember our postulates), we need not have cumbersome and precise procedures for doing the simple things that come naturally when people (nice people) get together to work out their problems. A meeting (of the kind we are talking about) is seldom so large or so highly structured that an individual has difficulty in getting the attention of the chairman. And this observation gets us back to our starting premise that the chairman will be expert, solicitous, and ever conscious of what "his" conference (every last person in it) is *thinking*. If just one individual develops a frown or any other facial expression that is different, the chairman should react to it immediately.

5. *"Move the previous question."* This statement has no place in such a deliberative conference even if somebody in the room *does* understand what it means. *Demeter's Manual of Parliamentary Law* states: "This is a motion. Its name is misleading and hence it is frequently misunderstood and misapplied. 'Previous Question' is the technical term for proposing to terminate further discussion and amendments on a question before the body."[1] Pages and pages have been written in all the literature on this motion and the form and function of it. In 1801 Thomas Jefferson was explaining, in his manual, why it *had been* so confusing since 1604 when first used. General Robert was explaining it in the early editions; and later editions today explain why it is still confusing.

[1]George Demeter, *Demeter's Manual of Parliamentary Law and Procedure,* copyright © 1969 by Little, Brown and Company, Boston, by permission of Little, Brown and Company, p. 92.

Today, almost all authorities concede that no substitute words should be attempted to avoid the confusion. The term is correct, there is no other acceptable term, and the *proper* term *must* be used in parliamentary practice. Yet, I believe that in an informal meeting of friendly adversaries the term should never come up. If the chairman is the perceptive individual I have said he must be, *he* will usually be the first to discover that the consensus is as nearly complete as it can be. He, therefore, will be the one to suggest to the group: "Time is running out. Are you ready for another opinion sampling on Joe's proposal?" If the members are, the chairman should find it out in about 2 seconds without any formal words or pragmatic niceties. If more discussion is appropriate, the chairman should soon know it and encourage further airing of the issues. Opinion sampling, repeated and informal (which, incidentally, most certainly *is* encouraged by many experts), is the best means invented to date for the participants, as well as the chairman, to learn the members' feeling on a proposal. That, more than any other means, will indicate when the time is at hand to cease debate on a particular proposal. When repeated samplings show that opinion is fixed and no longer changing, there is little point in continuing the debate unless someone has a *new* point not already hashed over. It is the opinion sampling that finally convinces the minority that it cannot win its point and that it should concede and get on with bigger and better things. If a sufficient number of opinion samplings has been taken on a proposal, an action in concert with majority opinion will most likely stick afterward. Note, again, that there is a basic parliamentary rule that makes such a cloture and vote legal: Demeter emphasizes in his manual that, despite the parliamentary requirement for a two-thirds affirmative vote to stop debate, an inadvertent ruling of cloture by the chairman *to which no one objects* is just as legal as if the proper two-thirds vote had been given *before* the chairman closed debate.[2] Demeter explains several cases in which this situation can arise even when proper strict parliamentary procedure is being followed. But I must emphasize that a chairman who has not been considerate of the wishes of the meeting stands a good chance of being censured or of having his decision generate an appeal from the meeting if he attempts such action without a trusting conference.

6.   *"Call to order"* or an *"adjournment."* This is not a legal requirement for the conduct of business in most such deliberative conferences. Neither is the strict enforcement of any quorum rule of particular importance. Remember that we are assuming that the chairman is giving due

[2]George Demeter, *Demeter's Manual of Parliamentary Law and Procedure,* copyright © 1969 by Little, Brown and Company, Boston, by permission of Little, Brown and Company.

consideration to the absent members and others who would not expect to be present and yet would undoubtedly be affected by the decisions of the body. Therefore, whether or not the body is in formal session isn't very important under these ground rules.

7. *Other requirements.* Such requirements generally do not apply to these conferences. Very few requirements of parliamentary law apply to such a conference, once the informal nature has been accepted by the conference itself and the members have found that they are happy with informal procedures which aim at the basic premises of parliamentary law rather than the strict rules and procedures of parliamentary law. The point is perhaps best summarized by Demeter in his manual, in the section dealing with the responsibilities, duties, and *privileges* of officers, in which he states his "privilege #4":

> 4. To exercise informally such prudent leadership and initiative (without strict compliance with the rules) as in the exercise of sound judgment no one would be likely to object to—as when suggesting cessation of further debate, or allowing only one or two more speakers on each side of the question, or taking some other necessary routine or informal action as would expedite accomplishment of business—but to instantly desist if anyone objects, or put it to a vote for approval.[3]

In dealing with such other requirements, the chairman must be aware of his obligation to the conference at all times and, as the closing phrase in the foregoing quotation admonishes, he must be prepared to revert to proper parliamentary rules if things get sticky.

"Running" the Conference

As long as the chairman is properly managing the affairs of the conference and of everyone in it, including members of the minority and the absent, he should have no reason to fear reprisal or censure. But even if he errs by mistakenly believing that the group wants to decide a question in a particular way, he should take it as no personal censure when someone calls his attention to his error; he simply backs up and starts over at the point from which he started in the wrong direction. This can be done very effectively and with very little lost time and motion. It also serves further to convince the conference that the chairman has no preconceived notion of what he wants the meeting to do. Such double takes are normal and likely and should be spontaneous.

[3]Ibid., p. 251.

Members of the group should be encouraged to interrupt the chairman whenever they discover something that he himself (the expert) has missed. Never allow a meeting to proceed when anyone discovers or even suspects that it is headed in the wrong direction. It is far better to stop and reconnoiter at once than to risk wasting time chasing down some blind alley. Fast response *by* the chairman to such queries can encourage faster response by the conference itself when it suspects such departures from the proper path to a course of action if the chairman is awake, perceptive, and obviously solicitous of suggestions.

Watch the Basic Premises; Know the Rules, but Don't Overemphasize Them

It is an interesting learning experience that will go on forever, as a conference and its chairman together master the principles of good sportsmanship and conviviality in finding the best decision for the community. And, best of all, this simplified procedure does not require that the whole conference learn the intricacies of complex parliamentary procedure in order to get decisions with everyone a party to them. It does require that the chairman know the rudiments of parliamentary procedural rules even though he will seldom get an opportunity to apply them. Instead, he must read all the fine print in *Robert's Rules.* He must look in the back of the book, in the footnotes, in the Introduction, in the basic premises, and in the historical treatment and read what the manual calls the "genesis" of *Robert's Rules of Order.* Then he should read again, and reread over and over, the last paragraph of the Introduction, entitled "Principles Underlying Parliamentary Law," until he can quote it almost verbatim and get it engraved permanently into his forehead, if not actually into his brain. Also, the student of this simplified, basic parliamentary practice should review Chapter 1, "The Deliberative Assembly: Its Types and Their Rules," to gain a clear understanding of what the basic forms are and how they would differ in the informal processes of a nonhostile industry or community which must achieve maximum decision making per meeting minute. Other material in *Robert's Rules* is important, but it will probably not be remembered once the chairman has mastered the informal approach to the complete satisfaction of the conference itself, for the simple reason that he will never be called upon to use the material in *his* meetings.

Because readers may have few occasions to exercise their knowledge of parliamentary procedures, it is even more important that all, chairmen and meetinggoers alike, obtain their own copies of a suitable work on parliamentary procedure. The most useful information will probably be obtained from the oldest and most widely circulated work, namely, *Robert's Rules*, which sold more than 2,500,000 copies before the latest edition. Readers will want the latest edition, which in 1979 is the 1970 edition bearing the title *Robert's Rules of Order, Newly Revised*, published by Scott, Foresman and Company, Glenview, Illinois.

It should be obvious that a direct consequence of simplifying parliamentary procedures, as urged in Chapter 4, is the problem of maintaining some semblance of decorum and order in a meeting that may be almost devoid of the usual parliamentary stratagems and protection means. Yet, if the reader has taken careful note of the advice to chairmen given in Chapter 2 (supplemented with further instructions in Chapter 3 that will be expanded in later chapters), the methodology of the extremely large Goldfish Bowl deliberative conference will begin to make some sense. Now it is time to concentrate upon that major problem of the neophyte chairman: how must I act to maintain the order and decorum that must exist in the absence of the usual rules? This is certainly a ponderous question with a complex answer. Yet, I shall surprise that neophyte chairman by making a rather blunt statement: managing a large Goldfish Bowl deliberative conference and getting it motivated to make important and lasting decisions quickly and effectively is far easier than manipulating a small meeting into the same decision making. The large meeting may scare the neophyte, but it is the small meeting that really poses a challenge to neophyte and professional alike (you will learn more about this when you get to Chapter 17). Thus, after such a rash statement, let us proceed with the arguments and the procedures: this chapter will not tell all, but it will serve to induce you to take the rest of this text in the proper order. At the proper time, you will be given further explanation, which must, for practical reasons, be deferred from this chapter to later chapters.

5

How to Maintain Order in a Large Meeting: Practical Suggestions for the Chairman of a Goldfish Bowl Deliberative Conference

The Chairman: The Agent

In a Goldfish Bowl deliberative conference and in any meeting of any size and form, the chairman must be the fall guy, acting as the agent of the participants in keeping order and in ministering to their needs. To do this he must ensure that he does exactly what, and only as much as, the meeting collectively wants him to do. If any doubt exists over *whether* the meeting attendees *want* him to keep order and how it should be administered by him in their name, he can find out easily enough. He can ask them. But before asking, he should satisfy himself that he is willing to do what the participants will ask him to do. It does little good to ask a group this question and then, having received the answer "Of course we do," to discover that he is simply not up to it; he doesn't have the guts to do what has to be done to keep order. This is the usual explanation of why most meetings will not, collectively, ask their chairman to keep order. Most members concede that it is unfair to a volunteer chairman to turn him into a policeman for their benefit. Thus, they seldom ask, let alone urge, their newly elected chairman or president to do anything other than sit in the chair and preside. Everyone hopes that the meeting will be "nice" to him. Yes, it probably will, but only until a controversy breaks out over some mammoth question, such as whether the coffeepot should be half full or two-thirds full at meetings or other equally tantalizing debate issues.

HOW MUCH DECORUM IS WANTED?

To get this question clearly understood by the learning chairman, let us *assume* that he is up to enforcing whatever reasonable rules of decorum and procedure the group establishes. What rules *should* he ask them their wishes about establishing? Here is a list of candidate rules, good and bad:

1. *Start on time?* We put this proposed rule first because it is probably the most difficult one for a neophyte chairman to accomplish (*not* promise to accomplish—that's easy; *not* start "kinda" on time—that's very easy, by simply defining, subjectively, what "on time" is). Really, actually, regularly, truly to start on time is a mammoth undertaking that *can* be accomplished, but it requires real guts, finesse, and terrific motivating force; it is the subject of separate treatment in Chapter 29. For the moment, let us assume that you will *not* ask the meeting for its desires on this point, but, instead, that you will do about what *Robert's Rules*[1] suggests for the first meeting of a permanent society (and you must locate a copy of some earlier edition of *Robert's Rules* such as the

[1]See citation at the end of Chapter 4.

1907 edition recently reprinted, to find this *quantitative* suggestion inasmuch as the 1970 edition is not quantitatively specific): "It is not usual in mass meetings or meetings called to organize a society, to commence until ten or fifteen minutes after the appointed time, when someone steps forward and says: 'the meeting will please come to order. . . .' " Oh, if it were only that easy simply to "ask" the meeting to please come to order!

2.   *Maintain order when a disturbance takes place?* The maintenance of order is a most important requirement that any sensible body will certainly "want" the chairman to administer for them. But seldom will a member of that body, despite his frustration in being unable to hear another individual speaking, ask the chairman to do something about it. Unfortunately, the practice of most conference attendees, even professional meeting attenders, is simply to ignore the breach of rules or etiquette and to pretend that nothing is wrong, hoping that a subsequent speaker will explain or give some hint of what was being said. When this happens, it is a disgrace to the chairman for allowing it to happen, it is a disgrace to the body for not calling the attention of the chairman to the problem, and it is a disgrace to the speaker that no one cares sufficiently about his words to want to hear what is being said. The chairman is the one, *and the only one,* who can put the matter right (with one exception dramatized in Chapter 9 and further explained in Chapter 33). When a speaker is duly permitted to speak, he has certain obligations to the chairman and to the body.

The speaker is taking valuable time of the body; he should be allowed to continue only as long as he makes himself heard and *understood* and speaks on the point of issue (he is being relevant). When any of these requirements are not met, he no longer has any right to continue *if* the chairman interrupts him to tell him that he has exceeded his right. When the noise in the hall makes it evident to the chairman that members are no longer able to hear the speaker or understand him, the chairman must act immediately to have him wait for order to be restored and then tell him to continue from the point at which he was when the interruption started. The chairman should do this even though the interruption is not noise but members passing papers back and forth and thereby disrupting other members' concentration on the *content* of the words, although they can still hear the speaker. The chairman must watch for the *signs* of interference as well as the *sounds* of interference. Only the chairman is in a place where he can observe the members and observe their degree of concentration. But sometimes it is not the fault of the body but of the speaker when the participants cannot hear or understand him. Still, the chairman, although he should be courteous to a speaker unable to express himself loudly or sensibly enough, has an overriding obligation to the collective body itself that he must not relinquish. He *must* stop the speaker and have him move to a better position, where perhaps the amplifier system will better convey his words, or if the subject is not relevant, he has the obligation to call this to the attention of the speaker and *have the speech made relevant* or stopped. If *one* speaker is allowed *one* irrelevancy, the chairman, in proper fairness to all, must allow others their irrelevancies. The situation can get out of hand very quickly.

One common mistake occurs when a speaker gains the floor and inadvertently starts a lengthy argument for or against some point that the body has already either adopted or rejected firmly in prior debate. If a chairman, either unwittingly or stupidly, allows this type of speech to continue without informing the speaker of his error, he is committing another error on top of the first error (of the speaker). It is better to take a chance of embarrassing *one* member of the group than to risk embarrassing the whole meeting and the chairman by allowing a lengthy irrelevant speech. Eventually, the erring speaker would discover his error and be embarrassed anyway, and even more so. Remember your responsibility for kindness to the most people, not kindness to just one nice guy. Don't take what looks like the easy way out.

3.   *Require attendance and attention during meetings?* This is a question that you should *not* ask your group to have you enforce. Except for certain legislative groups, paid board members (with not just paid expenses but paid fees), and a few other exceptional cases, you should not expect people to attend a meeting or even a particular session of a conference that they themselves do not choose to attend. (You will find more coverage of this topic in Chapters 16, 21, 25, 26, and 29.) Be reasonable in trying to control a meeting; confine your control to those things which are reasonable and proper, and don't get so carried away by your responsibility to manage that you feel the urge to drive everyone beyond the proper limits of your authority.

Instead, let the motivation of the attendees work for you and for the meeting, and you will discover that you have produced a far better climate for the free and open exchange you need to find a consensus in a large and complex meeting. Showmanship, not a bullwhip, is the real answer. Once you realize that people will come in droves and work hard when they discover the proper relaxed atmosphere of encouragement, along with entertainment that is really interesting, you will find that they will work better than paid factotums for you and for each other, as only free volunteers can work. A Goldfish Bowl conference is really an intriguing adventure. It is an experiment in psychology; and it is always generating something new, something that is more appealing than a bevy of paid entertainers. A Goldfish Bowl deliberative conference is spontaneous; it is live entertainment of the best kind because the actors are real and the stage setting is real life, with commerce as the backdrop. And the stakes are high, with real money soon to be expended, based on the outcome of the meeting. There are no dull, dreary speeches about ethereal politics, or unreal science fiction, or staged soap operas. Instead, all the drama of history in the making unfolds before the actors themselves, who gasp at what they have produced, and every attendee is a part of that stage action of real life. Though not every participant can claim that he alone came up with the winning idea that solidified the consensus, everyone can brag that he was a part, an important part, of the group that made that important decision.

But hold everything. Are Goldfish Bowl deliberative conferences really *that* good? Are they *that* entertaining? Not ordinarily. But in the hands of a capable chairman who has studied the problem and knows the solution, such affairs can be highly intriguing and worthy of being classed as solid entertainment. If they aren't, the meetings will probably fall apart, and everyone will go home (as explained in Chapters 25 and 26); the chairman will wonder why no one comes any more. He should recognize the Goldfish Bowl for what it *ordinarily* is: a difficult working meeting that will take a lot out of every participant, a dreary, tiresome, soggy event that is frustrating, unsatisfying, and oftentimes meaningless to the onlooker. The chairman is the key to success of such an event. If he has studied the art of entertainment, the art of serving as a master of ceremonies, the tricks of the performing arts, and the methods of a good lecturer and public speaker and if he can combine all these with the skill of a director and producer, he will turn a dreary obligation meeting into something that is alive: a Goldfish Bowl deliberative conference of the best kind, the kind that attracts more and more attention from the people and organizations that you need to make your decisions broader, more nearly complete, more salable, more interesting, and easier to publicize.

Nope! Don't ever blame your participants for sleeping or for walking out of *your* conference. If you organize it, orchestrate it, blend it, and administer it with the deft hand of a pro, you will have them flocking back again despite the dull and dreary sound of technical topics on a conference agenda. You, and you alone, can do this. No committee can do much to help. Study the practices of masters of ceremonies, entertainers, and performers to learn the principles of *communicating* with an audience. (Study the principles of Chapter 16 to make committee reports bearable.) Don't be obvious, but be a *showman* as well as a perfect chairman. The conference will improve, the work output will go up, the participants will be happier, the seats will *seem* softer, and every attendee will praise you for your "chairmanship," not realizing that it is the showmanship that makes them like your chairmanship. No, never insist on attendance or attention.

4. *Insist upon formality in parliamentary practice?* This is another rule that you should *not* ask your group to have you enforce. Now we are getting on very touchy ground parliamentarily, because almost every authority on the running of meetings, conferences, seminars, and so on, is of one mind on this question. *All* insist that the chairman should *always* not only employ strict parliamentary procedures but do so with a high degree of formality. Never is it admitted that a member may address another member directly or that the chairman may break down the barriers of tradition and search for the *feelings* of the participants in a friendly manner. Instead, for the historical reasons explained in Chapter 4, the chairman is expected to remain aloof and impersonal to protect the minority. Yet, the early writings of General Robert[2] suggest the exception which I am stating here: *for deliberative conferences that are motivated by commercial pressures for finding a consensus and in which far less serious divisions of opinion exist.* I do not suggest that divisions of opinion will not exist; I suggest only that the serious, formal approach can intensify divisions of opinion rather than soften them. Further, the usual insistence by all works on parliamentary procedure that *all* members' words must be addressed to the chair and that a member can never speak directly to another member is *not* conducive to an efficient and effective deliberative conference. If the chairman is new at the task, he may have to follow such ponderous and pompous procedures until he and the group begin to learn how to simplify and unsnarl the procedures. But unless the chairman is willing and able to conduct the meeting in such a form that any extraneous speech is *immediately stopped,* the informal approach cannot be effective.

In order properly to apply the wonderful salutary effect of informality, the chairman must become a name expert (for first names), and he must give everyone the message, loud and clear, that he wants to be on a first-name basis with every member and participant regardless of the organization, motive, or position of each participant. If he is open about this, he can greatly expedite the conduct of business by disarming everyone with a frank, candid welcome to the Goldfish Bowl and a friendly invitation for anyone and everyone to speak his piece. As an example, when he sees a hand go up in the back of the room from someone who has not spoken before and is quite timid, he may be able to introduce the individual while the man is moving toward the microphone. If the chairman (who should know all the players in the com-

---

[2]See Chapter 4.

mercial drama) knows the man's organization and background of experience, he should say something nice about him, even though he knows that the individual will speak *against* the favored proposal and may wreck it with extraneous material. When an individual is properly welcomed and offered the floor in a sincere manner, his remarks become less pointed and more conciliatory. It is the chairman's *duty* to get controversial points before the group so that it can deal with them. There is nothing worse than an objector who will not speak up until after he has left the meeting. By informality the chairman may succeed in getting a message presented that otherwise would remain hidden.

There are many memory aids available so that the inexperienced chairman can remember enough about a man or his organization to allow a *good* introduction for a newcomer. For example, if the chairman does not know the man's name but can tell from his seating location that he is with the X Corporation, he can introduce him in something like these words: "I see that X Company has a comment—you will recall that they build the AC-47 aircraft and have a new design about ready for customer inspection, and we have all been wondering what they think about George's idea for grounded grids. Would you please tell us your name and the division you represent?" By this time Joe has reached the microphone and will be pleased that he has already been introduced, and he will *certainly* give his name and other identification before speaking.

In informally recognizing at the conference an old-timer who has been speaking regularly and repeatedly and will be quite reticent in giving his name and affiliation each time, the experienced chairman may introduce him this way: "I see Jim has his hand up, and we should hear from him to learn Y Company's views on this point." Turning to face Jim, he says, "Jim, would you please tell these nice people who you are and what company you are representing now?" Presented in an informal, friendly way, this is an ideal cover-up for a chairman with a lapse, every so often, of memory for last names. If he does this bit frequently during a meeting, it serves to help others learn people's names and organizations. This procedure will help to dispel the impression that so-and-so is *not* very important and, therefore, that nobody need remember his name. It is this "importance syndrome" which keeps people from announcing their own names when they start to speak and which makes the use of formal parliamentary procedural forms universally necessary unless something as good as an introduction for people can be substituted.

If the experienced chairman will have consideration for the participants' *need* to know *who* is speaking at all times and *if* he will treat everyone fairly and in an equally friendly fashion in welcoming them to the microphone, he can expedite the meeting greatly by that informality. He should not forget the human nature of participants to pay no attention whatever to a speaker's name and affiliation *before* he speaks. This is a characteristic of people which causes them to be uninterested in anyone else until they discover that the individual has something important (to them) to say. Thus, an experienced chairman will also de-introduce a speaker as he moves to his seat after speaking by saying: "Thanks, Jim Brown, for giving us the Y Company endorsement [or objection] to the grounded grids." Not only does this tell people whom to work on if they don't like what has been proposed, but it also summarizes what is often a lengthy and confusing dissertation that leaves people wondering whether the speaker is in favor of or opposed to grounding the grids. In case the chairman can't figure out the speech either, he can help the audience by saying: "Jim gave us some good arguments, but I am not exactly clear whether he was for it or agin' it. Did you all get it clear which it was?" At this point, Jim will realize what he did; he will smile and whirl around and head back to the microphone and probably say: "I'm agin' it, because we don't want to trip over the grids in the aisle of the aircraft." Now all the people in the room and out in the corridors have the message loud and clear, and they know that they had better find a substitute for George's proposed grounded grids. The chairman should immediately follow this up with a question to Jim (we assume that everyone else is sitting quietly, wondering "Now, what do we do?"): "Jim, what do *you* have in mind instead?" Jim will probably have a solution or at least a suggestion that can lead to a solution.

The important message here is that the chairman, through his informality, has been able to drag out the real facts that may have remained hidden: that an important member of the industry has a *serious problem* with a proposed action but is willing to work hard to find an acceptable alternative. Once the speaker has been pinpointed to everyone as *the objector,* he assumes his obligation to find a solution that *he* would *not* object to. Now Jim will be the hardest worker in the group because *he* is on the spot. If his objection had not been gotten across to the meeting, he would simply have clammed up and sulked in the belief that no one was paying any attention to his serious problem. If you watch carefully in meetings, you will find this same case developing time and time again because a chairman and a conference are so stilted in their ways that they believe their only responsibility is to *let* people speak, not for the speakers to get their message across or for the meeting to *hear* and *comprehend* what is being said.

Let me repeat again the admonition to the chairman to concentrate on everything that is being said and to assess its relevancy, its content, its comprehensibility, and its applicability to *the very next move by the chairman and the conference*. In the typical case postulated above, for example, what good would it do for the chairman sleepily to recognize the next speaker, who, oblivious to the serious objection just raised, drones on and on about the merits of George's grounded grids? Consider the confusion, the time wasting, and the upset people (particularly Jim, who was trying to be helpful). Imagine what would happen if the matter came routinely to a vote and everyone except Jim voted *for it*. It could be much later, long after the spec had been promulgated as the supposed product of the majority, that someone would discover that Jim and his whole firm have a solid problem with it. All this would happen because of a nonlistening, pompous, erudite but sleepy, formal chairman.

The words of George Demeter confirm the proper action by a chairman when it is impartial and for the benefit of the meeting itself. After explaining why an intervention by a chairman may be construed as taking sides, he adds this paragraph:

> On the other hand, in the exercise of sound leadership and initiative, the presiding officer is within his rights to shed light on a motion, to inform the members of the status or effect of a question, or to enlighten the assembly on facts within his knowledge to spur the assembly to action; and if such liberty is not abused by him the practice is not only tolerated but frequently welcomed.[3]

We should note Demeter's next paragraph and the consequences of abusing the chairman's rights given above:

> But the Chair's comments and remarks commending or condemning speeches or opinions of members expressed in debate are unwise and unparliamentary. Judicious and efficient presiding officers avoid it; they are expected to be outwardly impartial and nonpartisan.[4]

Don't argue with a speaker or with a speaker's opinion. But *do* ask him to be clear in what he is saying, what the effect of his opinion would be on the action, and what enlightenment he can give the group on why it should accept his opinion. If the chairman does this for the group and if he does it in a frank, nonpartisan manner, the members

---

[3]George Demeter, *Demeter's Manual of Parliamentary Law and Procedure,* copyright © 1969 by Little, Brown and Company, Boston, by permission of Little, Brown and Company.
[4]Ibid.

will usually appreciate it. Informality, on a first-name basis, is a tremendous help.

"But hold everything. You don't really expect a chairman to know the names of people, do you?" is what you are saying. Before you put forward the old saw that *you* have an excellent memory for faces but can't remember names, I urge you to withhold judgment until you have reviewed the reasons in Chapter 28 why names are so important and the case histories of name remembering in Chapter 13, along with the several suggestions given there for cultivating the capability. I should mention the problem of first names in international conferences. Not all nationalities like to use or even divulge first names. The French abhor it, the Russians have long-standing customs against it, and even the Germans, English, and other Europeans have a lot of resistance, at least among the older generation, to the use of first names in a nonfamily application. I have found that younger people accept the American practice pretty well, older people tend to tolerate it in the interest of getting the job done, and those who do not wish to use first names can be accommodated by title (the American Mr. is acceptable for United States organizations even when meeting in Europe). However, don't be surprised if your Europeans (even the French and the Russians) start registering for your meetings with *complete* names and start using their first names after a few minutes of watching the American practice.

5.   *Hold opening and closing ceremonies?* Ceremonies are favorites with pompous organizations and those looking for something to fill time or something to justify some bootstrap stature raising for publicity or other reasons. If you ask the members of your group this question, they will probably be about equally divided on the benefits and penalties of an opening ceremony. Remember that such events are *not* part, parliamentarily, of the deliberative conference. No quorum is needed. No formalities other than proper protocol are necessary. If you want a ceremony, follow the protocol carefully, and when it is over, start the meeting.

And if you do not have opening ceremonies in the usual sense, your group may believe that you must formally open the meeting with a gavel and with a call to order just to make it legal. In an informal conference of the type postulated, "legality" is more likely just a word rather than a requirement. Meetings don't have to be called to order; meetings of a disciplined group, however large, can simply start at the appointed time. Calling a meeting to order does not produce order in the conference room. Banging on a gavel to drown out someone else is not only bad parliamentarianism but bad manners. There are better ways than that to get order in a meeting. If you are not an expert, the easiest and most surefire way is the oldest way: have someone (not you) give an invocation. That's how the practice got started. It's the best method ever invented for getting a crowd quiet. But be ready to start the meeting immediately afterward before everyone goes back to his other conversations again. (See Chapter 29 for more details.)

If calling a meeting to order is unnecessary, adjourning it is of even less use. Recall that a motion to adjourn can almost always be ignored (not actually ignored but simply noted and rejected with the proper explanation that business still remains to be handled and adjournment motions are out of order) when it is inappropriate or untimely. Thus, when business is finished, the meeting knows it, and the chairman knows it; and if there are no announcements or other ancillary things left to do, it is quite sufficient just to stop. Gavel pounding does nothing to legalize an adjournment. This chairman has been conducting large industry international deliberative Goldfish Bowl conferences for over a quarter century, and neither the organization nor the chairman even owns a gavel.[5]

6. *Establish and enforce a quorum?* This is also a matter that is more pompous than useful in a carefully run deliberative conference. If you ask, your group will say, "Of course, we must establish the proper number for a quorum." But if your organization operates with a useful output of accomplishments that stick after everyone goes home, you, too, will discover that the quorum you so carefully established has long been forgotten as just so much useless drivel. But, is it legal to take action without a quorum? Suppose someone objects afterward? I predict that your action would be the same in any case; if objections come up afterward, the organization must deal with them adequately anyway, quorum or no quorum. *Demeter's Manual of Parliamentary Law and Procedure* cites numerous court cases that have a specific bearing upon parliamentary law and makes a specific point of one that answers this question: "If the absence of a quorum is not noticed or is not raised when an act is done or is not raised immediately after its completion, a quorum is presumed to have been present."[6]

7. *Keep a record of voting?* This practice gets a mixed reaction from members for all the reasons set forth in any manual or treatise on parliamentary procedure. Members do not always like the idea of their vote being publicized at a later date; yet there can be good reason for an organization's accepting such voting for the record. If members of your group will talk themselves into accepting a record of voting (even

---

[5]This statement was strictly correct only until corporation legal counsel Rick Lowery heard about it. Soon there arrived from the law firm Kirkland & Ellis a large package containing a beautiful gavel set from Rick Lowery, bearing the inscription:
W.T.C.
For over a quarter century as chairman you never needed one
R. C. L.

[6]Demeter, op. cit., chap. 15.

though the actual voting of individual members may not ordinarily be made public), this can help by making people far more careful in deciding a course of action; it produces far more responsible action than a simple off-the-cuff voice vote or show-of-hands vote. It is surprising what a recorded vote will do for any organization. But remember that many actions of an organization never need or could justify such complexities as a recorded vote or even any vote at all. Common consent is an ideal means of getting a noncontroversial action established. But this is proper only when *no one objects*. Recalling the postulate for the type of deliberative conference we are discussing, we must remember also that decisions that stick are the only ones with any utility. Common-consent actions must *really* be that. Otherwise, voting by some acceptable means is called for, and a record of that voting is highly desirable inasmuch as the action taken must be sold to an entire industry or community. A record of the vote helps that selling, and it also helps the acceptance of the action by others who were not present but are affected by the action. (See Chapter 14.)

8. *Other points?* Many other points will occur to you as you proceed to consider the intriguing aspects of a Goldfish Bowl deliberative conference. Yet the foregoing are the major questions of decorum and procedure that are necessary to get started in decision making and that should be endorsed by your group to ensure that all members know the limits of the authority they have extended to you, their chairman, as *their agent* in expediting the decisions that must be made for their mutual benefit. You must never forget that you are making certain determinations of what should be done *in their interest*; they, too, must remember that your only motive is their best interest rather than self-aggrandizement. If, at any time, your action as chairman seems to be aiming at the latter rather than the former, they should put you in your proper place immediately.

Now, after completing the second of three chapters concentrating upon the simplification of parliamentary procedures and substituting alternative decorum management practices, I need to present some examples of how this can be done, and *is being done*, in the real world. Chapter 6 will apply these practices to some organizations that would not ordinarily be expected to depart so far from strict parliamentary procedures. These real-life examples show what can be done when a chairman accepts his responsibility for the good of the organization and exerts strong leadership and direction. Note these examples well, dear reader, because the key to successful deliberation by any unwieldy body is good leadership by the chairman, exactly as I have emphasized in all the preceding chapters.

Yes, informal parliamentary procedures can be highly effective in the formal proceedings of a body which must, under its own rules, conform with established parliamentary laws and procedures. But they can be effective only when in the hands of a pro.

The Arthur Lebel Procedure

Dr. Arthur Lebel was a highly respected and much-loved personality in the U.S. Department of State. Prior to his retirement some years ago, he was known as Mr. Telecommunications, the man who had chaired more international telecommunications conferences (in the International Telecommunications Union and the International Civil Aviation Organization) than any man alive. The world knew and loved Art Lebel as a most gracious and fair chairman. All of us learned from his immense background of experience gained in serving so many complex international conferences.

Art Lebel favored the informal approach and welcomed the opportunity to observe how we handled it in our airline meetings. After attending several such affairs in which we employed the simplistic method in our deliberative Goldfish Bowl, he indicated his endorsement of our practice and told us a story.

It seems that he was chairing a particularly complex conference in the UN International Telecommunications Union at which every nation was battling every other nation over frequency assignments. It was no simple conference; he said that no one seemed even to *want* a solution, and complex parliamentary procedures seemed to be the consequence of the battle. Conditions finally got so bad that motions on the floor

6

Informal Parliamentary Procedures in the United Nations and Their Application Elsewhere

were becoming encumbered with many amendments of such complexity that the whole meeting seemed lost in a quagmire of rules. Art felt that nothing could be accomplished in that environment, and he decided to make a speech. He stopped the proceedings, gave the meeting a moment to relax, and then started with something like this:

"Aren't we all here from our respective countries to find some solution to this complex problem rather than to make the problem worse by gross disagreement?" He paused at this point to see what reaction he would receive. He waited. Yes! Some of his hearers were nodding sympathetically. Slowly the participants in the meeting began to realize what they had been doing. They had forgotten where they were in the complex parliamentary procedures of amendments on top of amendments cluttered by parliamentary "exercises." After the participants had a few more moments to ponder what had been happening, Art knew that he had the meeting waiting for *him* to straighten everything out. As Art described it, the meeting was now ready for *any* suggestion or proposal that would bring some progress. He asked the participants whether they were willing to forget all the proposals on the floor and start over with a new proposal that would point toward a solution. The reaction was immediate. As Art tells it, he received a gracious offer from one of the warring factions to compromise, and within a few minutes the meeting had found the solution. Today, many years later, no one would remember what the battle was all about; no one would remember what the ultimate solution was; but I am sure that everyone who was present in that meeting, so long ago, would remember until their dying day the finesse with which Art Lebel resolved an important international dilemma.

Is such a situation likely to occur only in such ponderous and mighty conclaves as those of the United Nations? Is it a problem only in organizations with thousands of participants meeting for lengthy debates on esoteric topics? Is it a dilemma that only high and mighty chairmen need know how to resolve? Of course not. Whether at the United Nations or at your local Saturday afternoon tea club, all chairmen will sometime, if not frequently, face the problem. Whatever the cause in *your* group, the Arthur Lebel procedure will help you solve the same dilemma that has confronted countless experienced and inexperienced chairmen through the centuries. Let's take a look at several other cases to see how the pattern develops and how a meeting, once in the mire, can extricate itself.

The Achievement of Bishop Mathews

Bishop James K. Mathews, of the Washington Area of the United Methodist Church, reported a quotation attributed to an important political figure of some years ago that goes something like this: "The three major deliberative bodies in the world today are the English Parliament, the United States Congress, and the General Conference of the Methodist Church." Bishop Mathews concurs in that statement for two important reasons: first, because he believes that the central management structure and historical origins of the Methodist Church have necessitated a complicated means of sorting out problems arising through the differences of geography, mores, and precedents of the constituent parts that have produced one of the largest churches in the whole of Protestantism; and, second, because he found himself in a complex parliamentary flap a decade ago.

Bishop Mathews says that he will always remember that flap and how he was dragged out of another meeting and conscripted to fix things after another presiding bishop asked to be relieved at the height of the debate. It makes an interesting case study for the neophyte and the experienced alike; so we should explore the circumstances and see how nice, friendly church people can also get snarled in parliamentary battles.

To understand the circumstances we must remind ourselves that the United Methodist Church in America got its start in the period just before the American Revolution and remained in one piece only until the early nineteenth century, when the black groups, the Southern Methodists, the Methodist Protestants, and others broke away. Although most of the groups kept some Methodist name, they were separate entities. Then, in 1939, three of the factions succeeded in getting back together again in the first uniting conference in Methodist history, which produced the Methodist Church.

And now we come to 1968, Bishop Mathews's problem date, when a separate denomination, the Evangelical United Brethren Church, met with the Methodists in a 2-week uniting conference starting on April 23 in Dallas, Texas. Although the uniting ceremonies took place the first day, the conference had to sort out numerous technical and Discipline problems that would require many sessions extending into the late hours every night. Not surprisingly, things didn't get glued together easily. The 2 weeks went by rather quickly, and a lot of unsettled matters were still being debated. So, what's new? The last business session convened at 7:30 P.M. on May 3. Numerous committees had reworked the still-unaccepted resolutions and the new Discipline. The Discipline was sorely needed, particularly for the local churches, and it didn't seem conceivable that the Discipline could be passed over. Neither could it be accepted without considerable floor debate and amending. The bishop who had been chosen to chair this last session had never chaired a General Conference session before.

Although the record of the conference shows that the bishop did a remarkable job for someone with such a lack of experience, he became hopelessly tangled in the parliamentary maze of amendments, motions, technical questions, parliamentary inquiries, points of order, and everything that I have urged neophyte chairmen to avoid in the first place (see preceding chapters). The conference was so mired in complexity that motions to adjourn were being made in desperation despite all the unfinished business. Then, several participants proposed a solution: a 10-minute recess for the Committee on Presiding Officers and the Committee on Committees (whew!) to "work out a procedure." A motion to this effect was carried.

The presiding bishop called the meeting to order to announce that he had asked to be relieved (he was to retire from active service immediately after this conference) and introduced to the conference his successor in the chair, Bishop Mathews. Bishop Mathews accepted the chair and, after acting upon a resolution of thanks to the retiring chairman, opened the meeting to business. The reader should not assume that with this experienced chairman all problems melted away. Certainly not. The legislative logjam was still there. The dilemma hadn't gone away; time had passed, and the conference was more tired and more behind than ever. This was not a particularly nice situation for a new chairman. Also, remember that the new chairman had not been in the meeting; he had been occupied in a committee meeting and had no knowledge of the quicksand that he was stepping into.

As Bishop Mathews recounts the episode today, a decade later, he says that it was that *lack* of knowledge of the pending motions and amendments that gave him the "out" which allowed him to survive with dignity and aplomb the first minutes of confusion when the conference was expecting him to work some miracle and settle everything in a few moments by profound decree. Nope! No such miracle occurred even with all those ecclesiastical pressures and capabilities. The report of the uniting conference, published in the May 6, 1968, issue of *The Christian Advocate* (The Methodist Publishing House, 201 Eighth Avenue South, Nashville, Tennessee 37203), contains ten more pages of fine print to document the remaining discussion and action that late Friday night before everything was amicably settled. But those first few minutes produced the key to the mood of the conference. As Bishop Mathews sighs and recalls that long night, here is what he says was the key to his actions:

> I knew that I could not take over that conference with its pending motions and amendments intact, or I would simply flounder in the same complex procedural problems of my predecessor. I knew that I must somehow get things started over procedurally, so that some solution might come out, as I gained knowledge of just where the

conference really was in its deliberations. Thus, I asked common consent of the conference to dispense with all pending motions and amendments. The participants graciously accepted my request, and that acceptance left us open for a new proposal in which a proper order of priority of business could be ensured; thus we would not spend time on the lesser items of business until after we completed the most important items.

As we read today the lengthy report of what followed on that late Friday years ago, we can, with our perfect hindsight, see that Bishop Mathews was right. He succeeded in changing the mood of the conference to one of "prioritizing" (there's that Washington buzz word) the work and in *keeping the conference's collective mind on that point*. Conferences are funny: they don't think as smart people think, and they do silly things that the constituent members would not do separately. Conferences waste time on unimportant things that people would never waste time on. A conference needs a strong chairman to keep its collective mind on what it is doing. The prior chairman had not kept sufficiently tight control over the uniting conference to keep its mind on its business: he had not concentrated sufficiently on *hearing* and comprehending every proposal made to the conference so that he could rule out of order those proposals which were extraneous to the immediate need for action. He had seemed simply to float with the conference and to let it follow its every whim. Careful listening (and hearing and comprehending) is an important attribute of a chairman which we shall discuss later (Chapters 12 and 13); searching for or developing a consensus is a complex art (Chapter 21), particularly when time is running out (Chapters 25 and 26).

Bishop Mathews used the directive that he had received from the Committee on Presiding Officers and the expressed view of the conference itself to justify the firm hand he employed in keeping the conference on the track for the long debates that were still to come that night. As every chairman will know when he finally faces a situation like this, there is no simple formula for getting a consensus when no consensus exists. But there is a potential for finding or developing one if the chairman has the guts to do what is required of him and to do it with fairness and gentleness to all. *How* to do that is treated in a later chapter; here we simply emphasize the problems of a chairman that can be helped to a resolution by firm gentleness for the total good of the meeting itself.

The Author's First Experience as Chairman

Sometimes a melee develops despite a good chairman, as in the example of Arthur Lebel in an international conference. Sometimes the dilemma is one that was handed to the chairman by another, as with Bishop Mathews. In either case, something that is *different*, perhaps seemingly revolutionary, must be done. In any event, a chairman should be prepared for a situation that requires some specific action by him to resolve a dilemma. Hopefully, you will find an opportunity to experiment with such dilemmas, as I did many years ago, before you are faced with a real-life situation of immense proportions, as the predecessor of Bishop Mathews was. Here is the experience I went through many years ago that made me aware of what can happen to an unwary chairman:

In the late thirties I was assigned by my firm to a public-speaking course aimed at industrial organizations and their personnel. Included in that management course was a short, concentrated emphasis on parliamentary practice. As the youngest member of the class (among experienced management people), I was rather outspoken compared with the old-timers, and this led me into some interesting situations. For example, when the instructor suggested a simple practice session as the easiest way to illustrate parliamentary procedures, no one seemed willing to volunteer as the chairman except (you guessed it) yours truly.

I didn't know until later that I was being set up for this job; yet it was the best experience I could ever have had, though mighty embarrassing at the time. The instructor suggested, quite disarmingly, that perhaps other members would propose something simple, such as a picnic, and give the group practice in amendments. They did. In 5 minutes there were so many complex motions and amendments on the floor that this chairman was utterly lost. I tried to keep track of where I was, but to no avail. I thought I knew all about parliamentary procedures, and I never dreamed that such a simple subject as a picnic could get so bogged down. After 10 minutes we were hours away from a consensus, further away than when we started. I kept at it doggedly, trying to unravel one amendment at a time, but new ones came up faster than I could get the old ones untangled.

Whew! I shall remember that experience longer than any problem I have had since then in years and years of chairing large, complicated conferences with heavy work schedules. It is that memory and the ultimate solution of that dilemma that have kept me thinking in the four decades since that time about the processes of proper chairmanship and proper parliamentary procedures as espoused herein. But back to my story: the instructor finally took me out of the chair and asked for another volunteer to straighten things out. He got one quickly, and in about 5 seconds the whole dilemma was resolved, and our "picnic," the most complicated picnic ever, was decided upon.

Thousands and thousands of practice parliamentary sessions have planned picnics before and after my experience 40 years ago, but I wager that none has ever been as complex as that one. I was let in on the little secret afterward when I learned that two of the members of the class had just arrived in town from Washington, where they had spent their spare time coaching senators and congressmen on parliamentary procedures. The rest of the class had been in on the whole thing and had helped to tie this chairman into parliamentary knots. The instructor expounded on the point that is the major theme of this book: the chairman will always be the problem in any conference, as even the best chairman will be inadequate in some respects. He pointed out how important it is, under parliamentary law, for the chairman to accept the need to keep order and avoid the deleterious happenings or dilatory actions of a meeting. A chairman is not helping a conference when he bends to its every whim and lets the participants float, willy nilly, from topic to topic and from motion to amendment to amendment. The conference deserves better than that; it is the chairman who will cause better things to happen if better things are to happen.

Perhaps not every chairman will have an embarrassing opportunity as I did to learn under the best teachers in advance of having to handle the job in a real-life situation. Not many chairmen will ever be caught in a United Nations chair with the problem of Dr. Arthur Lebel with which we started this chapter. Nor is it very likely that the dilemma of 1000 tired delegates, needing action on a complex book of procedures on the last night of a long, dreary conference, will be thrust into your hand to deal with as you choose, as was the case with Bishop Mathews. No, you are not very likely to be treated to such problems as these. But, just wait: your time will come. The occasion will be a dilly when it does come. You had better be prepared for it as best you can. Hopefully, this text will help to scare the daylights out of you so that you will concentrate on getting better prepared for that eventful day.

I shall, in the next several chapters, shift gears to some other topics that come next in order, but in Chapter 9 I shall give you additional horrible examples before I start offering solutions in Chapters 10, 12, and 13.

My account would be incomplete if I were to prognosticate conference management techniques without a chapter on committees. With so much written by others about the fun-and-games side of conference activity, I must assume that committees will always be a subject fit for ridicule, and I should accept the premise that membership on a committee is almost sufficient in itself to cause ripples of laughter over "What kind of camel is *your* committee going to invent?" I shall probably fall short of any contribution to the humorous side of committee functioning, but I must take note of the many truths contained in the proliferation of gags. The foibles of committees are the foibles of *people*, and we must understand those foibles if we are to understand the functioning of committees and of the whole deliberative process.

Description of a Committee

One of the best descriptions of a committee was given by former Secretary of Defense Robert A. Lovett to a congressional group, known as the Jackson Subcommittee, that some years ago had uncovered about 900 coordinating committees within the Department of Defense. Here is his definition of a coordinating committee: "Lonely and melancholy men who coagulate into a sort of glutinous mass suddenly come out as a 'committee.'" Perhaps you prefer the cliché "an aggregation of the unwilling appointed by the incompetent to do a task that is unnecessary."

There are many more descriptions: all have their humor at the expense of the committee, but all contain a considerable measure of truth, and it is that truth which we must search out and dissect in order to understand and utilize properly the thing we laughingly call a committee. But before we launch into the search for truth, let us remind ourselves of what was probably the best dissertation on this subject ever written, a paper by Dr. Bruce S. Old of Arthur D. Little, Inc., Cambridge, Massachusetts, entitled, "On the Mathematics of Committees,

---

7

The Inefficiency and Ineptitude of a Committee

Boards, and Panels," published in the *Scientific Monthly* (Volume 63, August 1946, pages 129–134). It contained a whimsical but accurate analysis of committees and of how they operate under "scientific" laws. I can certainly not give full justice here to that erudite treatise, but I shall quote from it, with the permission of the American Association for the Advancement of Science, Washington, D.C., what is possibly the most important conclusion of all time with regard to the functioning of a committee. Dr. Old confesses, in the conclusion of the treatise, that a certain lack of correlation seems to exist. He then states this worry: "One point which particularly baffles the author is the peaking of the efficiency of output of a committee versus number of committee members at seven-tenths of a person." Unlike Dr. Old, I see no reason why this should have to be explained.

My contribution to the understanding of the deliberative process is summed in two postulates which I call Small's law and the Country Club syndrome. Let's study these two postulates:

SMALL'S LAW

Deliberative bodies appoint only small committees.

And a small committee is defined by:

THE COUNTRY CLUB SYNDROME

A small committee is one barely distended to include me and other consummate paragons, but contractile in preclusion of you and others like you with odious propensities.

Composition of a Committee

How many times, if ever, have you heard a chairman state to a meeting "We must add everyone to the new committee who has a view on any aspect of the subject if we are to get a balanced consideration of the problem"? (Now, be truthful.) Have you heard such a blasphemous proposal out of *any*, let alone many, chairmen?

It would seem that the least-read passage in *Robert's Rules* is that on page 414 of the 1970 edition (pages 131 and 132 of the 1951 edition or page 169 of the 1907 edition) on a simple but important topic, proper composition of committees. People everywhere seem oblivious to the admonition of General Robert to consider the *purpose* for which a committee is constituted and then to select the composition accordingly. A simple pondering of the circumstances surrounding the use of committees should make it obvious what *Robert's Rules* is trying to explain: one of the most useful things about a committee for a deliberative assembly is its flexibility, and even its informality, to the extent that business that could not easily be handled in a large deliberative assembly (because of the person-hours required for complete discussion and investigation) can be organized and put into better shape for the assembly to consider if a committee is assigned the task first. Here is the advice on size which people seem to have missed seeing and understanding, ever since General Robert stated it as far back as 1907 and actually far earlier than that, since the 1907 edition was essentially the same as the 1893 edition: "A committee for deliberation or investigation, on the contrary, should be larger, and represent all parties in the assembly, so that its opinion will carry with it as great weight as possible." The *last twelve words* of that advice give the most compelling reason for such broadness in the scope of an investigative committee. For a commercial activity, which may influence a whole industry or community rather than just the *organization* that is deliberating, it is even more important to have broad coverage of every possible opinion so that the decision, when finally made, will be salable to one and all, without long delays while the problem and the solution are explained and further debated by those who were not present but who wield enough influence to preclude *implementation* of the action.

It is most certainly true that a small committee (preferably seven-tenths of a person, as Dr. Old recommends) is the most efficient and the easiest to control when the chairman is inexperienced. But who will explain the rationale for the decision to the deliberative body or to the community at large? The answer is that no one will. And the deliberative body has to start over again with its deliberation to sort out the needs of the community or industry. High efficiency is not what we want in a committee or in a deliberative process. We want results, and results that will stick through the implementation phase.

One complaint often heard against large committees is that they are unwieldy. He who makes this complaint is usually rather naïve in believing that constricting the size of a committee will somehow reduce the number of people concerned with the decision of that committee. No way! By excluding the affected people or organizations, we are simply lengthening, rather than shortening, the deliberative process. Drag 'em in, shove 'em in, get them in somehow, and keep them meeting together until they find a common solution. Naïve chairmen seem to have the view that a large meeting is harder to manage than a small meeting. Not so. Management problems are a function of how many people are participating in the discussion, not of how many are in the room. A large meeting with five active debaters is no more of a problem than a small meeting with five active debaters. (Chapter 17 explains why a small meeting may actually be more difficult than a large meeting.) One hundred quiet listeners are no problem. These quiet listeners may be good advocates for selling the committee's conclusion to the deliberative assembly. A large committee for deliberation, investigation, or recommendation is quite often an advantage rather than a liability. One hundred years' experience with *Robert's Rules* proves the correctness of the advice on small committees.

We must not leave page 414 of *Robert's Rules* without emphasizing the difference between the makeup of a deliberative committee and that of an action committee. Here the advice is to keep the committee small and constitute it from *supporters* of the action. Since Small's law seems to be applied by most chairmen, the smallness will take care of itself.

Inadvisability of Manipulation

Sometimes, despite the admonition of a naïve chairman and an equally naïve conference to keep the special committee small so it can work effectively, the Country Club syndrome produces a larger-than-hoped-for committee. Now we see the start of all kinds of shenanigans by the chairman and the conference to get the effect of a small committee despite large numbers of members. They may try to avoid actually having meetings of that committee and to get a few members together at lunch to work out a "committee recommendation." Or the chairman may suggest deferring the meeting of the group until late in the session (after most people have gone home) in order to reduce artificially the size of the committee. Or he may defer the meeting in the hope that the problem will go away and the committee will decide quickly, as all the members wish to pack up and go home.

Not only is this type of procedure very bad manners, unparliamentary, and amateurish, but it serves no practical purpose. It simply frustrates the deliberative process—the process that all deliberative bodies depend upon for continuity, stability, accountability, and credibility. Such shenanigans (and that is what they are) are a waste of deliberative bodies' time. I wish I could get one point across to those searching for solutions to real deliberative issues: bring the problem out into the open, ensure that those who are, in any way, involved in or affected by the decision are either present or have provided their views, and ensure that sufficient time is given to allow all ideas, problems, objections, and even irrelevancies to be thoroughly debated and mutually understood before the discussion is closed. (This problem and how to cope with it are examined further in Chapter 21.)

Certainly, length of debate can be compromised with the will of the majority, but there can never be any justification for excluding people whose views are controversial but who are authorized under every known precept of parliamentary law to speak out and be heard. The message I am trying to impart is that it is in the best interest of every organization to know and understand the *reasons* why such parliamentary-law precepts are made and why even if there were no such thing as parliamentary law, it would still be not only the right thing to do but the most effective way of doing business in a democratic society.

Value of Committees

As I stated when I started this chapter, committees (and other similar deliberative bodies) will always be subject to ridicule as a very inefficient way of doing business, as a most unsatisfactory way, in principle, for inventing camels, and as time-wasters because of the person-hours spent in making absurdly simple decisions that any *one* individual (or a committee of seven-tenths of a person) could make more efficiently. But camels are highly useful animals, a committee can move a mountain of opinion, and a deliberative body can run the world and keep some measure of contentment among constituents. As stated in the old cliché, democracy may not be good, but it is well ahead of whatever is next best, and committees are the *only* mechanism we have ever invented for doing certain things we must do in our society. Bad, yes, but still far ahead of the next-best alternative.

DONKEY'S PRECEPT

So your committee invented a camel while trying for a helicopter. Remember that people will walk a mile for one but not the other.

It has often been stated that if a group of people are locked in a room, one of them will emerge as the leader, just as elsewhere in nature, with chickens, camels, monkeys, or dinosaurs. Such a conclusion seems obvious, yet *who* becomes the leader when a group of people meet together with a problem to solve? This is a very difficult situation. Usually a deliberative body solves that problem for one of its constituent committees by appointing the chairman. Is the best man appointed chairman? Not necessarily. We have grown up around the principle that we should respect the chairman whoever he is and whatever his qualifications are or are not. Too many times we hear these words expressed about some committee election: "It should *not* be a popularity contest." Then, the nominating committee, which itself has been selected by the same sort of popularity contest, proceeds to select the most popular individual for the job, after having dutifully stated that it had reviewed a long list of names to ferret out the best and most capable individual for the position. So, what's new? Must we keep on pretending that we search for the *best* rather than the most popular candidate for the post? Fortunately, our parliamentary procedures have grown up around the principle that the *rules* must protect the body from the ravages of an incapable but popular chairman. But unfortunately, we have also acquiesced to an unwritten rule that we should honor the chairman, despite his limitations, because tomorrow we may be occupying his chair and we want honor bestowed upon us as well. Thus committee members can be, and are, mighty accommodating to a chairman they have helped select. They know which side their bread is buttered on.

What does all this have to do with our deliberative process? Quite a lot.

8

The Hierarchy of Committees, or the Pecking Order of the Unctuous

Choice of a Leader

All who have at any time been members of prestigious clubs or societies know what is meant by "going through the chairs": the slow process of starting out in some menial function and slowly working upward in the organization in the hope (if we live long enough) of eventually becoming the chairman or the president. Seniority is an important attribute in gaining such a distinction even though it takes no brains to accumulate seniority. Even an imbecile accumulates it rapidly. Everyone knows that the extrovert will advance over the introvert, the popular over the less popular, and the erudite over the unlearned. Those who hold the popular view, whether sound or absurd, will advance.

Everyone upholds the prestige of leading a prestigious society. But what about our commercial endeavors, which this text has so heavily emphasized as being highly important? Sorry to say, often the same so-called attributes are the factors that determine the leadership of commercial efforts. But it doesn't have to be that way; the most successful commercial endeavors that this observer has seen are those in which the leaders were chosen for their enthusiasm and motivation and their capability of keeping a project active until an answer could be obtained. Everyone who has ever attended any sort of commercial deliberative meeting in which a committee was needed to work on a subset of the total problem knows all about what I call:

The Fulsome-Caviling Syndrome

> The propensity of a deliberative body to select the member who carps the most to be the chairman of the committee to resolve the problem.

While most committees are simply overreacting in doing what this syndrome predicts will be done, they are really reacting quite properly in getting the individual or organization most deeply affected by the problem to take a direct part in getting it solved.

Arranging a Meeting

Once a committee has been formed, the difficult part starts: now somebody must call a meeting. But how? Here is where the presence of a permanent professional secretariat in some parent organization is so very important. The secretariat can gently prod the members, arrange a meeting, and get it all started even with an inexperienced chairman. If the job must be left to the chairman, forget it. Little is likely to happen until someone else pushes. And now I have to tell an anecdote to illustrate this problem.

It was many, many years ago. I had just been appointed to membership on my first industry committee. Bright-eyed and bushy-tailed, as the saying goes, I was ready to conquer the world. Not knowing or understanding the principles of the Fulsome-Caviling syndrome, I pointed out all the apparent problems with industry specs and urged that a new spec be prepared to fix one particularly bad problem. You guessed it. The chairman of the body made me the chairman of a subcommittee to prepare such a spec. I went home and spent many a sleepless night trying to figure out what I should do next. The other members of the new subcommittee were thousands of miles away; when should we have a meeting? Where? To do what? Why? Obviously no meeting was scheduled immediately, and the longer I waited, the less important the whole exercise now seemed. Weeks went by. The next meeting of the parent body was announced by the secretariat, and I went, waiting for the ax to fall upon me when I would be asked for a status report on my progress. There would be recriminations; everyone would criticize my failure to act on such an important matter (*I* had said it was important). The meeting came and went with nary a mention of the subject or even of the subcommittee. That was more than 30 years ago; later I was made chairman of the parent body and served in that post for 26 years. But never has the subject been mentioned by anyone. Here I am trying to write a book on how to run meetings, and I am admitting to having failed to run the very first industry meeting to which I was assigned.

Perhaps the reader will now understand how compassionately I can sympathize with the nonprofessional first-timer who starts off in a burst of glory but never gets even the first meeting organized. Lucky is he who has a professional organization to get him started and provide the backup for his complicated meetings. This anecdote (it's absolutely true) leads us to:

Carnes' Glory Law

1. Select the most useful task that can be done quickly.
2. Expedite completion *and publicity* before the glory expires.
3. *Then,* and only then, tackle the intricate, long-term problems, supported by a fully charged glory battery.

The Glory Battery

All new endeavors run from a glory battery which will soon run down. The chairman and every member love to bask in reflected glory when they are heading or helping an important undertaking. But basking wastes battery power without accomplishing anything. If a committee doesn't do something useful before the glory wears off, there will soon be no further motivation. Motivation is highest immediately after appointment; from then on everything is downhill. The glory battery is running down fast. Someone or something has to keep that glory battery charged. The only assured source of a recharge is accomplishment. Each accomplishment generates new glory for the chairman and the committee, keeping the battery charged for those monotonous pulls up steep hills and through the quicksands of fruitless mistakes on the long road to final success. A smart committee doesn't waste time on nonessentials that just run down the glory battery without producing useful work output. Writing lengthy terms of reference or debating endlessly "What are we here for?" is not productive work output, although most groups go through periods of preoccupation with such nonessentials (Chapter 10 suggests how to expedite such matters when they are inevitable).

Most effective commercial organizations have few if any hierarchical pecking-order and charter-writing compulsions. Social clubs and societal organizations are usually overpopulated with club officers, committee structure, understructure, superstructure, folderol, procedures, gobbledy gook, precedents, and an abundance of work programs that are centered more on the self-survival of hierarchy and on verbiage than on work output. While the noncommercial organization thrives upon folderol, with the intent of producing the maximum number of positions and committee posts to keep the maximum number of people occupied in the organization (they all pay dues), commercial organizations would expire instantly if they were saddled with all that excess weight. Commercial organizations are formed to *do* something, not just to make elaborate plans for doing things. Commercial organizations are costly, in time and effort if not just in money, and no such organization can survive for long without a commercial reason for being. Economy of the small glory batteries is highly important.

It may take time for a new commercial entity to complete its first accomplishment; it may mush around at first trying to act like a club or a professional society, simply because everyone is knowledgeable about such organizations. While it is mushing around in the folderol of a new organization, time will be wasted. Just the expenditure of time to get a charter or terms of reference adopted may be all that is needed to run down the glory battery, and the organization then goes kaput. It would be much better if the organization could do something useful for society (industry) *first* and fiddle around with its charter afterward. Organizations that *could have* been useful to the community may get started, float around in folderol, and then expire before anything useful comes out. In my own experience, I can admit to an early preoccupation with trying to legislate success by elaborate terms of reference. It is like trying to lift yourself with your own bootstraps. For the Airlines Electronic Engineering Committee (AEEC), it required 20 years to progress from a sixteen-page complex charter which spelled out everything imaginable in infinitesimal detail, just for a committee of seventeen members which held private meetings and wasn't known outside its own backyard, to a one-page summary that now governs a thirty-member international airline body involving the development of avionics by the airframe and electronics suppliers for the world's airlines. This group has never missed the elaborate document that we wasted so much time on in those early years. We spun our wheels for several years trying to boost our prestige through elaborate terms of reference before we learned that an elaborate charter was not a substitute for hard work.

More organizations have bit the dust while trying to broaden their scope of endeavor in writing and rewriting charters rather than in doing something for humanity or industry. While one organization is debating whether it has jurisdiction to engage in a particular activity, another organization is actually doing the work and building up the charge in its glory battery. Accomplishments pay off handsomely in glory and in charged-up glory batteries; writing charters is useless friction and is only a signpost on the way to oblivion.

Dealing with the Parent Organization

As I have explained, it is quite advantageous to have a parent organization, such as a trade association or its equivalent, handy when a job needs to be done. Forming a committee under such a parent organization is much easier and more likely to be successful than if a nonhomogeneous group must start out without such help. But because needed committees generally start their life under the aegis of some parent organization, hierarchies are expanded with every such committee, and the battles of the pecking order spread with every new committee. Some organizations believe they can solve that problem by the simple expedient of having a plethora of standing committees so that everything conceivable will fit under at least one such committee; thus, new committees are never needed. That solves one problem while generating lots more (see Chapter 9). Now interjurisdictional disputes develop between and among the permanent committees over which one will get an interesting new job. And then, when one committee completes a particularly important task, with lots of compliments and publicity, the parent organization and all the competing organizations rush to divert some of the accolades to themselves. Certainly this will happen as sure as God made little green apples. The parent or some other organization may even try to take the job away so it can have some of the fun and all the glory. This will happen. It does happen; jurisdictional disputes will keep on happening as long as God keeps making little green apples. The ancients tried to stop it; Congress doesn't know how to stop it in its own family; no one can stop it. But always remember that your group might never have gotten its start without the push of a benevolent and helpful parent; perhaps the parent deserves as much of the glory as it can divert. The parent *is* your own flesh and blood; the new committee is its progeny; speak kindly of your father.

When your father attempts to steal your projects from you, just remember that he may be getting old and may have little glory to bask in except the glory reflected from your efforts and success. Be kind. Don't overreact; don't fall for the ploy and spend an inordinate amount of time in trying to shore up an incomplete charter. Perhaps the parent organization will be wasting time in trying to prop up its own charter to get responsibility for the things you have been doing so successfully, and it may run down its glory battery while doing it. While the parent organization is artificially boosting its stature, you can do more work, with more accomplishments, and charge your glory battery even more. A successful effort needs no justification for continuation. In the words of Alexandre Dumas, "Nothing succeeds like success." And you should remember:

Foil's Law

No committee can serve two masters:
1. Folderol is a fallow and fickle fiend who foils fulfillment.
2. Fulfillment is a frugal and faithful friend who forestalls failure and foretells fame.

Having departed in this chapter from an emphasis on parliamentary procedure and how it can be simplified, I shall continue that de-emphasis in the next chapter to illustrate many of the points I have stressed by means of a lighthearted tale of the life of a committee. Then, in Chapter 10, I shall return to a typical parliamentary problem (of a charter), and in Chapter 11 I shall tackle another parliamentary question that has wasted time in everybody's conference on one occasion or another: the technical question of proper word usage in the approval process for reports and other things.

How does it all start? What determines whether a new committee will be just another lost cause, with wasted effort, frustrated tempers, and unsolved problems building up to immense proportions and eventual demise?

Let us hypothesize a situation. Several manufacturers of poofduffels (used on many automobiles) are worried over shortages of industrial rubands employed in the manufacture of poofduffels. Contributing to the high wastage of rubands is a spherical shape which allows them to roll off the workbench. Cubical or even pyramidal rubands would be usable, but new processing machines would have to be obtained, and the shape must be standardized if any but spherical rubands are to be used. How to standardize? Joe Tokalott, president of Super Poofduffels, Inc., tries to get some action started at the 146th annual meeting of the American Poofduffel Association, but no one seems willing to put effort into the problem. No new committees can be authorized this year. Joe next tries the International Spherical Ruband Association, but it has just held its annual convention and can't consider any new activities until next year. Poor Joe! A friend says that the government must have some committee structure somewhere and suggests that he write to the Undersecretary of Commerce for Poofduffels. Joe does, but after 3 weeks of waiting he learns that any such activity would have to be interpreted as "advice" to the Department of Commerce, and that would require chartering as a federal advisory committee under the Federal Advisory Committee Act; this would take lots of time (probably at least 4 years), some large appropriations, and some new legislation to establish the Defense Department's need for government usage of cubical rubands for instruments. Although officials of the Department of Commerce do not offer Joe help, they do offer some advice: "Be sure your dimensions are in metric units." Joe is having his problems, but

9

The Birth of a Committee or "The Booming Deus": A Playlet in 2¾ Acts

they are not unlike the problems of others in industry. He next turns to the American National Standards Institute (ANSI), but it has no committee activity that can work on square rubands, and it suggests that he get his own trade association to sponsor the work; then it would be glad to consider the resulting spec for ANSI adoption in due course. Joe is in trouble. His supply of spherical rubands is running out, and they keep rolling off the benches. He phones all his friends in the poofduffel business, and they, too, admit coming troubles. But they, unlike Joe, cannot justify taking the lead in hunting up some alternative source; some day they may get out of the poofduffel business and go into piffelpoops, which can be made from glass beads. Now what?

Joe has been attending poofduffel conventions for 10 years or more and knows something of the committee structure in the association. He looks up his old files and discovers something: in 1928 there was a Poofduffel Standardization Committee which had completed some remarkable work in the olden days of poofduffels. The committee was regularly assigned funds, but no chairman has been appointed for at least 4 years since Chairman Ritemore retired. No members are listed either. Aha! Why not? Joe writes to the association again, pointing out the importance to his organization and to the stature of the American Poofduffel Association of that most prestigious committee. Why has it been dormant so long when so much important poofduffel standardization needs to be done? He has found his angel. The staff has to agree on the importance of that particular committee; guess who is immediately appointed chairman of the reactivated Poofduffel Standardization Committee? Joe is in business.

Quickly he writes to ANSI, the Department of Commerce, and the Defense Department to alert them about the new activities soon to be starting on poofduffel standardization. Will they participate? "No," the answers come back: there is too much other work of higher priority.

Joe has half a dozen friends in the poofduffel business on whom he can lean for help; so he arranges with the staff to get them appointed, at least temporarily, to his Poofduffel Standardization Committee. After dozens of letters to the staff, they finally set a time and place for the first meeting, using the staff office in Gaithersburg, Maryland, just outside Washington, D.C.

First Committee Meeting

Joe shows up at the appointed time, and so do three others; Joe convenes the meeting, and he is immediately besieged with questions: "What are we here for?" "What time will the meeting adjourn?" "Who is going to do all the work?" "How can we *possibly* get any results?"

"Who is going to rewrite our charter so we can do all this?" No answers—just questions.

Joe has been awaiting the opportune time to pass out a paper which includes a proposed spec on cubical rubands, but now prospects are not looking too good. He had better hold the paper back for a while. Jane has taken a plane schedule out of her pocket and seems more engrossed in that than in the questions of Dick and Marian. Jane asks, "Will we be through by 10 A.M. so I can catch that 10:30 flight, or must I plan on the noon flight?" No one pays any attention to Jane, as Marian now seems engaged in looking at Dick's *Time* magazine, while Dick turns the pages to find the story on ruband production. Joe is still trying to answer some of the questions, but nobody seems interested until he mentions the latest price quotation just received on spherical rubands. Jane drops her plane schedule and interrupts Joe, "What did you say you had to pay for the latest batch?" Dick senses that something has been said that he *should have* heard: "What was that about ruband prices?"

Now, with *money* inserted into the discussion, Joe has everybody's attention, and he makes his point quickly: "If we don't show the ruband suppliers that we have an alternative to their spherical rubands, *and a standard alternative*, we are in real trouble." He makes his plea as passionately as he can while they are still listening.

Not only do the others get his message, but they all want to contribute, and they start talking at once, agreeing with each other on the premise but urging opposite approaches to a solution. Jane is pushing for flat, square rubands because they are easier to define; Dick wants egg shapes; Marian wants cylindrical shapes to facilitate their counting; Joe is still pushing his cubical shapes. But they all are talking at once; everybody believes his or her view is the one best liked.

Jane jumps up and heads for the door, saying, "You don't need me to write the specs on the new shapes, so I'll catch that 9:30 plane and leave you to work out the details." She rushes out the door leaving the three still talking and believing that she has just gone to the coffee urn.

It takes a while before Joe, Dick, and Marian all discover that standardization won't be so very easy. The debate goes on until midafternoon before Joe has convinced Dick that cubical rubands are all right, if not actually the best; but Marian is not convinced. Now the debate centers on what Jane agreed to before she left, but they finally conclude that no one knows what Jane wanted or said. Dick keeps suggesting that they should vote on the matter democratically, but Marian can see that she would be outvoted by Joe and Dick; so she keeps trying to convince the others that they are *both* wrong. She is the largest buyer and must have a greater say than either of the others, and, besides, she has had more experience with rubands of different shapes than anyone else. Marian successfully avoids a vote until 4:30, when Joe announces that they have to get out of the conference room at 4:45, and they must decide, at once, whether to continue on the next day or to adjourn today.

Marian keeps right on debating the issue, claiming that she has to get to another meeting tomorrow and the matter must be settled today, and that it has to be *her way*. The office closing time arrives; they are walking out of the office with no decision; they stand on the curb in front of the building for 10 minutes until Marian gets a taxi to the airport, all the time still debating the shape of rubands to come. The taxi starts up, and Joe yells, "How about a meeting next Tuesday, same place and time?" Marian seems to be nodding as the taxi speeds away. Joe and Dick stand on the corner talking for a few minutes before going their separate ways. About all that is *sure* is that next Tuesday a few, if not all, of the original four will be back in Gaithersburg.

Participants' Reactions

Let us now interrupt this fictional story of a great conference to summarize what each of our committee members has learned so far:

Jane's Conclusions

1. I'm glad I learned about those cost increases.

2. But there is no problem. They liked my suggestion for the flat rubands, and they will write a spec that will solve all our problems.

3. I'm glad we got that meeting over so soon; I hate meetings.

Marian's Conclusions

1. Costs are getting high; we need a spec.

2. I just about had them convinced on the cylindrical rubands. Another few minutes would have done it.

3. I guess next Tuesday's meeting is necessary; we need to get the spec done on the cylindrical rubands.

4. On second thought, I don't need to be there. I'll write to Joe and give him all the good reasons; I'll let them write the spec.

Dick's Conclusions

1. What a problem! Costs are going up, and we don't have any consensus, let alone a start on any spec. I would have given in to Joe's cubical rubands if Marian accepted them too, but she wasn't willing. Now we have to have another meeting.

2. This next Tuesday's meeting won't last long; we just have to explain to Marian why Joe's idea is acceptable. We'll get the job done quickly.

3. I still like the egg-shaped ones better; I think we would have a better chance of talking Marian into a standard egg shape than into that stupid cubical shape that Joe wants. Joe isn't that smart. My idea is better. I'm going to write to Joe.

Joe's Conclusions

1. What a mess! Now we have to have another half-day meeting to finish up. Why wouldn't they listen to me? They must know that cubical shapes are the only practicable alternative to our present spherical shapes.

2. Anyway, we'll get it all settled next Tuesday morning. I'll announce early that I have a noon flight; that'll speed them up.

3. I will be firm with them at the next meeting; I was too lenient. Don't they know *I'm the chairman?* Also, I'm the best qualified of any of them. I'll lower the boom on Tuesday, and we'll see who's boss.

4. Yuh know, we really did have a problem today. They are all stubborn. I'm knowledgeable. They will see the light next Tuesday.

5. I remember something I read about issues and conferences. It was something like this: small deliberative conferences over large issues are just as complicated as large deliberative conferences over large issues, and all issues are large complicated issues.

6. Next Tuesday, at the very beginning of the meeting, I shall present my draft spec and insist that they all adopt it. I'll be a *real* chairman.

Second Committee Meeting

But, alas, when Joe gets back to his office he has several letters from other poofduffel manufacturers wanting to "help" with a spec; no two seem to have any common views on anything. Later he receives letters from Jane, Dick, and Marian, each urging acceptance of a pet shape.

Joe has asked the staff to circulate an announcement of the Tuesday half-day meeting to Jane, Dick, and Marian; now he must invite a few others. More letters arrive; the size of the Tuesday meeting is increasing.

Tuesday arrives right on schedule. So do fifty-odd poofduffel suppliers, four ruband manufacturers, and even one large user of poofduffels (users have not been invited). Joe starts the meeting right on schedule, with everyone ready to go. He has decided to brief everyone (10 minutes) on what happened at the first meeting and where the project stands now (5 minutes) rather than pass out his draft spec. Joe starts, but 10 minutes are insufficient; an hour passes; there is more discussion: another hour. Joe suddenly realizes that he will miss his noon flight, and the meeting hasn't gotten past the status of the project at the first meeting. He waves his arms; he interrupts Marian, who has been trying for an hour to get a word in on cylindrical shapes and has just gotten through her first sentence: "Sorry to interrupt for a minute, but we have to settle an administrative matter right quick!" Joe looks around at the group to see whether they are all listening to him rather than to Marian. No! There seem to be two other small meetings going on in the back of the room that he had not noticed until the rest of the room was quiet. He bangs on the table with an ashtray, and the two meetings stop: "We have to decide *now* how long this meeting needs to go on. I planned a noon flight. Shall I have it changed to a 3 P.M. flight?" Joe looks around at the people, all of whom seem confused over what he is talking about. A few people nod; both of the meetings in the back of the room have started up again, leaving Joe saying to himself, "What am I doing in this madhouse?" He ponders the situation further and states loudly: "I'll have my schedule changed, and we'll go on until midafternoon; I'm sure we can settle the spec business by then." Joe isn't sure but knows he must appear optimistic. He asks the staff to rearrange his schedule and again turns his attention to the meeting, which by this time has broken up into five separate affairs plus other individuals who have gone out to the water cooler in twos and threes to debate parts of the problem.

Joe bangs on the table with the now-cracked ashtray, yelling, "Order, order, please, order." A wisecracker halfway back yells out, "One hamburger, please, with the works." This seems to get the attention of the others, so Joe joins in the laughter, still banging on the table with the largest piece of the broken ashtray. Dick, who is seated in the front row, tries to be helpful by suggesting something: "I think we ought to give it a try, now that we have discussed all the possiblities, and we know now that only that one will work, just as Marian said last week when we were standing on the curb discussing . . ." (his voice trails off in the general noise and commotion, so only Joe knows that Dick is speaking). Joe is willing to consider anything at this stage, so he looks at Dick and says (his words are unintelligible to anyone beyond the second row): "Dick, what was it you were suggesting? I didn't hear what you proposed." Since no one except Joe could hear Dick, the other participants in the meeting have now gone back to their own private conversations, almost drowning out the two "meetings" going on in the back. Dick says something, but Joe can't make it out; Joe moves away from the head table to Dick's side, and they go on with their conversation, no one else hearing or caring.

Joe is interrupted by a booming voice from halfway back: "What kind of a lousy meeting is this? No one seems to be running it! We're wasting good time and money here." The Booming Voice has captured the attention of Joe and Dick and a few others. "Don't you people have any desire to get this thing settled? Can't you settle down so we can hear someone with an idea make a proposal?" The two meetings in the back of the room have quit their yelling and are watching the Booming Voice. "I don't know what the problem is; will someone who *knows* please tell us and let us have a little order here so we can get on with this matter and then all go home?" The Booming Voice is obviously in total command of the meeting. Joe looks around, too; nobody knows what to say. Joe finally comes to his senses and states: "He is absolutely right; that's what I've been trying to tell you people! We *have* to have some order here and take this matter up logically, with only one person speaking at a time. As your chairman, I now recognize Dick, who had the floor just before this interruption." He turns to Dick.

Dick, completely taken aback by this new attention focused upon him stands, facing the chairman, and speaks, "We have been holding an important meeting. . . ." He is interrupted by the Booming Voice. "We can't hear you back here, please speak up, and please face this way; I'm sure the chairman won't mind your not facing him." Dick looks at the chairman, who shrugs, and then Dick turns halfway to face the audience partly and still face the chairman: "Our meeting worked very hard to find an acceptable. . . ." One of the meetings in the back of the room starts up again, since nobody can hear Dick in the back. The Booming Voice takes over again, "We still can't hear you. *Please* face the audience." The Booming Voice emphasizes the "please," and Dick turns completely away from the chairman toward the audience, facing particularly in the direction of the Booming Voice: "Our meeting. . . ." The Booming Voice interrupts him again: "Don't face *me*, face the audience. That bunch in the back [they stop their meeting each time the Booming Voice speaks] needs to hear you—not just me." Now, the two groups in the back seem to have decided that they may be missing something up front, so they turn toward Dick with complete attention. Dick starts again, "Last week's meeting was very productive, and we all learned a lot about the problems of poofduffel usage of rubands. . . ." The Booming Voice interrupts him again: "We keep hearing you say *that*, but you never get to the point of saying *what* you learned, or *did*, last week that we should all know about." Joe feels that he really should be running the meeting instead of the Booming Voice, so he chimes in: "Yes, Dick, please tell us what we should do."

Dick has the attention of everyone, and he now realizes that he has nothing *really* to contribute, but he ponders and addresses the audience with a full breath and some better-chosen words: "We *settled* [he emphasizes that word] upon the cubical rubands last week as the consensus of everyone present. [He realizes that he is stretching things a bit, but it might work.] We didn't have time to write the rest of the spec, however, but we could finish up this whole job fast if we could get a consensus today on the cubical rubands we picked last week." Dick looks around expectantly; Joe looks around expectantly; one of the meetings in the back of the room starts to generate some noise, unintelligible to those up front. The Booming Voice interrupts the back-of-the-room meeting: "I could accept that; it would be better than spending another couple of days here in Gaithersburg. Why can't you others put aside your favorite whims and work together on a common solution so that we can all start saving some money on our poofduffel manufacturing?" Joe looks around the room. Dick can't believe what he has started; people are nodding their heads all over the room. A voice in the back, which Joe recognizes as Marian's (he really *should* get some new glasses), comes through loudly, so Joe hurriedly points toward her as an indication that Marian is recognized by the chair, although she obviously hasn't been going to wait for recognition. "That's what I have been trying to suggest all morning." Marian's voice is firm, even though her facts are faulty: "We have to settle something so we can get out of here and get back to work." Marian has made contact with the meeting, and almost everyone seems ready to affirm what she has said by nodding. Now Jane has to get into the act: "I'll make that a motion."

Joe doesn't know what should be done next, but he hears the motion plus several echoing seconds from somewhere in the back; so he does what any red-blooded chairman would do: he bypasses all the rules and procedures and shouts, "All in favor, say aye!" Lots of ayes greet him. Now that he is ahead, he forgets all he has ever read about parliamentary procedures and says, "Looks like we have it all settled, and a new spec is done," forgetting for a moment that no one has even known he *has* a draft spec with him for cubical rubands. Jane jumps to her feet and starts for the door, speaking above the din that is now swelling, as each compliments a neighbor on having settled everything, "Now that we have it all settled, we can leave the 'grammaring up' for the staff to do so we can go home; I'm going to catch the noon flight," and out the door she shoots without waiting for any response.

True, the difficult work *is* now done through a fluke, but nevertheless it is *done*, and Dick is still scratching his head in wonderment over how he has been goaded almost against his will and his better judgment into offering the winning suggestion, by the Booming Voice, whoever he is. Dick looks around the room to get a better view of whoever the Booming Voice is. He can't see. Joe must have come to the same conclusion at about the same time because he, too, is straining to see halfway back in the large conference room ("I *really should* get some new glasses"). The others must also have had the same idea because all the attendees are surprisingly quiet, craning their necks to look backward from the front or forward from the rear. No success. Joe speaks out, "Will the person with the heavy voice who made such helpful suggestions please identify yourself; where are you?" No answer. No Booming Voice. Absolute quiet, for the first time all day. "He's gone!" Joe exclaims. "Did anyone see him leave? Did anyone recognize him? Is he a poofduffel manufacturer? Who is he?" No answer, but there is lots of horizontal nodding even from those near the middle of the auditorium where the Booming Voice seemed to come from. Marian calls out, "I don't think anyone except Jane has left. It wasn't Jane's voice. I think we have a real mystery here." She pauses, then says, "Let's go to lunch now, and meanwhile maybe the staff can check the attendance sheet to see who is now unaccounted for." George, from the staff, speaks up quickly, "I already did; everyone is explainable except for one individual who seems to have three initials, D.U.X. His last name seems to be Machina, or something like that, if I can read his writing. I've never heard of him."

By now the group is moving toward the door. Then Marian gets an idea and pulls Joe aside to the office and to a large dictionary opened on a stand. She turns pages, saying "D . . . E . . . U . . . S." A broad smile comes over her face, and she closes the dictionary before Joe can see what she has turned to: "Come on, Joe, let's go to lunch; no one would believe it anyhow." And she pulls the surprised Joe out the door, and off they go.

Aftermath

Certainly the poofduffel ruband job is not yet done. But the difficult part is over; now the basic issue has been settled, hopefully to stay settled, and, most important, the combatants are now talking to each other. All are aware that each has had to give up a favorite whim to get some consensus so that they can move forward. All are hurting because of rising costs; those costs can't be curtailed without a new spec and a new concept, over which everyone disagreed at first. When failure to find an answer (plus the boredom of Gaithersburg for another day), was hurting everyone enough, *then* the people were ready for a suggestion that would solve the problem quickly.

We may not have a chairman with both technical knowledge and conference management knowledge; we have to accept what we have available. Sooner or later, there will develop a *will* to negotiate, motivation to negotiate, then even *fear of a failure to negotiate*. When the time is right, someone, either one of our meeting attendees, as described in Chapter 33, or possibly even a *deus ex machina* will materialize to help the chairman find the answer. Such answers are *there;* we must simply find them. Watch for signs of a *deus ex machina* arising in the middle of the conference from the spot where everyone least expects him.

Reprise

Perhaps you may recognize this whimsical fable as an allegorical composite synthesis of your worst meetings, in which participants have reached the beginnings of a decision, but won't take the extra time to tie things down before they leave. As I explained in Chapter 4, a decision made as in this fable is unlikely to stick unless certain follow-on steps are taken to *explain, document,* and *publicize* the decision. Perhaps even another meeting should be held to tie down the loose ends and ascertain that other alternatives have been properly evaluated as part of the decision. Yet, my purpose with this fable is to illustrate the odd ways in which a consensus may evolve despite the inexperience of a chairman and a whole meeting. With an expert professional staff, such a decision *may* be made to stick, however irrational the process of its development may seem.

Human nature being what it is, with everyone an "expert" parliamentarian, it becomes almost impossible to put a new constitution and bylaws document into effect without far more time and effort than seem justified. Everyone wants to kibitz on the draft. Everyone feels an obligation to "expert it" to an infinite degree. All will help with the nit picking to ensure a perfect document. And if the individual who drafted the paper can survive the nit picking, the paper will finally be adopted, weeks or months later, and the organization will have its new charter. Now it can start holding meetings and get down to business.

But is all that *really* necessary? Do we have to have all that folderol? Here is a true story of how a new civic organization was bamboozled into simplifying its charter development.

A Case History

This happened several years ago in the Maryland suburbs of Washington, D.C. A local realtor had petitioned for rezoning to build apartments in a residential development (this is the same old story of many citizens' associations). Horrors! We couldn't raise any Cain with the authorities because we didn't have an official citizens' association. Now we had *motivation* to get organized. How could we do it expeditiously? An "accomplice" agreed to organize the people in the neighborhood, and I accepted the task of drafting a charter consisting of a constitution and bylaws. Having done that many times for other organizations, I had no problem with the *drafting*, but how could I get the charter adopted without the usual fiddling around? I developed a carefully laid-out plan. I started with the charter of a neighboring citizens' organization, deleting all the portions relating to complex hierarchical committees that seemed unnecessary for our organization with only *one specific job to do*. All the other words were left exactly the way they were. Now I was ready.

My accomplices had already picked the chairman, the vice-chairman,

10

How to Get a New Charter Adopted in One Meeting

the secretary, and the treasurer, so all we needed at the first meeting was the acceptance of those officers (that would be easy) and the adoption of the charter (that was our worry). Announcements were mailed for the first meeting at the nearby public library, and we awaited the meeting.

The night came. Everybody in the neighborhood showed up. As I had predicted, they were quite happy to vote our proposed people into office. Then we faced the real test. The chairman was a lawyer from the U.S. Department of Justice, and he started off with good knowledge and good stature to run a precise meeting. But we had guessed right. All the participants in that meeting were authoritative experts on charters, constitutions, bylaws, and all the intricacies of *Robert's Rules*—at least they all thought they were. I had selected a seat not too near the front, and I carefully stayed out of the brewing battle for about 45 minutes. Now was the time. So many people were waiting to be recognized that after I raised a hand, it was quite a while before the chairman gave me the floor. Now I was ready for my fun. I went up front and faced the group. I was smiling—nobody else was. The others were all quite serious about their fiddling with the constitution and bylaws. I started by reminding them how long they had been debating the first few sections, and then I predicted that, at the rate at which they were progressing, they could expect several long evenings of debate just to get through the document. Then I would redraft the document for subsequent consideration, and that could go on for weeks, if they would like it that way. And, in the end, the constituion and bylaws would go into someone's file, where no one would ever refer to them again, as happens with almost all such documents. In the meantime, the coordinated effort against the apartment building would have to take second priority while I finished the constitution and bylaws. So I explained that I had hoped they would expedite the action, and this was why I had carefully based the draft on the constitution and bylaws of a neighboring citizens' association which had found them quite satisfactory for several years. I had deleted the unnecessary sections not applicable to our small association, as I suspected that there would be no need for so many committees and so many officers. Thus, the words that were now in the draft were the basic minimum to get the organization chartered with a minimum of controversy. I concluded my "speech" with an offer to stay with the group for as long a time as the members thought they needed to finish the document in but perhaps they would like to watch the time a little more carefully so that we could get to the apartment matter tonight. I was still smiling, trying to look friendly. I sat down. There was utter silence.

A long list of speakers had been waiting their turns. The next speaker in line continued his nit picking, and I was wondering whether the group would accept my challenge or simply ignore it. But then it was evident that the mood *had* changed; someone found a small point to fix on the last page, and there were no more changes. The struggle was over.

Lessons to Be Learned

In this particular case the chairman of the meeting was not the one who pointed out to the participants of the meeting what they were doing improperly; certainly the chairman was in on what was to be done, and he cooperated with that effort to bring a touch of reality to the meeting. In most cases, it will be either the chairman or no one. Seldom can the chairman expect someone else to act as his factotum in doing what *ought* to be done. The case described is a true story. It is quite typical of what a meeting will almost always do in the beginning if left to itself. A meeting is generally not a thinking entity, at least as far as parliamentary shortcuts are concerned, and its components are simply people, with no one ostensibly in charge. If the chairman is willing to take charge or if some individual who has a breadth of experience is willing to exert himself, the meeting quickly can be made aware of its foibles. Then, and only then, can a meeting make a cooperative effort to act rationally and *cost-effectively*. But if no one, not even the chairman, takes the initiative, the meeting will have to plod wearily along through all the monotonous rules of parliamentary procedure with nary a shortcut, leading eventually to that same end point at which the final consensus is obtained. People are people. The chairman is the most appropriate one to take charge and expedite the action, but if he doesn't take charge and if no one else does it for him, the meeting is doomed to dreary, tiresome monotony.

Chapter 6 gave some examples of knowledgeable chairmen, and Chapter 33 discusses ways in which a member with experience can help an inexperienced or inept chairman run a meeting, if that member has the guts to do it.

Almost every organization has, at some time or other, spent an inordinate amount of time debating with itself the proper parliamentary manner of acting upon a report (the presenting of sensible reports is a whole separate topic that will be deferred until we get some other matters out of the way; see Chapter 16). Because deliberative bodies seem to have such a propensity for being very accurate on *this one matter* of nomenclature and procedure and yet seem unable to read and comprehend what is written in parliamentary handbooks on this question, I feel obligated to assign this chapter to this major time-waster of a problem. If *you*, dear reader, are an expert on this matter, you may bypass this chapter, but I'll bet you aren't, as most parliamentarians seem quite unsure of themselves on this confusing question. So now I shall address the question in the title of the chapter.

Formal Procedures

A body *approves* a report, of course. But wait a minute. Is that right? If the proposer of a report asks the deliberative body to "accept" his report, what does he intend to happen? Perhaps the chairman will state, "It is time now to receive committee reports." What does that mean? Or perhaps the proposer asks whether the meeting "agrees" to the report, or he suggests that the meeting "ratify" the report. Many words get used. Which word means what?

Most organizations get their feet wrapped around these words and have great difficulty in extricating themselves from a morass of complex words and meanings that takes a lot of careful study of *Robert's Rules* to untangle. You have probably been in several meetings in which the participants, all at once, get worried over the implications of possibly signing their lives away by giving their approval to some lengthy controversial report of a lesser entity. Does "approval" of the report indicate that we have authorized the expenditure of funds to implement something that is referred to in the report as "nice"? Have we become

11

What Does a Committee Do with a Report?

a lobbying organization by approving some lengthy endorsement of lofty principles of trade unionism? Are we all subject to criticism, if not lawsuits, when we "receive" a report criticizing some action of Mr. Doe of the Gravy Train Oil Company? It might be advisable to know the difference, if there is one, between "taking note" of a report and "making it our policy."

You may remember a time in some board meeting when such a question was a burning issue. Then everyone went home and researched *Robert's Rules* and came to the next meeting armed with words and definitions and quotations galore, so that the whole meeting was spent in debating which words applied when and what "we should have done with that report at the last meeting instead of what we *did* do with it." No, the question was not resolved adequately. Probably everyone just tired of debating the matter, and the participants in the meeting decided what they were going to do in the future if the matter ever came up again. They decided this question by voting on what the preference of the group was. So that deliberative body always uses the exact word they decided upon, with a presumption that it is correct. Many organizations do the same thing. The words *are* complex. Let us first try to unsnarl this tangle by separating the actions desired from the words that should be used to describe those actions properly.

Members of a group really have only two choices with respect to something they are considering: they can simply have the matter read to them (or have it handed to them in writing, which is essentially the same), or they can embrace the words as their own. In the first case, if they choose nothing more than that, the group has simply received the report (or whatever it is), because it need not determine, as a deliberative body, whether it likes the report or hates it. As parliamentary texts explain, there is nothing that a body need do to receive a report. If the report is on the agenda (the orders of the day), it is preordained that the body will have received it when it is presented to it. The body simply has been notified that such a report exists; it has given no sanction to anything in the report; it has neither "adopted" it nor "rejected" it. It has done exactly nothing with the report. The 1970 edition of *Robert's Rules* cautions against adoption of an entire report except when the organization is to publish it in its own name. The reason, of course, is that an affirmative vote on a motion to adopt has the effect of the body's endorsing every word of the report, including the indicated facts and the reasoning as though they all were the body's own statement. Even as far back as the 1907 edition, General Robert warns his readers to be alert to another dangerous possibility of error: someone may move for acceptance when he is simply trying to note for the record that the report has been received. In fact, "accept" is equivalent to "agree to" or "adopt" in *Robert's Rules*. When you search that volume for preferences among these three choices, you begin to detect what has been the problem in the past. Some of the earlier editions (1907–1951) of *Robert's Rules* state that "accept" is the proper term to use with respect to a (simple) report; the 1970 edition suggests that the term "accept" is too often misunderstood, and although the equivalence of the several terms is affirmed, the 1970 edition and a footnote in the 1907 edition prefer the word "adopt" for all reports, since it is the least likely to be misunderstood. But what about the other one of the three equivalent terms, "agree to"? If a lawyer is taking part in a deliberative conference or providing technical advice to it, you may note a degree of shuddering whenever the term "agree" is mentioned as the action of the conference on a report. Although I have never seen anything in any prior reference work on parliamentary law that would outlaw the parlimentary usage of "agree to," I shall tell a parable to explain the real problem in the use of "agree to" in a nonlegal sense:

LOWERY'S PARABLE

It seems there were two lawyers who were good friends one to the other, and the first one spake to the other, "Jehoshaphat, as good friends let us agree to break bread together come Tuesday noon and then take ourselves to the golf course for proper relaxation and to ponder ponderous matters in a serene manner." Jehoshaphat spake likewise, and it was to come to pass next Tuesday. But Jehoshaphat was delayed in court; his friend sued him for breach of contract, with multiple damages asked. End of story.

Although legal definitions of "agree" or its equivalent, "agree to," are very similar to dictionary definitions and do confirm that "agree to" is a suitable equivalent of "adopt" or "accept" in parliamentary usage, legal definitions include such usage as "to exchange promises,"[1] which would not appear in the usual dictionary definitions. Thus, the parliamentary preference is well stated in the 1970 edition of *Robert's Rules* for "adopt."

But, what about "approve," which is the simplistic word often employed in acting upon meeting reports? Now, we get into complications that are not easily resolved but should be understood if we are to avoid more confusion. In looking for *definitions* in the texts on parliamentary law, we shall be pretty well confused; instead, let us look for the typical *usage* that is condoned by those texts. All editions of *Robert's*

---

[1]*Black's Law Dictionary*, West Publishing Company, St. Paul, Minn., 1976 ed. copyright by Charles Scribner's Sons, New York, 1976.

Rules[2] will be found to be consistent in *not* using "approve" except for one specific thing: the approval of minutes. The word "approve" is used more often in the 1970 edition than in earlier editions, but it still is a term employed in an indefinite sense. Although minutes are approved, amendments to minutes are "adopted." Inasmuch as parliamentary authorities state that a motion to approve minutes is an incidental main motion, it is obvious that the *motion* will be adopted rather than approved; that action makes the minutes approved, although it is not incorrect to adopt or accept the minutes. *Robert's Rules* (1970 edition only) describes the action of approval of minutes under a section entitled "Ratify, Motion to" and states an equivalence between these two terms and a third term, "confirm," to describe validation of a prior action. Demeter gives a pertinent example of proper ratification action by assuming that a treasurer has spent some money for a particular charity. If the body ratifies the action (already taken without prior approval), the treasurer gets his money back from the treasury; otherwise he is stuck with the expenditure out of his own funds. The connotation with respect to minutes is that they have been prepared and partially published without formal authorization; thus, the body will ordinarily ratify them as written or, at the most, modify them somewhat and then adopt those amendments and the minutes simultaneously. All texts make an *assumption* that minutes will usually be ratified by common consent. Demeter suggests the words to be used by the chairman: "There being no corrections, the minutes will stand approved as read." He states that this constitutes acceptance of the minutes, assuming that no one objects, as is usual. He states that if a member wishes to take a more formal action, the proper words would be: "I move to accept the minutes as read."[3]

Simplification

In the foregoing, I have attempted to be rather more pedantic and exact than I would ordinarily expect a group to be in the handling of minutes. I have used exact terms and proper parliamentary forms for tutorial reasons, to allow the best understanding of the principles involved so that any simplification will be predicated upon sound parliamentary principles and be unlikely to confuse anyone. I have shown how confusing the whole topic can be even when handled exactly in the form sug-

[2]See citation at the end of Chapter 4.
[3]George Demeter, *Demeter's Manual of Parliamentary Law and Procedure,* copyright © 1969 by Little, Brown and Company, Boston, by permission of Little, Brown and Company.

gested in the usual textbooks; thus, I must clarify rather than further confuse if we are to make a proper abridgment of the formalities. The foregoing tutorial exercise brings out several points that are important:

Summary Points

1.   To avoid misunderstanding in reporting an *action* on a motion, report, minutes, or recommendation, use the term "adopt" rather than "agree to," "accept," or "approve." Although these other terms *may* be correct, they may also prove to be misleading and confuse rather than clarify the action you are reporting.

2.   When exactness is extraneous (as with uncontested actions) and a sense of informality is appropriate, it is better to avoid any and all of the terms defined in parliamentary-procedures texts and employ self-explanatory phrases such as "concurred in this action," "decided to reject the proposal," "were unanimous in their choice of that alternative," "chose to adjourn early," or "confirmed the committee's choice of words" as suited to the action taken or the action that was proposed to be taken.

3.   Be absolutely clear on what *specifically* the action was taken. If it was on the whole report, say it *clearly*. If, in the usual case, it was on one or more recommendations within the report, make absolutely certain that the deliberative body knows *what* it is and that the minutes or report of the action make it abundantly clear that the body simply took note of the rest of the report but took no action on it.

In discussing simplification of assembly actions on reports and recommendations, it is well to go one step further and suggest one simplification that can effectively be introduced into the reporting process with respect to minutes describing the action of a body. Demeter points out that minutes are known by at least three other names, "record," "report," and "journal," and that all are synonomous.[4] It seems to me that almost all organizations in my experience use the term "minutes," and that term is associated with a degree of formality that is unfortunate. This brings us to the typical problem: how can we prepare minutes so that they can be quickly distributed to record the actions of a deliberative conference? Minutes, by their very nature, cannot be validated instantaneously, and valuable time is lost with working subcommittees and even deliberative assemblies because of the impropriety of circulating the minutes of a meeting until they have been adopted by that meeting. Thus, we are faced with the natural protectionist nature of an

[4]Ibid.

attendee at a meeting who fears that something will be attributed to him "which he didn't really say." Once a member has found an objection to minutes, he is not likely to authorize any distribution of future minutes without *his* authorization. Such objections to minutes fit generally into several distinctly different categories. Let's take a closer look:

Reasons for Objecting to Minutes

1.   Outright mistakes in reporting. This is the least of our worries with an experienced recorder of minutes but is the reason usually given for complaints against minutes.

2.   Correct but unkind or untactful reporting. This is the next least of our worries with adequate experience by the recorder and is one we shall *never* be accused of, but we still must learn how to avoid untactful reporting.

3.   Unnecessary reporting. This is the most usual problem of the amateur recorder who thinks he should cover every detail and finds everyone objecting, not over the conclusions but over the reasons given for the conclusions.

4.   Black-and-white reporting of matters that should have been a shade of gray. This is a usual problem of an overenthusiastic recorder who hates to admit that some things were not definitively settled in the meeting. Thus, his minutes generate complaints from those who didn't see any black-and-white action but recall the unfinished debate and unresolved issues.

To improve our reporting of meetings, it is important first to understand clearly what the *purpose* of the minutes is or what it *should* be. Minutes should be optimized to provide three functions: memory refreshing for those present, information for those absent, and a history of acts and accomplishments. They must provide a bridge between one meeting and the next meeting to ensure continuous action rather than duplicated action or counterproductive action. Timely minutes, carefully optimized to do these things, are time-savers and money-savers for any organization which meets regularly to accomplish something useful in the commercial world. The emphasis must be on *timely* minutes, because, failing timeliness, minutes are less than useful in meeting *all three* of the functional needs. Therefore, it behooves the recorder to reduce the details sufficiently so that he can ensure no major criticisms of the material by the participants and that the group will accede to rapid distribution *without prior approval.*

Now I come to a possible shortcut. Years ago, the Airlines Electronic Engineering Committee, like every other organization, was strapped with a demand for advance approval by the official members before *any* minutes could be distributed outside the membership. Then, exercising the chairman's prerogative (as I have consistently urged throughout this book), I made an administrative decision that has survived for more than a quarter of a century without a problem. I decided to substitute a chairman's report of each meeting for what we had previously called minutes. No flaps. No objections. Nobody has missed the minutes of the meetings in 25 years. The reports are prepared by the technical staff and distributed publicly to international mailing lists of hundreds or thousands, depending upon the topic and degree of interest, and there are no objections. Certainly it isn't just the different, informal *name* that does it. The technical staff now knows how to report a meeting properly to provide maximum exposure of the discussion trend without infuriating someone who didn't get his pet idea accepted. Credible and careful reporting serves the purpose, along with an open and friendly invitation for anyone to correspond with the chairman over anything he believes has not been covered properly. By showing (and meaning) a willingness to let the opposition air its views not only in the meeting but in working papers which the chairman will circulate, we can avoid that old problem of recorders everywhere: a long time cycle due to a necessity for advance approval of everything of record that is circulated.

What I am saying, again, is that there can be no substitute for graciousness and openness on the part of a chairman as well as of his whole staff in encouraging all the divergent opinions of minorities as well as the favored majority view. That same openness should exist in the dealings by correspondence that exist in a Goldfish Bowl deliberative conference. The Goldfish Bowl is a continuing activity; it doesn't cease when the people go home to the far corners of the earth after a public meeting.

What Comes Next?

In our first eleven chapters I have skipped around quite a bit, taking tutorial potshots at practices which my experience shows to be major time-wasters in the transition from the ordinary, usually rather clumsy, deliberative conference to a more effective Goldfish Bowl deliberative conference, at which everyone likely to be affected by the decisions is brought into one meeting so that the decisions can be made in parallel rather than in the slow, ponderous serial manner of the usual decision making of industry and government. Now, it is time to delve more deeply into the finer points of conference management as applied to the

Goldfish Bowl deliberative conference. From here on, there will be more emphasis on how to go about doing what I admonished you to do in earlier chapters. Intermixed you will find some duty topics that must be included in any book on conference management, such as "Advance Planning" (Chapter 27) and "How to Negotiate with a Hotel" (Chapter 30), each of which contains new ideas not found in the usual conference book.

As you concentrate on Chapter 12 and the chapters that follow it, you will find yourself squarely in the middle of things that count in improving the effectiveness of chairmen and participants in any kind of deliberative conference, particularly the Goldfish Bowl deliberative conference. Now we are into the small points that add up to immense savings of time and money in industry conferences.

We all laugh at the old saying "I can hardly wait until I open my mouth to find out what I have to say." But there are two aspects of that saying. There is much truth in the instructions to would-be debaters to plan what you will say *before* rather than *during* your speech. But there is also truth, as I shall explain, in thinking on your feet so that every word you utter has an immediacy and a timeliness that would not be present if your speech were planned in advance.

Impromptu Speaking

Public-speaking instructors with experience in industrial training fully anticipate this need for explicit timeliness in most commercial speaking, as opposed to college speaking and debating. One department head in public speaking in a Midwestern university explained it this way when he discovered that I was returning to him for industrial training in speaking after having taken his courses several years previously as an engineering undergraduate: "You people in industry have an entirely different need for speech training from what you had as an undergraduate. You don't have the opportunity to prepare your speeches in advance; you must think on your feet. In college you may need extemporaneous speaking ability, but seldom impromptu speaking as in industry, where you will be called upon to speak *instantaneously* and explicitly." As a consequence, the industrial members of his speech classes were encouraged to work with only a very general advance preparation of specific speeches. The environment in the commercial world is not one that will allow an individual to plan his remarks in advance. While he is making plans for his "words" when he next gets the floor in a commercial conference, he will miss the specific point of the preceding speaker and find his words inapplicable, inappropriate, and probably wasted. To get anywhere in a complex, fast deliberative conference, an argument must be developed *after* the preceding speaker finishes his argument, not during the beginning of the

12

The Art of Expert Argument, or One-Upping Your Competitors

last sentence. An argument must get the attention of the meeting in the first few words, it must hold its attention until the point is reached, and it must have no irrelevancies that will distract listeners from the specific point.

Now that I have gotten your attention, dear reader, let me back up and take the subject a little more slowly by repeating a basic premise of this text. Remember that I have stated that the commercial motivation for finding an answer in industry deliberative conferences is *money,* either to save it or to make it. Remember, also, my premise that the chairman is responsible for the success or failure of every conference and that the participant can do whatever he is allowed to do by the chairman; that is, the chairman is responsible for decorum or lack thereof in a commercial or any other conference. But that is not all of my premise: I suggest that a representative is sent to such a conference, not for fun and sun, but for business reasons when the sponsoring organization has a money reason for getting the right decisions from the conference. Therefore, even though the chairman has the *responsibility* for success and for establishing decorum, every participant has a *monetary stake* in getting results from the conference. With an expert chairman, participants will have equal rights in speaking and sufficient opportunity in a logical, orderly conference to express their views. But with an inept chairman or even a sleepy chairman, rights will be unequal. If you can be assured of freedom from interruption in speaking (Ha, ha, ha!), you need only conventional (no pun intended) speaking ability. But if you must make every word count, you had better learn *impromptu* speaking.

Getting Your Views Heard

Now that I have put this chapter into its proper perspective, I shall continue in the understanding that I am not condoning imperfect chairmanship but am simply recognizing and reaffirming what I have said before, that there are no perfect chairmen, only various degrees of imperfect chairmen. Our aim must be to survive in an imperfect commercial world where it is almost literally true that only the fittest can survive.

Let me hypothesize a case to illustrate the options open to you as a conference speaker attending a deliberative conference at which you want to find a suitable solution to some complex government regulations affecting your industry. You note that several government spokesmen have been invited to present suggestions for improving the regulations. Most of the suggestions are too general to be of any utility. Although one speaker has made some suggestions that come close to being specific enough to solve the problem, he has stopped short of making the proposal, and the group seems not to have seen the solution. Should you get the floor and suggest the solution? You have discovered that time is short (Isn't it always?) and that the individuals who gain the floor for a comment seem to be pressed by the chairman into making very incomplete statements, probably because so many presentations have been arranged that the chairman is worried about time. In that environment, a floor proposal seems useless; you would never get even the background explained. Noting that others had been allowed presentations, you suggest to the chairman at the coffee break that you could add to what one other speaker has suggested to make a useful proposal upon which the group might act. Could you have a few minutes to make such a proposal at whatever time the chairman feels would be best? It works. (It will always work when you do it right.) Since the chairman is now more worried than before about time, he does what you thought he would do; he asks the group if it will be OK for you to make this proposal, which may provide an answer to the meeting's problems. Naturally the participants answer "Yes"; they don't know anything about the chairman's worries about time. The chairman spends the next hour giving you more and more publicity on your "speech," as he keeps explaining to the meeting *when* you will be making your speech. Bully! Just what you wanted.

Soon the time comes, and you are offered the podium, which you politely refuse so you can "save time." Besides, you would rather stand at your seat because you are closer to the center of the audience and can better observe its reaction from that point. You rise. An aura of expectation surges in the audience; who could be so bold as to ask for permission to make a speech to this audience? The members are thinking that you must know what you are doing. You have deliberately *not* made an outline. You have deliberately covered up all your notes taken during the meeting and now lying on the table. The group can see that you have no notes and no outline and thus that you *must* have something pretty important to say. The participants are all ears. Your purpose in having no outline is to avoid any commitment to specific words or content. You can start with the necessary background, but you watch everybody carefully for any sign of restlessness. You watch the chairman, but so far, at least, he is sitting down, relaxed. If you can just get your introduction done before the participants get nervous! Now that you have started out with perfect attention, you can use your feedback to measure continued attention. You sense it immediately when you say something that the participants already know, having remembered it from the earlier speaker; you sense it when you remind them of something they have forgotten from the previous speaker. You compliment them on remembering some things even though you know (your feed-back tells you) that they have missed some points earlier. Now you have kept their attention long enough on preliminaries; it's time for your proposal. They are ready. They get it. They even like it. Success! Sit down quickly. The chairman is quite surprised. He had expected a long speech. He has gotten your point, and it will appear in the meeting report as *his* assessment of the meeting consensus. You know this by his reaction to your words and the nodding heads of the meeting atten-dees. There is no need for any motion.

This time the method has worked well. Sometimes you will be resisted by the group. Sometimes you will be put down by the chair-man even before you get an opportunity to open your mouth. It doesn't always work so well; sometimes you win, and sometimes you lose.

Feedback from Your Audience

What I am trying to illustrate is that the speech must be tailor-made for the *topic* and the *environment* and the *chairman* and the *audience* and the *general circumstances* and the *time*. Your speech can be most effec-tive if you have heard and comprehended everything said on the topic before you get up to open your mouth. You should ascertain the most effective time to say what you must say. You should search for some gimmick to establish immediate contact with your audience. One way, as in the foregoing example, is to build upon something that has been said previously by someone who has some stature and degree of accep-tance; you bootstrap yourself into the conference and into the ears of the audience and, particularly, into the mind of the chairman. Once you have established contact with an audience, it is quite easy to keep a perfect feedback connection that will tell you when your contact is breaking. You simply know how well your audience is reacting and whether it is confused over something you say or is ready for you to move on to something a little more meaty. *What you say in every sen-tence should reflect the feedback from the prior sentence.* Don't waste time on preliminaries that are already understood by your audience. Don't skip over preliminaries that your audience shows it has not assimilated. Don't take your eyes off the members of the audience; don't lose brain contact. Watch their faces, their hands, the shifting of their bodies; watch their eye movements, as these can give you better feedback than anything else. Take the arguments in small steps until you have paced the audience and its concentration in following your points.

As in the example described here, you will have much more freedom when you are introduced by the chairman and are offered the podium and when the chairman sits down and looks relaxed, rather than standing, looking at his watch, shifting from one nervous foot to the other in the hope that you will take the hint and shut up. In any event, whether invited in advance or not, you must optimize your presentation for the greatest effectiveness. If you take undue advantage of a proffered podium, a gracious chairman, or a friendly audience, you are cutting your own commercial throat. The chairman might be smarter than you give him credit for: perhaps he knows that the best way to get you put down is to let the audience put you down if he believes that is what the audience wants to do. He can simply recognize another speaker on a loosely related aspect of the same topic and leave your proposal hanging in midair. Many chairmen will do this anyway simply because they don't know any better. Unless you are austere with the audience's time and cater to its needs for a solution rather than emphasize your commercial whim, it will simply return the favor and ignore you and your proposal. Once spurned by a busy and articulate meeting, you will need the best of luck in trying to get started again on any proposal.

To illustrate the audacity of an audience, I must tell the true story of a preacher in a church in the outskirts of London who was treated to "listener control" by one of his parishioners. The man had long ago lost his hearing, but he came to church regularly and sat in the front pew, proudly displaying to the rest of the congregation his fine hearing aid provided to him by the British government. The old man always allocated the preacher just 20 minutes—no more. When the 20 minutes were up, with obvious ostentation he would remove the earpiece from his ear, place it in his pocket, turn off the hearing aid, and sit back in the pew looking glumly at the preacher. The preacher had a foolproof feedback system that all the other members of the congregation could take notice of.

Not every chairman and not every speaker can have such a perfect system of feedback to signify when the listener ceases to be a listener. Perhaps we would have better conferences if everyone had his own listening device, as in the United Nations, where simultaneous translation is employed and everyone needs headphones.

Speaking to the Point

Our message here is twofold: not only will feedback-controlled speaking produce fewer orations and more to-the-point explicitness, but it will enhance your success in winning your desired point with a busy or a sleepy audience. Since winning your desired point is probably the commercial reason why you are there, it is worth money to you and your organization. Yet one of the public-speaking errors regularly observed in deliberative conferences is the error of not looking at the chairman or the other participants. Some people have the idea that if they don't look directly at another individual while speaking to him, they are lessening the chance that the other individual will interrupt before they are through. Yep! It does that. But the practice also frustrates the other guy, who may see an obvious fallacy in an assumption on which your argument is predicated. The listener must listen dejectedly to the long harangue, only to explain at the end that it was all based on an absurd, fallacious assumption. Time has been wasted because the speaker has turned his eyes away and has also turned a deaf ear to the listener; and the oration (that's what it has now become) dribbles on and on and on. Speakers who have developed this inane practice in personal conversation will often try to apply it to larger groups of people in a deliberative conference with horrendous results that stultify the true deliberative process. Not only are they hurting the whole conference, but they are embarrassing themselves and making it abundantly clear to all knowledgeable participants how naïve and unprofessional they are. A proper chairman should recognize this tactic immediately and, from his own feedback from the audience, press the speaker into making an explicit proposal rather than an oration.

At this point, I should state that the main reason why a *large* deliberative conference is believed to be more ponderous than a *small* deliberative conference is the prevalence of orations in the large conference that would never develop in the small conference, in which people don't usually feel so great an urge to orate. But if the chairman sets the proper mood for the large conference and if he can get the participants motivated to *listen* carefully and speak to the point, no sluggishness need be associated with a large deliberative conference. The chairman must set the mood and ensure proper continuity so that the large deliberative conference does not take on the character of a Roman forum, with orators standing in line to orate. But whether or not the chairman can set this proper mood, the individual participant can help his case by turning on his own feedback system, by listening to everything said or even alluded to, and by gauging his speech making to the exact needs of the listener, tailoring his speech as to supply just what the listener needs, no more and no less. The commercial advantage to be gained is immense; in addition, he is helping an inept chairman form the proper mood and setting for deliberative success.

With the recent experimental use of television and radio coverage of the proceedings of the U.S. Congress, we may discover less than the usual degree of disinterest by senators and congressmen when a colleague is speaking. In Congress the system is different; everything that is said (and even everything that is pretended to have been said) is made a matter of record. Speakers are speaking to posterity, not to each other. They speak from prepared scripts rather than from urgency. The system requires such ponderous methods that spontaneity is not as much of an asset as in a commercial conference. True, some speakers apply extemporaneous speaking, but some wish that they hadn't when they read their unpracticed words in the *Washington Post* the next morning.

My message is addressed to participants in money-motivated commercial deliberative conferences rather than to congressmen and senators. Every word you say ought to be effective; you should concentrate your entire effort on making even the first word uttered count. Think fast and effectively before you open your mouth, but don't wait until you have organized a Gettysburg Address: the meeting will be over, and your point will never have been heard, good though it may have been.

Principles of Conference Speaking

So far in this chapter I have hardly mentioned the usual points for extemporaneous speakers to watch out for, let alone the points for impromptu speakers to follow. I cannot give them all here but must simply refer the reader to the usual texts for the basic rules of public speaking. However, I must emphasize a few points that are so very important in commercial debating but are so often ignored. Let me take a few examples.

Perhaps the most often ignored principle is the rudimentary principle of all successful debating. Don't jump from one point to another before the first point has been accepted by the meeting. Time and time again, a conference speaker will make a good point and then jump to his second point, leaving the meeting hanging. Once you have made a point (and your feedback should tell you whether the meeting accepts the point or resists it), you should make sure that the chairman follows up with an action at that time. With an inexperienced chairman, you will have to make the point in the form of a motion to get the action you desire. With an experienced chairman, it should come immediately and automatically by the chairman, who will state what seems to be the consensus of the meeting in favor of what you have proposed. In either case, don't let the point float but get it voted in or out. As I have urged throughout this text, don't assume the concurrence of the meeting on your point; get it made a matter of record while the meeting is in an accepting mood.

A second problem with many speakers is their failure to follow the proceedings. They will propose something that is unrelated to what has been discussed immediately before. Perhaps the preceding speakers have been working the group up to the point of making a specific proposal but have not quite gotten to the point of action. You may inadvertently ruin the whole train of logic by proposing something that does not logically come next. You will discover a very upset meeting, and if you haven't been listening, you may not understand just what you have done wrong.

Another principle that is often violated, to the detriment of the speaker, is nonspecificity in a presentation or even in a short comment from the floor. Too many speakers express their opinions in the form of vague generalities that point the meeting nowhere and do nothing for the stature of the speaker. Are you for or against a proposal? If your only contribution is a vague worry over some possible remote consequence of the action or inaction, you are not being very helpful to the meeting or to your own commercial cause. Meetings are very slithery things; they cannot react to vagaries but need points of substance to react to. If you propose a generic solution rather than an explicit solution, you can expect the meeting to drop off to sleep. There are times when a group must explore broad avenues before it is ready for the direct route to a solution, but try not to be the one that pushes the group back into the open field of generalities when it has started to focus on specifics. If a prior speaker has suggested a general approach simply because he hasn't gotten the end result clearly in mind and thought it through, try to make a contribution that will build upon that thought, mentioning him by name with a compliment, followed by your specific proposal. Give him due credit rather than attempt to take all the credit as though you had independently arrived at your proposal.

A related problem is your countering of a prior proposal, thereby placing *two* contradictory proposals before the group. Now you will have thoroughly confused the meeting, to your own detriment, because both proposals now are mired in a conflict that need not have been generated. When you hear the exact opposite to your view being made a specific proposal by someone, it is human nature immediately to ask for the floor and present your counterproposal to the meeting. Resist that impulse. Hold your horses. Watch the meeting for the group reaction to the proposal, and wait for the proper opportunity. Properly, that proposal should be acted upon, be either accepted or rejected, before a different proposal is injected. If the meeting were following strict parliamentary rules and procedures, you would be within your rights to move to substitute *your* concept for the one being debated. But there are at least a few reasons why that will not be appropriate in the usual commercial deliberations I am assuming. First, it is very, very unlikely that the proposal will have been made in the form of a motion in the usual commercial conference. Second, even if it were, it is highly unlikely that the chairman would have the least idea of what you are talking about and of how to manage it parliamentarily. Third, even if he did, no one else is likely to understand the workings of such an action. Fourth, even if it were understandable, it would be such an abrupt action that the group would tend to resist your proposal on the grounds that you were being unfair, ungentlemanly, and downright pompous in showing off your knowledge of parliamentary maneuvering, because your action would invariably be interpreted as just that. In Congress, yes; in a club meeting, yes; in a commercial meeting, never.

So what should be done instead? You have several outs. Some are a trifle sneaky; others are safer. One sneaky way is to wait for someone who holds the proposal in disfavor to raise some objection to it (there are always those who object to everything and don't mind expressing their minds against everything), after which you can either wait for some further show of displeasure with the proposal and then offer your counterproposal, or you may jump in immediately and express your concurrence with the other speaker, following it with your alternative plan. This diverts the meeting's displeasure to the other guy and puts you in the position of helping out the meeting. Always remember that if things are generally equal, a meeting will prefer the latest proposal made to it. Thus, it is better to have your proposal made as an alternative to some untenable proposal instead of as a first proposal. Of course, you do not want to wait so long, in the hope of following some untenable proposal, that you miss your chance. Still, the only proper way, and the safe way, is to let the first proposal work its way through the group discussion and be rejected or accepted. You may hate the idea of losing out because of mistiming, so that someone else gets his idea before the group and accepted just at the time yours should have been presented, but that is the curse of cautiousness. You can't win them all.

Paying Attention and Getting Involved

Throughout this text I have repeatedly urged careful and expert watching and listening by the chairman. By analogy, I have extrapolated that advice to fit the potential chairman. By further allusion, I have urged everyone who has a commercial purpose in attending a deliberative conference to look out for his own interests, and that requires some very careful attention to what the chairman does and what he fails to do that he should have done. It requires careful watching, careful attention, careful listening, and some quick thinking. It also requires advance planning of alternatives that are likely in any conference.

With experience as a chairman, this planning, thinking, and listening will come more easily. But to one who has not had lots of experience as a chairman, this advice may appear meaningless. You may say that you hate meetings. You may admit to always getting sleepy in meetings. You may question how anyone can really pay attention to intricate details when his mind is on relaxing on the beach or in the casino or focusing on that lobster dinner he will soon be enjoying. You will also say that this text states elsewhere that it is the job of the chairman to make it all good theater so you will not have to work so hard to pay attention; it's *his* meeting, not yours. Right again. Meeting participants, as a general class, have one thing in common: all *want* to sit in the back row, on the end of that row, next to an open window, with perfect access to the water fountain, the washroom, and the nearest bar. No one but the hardiest of meeting attendees wants to get involved in what is happening. All want the others to do all the preliminary work, the preliminary sorting of ideas, the preliminary drafting. You must be dragged into the problem when the solution is ready for final approval and after it has been developed in exact accord with your wishes. Certainly you would be willing to give the working group the benefit of your experience by making a presentation at the appropriate time. But you have every intention of arriving just before you speak and of leaving the meeting room just as soon as you have made your presentation, before any questions can be directed to you (there won't be any questions; *your* ideas are always sound): "If there are any minor uncertainties, the working group can sort them out after my presentation. I am interested only in 'the big picture,' not the intimate details." If pressed for detailed information, you will arrange to have an underling (a technical expert) present to explain all parts of your proposal. "The technical expert won't need me; I'll be on the golf course making sales contacts."

Unfortunately, it is this disassociative syndrome that ruins many deliberative conferences, keeping the people we all need out of the meetings until something has been decided. Then it has to be debated all over again with the involved people present. Those in industry who have had long experience with industry organizations realize that they must be present if they are to get their ideas across; otherwise, they may find it necessary to accept a less satisfactory outcome. Deliberative conferences require deliberative people deliberating. It is not easy, but there are many rewards for those who help. Sometimes it is only the knowledge that you helped; at other times it is the difference between an industry standard compatible with your practices and one that costs you a fortune to conform to. Whatever the motive, altruism or personal glory, money saving or accolades from a boss, there are benefits from working out industry problems in a common arena. But none of those benefits come unless the knowledgeable people and organizations get involved from the very beginning and stay involved until the problem has been solved. To get involved, individuals must *observe;* they must *listen;* they must *think;* they must *concentrate.* And they must put the welfare of their industry above the welfare of their own organization if they are properly to help their own organization and keep the esteem of their colleagues in industry.

A quotation:

> The best kind of conversation:- That conversation is the best which furnishes the most entertainment to the person conferred with, and calls upon him for the least exercise of mind. It is for this reason that argument and difference are studiously avoided by well-bred people; they tax and tire. It should be the aim of everyone to utter his remarks in such a form that the expression of assent or opposition need not follow from him he speaks with. (*Decorum: Treatise on Etiquette and Dress of the Best American Society*, J. A. Ruth & Co., 1878)

Even though the frontispiece of this 100-year-old book states that it is sold only by subscription, it would seem that almost everyone who has attended the meetings I have attended must have read this passage and *believed* it. Committee chairmen and participants all seem to go out of their way to avoid speaking directly on any topic in any meeting. But now that I have said that and now that I have written the preceding chapter of this text, "The Art of Expert Argument," I must still state for the record:

CARNES' COMMUNICATION CANON (CCC)

Communication is our most important problem.

And that leads to:

CARNES' CRITICAL COROLLARY TO CCC

Inasmuch as the prerequisites for accurate communication are accurate transmission and accurate reception, it is inconceivable, in an actual committee environment, that *anything* could be accurately communicated.

13

The Prerequisites to Expert Debating: Expert Listening and Expert Remembering

Since it is almost impossible, with the English language, for even two Englishmen to communicate reliably, our problems multiply when we put several Americans in a meeting, particularly if they are from different parts of the United States. Imagine what the error rate will be when we put a few Englishmen, Germans, Italians, and Texans together even if all are experts on the subject being discussed. Then throw in some non-American Indians, some American idioms, and some modern slang. Stir in a Scotsman, a Russian, and a couple of government people, and we are in trouble. Acronyms and American slang flow like vodka in the Ukraine.

And then, just to make it worse, we have the People's Propensity for Plenteous Pleonastic Pedantry syndrome. Committee participants simply refuse to answer a simple question with "Yes" or "No": a speech, particularly a pompous, pedantic speech, is much better than a simple answer to a simple question.

Thus, while individual affectations caused by the fashion of society will always regiment an individual into such pedantry, no such affectations or fashions interfere with perfect listening. No one can ever criticize a person for the quality of his listening, for the simple reason that his listening is private; no one knows how well he does it. While he may be forced by society and protocol to make a speech when none is necessary, he is never restrained by society from careful listening, as long as he does not do it at keyholes.

Now we come to the root of our communication problem: rather than attempt success in communication by making transmission more accurate, we are generally constrained to do all our improvement at the listening end of the circuit. Impossible though the task may seem to be, that is exactly where we must make most of our improvement in oral communication. If that is where we must make our improvement, let's admit it and get on with it. For the purpose of committee communications, listening must be discussed under two headings: (1) listening completely (to everything) and (2) listening accurately. While the former is a prerequisite for the latter, it is not a substitute for the latter. Let's take the two separately and see what can be done, first, to improve our listening to everything and, second, to improve the *accuracy* of our listening.

Listening to Everything

While listening is not akin to hearing, it is the start: Let us note what our 100-year-old textbook on decorum tells us about listening as it was practiced way back when:

LISTENING

"A dearth of words," says Young, "a woman need not fear,
But 'tis a task, indeed, to learn to hear;
In that, the skill of conversation lies;
That shows or makes you both polite and wise."

Listening is not only a point of good breeding and the best kind of flattery, but it is a method of acquiring information which no man of judgment will neglect. "This is a common vice in conversation," says Montaigne, "that instead of gathering observations from others, we make it our whole business to lay ourselves open to them, and are more concerned how to expose and set out our own commodities, than to increase our stock by acquiring new. Silence therefore, and modesty, are very advantageous qualities in conversation."

Though many of society's mores are different today from what they were generations ago, we can see that writers were admonishing everyone then, exactly as now, to *hear* as well as to listen. Today, we all recognize the rapid cadence of business activity; no more can we conduct our business as was deemed satisfactory in the days of the pony express. Fast business communication by satellite telephone or by computer-to-computer data transmission has been thoroughly exploited to gain every bit of speed possible in information transfer. How can business have become so much more efficient in all activities except in the holding of meetings and in even the most rudimentary exchanges of oral communication? Business firms offer their management people training courses in almost everything, including public speaking, but when has anyone offered a course in public listening? Possibly because public listening is so private (unlike public speaking with everyone watching), it is unobservable. Almost everyone listens badly. Almost everyone hears very little of what is said. Speeches contain dripping redundancy; it is almost as though the listener were expected to engage in only part-time listening. What should we do about it? Let's start with the motivation for careful listening.

The best motivating force for careful listening is direct involvement in what is going on. When we listen to a Sunday sermon, we are not involved directly in what the preacher is saying; even though Judgment Day might be near, it is not today, and we must think about that new manufacturing process we are introducing tomorrow. And in our annual convention of the Fiddlewhopper Association, the speaker seems to be concentrating on next year's improvements to fiddlewhopper marketing, so why get concerned? We can read his speech after we get home. And even the meeting of the Fiddlewhopper Engineering Committee isn't likely to produce anything to help us for many months. But, wait a moment: the Ad Hoc Emergency Assessment Committee is meeting this morning. It says here that the committee has been given the power to decide how much each firm's assessment will be for that big advertising campaign the Executive Committee adopted last night. My share could be as much as $27,000; I think I should attend. Now I *am* motivated, right down in the depths of my pocketbook.

So when an individual gets *motivated*, he not only attends a meeting but *participates*. You bet he listens. You bet he hears everything that is said. He even intercepts the murmurs of another guy who is suggesting to his neighbor that the "big firms" ought to bear the brunt of this campaign. I have an old saying about those who *are* involved and must listen:

CARNES' LISTENING PRECEPT

To get the message, listen between the lines of the unwritten handwriting on the wall.

For those who are automatically involved in what is happening, listening will take place automatically. You will suddenly discover how much is happening in a meeting, and you will get it all. Not only will you be listening to every word, but you will *hear* every word. You may or may not hear it *accurately;* that subject I shall treat later in the chapter.

The foregoing hypothetical situation of an immediate monetary assessment gives us one suggestion for getting involved as a means of developing concentration and thereby developing better listening habits: even though we may not be subject to an immediate assessment, we *can* get ourselves involved through other means. Developing a friendly interest in others and their problems is an ideal way to practice the art of listening. Put yourself in the place of your competitor, or develop an altruistic determination to get the best answers for your whole industry or community and offer your help to work on solutions to industry or community problems. Once you have elected to get involved, you will discover that you are making new friends, you are opening new vistas, and you are no longer drowsy during the same committee meeting. You will also discover that you are hearing, as well as listening to, everything that is said by anyone and everyone. Involvement for almost any reason will generate *motivation* for listening. Probably one of the best methods of learning the art of quantitative listening is to offer to be the secretary of a committee. Now you will have perfect motivation for hearing everything that is said, and this will lead you to the second part of the problem, listening carefully and accurately.

Listening Accurately to Everything

Although we must start by learning to listen to everything, we cannot graduate from the course until we have learned, first, to hear everything and, second, to *hear everything accurately*. Remember my introductory proposition that speaking is seldom precise and explicit enough to allow translation into correct thoughts that reflect what the speaker has in his mind simply by listening to what he says. The accurate listener must understand what the speaker *intends*, not just what he *says*. A rudimentary example might involve a speaker, urging another committee meeting on Wednesday, who trips over his own tongue and says "Tuesday" in the middle of a sentence when he has said "Wednesday" in the rest of his speech. A careful listener and a professional secretary of the committee would transliterate his Tuesday into the intended Wednesday without even calling the speaker's attention to the error so that his train of thought is not broken. A not-so-careful listener might miss one or more of the Wednesdays and take a lot of time in the meeting to object to Tuesday for the proposed meeting. Partial listening and inaccurate listening can slow down many a meeting. A secretary's recording of the wrong day in the meeting minutes (a literal transcription of what the speaker said rather than what he meant) can confuse those who read the minutes later and don't know when the next meeting is to be held.

Most presentations of ideas to a meeting are imperfect; usually the speaker will try to explain views in several ways, and the several ways may not produce the same ideas in the mind of the listener. The inexperienced listener will immediately object to the proposal because he takes offense at one of the several explanations given; he simply ignores the other explanations. Extra time is required as the meeting debates the *motives* rather than the *proposal* of the speaker. The reason, of course, is that several contradictory explanations of the same proposal will usually be interpreted as weasel words offered by an individual who is trying to court both sides by making a proposal that is unspecific. The proposal therefore becomes suspect. Though the speaker may try hard to explain that he inadvertently said what he had not intended to say, the damage will have been done, and his proposal is probably lost; he has lost his hearers' trust.

Certainly I am in no way suggesting that redundancy in speaking can be eliminated just because it is unnecessary. Even though redundancy is unnecessary, it will never be eliminated in oral communications because that is the nature of oral communications and it will always be that way until some new language that has no redundancy is invented and that language is digitized for rapid oral communication, and *that* isn't going to happen in this century.

No! All I am suggesting is that redundancy, particularly imperfect redundancy, is a basic part of all oral communications and that we should learn to live with it. It must always be our hope that, through expert listening, we shall learn how to correct the inaccuracy that will never be corrected in the inexpert speaking we all hear at every meeting. We observe this inaccuracy in our own conversations all day every day. We cannot correct it *at the source;* we must try to correct it through careful listening.

Students of language know that English is not a precise language and that French is far better. United Nations bodies have made numerous studies to learn just how imprecise the English language really is. One set of studies took some typical speeches and translated them from the original language through all the United Nations standard languages and back into the original language, just as we have all done on a lesser scale in the old parlor game of our childhood. As might be expected, these tests showed how much was lost by simple simultaneous translation in sequence through the various languages. It is a common tale throughout the various United Nations entities that the imprecision of English can be checked by translating the suspected words into French and back into English. If the original English can stand this exercise without losing its meaning, it is acceptable.

Even computerization of the translation process suffers from imprecision and odd expressions. The story is told of one experiment in computer translation in which a term widely used by mechanical engineers, "hydraulic ram," invariably came out as "water goat." It is evident that for successful computer translation the programming of the computer must take into account many factors, including the state of knowledge of the writer, if accurate translation is to be possible. Committee meetings suffer from the same malady, and the malady is more disturbing in commercial conferences because of the fast pace of business and business communications in meetings.

Once an individual has been motivated to want complete and careful listening, he becomes almost paranoid as he observes the wide disparity of opinions on "what he said," Here I must return to the very first admonition in this text addressed to the chairman, the one individual who supposedly is best equipped by training and experience to cope with the many interpretations possible from everything that is uttered in a meeting. As I said many chapters ago, if the chairman cannot understand what is being said and *meant*, how can we expect the rest of the meeting to advance toward a consensus? It is the chairman's duty to help. If the chairman can't figure out a proposal, he should either ask the speaker to clarify it or give his own interpretation succinctly and ask whether that is the speaker's proposal. Even if the chairman can figure out the proposal, we can be reasonably certain that many in the meeting won't get any idea of what is being proposed; here again, the chairman can help immensely if he will try an explanation and test it on the speaker.

One additional help for speakers and participants is to know the other participants well. An experienced chairman and an experienced secretary often will know their participants very, very well and be able to read them like a book. Despite a long, rambling dissertation that seems to point in all directions, an experienced chairman can translate it into a short, succinct proposal that all can consider. The reason why an experienced chairman or secretary has this capability is his capacity for *complete* listening. This capacity can do wonders in sorting out imperfections and inconsistencies in a speech or series of speeches. By building up experience with particular individuals, the chairman or secretary can often know immediately what an individual *is going to say before he starts*. The chairman starts his listening process with a premise which he then adds to or subtracts from as the lengthy speech unfolds with all its inconsistencies, redundancy, and incomplete concepts. When the speaker is through, the chairman has his original premise, possibly only slightly modified, to present to the meeting in a few well-chosen words. How efficient it would be if everyone in the meeting could be motivated by direct involvement to listen so well, so constantly, so consistently, so perfectly, and so accurately to what the *speaker has in his mind rather than to what he puts into words*. There is one very good reason why the inexperienced debater doesn't listen so expertly even though he is involved, is trying, and is taking a highly active part in debating the issues. This one handicap of the inexperienced is a major cause of poor listening; it is a factor even in ruining two-party conversations and debate, it is successful in undermining almost all two-way discussions, and in a meeting it slows the search for a consensus probably more effectively than any other bad trait. I shall call it:

DUPLEXER FAILURE SYNDROME

The propensity of a debater to turn off his listening apparatus while organizing his next rejoinder.

One would think that anyone engaged in a debate would plan his next remarks *after* he has heard what his opponent has just said. Not so. Too many debaters get carried away with planning their debate arguments and start reviewing their prior arguments and planning their next ones while their opponents are giving their own best arguments. But they may not realize that they turn off their listening facility while planning their next retort. They never even realize that they are often out of synchronism with the debate: they are arguing a prior point already passed over by their opponent as lost, and they are so engrossed with their coming oratory that they fail to concentrate on what their opponent is now saying. Like those admonished in the 100-year-old quotation from *Decorum*, we are preoccupied with exposing ourselves instead of concentrating on acquiring information. We shall certainly need that information if we are to win a debate through sound argument and logic rather than through noisy oratory unrelated to the issues. Thus, I urge self-examination to see whether we are *thinking* simultaneously with our expert listening. If we must decide between two capabilities, only one of which we can use at a time, my vote is for listening first, holding up oratorical preparation until listening is finished.

If we practice faithfully, we shall soon discover that *both* capabilities can be used at once without interrupting the all-important listening. Knowing our failings is the first step in their correction. Concentrate on listening until you are sure that you are hearing more than anyone else in the meeting; be sure you can anticipate what will be contained in the minutes when you read them later (assuming an experienced professional chairman and secretary). Experience as a chairman will make you an expert listener in a conference, but even without that experience watch, carefully observe, and listen to everything in other people's meetings. It may seem difficult at first, but it can be an interesting and rewarding experience that will be of inestimable value to you as you go down life's highway, attending more and more long business meetings. Instead of sitting through what you thought were boring conferences, you will discover the mystery of "people watching," that great pastime of so many. But you will be applying the precepts of people watching in an environment in which it can aid you in business, save you time and money in the meetings you must attend, and even rub off on your fellow participants, who may not yet have learned the potential of this exercise for improving *their* business.

Having discussed both the quantitative and the qualitative aspects of listening, we still must not leave the topic of listening without some mention of the process of recalling what we have heard: a memory for the results of listening.

Remembering What We Hear

It serves little purpose to practice the art of listening until we become proficient if we then discover that we cannot recall what we have heard. And so we come to that great cause of differences of opinion: how to recall what we need to recall. Some secretaries of committees swear by the process of note taking; others insist that only superficial notations should be written and the time spent in listening rather than in writing. Others may have had experience with Speedwriting or even formal training in shorthand, and some may even be able to read their shorthand notes after these get cold. I know one individual who has trained himself to take such elaborate notes in longhand that he need only hand them to his secretary for transcription and he will have a complete report that can be published with no further work. That ability is exceptional. But even experts at note taking usually discover that they have trouble when called upon to chair a meeting. Note taking is essentially an activity for the passive, or at least the not so very active, participant, and seldom is it suitable for the chairman. Some people choose to depend upon memory for the happenings of a meeting and can produce a detailed, accurate report of a meeting long after the meeting is finished by simply recalling the action, the debate, the views of participants, the eventual outcome, and the processes of getting to that point, all from memory. In my own case, memory rather than note taking was employed because of horrible penmanship and very slow writing, which did not lend itself to a fast meeting when I was faced with the necessity of serving as the chairman *and* the secretary. I don't necessarily recommend this method, but if it is the only possible choice, it is the only possible choice. So, get on with it. It can be learned.

As with all other memory problems, everyone has the *inherent capability* to remember; not very many have the motivation to work on their memory; fewer have the stamina to keep at it. Again, as with all the characteristics of expert chairmen and expert participants, there is one basic prerequisite for memory: motivation. Motivation itself has the same prerequisite stated before: involvement. If you find yourself forced to be a secretary and write a *definitive* report of what happened, you will find yourself getting involved. You will find yourself thoroughly motivated, and the memory of which the human mind is inherently capable will make itself evident to your great surprise. With more practice, your memory will develop further. Soon you will find yourself with an in-depth knowledge and understanding of everything of any importance that happens in a meeting. This does not mean that your report of that meeting will be particularly lucid; that takes further practice and some more hard work. But you will discover that you are blessed with a better recollection of events and their sequence than almost anyone else who attends that meeting. This will not come in one sitting; you will have to help your memory along by some simple exercises.

As repeated typing of each character helps with worn-out carbon paper, you can help your memory process if you run happenings back through your conscious memory a few times immediately after they have taken place. You will do this automatically if you are the chairman and summarize the events as they happen for the benefit of the other participants. If the chairman does what is his duty and what I have repeatedly admonished a good chairman to do, he will be exercising his own memory and ensuring that he is running the proper facts back through his memory and *engraving them there*. Furthermore, if the chairman will do as I have urged and remind the meeting frequently where it is in the deliberative process, he will discover that he has organized his thoughts far better than if he left them for sorting a week or two later when he gets ready to prepare his report. That simple exercise not only helps the others in the meeting but firms up the conclusions and the way they were arrived at so that a sensible, logical basis for action will have been developed. The chairman's summary will benefit everyone in the meeting, including the secretary and the chairman. All these benefits come about from getting involved, becoming motivated, and accepting responsibility as a chairman or a secretary. But even though you may not be serving as secretary or chairman, you can go through these exercises *as though you were* and gain the same benefits of a better understanding of what is happening for your own sake and for that of your organization.

At this point, I should mention one common failing in memory of many people who attend meetings. If you were to sneak a look at the business trip report of one of your colleagues after you both had attended the same meeting, I can practically guarantee that his trip report would emphasize the *one or several proposals he made to the meeting,* whether accepted or not. The reason is not one of immodesty; this is simply the only part of the meeting he remembers. Now, check your own trip report and see if you did the same thing. This gives us the key: we remember those things that have impressed us intensely; we remember what *we* say at a conference; we don't usually remember what someone else says. Knowing this quirk of our own memory process, we must get ourselves more deeply involved so that *everything* at the conference is impressed upon our memory. We must run it all back through our memory as we think about it or discuss it with another participant so that everything, whether we said it or not, gets the same emphasis in our mind. Yes, *you* can write up a 3-day conference from memory and have your account check with the conclusions of other experts. Remembering may be the easy part; the writing of the report in a logical format that others can easily read may be more difficult. It is the purpose of this text to treat, not the process of good writing, but only the process of conference management and the memory aids that contribute to it. All I can say here is that a careful review of happenings as they occur and a careful re-review of the same happenings several times before they get cold can give you the wherewithal to produce a sensible and complete report. Beyond that you are on your own.

Remembering Names

It is always disconcerting to the chairman of a meeting and to each and every participant when he cannot remember the names of people he should know. In Chapter 5, I exhorted the chairman to use names (first names) as a means of speeding up action and debate, and I promised to give further details later. While I cannot give complete coverage to that complicated topic here, I shall offer a few suggestions, and I shall state unequivocally that you or anyone *can* remember names if you decide you really want to.

How many times have you said to anyone who would listen "I have a wonderful memory for faces, but I just can't remember names"? Rubbish! If you say that, it is an admission that you can't care less about people and their names. You don't consider another individual's name important to you. You are denigrating his name while raising the importance of your own name. Now that I have said that, let me get a little more specific: it doesn't take much brainpower to remember people's names or anything else about them; it takes simply a desire to do it. Let us look at some simple cases.

In our hometown, as in yours, there are many parking garages and parking lots in the downtown area. Perhaps ours are bigger than yours because we have so many government offices of immense proportions scattered all over our town. In our town, as in yours, parking-lot attendants do not have the highest-paid jobs in town; seldom do we find a high-IQ genius, or even a Ph.D., attending a parking lot. Yet, time and time again, when I have occasion to leave a car in one of those lots (never in the same lot more than once or twice a year), I am greeted by the attendant, who tells me where the car is without even looking at the ticket. I don't stand out in a crowd any more than anyone else; parking-lot attendants, as a class, have an excellent memory and can associate a car with its owner. Take another example: if you have visited a high-class restaurant in Los Angeles, Miami Beach, or other cities where it is the fashion to have valet car parking at the door, you will recall the many restaurants where no tickets of any kind are ever used. But the attendants can usually remember your car without so much as a word on what kind of car you have. No Ph.D.'s here either.

Another example: now that I have mentioned restaurants, do you have the proclivity of ordering the same thing for breakfast in a hotel every day? If so, you may be surprised at how short a time is required for a waitress to get you associated with your regular order. I can recall one particular city I visited about every 3 months, where a waitress learned my favorite. After many months' absence, I was astounded to find grapefruit in front of me as soon as I sat down; she saw me coming. Speaking of hotels, the managements of certain hotels have made a goldmine by offering special attention. Some hotels may use card files to record the special needs of a particular infrequent guest, but others depend strictly upon memory. Still no genius and no Ph.D.

Now, let's get closer to our kind of work. Have you observed your preacher lately, how he greets everyone in his flock by their full names, and how he has an infinite capacity for remembering all the vital statistics of the family: names of grandchildren, ages of parents, birthdays? You name it, he remembers it without any notebook. Thousands of people attend a big-city cosmopolitan church (some not very often— Christmas and Easter only), but how well the preacher remembers! Now, let's look into your own office. Does your secretary keep some mailing list up to date? Does she have the task of answering your frantic inquiry when you can't find a telephone number and need it quickly? Does she depend upon a written record? Probably not. She probably produces the number right out of her head, along with file numbers, your children's birthdays, all your appointments and call-backs, and everything else. Perhaps you hadn't noticed these everyday examples of memory for names right under your nose while you have been lamenting, "I have a wonderful memory for faces, but I just can't remember names." I believe the foregoing examples (and there are many more) will properly dispose of the old fallacy that a memory for names is a God-given capability of only certain lucky people.

If it is so easy, why can't I remember names when I try so hard? This response is akin to that of the pompous individual who listened to a great violinist and then remarked to his friend, "I would give *anything* if I could play like that." When translated, what he *really* meant is that he would do anything that was no trouble but that he certainly would not take lessons and practice. Remembering names is most certainly within the capability of anyone, but a prerequisite is the same motivation and involvement that I have stated to be a prerequisite for almost anything else of importance in this text. There is no simple shortcut. It is work, just like everything else worthwhile. But the benefits are immense for a chairman and for anyone who wants to get ahead in his community, his social club, his company, his industry, or his world.

There are some alternatives to learning names. For example, if a man becomes important before he becomes smart, he can get by with an associate who will stand ahead of him at receptions and in business meetings and pass him the names of people. He'll be just like a politician shaking hands with constituents. But if he really needs to know people's names and wants to learn how, he should best start by *doing* it, tripping up, and doing it again.

I recall the time a quarter century ago when I was first called upon to chair what was at that time a very small Airlines Electronic Engineering Committee meeting. I tried every trick in the book because I was having so much trouble. But I kept at it, continually trying. Time went on; I knew that I ought to introduce all participants with their first and last names, their firms, their titles, and their cities, and I kept at it until I could. As I look back now, the practice caused quite a stir with only some two dozen people. But I kept at it; the meeting grew in size, attendance soon passed the 100 mark, and I was still doing it. I now had a reputation of being able to introduce hundreds and hundreds of people (an exaggeration, of course), and I was stuck with having to keep on as the meetings grew even larger. I couldn't really live up to the reputation, but I had to keep at it. Eventually, when the meetings got so large that I was spending too much time on such introductions, I had to cut the proceedings short and introduce only the thirty official committee members plus the other airline customers present. I still do that today, as a reasonable compromise, but even though I have not done the complete exercise in many years, I am often introduced to some newcomer as "the guy who knows everybody's name in the whole industry." A good reputation follows you everywhere until something happens to establish the opposite as a bad reputation. A memory for names is not impossible; in actual fact, it is as certain and as real as your *desire* to remember them. If you desire it, you can do it; if you believe you can't do it, it is only that you don't really want to.

How to help? The first element is, as I have said, motivation. You must generate a real *interest* in a person and his name, and not just in his name but in *him* as well. He must be a real individual to you. Then write down his name and read it over several times, impressing it upon your memory by noting how it is spelled, how it is pronounced, and how the individual wants it said. Once you have done this, you are on the road to remembering it. As with carbon paper that is heavily worn, you can still make a deep impression in your imperfect memory by repeating the name for emphasis. Any of the various memory aids suggested by memory experts can help; you may wish to associate the name with some characteristic of the individual, or you may not need to bother with this particular technique. All the methods are ways of emphatically becoming aware of the name and impressing it upon your memory until it sticks. Once you have written it down and pronounced it to yourself, you are on the right track; from then on it is simply a case of reemphasizing the name sufficiently to remember it.

People's Names: A Practice Method

To help you start the process, let us look at a specific example of how people are unconsciously learning people's names every day through the cocktail party, or reception, method. The next time you attend a "must" business reception, try this procedure: arrange to arrive so early that no one except the host and hostess will be there. After apologizing for your early arrival, inquire politely how many people are coming. Your hostess *may* start to name some people as she tries to make a count; note each name carefully, pretending that you recognize so-and-so's name and ask her if it is spelled with an *f* or a *th*. She will probably spell that name for you; concentrate on it. Then, if you can get somewhat away from the busy hostess, make a penciled list of the names you remember. If you have missed some, get her attention and ask how so-and-so's parents are getting along. This will produce more information and additional names for your list during the process of explaining to her who it is you are inquiring about. You will think of a lot of other tricks of conversation to get your list complete before any of the guests arrive. Hopefully, they will trickle in one or two at a time, giving you an opportunity to get the spelling of every name correct as the guests arrive.

You will also have an opportunity to watch the hostess as she introduces each guest to the others when the guest arrives; even if you can't catch the name each time, you can refer to your own list, now engraved in your memory, to determine which person it is. Watch the host and hostess, *particularly the hostess,* and note how she makes certain that she knows all the guests as they arrive, even her husband's business acquaintances whom she has never met. She has absolute motivation; she has complete involvement; she positively *must* learn everyone's name because she has to introduce everyone to everyone else. You will discover that the ordinary person can hold such a reception with some thirty to fifty previously unknown guests and get to know every one of those guests before the evening is out. If you watch what the hostess does, if you observe carefully, if you listen with care and concentration, if you try, you will discover how it is done, and you will be doing it the same way. You will know everyone's name at that reception.

Meetings are no different. Start with the determination to learn everyone's name and use the same procedure that the hostess used. It will work just as it worked for her, and you are now an expert with names. Although the hostess will get no credit for her memory exercise (everyone expects hostesses to know the names of their guests) and although few people will even notice how hard she works to do that little exercise, you can be sure that your memory exercise will not go unnoticed in a meeting. You will be credited with a fabulous memory. That's an extra bonus the hostess didn't get.

To summarize the process of memory development, I shall state again that when a human being has a need to remember, memory will develop as necessary; when there is no need, memory will atrophy. If an individual wishes to exercise his memory for names, places, facts, figures, or anything else, he must either develop a need or generate an artificial need to start the development process.

Other Aspects of Memory Development

There was another aspect of this topic that I wished to develop in this chapter with respect to memory and memory aids, but for the life of me I can't remember what it was.

> Your representative owes you, not his industry only, but his judgment; and he betrays, instead of serving you, if he sacrifices it to your opinion.
> —*Edmund Burke, 1774*

The foregoing words, paraphrased somewhat, were brought out in the musical play *1776*.[1] On the morning of the day on which the Continental Congress was supposed to take action on Virginia's resolution on independence, John Adams discovered Dr. Lyman Hall of Georgia standing in the shadows by the door in the congressional chamber before any other delegates had arrived. When he seemed to startle Adams, Dr. Hall recalled the above words, which he had once read, observing to Adams that he could not sleep in his dilemma over how he should vote. On the basis of the words in the quotation he had decided to vote for the resolution on independence.

Conflicting Responsibilities

Although Edmund Burke in 1774 and Dr. Hall in the play *1776* seem to have known what their responsibilities were with respect to their constituents, it has not been that easy for all the thousands upon thousands of representatives in the following two centuries to determine exactly where their responsibilities did lie. Many committee members who have never heard of Edmund Burke have pondered the philosophical question broadly when they find that they are expected by those who sent them as their representatives to do something or espouse something that does not fit within the bounds of their own judgment: "Now what do I do?" Time after time, a committee member goes through a period of soul-searching and then produces something like that statement of Edmund Burke (but expressed less eloquently) as an excuse for

[1] Text copyright © 1964 by Sherman Edwards; copyright © 1969 by Peter Stone; lyrics copyright © 1964, 1968, 1969 by Sherman Edwards; first published by The Viking Press, Inc., New York, 1970.

14

The Committee Member versus His Constituency

doing what he thinks proper instead of what his boss back home thinks he should do. Then the problem starts. Does he dare go back home? Can he hide what he did in the meeting from the prying eyes of his boss? Suppose that his boss reads the report, and it tells how strongly he argued in favor of the opposite side? Will he ever get another opportunity to represent his firm at a meeting? Almost everyone serving on industry committees has at some time had those mixed emotions. Is there an answer?

We know that a director of a United States corporation is required by law to give his first allegiance to the corporation. Yet he is a director voted into office by people who own large hunks of stock and want him to represent *their* stockholder interests. If he doesn't uphold their interests, he won't stay on the board of directors; if he doesn't do what is the best for the corporation, he is violating the law. So, what does he do when a conflict develops?

Often, the upshot of the complex pondering that invariably takes place is the conclusion by a body that committee members have a broad responsibility to *all* their constituents that transcends their responsibility to the particular segment of those constituents that elected them. The establishment by the committee of this premise as its policy seems to forestall the stomach tremors that the individuals might otherwise suffer in voting for something their own firms don't seem to like. At least, a committee member can now go back home and claim that the committee established this "statesmanlike policy" and that the members are required to work in that manner for "the total good" rather than for "our own private good." For a while this policy satisfies the two sides to the question, but only for a while. Once an important issue develops, the philosophical question arises again, never to be quite settled.

A Senate Debate

As I bring our study of English and American history up to date on this question of a member's responsibility to his constituents, I must report a particularly interesting turn of historical events in the early months of 1978, as the Panama Canal treaties went through lengthy debate in the U.S. Senate. On Thursday, March 16, 1978, the day of Senate passage of the first of the two treaties, I should not have been surprised (but I was) when I heard quoted *three times* in one period of 90 minutes these same words of Edmund Burke. This came about because on that eventful day several senators made speeches explaining their newly announced support for the treaty. It turned out that each senator was unaware that another senator had, just previously, called up exactly the same words as justification for endorsing the treaty. Even after three citations of the words, another senator quoted them all over again, stating that they were very important even though they were called up so often. Did that quotation and requotation settle the issue after 204 years? Not at all.

The next chapter in our study of history is set the next day following the adoption of the first of the two treaties on the Panama Canal. On Friday, March 17, 1978, the U.S. Senate started, in depth, the debate on the second treaty; now Burke's quotation was getting some more usage; it was quoted many times more by those who favored the two treaties, and it was rejected by those who did not favor the treaties. As an illustration, one senator had just requoted the statement as the basis for statesmanship when another senator asked him in which year the quotation was supposed to have been made. The first speaker said it was "around 1800," in the feeling that his opponent was being won over. But his opponent was using that opening only to call attention to the lack of electronic communications at that time, so that constituents were very ill informed. But in 1978 constituents could hear all the relevant arguments debated in their entirety on the floor of the Senate, as a consequence of the broadcasts of those debates by public radio. The debate continued, with the opponents of the Burke principle stating quite firmly that a constituent today has the background and knowledge to know what should be done; he does not live in the isolation of the late eighteenth century. Thus, the "world's most prestigious and important deliberative body," the U.S. Senate, could not resolve, satisfactorily, on March 17, 1978, whether the principle of Edmund Burke does or does not apply properly to the Senate. (Note also the follow-on discussion by the Senate of the same matter as reported in Chapter 20.)

Neither can I, in this text, resolve a matter of proper debate that has remained unresolved for the whole lifetime of the United States; nor shall I attempt to resolve it. Instead, my only contribution is to remind my readers that this is a complex topic. Do not believe that it is easily resolved, and do not expect a satisfactory and simple answer to this ancient problem, at least in the near future (your lifetime). But what do we do in an actual case? How can we survive in a committee environment when national legislative bodies cannot resolve a matter that seems basic to proper deliberative action? The only possible answer to these questions is to accept the principle that a deliberative body *by definition should deliberate and decide a matter on the basis of its best total collective judgment,* recognizing what I have noted many times previously, that under our principles of democratic action the "best collective judgment" is whatever a deliberative body chooses to do by majority vote (with the other usual requirements of parliamentary law carefully applied). It is neither possible nor desirable to ascertain *why* a particular member votes as he does.

Voting Procedures

We are given an insight into the broad general principles of parliamentary law when we review the procedures for voting. *Robert's Rules* establishes the simple forms of voice voting or show-of-hands voting as the basic methods, predicated on the basic principle that a member should not be required to divulge his vote in a truly deliberative body. If some members desire a roll-call vote, a majority is needed to require it unless the body's bylaws establish a lesser number. Robert urges organizations not to employ roll-call voting except when the members are responsible to a specific constituency and there is a need for a record so that the constituents can determine their members' record of voting. (In Congress, one-fifth of those present can require the "yeas and nays," as it is called.) What about absentee voting? Although Robert notes the several cases in which exceptions should be stated in the bylaws to allow certain balloting by mail and so on, the point made clearly is that a deliberative body should *deliberate* before acting; deliberation can occur only when the members are present before the vote. True, in today's electronic environment it is conceivable that a similar condition could be established through conference video transmission, and the time may arrive (although it had certainly not arrived by 1979) when teleconferences (see Chapter 32) could effectively replace actual conferences without voiding any of the precepts of parliamentary law for a truly deliberative meeting.

One other reference in *Robert's Rules* helps to give an answer to our practical question. With respect to proxy voting, Robert rejects it except for certain specific corporate requirements, established in some cases by law. Yet when the ownership of the "member seat" is transferable, as in a stock corporation, proxy votes are quite acceptable. The message which comes through based upon the parliamentary-law aspects of the question is that the member makes his decision (hopefully after listening to a full debate) and votes privately *on whatever basis he chooses to decide the issue*. He should not delegate that decision making to another; neither should he ask to give his vote *in absentia* (where he obviously could never take part in the deliberations that the other members take part in). The basis on which he makes his decision is his business and no one else's. He is answerable to his constituents to the degree that they make him answerable; he is answerable to his conscience to the extent that his conscience demands it. Any attempt by one member to force his own conscience on another member or an attempt by one member to discredit the reasons for a particular opinion of another member is highly improper and is about as likely to be successful as is a questioning of another member's motives.

Burke and His Constituents

Before we leave the historical aspects of this matter, we should perhaps take a last look at what happened to Edmund Burke after his famous statement in 1774. What did his constituents think about it? Did he go down in history as a great statesman? (Yes, he did, but not in the opinion of his own constituents.) Did he get trounced by his constituents?

Edmund Burke is widely quoted in the many books of quotations. He obviously fits into a particular niche in history. An account of the background of his representation in the British Parliament and the tribulations that followed his sojourn there is given in Simon & Schuster's *A Treasury of the World's Great Speeches*, edited by Houston Peterson. Burke had been in Parliament for 8 years when he became a representative of Bristol, then the second-largest city in England. It was after he found himself successful that he made that famous quotation as part of a speech to his constituents. Here is the portion of the speech from which the quotation is extracted:

> Certainly, gentlemen, it ought to be the happiness and glory of a representative to live in the strictest union, the closest correspondence, and the most unreserved communication with his constituents. Their wishes ought to have great weight with him; their opinion high respect; their business unremitted attention. It is his duty to sacrifice his repose, his pleasures, his satisfactions, to theirs; and, above all, ever, and in all cases, to prefer their interest to his own. But his unbiased opinion, his mature judgment, his enlightened conscience, he ought not to sacrifice to you; to any man, or to any set of men living. These he does not derive from your pleasure; no, nor from the law and the Constitution. They are a trust from Providence, for the abuse of which he is deeply answerable. Your representative owes you, not his industry only, but his judgment; and he betrays, instead of serving you, if he sacrifices it to your opinion."[2]

[2] Houston Peterson (ed.), *A Treasury of the World's Great Speeches*, Simon & Schuster, Inc., New York, 1954, 1965. Reprinted by permission of Simon & Schuster, a division of Gulf & Western Corporation.

Despite the statesmanship of that speech, Burke was in trouble with his constituents. Bristol was too far away, for good representation by Burke, and he served most of his 6-year term without canvassing his people for their views. Back in Bristol, he found himself trying to calm down a group of sullen constituents on September 6, 1780. Editor Peterson adds these words in comment upon this most remarkable speech: "His speech in self-defense has no parallel in the history of electioneering, and it was considered by Sir Samuel Romilly, the reformer of the penal code, 'the finest piece of oratory in our language.'"[3]

Burke's speech contains many other famous quotations, including the celebrated admonishment to his constituents who would continually debate the wisdom of a particular action on his part long after the action had taken place:

> It is not to be imagined how much of service is lost from spirits full of activity and full of energy, who are pressing, who are rushing forward, to great and capital objects, when you oblige them to be continually looking back. Whilst they are defending one service, they defraud you of a hundred. Applaud us when we run; console us when we fall; cheer us when we recover: but let us pass on—for God's sake, let us pass on!
>
> Do you think, gentlemen, that every public act in the six years since I stood in this place before you—that all the arduous things which have been done in this eventful period, which has crowded into a few years' space the revolutions of an age—can be opened to you on their fair grounds in half an hour's conversation.[4]

Burke makes many references to his inability to canvass Bristol:

> I admit there is a decorum and propriety in a Member of Parliament's paying a respectful court to his constituents. It I were conscious to myself that pleasure or dissipation, or low unworthy occupations, had detained me from personal attendance on you, I would readily admit my fault and quietly submit to the penalty. But, gentlemen, I live at an hundred miles' distance from Bristol; and at the end of a session I come to my own house, fatigued in body and in mind, to a little repose, and to a very little attention to my family and my private concerns. A visit to Bristol is always a sort of canvass; else it will do more harm than good. To pass from the toils of a session to the toils of a canvass is the furthest thing in the world from repose. I could hardly serve you *as I have done,* and court you too.[5]

[3] Ibid.
[4] Ibid.
[5] Ibid.

In noting Burke's inability to travel the 100 miles very many times in his 6-year term, we might compare that problem with those of a senator today. One who quoted on March 16, 1978, the words of Edmund Burke as his justification for voting for the treaty, was Sen. Dale Bumpers of Arkansas, who was elected to the Senate in 1974 and has found himself "frustrated to distraction by the Senate's disarray," using the words of *Washington Post* staff reporter Ward Sinclair in his April 23, 1978, story in *The Washington Post Magazine*, entitled "The Closing of the Senate Club." In that story, Sinclair quotes Senator Bumpers as saying very much the same about the problems of a legislator as did Burke 200 years ago. Here are Senator Bumpers's words, "The more complex the problem, the more time required for a solution. But the amount of time we have here has gone in the other direction. We have less and less time to deal with the problems." And yet, unlike Burke with his 100-mile-away constituency, according to reporter Sinclair, Senator Bumpers made at least twenty-eight trips back to Arkansas during 1977, meeting with and speaking to Arkansans at seventy-two public events.

Did Edmund Burke succeed? Did his constituents who had reaped much glory from his many public utterances decide to keep him as their representative? No. Peterson's summary states it this way:

> Masterpiece though it was in the long view of history, this speech did not win back Burke's alienated constituents. After two days of canvassing, he decided that his chances were hopeless and withdrew, "declined the poll," in a dramatic farewell.[6]

Edmund Burke, that great English statesman, did not remain out of Parliament very long. He went back into the melee, though not as a representative from Bristol, and he served a thankful country.

Does this historical account give us any further advice? I shall not answer that query but leave my readers to ponder it as they choose.

[6]Ibid.

I suspect that if you tabulate all the meetings, conferences, and get-togethers that you attend in any one period, you will discover that the majority of them have had something to do with some kind of standardization. That standardization may not have been concerned with things, but it probably has included standard practices, procedures, laws, formulas, rules, or even policies. Whether your meetings are industry or government, academic or commercial, social or business meetings, you will probably be spending a lot of your meeting time on some kind of standardization. You don't have to be involved in trade associations to get mixed up in standardization meetings: perhaps you attend union meetings to select your next fringe benefits, or perhaps your office social club has been invited to draw out employees' opinions on sporting events. You will be engaged in standardization whether things are involved or not.

Although things may not be your province in standardization, the processes are quite similar whether things, material or ethereal, are involved or not. While my standardization examples in this book have been primarily things (rather than policy statements, for example), they have been chosen only to make the examples more tangible and solid.

Growth of Product Standardization

Even if you believe that you will not have any direct involvement in any product standardization and, therefore, should be concerned only with procedure or policy standardization, I prognosticate that you may be surprised in future years by the increased emphasis on new-product standardization that I see coming. Those of us who sit in meetings around Washington are beginning to see a new trend that will

15

The Goldfish Bowl Deliberative Conference as an Aid to Product Standardization

undoubtedly influence the future proliferation of product standardization in many industries and in many areas of the United States where it would never have been believed likely to develop. Not only is the trend in foreign commerce making a shift that can cause such activity, but the whole mood of Congress toward government buying of commercial products rather than special products will result in government dependence upon commerical specifications as never before. This means that industries and product fields which have never needed product standards may now be forced, through commercial pressure, to follow a route that is quite foreign to them. And *you* may find that you and your organization are being caught up in a new activity.

Furthermore, I cannot, in my rather superficial look at product standardization in this chapter, cover the historical background on how the Goldfish Bowl got its start through product standardization of electronics in commercial airlines. Since the Goldfish Bowl is so ideally suited to product standardization, it would seem that any industry effort should make use of the experience of the airline industry through which the process evolved. That experience, set forth in historical perspective, is contained in Appendix 1.

Therefore, this chapter will simply introduce a complex subject, that of product standardization, to suggest some of the pitfalls of any standardization process, and offer some critical questions for assessing a potential program.

Importance of Product Standardization

Standardization is important in our world. We see the benefits of it all around us in every place, in every industry, and in every activity of modern life. When we plug in an electrical appliance, at least in the United States, we expect the plug to fit the wall socket and the appliance to work. When an American man takes an electric razor out of his luggage in some far-off country, he expects to be able to plug it in, in the bathroom, and to get a shave without burning out the razor. We Americans expect the whole world to be standardized in our way, just for us, and a lot of it is. When we buy new tires for our automobiles, we shudder at the new standard numbering system that bears no relation to the numbering system we learned in a prior generation. Somebody changed the standard. When we take apart our new Japanese tape recorder and discover that the bolts and nuts are different from the ones we bought at a hardware store, it matters not that the Japanese may be conforming to an International Standards Organization (ISO) machine screw standard; we don't like it because we don't use the same standard. Now we hear from the Department of Commerce that metrication is growing, although on a voluntary basis, and that we should expect to make greater use of metric units of measure in the future.

We expect standardization to exist, but we don't want to change any standard we already have in order to get standardization with someone else. Thus, standardization is something all people are *for*, as long as they don't have to give up anything.

How do we get standardization? We get it by giving up something we now have in favor of something else, simultaneously with other people giving up something they like for that same something else that neither of us likes. With all that complexity, how can we ever get any standardization? We get it by holding meetings and holding more meetings and then by fighting over each other's proposals, just as all meetings fight over something or other. If we gradually sort out some sense in those many meetings, someday we may have a little bit or a lot of standardization that we didn't have before.

International commerce wants to expand, and such commerce needs standardization; so all the pressures of commerce encourage standardization for the long term, even though the short-term penalties are quite great. History shows that when one particular country or one particular community has been the major supplier of a commodity, the standards of that particular commodity in that particular country or community have become the standards everywhere for the commodity. The classic difficulties with standardization occur for commodities or industries that develop simultaneously in a number of countries: during both world wars the American railroad rolling stock wouldn't fit the European railroad tracks because the gauge and other standards were different.

Perhaps the classic example of good modern-day standardization of consumer products is the cassette tape recorder. Many people may have first discovered this standardization, as I did, in the Roman Forum, where visitors can rent a machine with a cassette tape developed in the Netherlands and manufactured in just about every country in the world to the Dutch standard. Anybody's cassette fits anybody's machine: the ultimate in standardization.

A Proper Approach

As I pointed out earlier in this chapter and will explain in greater detail in Appendix 1, standardization of *everything* is just not a proper approach. With the recent pressures of Congress on government agencies to standardize and, particularly, to standardize on commercial products, I see an unreal and unjustified race to apply standardization to just about everything, whether appropriate or not. I find myself, after a lifetime of encouraging standardization, now trying to talk government and military agencies *out of* some impracticable standardization programs. Thus, my advice in this chapter is to be quite perceptive and careful in selecting candidates for product standardization. Here I feel my greatest contribution may lie in slowing down what may otherwise become a mad race by the federal government to standardize everything in sight, carrying commerce right along with it in its fierce drive.

And so here are eleven guidelines that may help to keep product standardization moving in the directions where it can be most useful:

1.   Before starting any product standardization process, it would be wise to ponder the needs of the industry or community to see what the ultimate aim and purpose are. Above all, never forget that standardization just for the sake of standardization is not only a lost cause but an absurdity. If, for example, interchangeability of parts is believed necessary for some reason or other (as with airlines), remember that the airline industry does not deem such interchangeability cost-effective in very many circumstances. At the black-box level in the aircraft, interchangeability of only the boxes themselves is important; inside those boxes, interchangeability of internal parts is not justified. Interface standards may be important between a fuel-truck hose connection and an aircraft, at any airport the world over, but standardization of the parts of that hose or of the fuel truck itself is not appropriate. *Selective standardization is more sensible than indiscriminate standardization.*

2.   Prioritize your standardization effort to concentrate on the forms of standardization that will save the most money or produce the best operational improvement. Don't fall into the trap of working on the easy standardization jobs that don't do much for anybody, at the expense of the really important but harder jobs. Remember the problem of the glory battery and Carnes' Glory Law of Chapter 8 as you select your first standardization tasks.

3.   Remember that difficulties in setting a particular standard increase with time as products come into being outside that standard. Before any product gets into the market, standardization may be a lot easier. But it may also be unnecessary. Are you certain you understand what the purpose of the standardization really is? Does your organization have enough stature to influence the industry and ensure that your standard will go anyplace? Or will the standard be just another pile of paper to go on someone's shelf?

4.   Have you clearly established who the customers will be for the product on which you intend to develop a standard? If you have contact with a segment of the user community so that you can determine what

it wants, is the segment enough of the total community to ensure a customer-endorsed standard? Or will it fail simply because few of the customers know or care about the standard and because no supplier takes notice of it? And if you do command the attention of the user community, what about the suppliers? Will they ever hear of it? Will they help develop the standard? Will they fight you at every step?

5.   In your business, is there a middleman who carries a lot of weight? The manufacturing community is often called the original equipment manufacturer (OEM), and this segment can be highly influential in any standardization of parts or related aspects of a product that your industry would like to see standardized. How does the middleman fit into your standardization effort?

6.   Have you discovered the "credibility factor" in spec writing, or do you consider the typical practice of "mil specs" the ultimate solution? Remember that present Department of Defense (DOD) policy on spec writing is to *avoid* such past practices as are exemplified by traditional mil specs and to specify only features that are necessary for the purpose. The DOD does *not* now condone the former military practice of specifying everything including the kitchen sink just because suitable standard boiler-plate spec material is available and has traditionally been included. There is a new philosophy in the DOD; admittedly the DOD and the military services have not yet completely established just how they will manage to keep such mil spec practices from continuing, but the policy now encourages the ARINC/AEEC type of spec that emphasizes what the customer would like in simple language rather than dogmatic how-to-design-it language.

7.   In developing a credible spec, have you included candid explanations of just what is wanted and *why it is wanted?* Or do you still endorse the precept of the old school that pretends that suppliers are stupid, that they would never provide what a customer wants if you give them any out, or that suppliers don't want to be bothered with explanations of why something has been specified?

8.   Do you still subscribe to the old view that a spec writer must be protected from blame by including every possible, known, or conceivable spec paragraph predicated on the record of all the mistakes that all industry has made in product development since the days of George Washington and his cannon spec?

9.   Have you recognized (as even the DOD has now recognized for the first time) that cost is a proper trade-off factor right along with performance, reliability, and delivery schedule? Ordinarily, industry is more likely to emphasize cost than is the DOD, but have you included the other factors in your trade-off analysis?

10.   Have you made proper allowance for the stultification of a product as a consequence of the standardization you propose? How often do you believe your industry or community can accept a complete change from one spec to an updated, different spec? Is the time measured in months, years, or decades?

11.   And last if not least, have you made allowance for the antitrust aspects of the problem? Have you explored the effect your standardization will likely have on an industry? Will it constrain trade? Will it *appear* to be in constraint of trade? Who could possibly be hurt if your standardization goes forward? Who could possibly *believe* they might be hurt?

The foregoing points may seem to suggest that I am encouraging the reader to forget all about standardization. I may seem to be placing all kinds of roadblocks in the path of standardization. Am I against standardization? I shall be candid: I most certainly *am* against standardization. If the only argument is just that standardization is good, I am most certainly against it, for the reason that it will possibly do more harm than good, unreasonably restrain trade, and waste a lot of time on useless meetings, of which we have enough without encouraging any more.

I must dutifully point out the pitfalls that I am afraid not everyone watches for in the mad rush to standardize something or other. Oh, if I could only get the point across that standardization at its best is difficult, and sometimes almost impossible, and that it does have many side effects that are not particularly good! If I can only ensure that *prospective* standardization is thoroughly thought out *before* it is started rather than afterward, I will have served a useful purpose. My purpose is not to thwart standardization but only to encourage some careful thought about the process to facilitate the work and get the proper results.

Efforts of the Federal Government

Now that I have given the pitfalls and some suggestions for critiquing the process, I shall describe the latest federal government standardization effort, to which I referred earlier in this chapter, and its likely fallout in industry. We now have, in the federal government, a new agency known as the Office of Federal Procurement Policy. Still quite new, it was spawned by the multitudinous studies previously mentioned. Certainly the major improvement effort will be applied to the DOD because the DOD buys more than other agencies do. A number of programs are getting under way at the time that this text is being written, but one such program should be of particular interest here. Early in 1978 a program centered in the new agency was being applied to the whole of the DOD with the help of the Department of Commerce. Identified as the Commercial Commodity Acquisition Program (C-CAP), it was aimed at establishing entirely new procurement regulations for the DOD in buying commercial products to commercial specs and with commercial procurement practices. The program was introduced to industry and simultaneously to DOD procurement people in a public conference at the Gaithersburg offices of the Bureau of Standards. The conference was keynoted by Lester Fettig, the Administrator of the Office of Federal Procurement Policy. He set the stage for the conference with his statement that the United States government (in this case, the DOD) must find a way of putting its procurement people in the same environment and frame of mind as those of the experienced commercial buyer selecting products in the industrial marketplace. He and others emphasized that a change *was* to take place; the DOD and other agencies most certainly would follow the edict from Congress to "buy commercial." Throughout the 2-day conference thereafter, working groups comprising DOD procurement people and a broad assortment of industry people delved into details of *what* to buy commercially, *how* to buy it, and *how to live with it afterward*. It was made quite clear that the complete DOD procurement regulations would have to be redrafted; the DOD wanted help from industry on what those revised regulations should contain and on how the DOD could best get on with the job.

The handwriting on the wall is clear; the DOD is already at work. Other government agencies will do likewise. The beginnings of the effort first observed in the DOD establishment back in 1970 have not died out; now the effort is governmentwide in scope. To buy commercially requires good commercial specs rather than the present array of complex mil specs. The process of developing such specs is not an easy one. Many industries are soon to face some quick learning; everyone will need an educational course on how to do it. This short chapter can hardly serve such a need but is only an outline of what a proper text should contain.

The assumption is made in the usual texts on a parliamentary procedure that committee reports are an important and necessary part of any meeting. Probably this is true, up to a point. Such a committee report is as much a traditional part of society and club meetings as is the traditional motion for adjournment. Unfortunately, few committee chairmen follow the advice in *Robert's Rules* to have the reports of committees and of officers reproduced and distributed in advance so that they need not be read to the meeting. There are only two classes of reports, those that are worth reading and those that aren't. Recalling the words from *Demeter's Manual* on the three purposes of the minutes of meetings, quoted in Chapter 11, we can generalize that the same three purposes apply to most written committee reports. Perhaps the same tradition which seems to suggest that we shall always have unnecessary committees also suggests that we shall have unnecessary reports from those unnecessary committees.

Even in the commercial conference world, we find a proliferation of unnecessary committees (I reported the experience of chairing such an unnecessary committee in Chapter 8). Fortunately, however, most of the unnecessary committees in commercial activities don't last long; but sometimes their much too late demise is quite painful to a deliberative conference, which for many months must listen to long, dreary progress reports (saying only that the committee has great plans for its future work!) and then, finally, to a death-wish status report that records the last breath of the committee. Hooray, it's dead. Now we can avoid long status reports in the future. But not so fast. Another committee is soon to be formed to engage in more nothingness, over a protracted time, and we shall be blessed by other useless status reports.

Problems of Committee Reports

The theme song of this text, "Let's Have a Meeting, and We'll All Be There," applies specifically to committees and, particularly, to unnec-

16

The Effective Oral Committee Report

essary committees. The phrase "Committees, boards, and panels, and such, are where we spend those happy days" tells the story of the committee life that seems so elegant, so eloquent, and so oratorically erudite. The participants love that life, where they can prioritize, reconceptualize, and actualize, to use the current Washington buzz words. And they love the stature-building effect of presenting (or "presentating") a committee report to a parent organization. Their moment in the sun may steal 30 minutes from a busy conference, at which committee reports are important items on an important agenda. Just think, if all the information-type committee reports of all meetings in a single year were placed end to end, it might be a good idea, so that we could get them out of *our* conferences into *your* conferences.

But whether we like it or not, there will be unending committee reports, committee reports, committee reports, ad infinitum. Is there anything anybody can do about them? Unfortunately, not very much. We certainly can't eliminate them; the most we can hope to do is shorten and improve them.

It seems that all committee reports, even those ending with an action proposition, start with a long oration giving the whole historical background before getting to the meat of the proposition. Before the conference can get to the recommendation (or, in a technical committee report, the spec for the product), it must sleep through the preface, the foreword, the antecedents, the precedents, the wherefore, the whereas, and, eventually, if anybody ever gets to it, the therefore. This is an old problem; it is a continuing problem; it is destined always to be a problem. If the front end is shortened or eliminated, there is always a fear that the conference will reject the proposition without knowing what it is. Thus, the whole dreary report has to be circulated in advance and even described to the conference in minute detail before the conference is presented with the proposition itself.

While in most cases the infinitesimal details that must be presented in support of a proposition are tolerated because of the known desire of the committee chairman to have everything made clear before any action is taken, the same justification seldom exists when a report is for information only. If you watch a conference carefully, you will discern a visible relaxation when a committee chairman announces that he has no recommendation at this meeting but only a status report. The conference breathes more easily; some participants get up and leave, and some go to sleep. Watch and see. Note the commotion that takes place, and the obvious worry of the attendees, when the agenda is not specific and the committee chairman neglects to say whether the report will lead to action or not.

The root of the problem is that a meeting is never homogeneous;

some participants study the advance papers carefully, and some never look at them. Some are so active that they know all aspects of a proposition even before it is ready to come before them, and others have no interest in it. The committee chairman must assume the worst: he must assume that everyone will be against his report until he has explained every last detail. This is his right; this is his worry over his report, for he is responsible to his committee for any failure to get it sold. He may not have a second chance; he feels that he must start the selling even before the report is ready for presentation. When we look at the pressures facing a committee chairman, we can see why, with even a very preliminary status report, the conference is doomed to hear it in infinitesimal detail.

True, we should be able to convince the committee chairman that he is doing himself and his committee a disservice by overreacting to the invitation (or the right he believes he has) to present a status report. But people are people; we all have the same human nature. That human nature does not allow anything less than an oration, to the extent that we are capable of an oration. And the long, dreary, unheard committee report is the consequence. Any admonition here toward shorter or better oral committee reports is probably doomed to oblivion. Yet, in the hope of completeness in this text, I feel such suggestions are necessary even though any consequential improvement is likely to be a figment of my imagination.

Improvement of Committee Reports

If I were to urge conformance with some fixed set of arbitrary rules, I know that I would be doomed at the start. Instead, all that I can do is to point out some of the advantages to the presenter of such reports if he were to try a different tack from the usual course. Perhaps all the basics have already been given elsewhere in this text; I need only point out where and how they apply to the oral committee report. Let me take them in simple sequence:

1.   My first advice would be the same advice that I gave in Chapter 12, which I might summarize as follows: Don't waste your time and the conference's time by broadcasting when people are not tuned in. No matter what the reason why people are not listening or comprehending, you should not speak. Nor should the conference chairman allow you to continue. Shut up and wait for quiet and for the attention that attendees at the conference most certainly will give you if you do your share for them. You may have to ask that the conference chairman maintain order. That is your right.

2. When you have the attention of the conference, start your pitch with *the most important summary statement* you can think of. Plan it in advance, exactly as was urged of all conference debaters in Chapter 12. More than that, you should assume that all persons in the conference hall have the right to get up and leave the hall after your first sentence if you have not captured their attention and interest. *Your* right is only the right to have quiet when you start; thereafter, you are on your own. You sink or swim on the quality of your presentation. (For the parliamentary basis for this premise, see the reference to Jefferson's rules cited in suggestion 5, in Chapter 25.)

3. Recall that in Chapter 12 the presumption was that the debater would be expert in listening (as pointed out in Chapter 13) and that he would have a commercial motivation for getting his point (in this case, the committee's point, too) sold to the conference before he was interrupted or tuned out by participants who had other more important things to attract their attention. Thus, in presenting a committee report, the committee chairman should keep open a perfect feedback listening circuit from all the participants to see how well they are receiving and to learn how well they are *accepting the premise.*

4. In presenting a report, the committee chairman should consider a lowered interest by the participants as a signal that it contains either too much detail or too much background that they already know and accept. He should be able to see from their reaction which of these two is the problem, and he should adjust his presentation to match their needs.

5. If his presentation meets resistance, he should know it by the feedback signals that are always there if he will just tune in on them. Merely watching facial expressions will tell him much about the reaction. For example, a little gag thrown in will indicate who is listening and who isn't (if the gag is not a subtle one). Gags or simple humor also help to redirect lagging interest.

6. The same principles of showmanship that were set forth in Chapter 5 for the conference chairman apply equally to the committee chairman, who must use his wiles to get his point across in the minimum time without losing his audience. He must do exactly as the stage professional does: he must develop a sense of timing and be ever alert to the feeling of the meeting to what he is saying. If he is not getting his point across, there is no purpose in plodding on and on with a losing or incomprehensible argument. If this happens to you, stop quickly. Establish a new rapport with the participants; ask a specific question that will focus their attention back on the issue, and wait for their reaction (you had better make it a question with a "Yes" or "No" answer unless you want the whole conference to take over the debate from you). Ask another question to localize their objections or their acceptance of a point.

7.   Remember that while you are presenting a committee report, you and only you are the temporary chairman of the whole conference. *You* may ask questions (within the bounds of the permission granted by the *real* conference chairman). You may carry the presentation of your committee's work in any proper direction that will move toward the resolution of an immediate or a future action on that report. Notwithstanding the rather explicit parliamentary rule that neither you nor anyone else can properly address anyone except the conference chairman, remember that even the prestigious U.S. Senate finds ways of bypassing this most formal rule, as the senators engage in rather informal debate and communication, yielding to each other repeatedly as they interrupt each other for questions or comments, all the time using the formal interjection "Mr. President" as their method of conforming to the formal parliamentary rule that every word must be addressed *only* to the President of the Senate. All that is necessary in a properly run commercial deliberative conference is that the individual presenting the report obtain the concurrence of the conference chairman (usually a simple query with a "Yes" nod is sufficient) to secure all the authority that is needed to conduct a question-and-answer session as a means of presenting the status of the committee project to the conference.

8.   If the committee report is intended to lead to a proposition, a recommendation, or even a specification for adoption, so much the better for the question-and-answer method. This is the fastest way known to get the *proper* questions before the group and to get the group *involved* in the issues. No participant can successfully remain aloof or uninvolved when the rest of the conference is engaged in asking questions on important issues. An individual's mind may wander during an oratorical presentation of a report, but his attention will be recaptured as the conference itself engages in a question-and-answer session.

9.   If a committee chairman lacks experience in question-and-answer sessions or in utilizing feedback signals from an audience, it is possible to suggest to him certain guidelines for such a session. First, he should select a specific limited time interval during which he may talk *at* the conference, after which he should be prepared to ask his first question of the group. If he ponders this guideline beforehand, he will undoubtedly select the best possible question to address the most important issue that the conference will face. His guidelines should specify the maximum number of minutes during which he can then continue to talk *at* the conference (usually half the number of minutes specified

before the first question), after which he should present his second question, prepared in advance and based on his expected success with the first question. With such guidelines, even an inexperienced chairman having no rapport with his audience (or *believing* he will have none) can present a report more useful to the conference than the usual report with long, dreary presentations that serve only to put people to sleep. If the conference can be tricked into hearing the message the first time it is presented, the chairman need not start all over again with an explanation after he has gotten to the action point and people discover that they haven't heard a word he has said.

10.   Although it is not easy to convince people that they should treat others in a conference kindly by refraining from orations, I would like to convince them that they can help their cause by skipping orations in favor of getting to the points that should be gotten to. They can accomplish this goal by using a feedback system while engaging in questions and answers prepared in advance.

11.   But with human nature what it is, we are all natural-born hams, and we love getting up in front of an audience, whether we orate or mumble inaudibly. Let us recognize this forcing function of nature and admit that we all do the improper thing and play to the audience. Our only hope is to substitute a different form of actor-audience interaction that can meet the needs of the hams among us while accommodating the needs of the audience for far better communications from a committee chairman who is destined to present the horrible, horrendous, monotonous committee report.

The title of this chapter may cause you to wrinkle your forehead as you contemplate whether anyone could be so foolish as to suggest that a large meeting is easier to run than a small meeting. Yet this suggestion most certainly is true; the smaller meetings are, the more trouble you will have in keeping order and in getting work done. A deliberative meeting of a chairman and two people is almost impossible to manage; it is almost entirely a three-cornered discussion, and an outsider who might walk into the meeting room could never figure out who the chairman was. Now let us look at the environment of the usual small meeting and find out why such a statement has been postulated.

Characteristics of a Small Meeting

A simple reflection on the circumstances of the typical small meeting will remind us that most such meetings are held for a specific purpose, with fewer time constraints than those of a large meeting that has many tasks. Most such meetings are more personal and, therefore, more informal than any large meeting could ever be. Participants in a small meeting and even the chairman seem always to feel a constraint to postpone starting the meeting until all those intending to come have actually arrived. All participants seem less self-conscious in a small meeting and feel no disinclination to interrupt the chairman or each other, just as they might do in the course of ordinary conversation, in which it is quite natural for several parties to talk at the same time. A small meeting of friends is simply that: it's a small meeting of friends

17

How to Run a Small Committee with the Same Finesse as a Large Goldfish Bowl Deliberative Conference

destined to do whatever they darn please, despite the prowess or the stature of the chairman. That's the reason and the rationale. When you have learned how to maintain absolute order and to accomplish results in a large meeting, then, and only then, should you attempt the almost impossible task of managing a small meeting. If you accept this premise, you will have discovered why most small meetings are so ineffective and seem to take so long for even the simplest business.

Although I may not yet have convinced my readers of this postulate, I shall assume, for the purpose of allowing me to continue with the chapter, that you, my readers, have, at least halfway, accepted my premise in order to see what I shall say next. Furthermore, I shall not take up the problem of *really* difficult small meetings (church groups, club groups, society groups, and so on, of a dozen or fewer persons) just yet but shall concentrate on business-related small meetings in which there is a good deal of motivation for having the meeting and for *getting something decided.* Let me use, as an example, the need that the Airlines Electronic Engineering Committee (AEEC) has found to have some time in which the official members (perhaps an executive committee) can meet to establish agendas, elect officers, or arrange details that are administrative in nature and need not take up time in the large deliberative Goldfish Bowl conference. The AEEC has this need and has sought the right time to fulfill it. But there is no right time: every possible time is inconvenient. People are so busy with the major problems of a large conference that it is difficult to find time for such meetings. Although no one likes the luncheon hour (Pete claims he has indigestion for weeks after one of our luncheon meetings), it turns out that all other times are hated more strongly, and so we have traditionally held our administrative sessions during the lunch period, with meals served to everyone in a suitable hotel meeting room.

At the appointed time, everyone convenes in the selected room (in our case, we have some thirty members plus a few staff people). To be reasonably polite, we don't start eating the appetizer until almost everyone expected has arrived; thus, private conversations have begun all around the table. When all are present, the chairman has the seemingly impossible task of getting everyone to turn off his private business conversation and take part in a meeting which nobody wants but which everyone has decided we must have for the good of the organization. Let me state quite candidly that although this chairman has no great difficulty in getting a meeting of 500 people to stop their conversations and come to order, he admits that this luncheon meeting is almost the hardest of all to handle. Why is it so hard? Simply because everyone has business to transact and everyone must be interrupted by the chairman for the meeting to proceed. A small meeting, as I have said before, has a personal character, with real *persons* involved; a large meeting is far less personal in nature and can be interrupted without interfering with real people.

To interrupt such a group of persons is difficult, but it has to be done, and it *is* done; then the real problem develops. A luncheon is an environment that is far from passive; all through a luncheon the people eating are being asked by waiters whether they wish more coffee; a member is being interrupted by his neighbor to pass the salt; he is repeatedly being distracted by someone or something; to cut his meat, he has to take his attention away from the technical or administrative topic the chairman is trying to focus upon. Everything works against such a meeting in such a place at such a time.

We are not talking about luncheon meetings of a passive nature or meetings at which the participants eat first and then hold a short, perfunctory meeting after the waiters have left with all the trappings. Nope, we are talking about decision-making meetings that start at the beginning of lunch and continue until 5 minutes before the large Goldfish Bowl conference is convened in a not-so-close ballroom.

To make matters worse, all the problems of acoustics in a big meeting are aggravated in such a luncheon meeting because the group cannot all be close to the chairman or to each other. Thus everyone will have difficulty in hearing over the din of silverware and the noise of waiters. Concentration on the topics being discussed is difficult. Public address systems for a luncheon are impossible. Good table arrangements by which everyone can see and hear everyone else are impracticable. Nothing is easy in such an environment. If you think it is difficult to keep the parties to the discussion concentrating on everything said in a large meeting, as I urged in Chapter 2, you will find that it is nigh impossible in such a luncheon meeting. Those of your group who have a propensity to start a separate discussion (or even to continue it when someone else starts it) will do so with even greater regularity in a luncheon meeting in which everything makes hearing the happenings difficult. Those who have not yet learned how to speak up and address the whole meeting will cause plenty of trouble in a luncheon meeting when they address their proposals just to the chairman in a timid voice that can be heard only by the chairman.

Such a meeting will try the patience and the wits of the very best and most experienced chairman. To make such a meeting accomplish *anything* is a miracle unless the chairman has the will and the audacity to insist upon absolute decorum at all times and to demand that no one speak unless everyone is hearing what he is saying. Failing to enforce every one of the rules of a large meeting in such a small luncheon meeting can be disastrous, and you should give up the whole thing until you have mastered the large Goldfish Bowl meetings and feel that you are now fully qualified to take on the tiny meetings that look so simple.

For the difficult small meeting (and all such meetings are difficult), the reader is admonished (yea, is pleaded with) to reread Chapter 2 and all the material elsewhere that covers the large Goldfish Bowl deliberative conference. I urge you to practice on the large meeting, in which you can really be impersonal in keeping decorum, until you have the principles down well and feel that you can do justice to the small meeting.

While small meetings with luncheon attached are almost the hardest to administer, all small meetings are difficult to handle. Again, the rules of procedure set forth in Chapter 2 that may seem to you to be optimized for the large conference are most certainly the rules that should be used for an effective small meeting. Inattention in a small meeting is just as wasteful of time and money as inattention in a large meeting. While the cost wasted by a small meeting may be smaller than in a large meeting, the ultimate effect of imperfect action in the small meeting may cause future wastage of time and money in a large meeting that adopts the results of the small meeting. Furthermore, since almost everyone has the belief that small meetings are easier to manage efficiently, you should not fail in your small meeting unless you want a reputation of lacking chairmanship capability.

Nice Little Old Lady and Gentleman Syndrome

And now let us turn to the meetings of nice little old ladies and gentlemen in a church or club group. If there is any one class of people that can give an experienced chairman a fit and ruin his ego as a qualified manager of conferences, it is this class of people in such an environment. I defy anyone (except *another* nice little old lady or gentleman) to get a participant to quit a private but noisy conversation with a friend during a committee meeting which you are trying to finish in record time so that everyone can go home. You may wheedle, you may implore, you may present all kinds of logical arguments that the meeting is taking a long time, you may quiet the participants down a little bit; but seldom can you get nice little old ladies or gentlemen to take an active part in a legitimate meeting. But why should you? Bless them. We can't get along without them. We shall all eventually be an old lady or gentleman if we are not already. We will probably react in the same way then and not understand why anyone would want to run an efficient meeting with logic and all that. Such problems of what I will call the Nice Little Old Lady and Gentleman syndrome apply to small meetings of other groups when *no* little old ladies or gentlemen are present. Just ordinary people can exhibit the Nice Little Old Lady or Gentleman syndrome, and they do so in many of the small meetings of church groups, clubs, and societies.

There are many ways in which you can discover the presence of the Nice Little Old Lady and Gentleman syndrome in one of your meetings. Here are a few of the symptoms:

1. The group feels a propensity to debate such complex issues as what meat dish they shall have for dinner, and though you successfully get them to adopt a motion, unanimously, to leave the selection to the dinner chairman, they will be right back in 5 minutes debating the matter all over again despite anything you can do as chairman.

2. They have unanimously decided to adjourn at 8 P.M. so they can all catch the 8:30 TV movie, but when 8 P.M. arrives, they insist upon continuing the debate on the dues increase despite your attempts to remind them of their prior decision.

3. After a 1-hour debate over the dues increase, they finally vote it down overwhelmingly. One of the committee chairmen then notes that meat costs have just gone up by 30 percent and a dues increase is inevitable, so they immediately vote a dues increase. An hour later, a member states that the dues are too high, so they vote them back where they were.

4. You, the chairman, discover that you have no status in the meeting and that everyone thinks he or she is the responsible head of the group.

Positive Suggestions for Running a Small Meeting

Now that I have given you all the reasons why a small meeting is so difficult or, in some cases, even impossible, I should, if only for the sake of my own ego, provide some positive suggestions in answer to the question posed by the heading of this chapter. We should use the fourteen "Responsibilities of the Chairman of a Goldfish Bowl Deliberative Conference," as stated in Chapter 2, as a guide. Here are the most important:

Rule 1 Certainly, you would expect me to emphasize the great importance of item 3 of Chapter 2, because any lapse into more than a single meeting will completely disrupt the affair and you will no longer be holding any meeting at all. Yet I shall surprise you by suggesting, instead, that sometimes in a small meeting you can get the same result from the opposite direction, as suggested in item 2 of Chapter 5. Rather than pounce on the *makers* of the noise or the people who are interrupting the speaker with their own little meetings, it is sometimes better to interrupt the individual who has the floor, explaining that what he is saying is so very important that you do not want the meeting to miss it. You will be following the advice for the effective presentation of reports in Chapter 16 and, particularly, admonition 1, that the speakers should not waste time broadcasting when people are not tuned in. If the speaker stops his pitch and you, the chairman, stop everything to wait for quiet, you will discover that those other meetings suddenly stop and that all the attendees are looking at you, wondering what they have been missing. So you will get the same effect as though you *had* interrupted the recalcitrant ones without actually having done it.

Rule 2   Always keep in mind the admonition in Chapter 1 about bullwhips and smiles and the mellowing of the chairman as the participants learn professional audiencemanship. Remember what I admitted at the beginning of this chapter, that a small meeting is not the impersonal affair that a large meeting can be. Any fixation on enforcing procedural rules in a small meeting must result in some hurt, some pain, or at least some bad feelings. The trade-off is not as simple to determine as in a large meeting, in which rules can be much more easily applied and accepted in an impersonal vein.

Rule 3   Once you have discovered symptoms of the Nice Little Old Lady and Gentleman syndrome, our best advice is simply to relax and let things go wherever fate takes you, unless you want to increase your ulcers. If and when any cure is discovered for that syndrome, I shall include it in a subsequent edition; but don't hold your breath.

This chapter should never have been included in this book. As I stated in Chapter 2, I had chosen to exclude from discussion all meetings which are chaired by the boss of the others who must participate in such meetings. The reason for excluding such meetings from such a text as this is that they are artificial; the boss is always the boss and can make decisions without the actions of any subservient committee. Such meetings may, in some cases, appear to follow the usual rules of democracy, but ordinarily not even this is the case. If they appear to be democratic, this is only appearance. The boss is the boss is the boss, and nothing can change that. Thus, all of this text except this chapter assumes that the committee is administratively free from control of the chairman. It assumes that the committee can act as it chooses without repercussions from a chairman who is also the boss.

Well, then, why was this chapter added? There is a reason. When the text was being prepared, a friend, who I shall pretend is named Horace, expressed interest in the book "so that I can give a copy to my boss, who runs long, dreary staff meetings. This book might help him out." Naturally that comment could have been made by any of about 3 million people just in the United States alone. I explained to Horace that the principles of good meetings just don't apply when the boss is also the chairman, but he said that the book could do some good anyway and urged me to add a chapter on that kind of committee just so that he could try and get some relief by giving his boss a copy. So here is the special chapter just for Horace and his 3 million fellow sufferers.

Why Staff Meetings Are Different

Before I start running down bosses, let us remember that we are all bosses over something or somebody; almost all of us run some office meetings that are far too long in the opinion of our underlings, and we decide everything in our favor just as Horace's boss does. Furthermore, let me note for the record what I stated in Chapter 17, that small com-

---

18

Beholden Committees: The Boss and His Staff Meetings

---

mittee meetings are usually much more difficult to run efficiently and effectively than are large meetings. Remember that the boss is trying to run a meeting under almost impossible conditions. I suggested in Chapter 17 that it would be difficult, if not impossible, for any outsider to determine who was chairing a small meeting that he might drop in on, because everyone takes an equal part in a small meeting. But even though the boss may allow such a display of apparent democracy in a staff meeting, the end result of all discussion is distorted in favor of what the boss wants done. And though the boss may state otherwise, the facts of corporate management belie his professions of democracy. True, the boss may allow the other members of the staff to do most of the talking; this may be his way of allowing them to let off steam. Or he may, quite seriously, feel that he should take their ideas into account before making up his own mind on what to do.

Perhaps the foregoing analysis may sound belligerent, pompous, and ungentlemanly. But the corporate hierarchy is not democratic. Corporate management goes to great extremes to build leadership within the organization, and top management wants very much to develop lower management. Democracy exists just as long as the lower level of management follows the precepts of top management; whenever a conflict develops, it is top management that wins and lower management that either gives in or moves out.

Leadership is that capability of a manager to get want he wants done by lower echelons of management that think they are doing it instead of top management. They may be given a large share in the running of a business, an office, a division, or whatever, as long as top management is satisfied with the final results and the manner in which those results are obtained. The staff meeting is just one facet of the management process that provides a measure of communication up and down. The staff reaction to a staff meeting is a function of the ability of the boss to make communications truly two-way rather than just one-way, downward. A boss who follows the precepts of a good chairman, as suggested throughout this text, will enjoy better relations with his staff during the command performances that are staff meetings. The staff members are captive; they cannot decide when to adjourn a staff meeting; they cannot decide the topics; they cannot decide the outcome of the discussion; they can only *suggest* changes, not dictate changes. If they don't like the chairman personally, they cannot vote him out; if they believe that they can get a better chairman for their staff meetings, they can do nothing about it: they are captive to the corporate hierarchy and its explicit pecking order.

True, many staff meetings are tailored to the particular vanities of the boss. The boss organizes them and manages them to meet his particular, sometimes peculiar, needs. In a division or a department of a large firm with broad vistas of endeavor, the boss probably does want a particular kind of staff meeting process to accommodate his needs rather than organize and optimize for the entirely different needs of the staff members. Thus, it should come as no great surprise that staff members generally do not like the staff meetings their boss holds. The usual argument will be that the meetings are too long and too detailed and are held at an inappropriate time for the staff members.

So, welcome to the club. Remember that your boss probably has the same complaint about his boss and those staff meetings he must attend. If you, in turn, were supervising a large staff, you too would hold staff meetings for your people, and your staff would probably complain a little bit. But *your* staff meetings would not suffer from those horrible things that your boss inflicts upon you in his staff meetings. Yours would be different; yours would be geared to meet the needs of your staff people. You know from experience what a staff member needs, and you would provide exactly what he needs and wants.

And so the circle continues, down the line of management to the bottom, where staff members have no one reporting to them. And they, too, will complain (but not *to* the boss, just *about* the boss), exactly as you did when you were in their shoes. Isn't it funny how you become so expert when you move upward and become the boss, and you do everything (including the running of staff meetings) so much better than the boss you worked for did?

Advice for Boss and Staffers

But in this chapter that was not intended to be written, there can be a message that is addressed to bosses and staffers: please try to understand each other; democracy cannot exist in corporate management. You have a right to complain a little, but if you want to be a part of successful management, you will have to play by the rules. The rules are not those of democratic deliberative conferences, in which one person is not beholden to another. The rules of a staff meeting are the rules of corporate management. Relax and accept them. Don't judge corporate meetings (staff meetings, sales meetings, and so on) by the rules of procedure for deliberative conferences. Neither should you judge deliberative conferences by the rules of corporate meetings. To each, its own; may the twain never really meet.

Here is a special message for the boss: try to understand the nature of the problem, and tolerate the lack of understanding on the part of your younger staff members concerning the elusive differences between your staff meetings and the deliberative meetings they have occasion to attend elsewhere. Help to explain those differences so that they may become tolerant of your problems while you are becoming more tolerant of theirs. Help them understand that their role in those other meetings is wholly different and that they can help to improve the meetings for your benefit, for their benefit, and for the corporate benefit. Emphasize why the two kinds of meetings must have different goals, different modes of operation, and different outcomes. Also, by understanding these basic differences yourself, you will probably discover that you can run better staff meetings than before and can better accommodate the needs of your staff members while still fulfilling your own corporate needs for the staff meetings. With that understanding, everybody will benefit.

Here is a special message for staffers: don't expect corporate meetings to follow the precepts of a good deliberative conference. Understand the reasons for those continuing differences, and learn to tolerate the differences. Learn the principles of the deliberative conference because you may attend more conferences of that kind than you will of the corporate kind. But even though you may feel that you are destined to spend far more time in corporate meetings than in the other meetings, you may come to the conclusion that you can probably do more to improve the outside meetings than the inside ones. Concentrate on the ones you *can* do something about rather than the ones you cannot. Keep in mind that someday you will be the boss and that there will be staffers like you who can't understand how *you* can consistently run such awful (in their opinion) staff meetings.

Organizing Problems

As I finish, just for my fictitiously named friend Horace, this chapter that was not intended to be written, we should look at one other aspect of the staff meeting problem. Did it ever occur to you that your boss may be writhing in agony over the staff meeting that he is required to hold? Have you ever heard about the organizations in big cities that do a thriving business in organizing staff meetings for managers who don't know the first thing about such matters, simple as they are? Perhaps you would never hear about such endeavors, but they most certainly do exist, and they do this job that you would naturally believe every manager worth his salt could easily do for himself.

Unbelievable? Perhaps. One such outfit in New York was managed by a young woman with a very small staff. She reported her various staff meeting jobs for big and small businesses. She told of managers who would get sick at the thought of running a staff meeting, even a very small staff meeting. She described the wide variety of clients she had and how she would prepare the agendas for the staff meetings, the various other papers that were necessary, and the reports of the meetings (when necessary). She provided the coaching and organization for big executives (and small executives, too), so that their staff meetings would be successful and the executives would get the credit. She had to remain out of sight and yet organize everything as though the executives were doing it. This is a good business, and a number of organizations make good livings from such activities. It is a specialty activity that the larger conference management organizations cannot handle very well; it takes quite a bit of experience to work for someone else in this manner, and it is a need that seems to have been met. Here we can see that a number of managers are so badly frustrated by simple staff meetings that they will hire an outside firm to organize them.

There must be countless others who have discovered the hard way what I have espoused in Chapter 17, that small meetings are much more of a problem to run effectively and efficiently than are large meetings. Perhaps your boss has discovered this little fact firsthand. You have never dreamed that your boss, a powerful manager of a major activity in your organization, could have such worries. Perhaps I have let a cat out of a bag by this dissertation on an unspeakable topic. Perhaps this chapter that was never intended to be written should have been written long ago. Maybe it is time that some of the unspoken pressures of corporate management be revealed for staff people, who might become a lot more tolerant if they understood better what those pressures really are.

Well, Horace, let's all work on those staff meetings. They can be improved; they should be improved. Yet some things cannot be changed: we should all be resigned to the fact of wished-for improvements that are just never meant to be.

You have established in your industry a committee with respect to some product standardization, and it has been busily engaged in such work for several years. The committee discovers that a government agency is considering some change in regulations that would cause a conflict with the committee standards that your industry has developed. The committee suspects that the government agency has missed some very important point and would change its regulations back again if it knew the real problem with what it is proposing. The committee asks that a representative from the agency attend the next meeting, and the agency head shows a considerable degree of interest in what the committee is doing because it obviously has a bearing on the regulations being contemplated. The meeting is announced, and the agency representative attends and finds the discussion and the arguments important to his agency. He makes no commitments but thanks the group and leaves.

Now what happens? From here on it doesn't make much difference whether the proposed regulations get changed or not, and it doesn't make much difference whether the committee changes its standard or not. What *does* matter is whether the Federal Advisory Committee Act of 1972 was, or was not, violated, and if it was, what should happen now. Probably nothing will happen. Lawyers could argue almost interminably over whether the act was transgressed. But they probably wouldn't argue over it, simply because this situation happens all day every day, act or no act.

But let us change the circumstances a bit and assume that the proposed regulations have something to do with consumer protection. Assume that, in the opinion of some people, the industry standard is at odds with the need for consumer protection. Assume, also, that the announcement of the meeting was sent only to member firms of the

---

19

How to Advise Our Government: The Federal Advisory Committee Act

association which was sponsoring the meeting. Assume that someone from a consumer-oriented publication learned of this proposed regulation and of the meeting and phoned the association to learn the date, place, and time, and the caller was told that the meeting was open only to association members. Now trouble can develop.

Civil Action No. 74-215

Situations somewhat like this hypothesized case have happened. Let us quote from Civil Action No. 74-215, U.S. District Court for the District of Columbia, *Food Chemical News, Inc. v. Rex D. Davis, Director, Bureau of Alcohol, Tobacco and Firearms, Department of the Treasury,* June 28, 1974:

Memorandum Opinion of United States District Judge Charles R. Richey

The issue before this Court is whether the two separate "informal" meetings with consumer and distilled spirits industry representatives relative to drafting proposed regulations of the Bureau of Alcohol, Tobacco and Firearms of the Treasury Department (hereinafter, "Bureau"), on ingredient labeling of distilled spirits were meetings of "advisory committees" utilized by Defendent Rex Davis, Director of the Bureau, to obtain advice within the meaning of Section 3(2) of the Federal Advisory Committee Act of 1972 (hereinafter, "Act"), 5 U.S.C. App. I, and, therefore, "open to the public." 5 U.S.C. App. I & 10(a)(1). The Court has concluded that the two meetings in question were subject to the Act and, accordingly, the Defendant was required to provide public access to each meeting pursuant to Section 10(a)(1) of the Act and to follow the Act's procedural requirements. The Court will, therefore, grant Plaintiff's Motion for Summary Judgment and enjoin the Defendant and his agents, servants, and employees from convening any future meetings of the advisory committees discussed herein, or meetings of any of their advisory committees, without complying fully with the Act's requirements, and from excluding plaintiff or its agents or employees from any such meetings in contravention of the Act.

This court interpretation of the act may suggest that almost any communication between some private body and government people implies "advice" under the act, and it may suggest that private bodies should stay a long way removed from any government people. If we read the further finding of the court in the above case, we might even become worried that any individuals who are members of a private body might also be construed to be violating the act even if they only communicate by phone or letter with a government office. Here are the further words:

> The Defendant's utilization of the industry and consumer committees in order to obtain advice on the draft amendments to agency regulations subjects the committees to the strict procedural requirements of the Advisory Committee Act including, among other things, that meetings between the defendant and private individuals comprising the committee be accessible to the public.
>
> It is the Court's opinion that the industry and consumer committees were "advisory committees" within the meaning of Section 3(2) of the Act which reads in pertinent part:
>
> "The term 'advisory committee' means any committee, board, commission, council, conference, panel, task force, or other similar group, or any subcommittee or any subgroup thereof (hereinafter in this paragraph referred to as 'committee') which is . . .
>
> "(c) *established or utilized by one or more agencies*
>
> "*in the interests of obtaining advice or recommendations* for the President or one or more agencies or officers of the federal government. . . ." [Emphasis added]
>
> It is undisputed that the Defendant utilized an *ad hoc* committee of industry representatives in order to obtain advice. Such a relationship, like that with the consumer group, clearly comes within the terms of Section 3(2) of the Act. *Aviation Consumer Action Project v. Yohe*, et al., CA No. 707-73 (D.D.C. June 24, 1974).

Department of Justice Interpretation

The quotation, within the court record, of the Section 3(2) of the act contains the words "or any other subgroup thereof," which would imply that individuals are intended not to meet with government people without proper authorization under the act. It is true that lawyers have argued over these words for several years. It is true, also, that the Department of Justice has had considerable difficulty in interpreting what the act means, with particular reference to two things: (1) what the true definition of a "committee" is for purposes of the act and (2) what the true definition of "utilized" is with respect to advice from such a defined committee. A memo prepared by the Department of Justice Legal Counsel, dated April 1973, has been widely touted as the authority for each of the foregoing definitions. The memo notes that these two questions are the important ones in determining whether the act applies. It states:

The question whether a group is a "utilized" advisory committee has two aspects: first, is the group a "committee or similar group" within the meaning of the act; and second, is the group "utilized" by a federal official as a source of advice.

Inasmuch as this text might be expected to identify committees and what they do, it might be well if I note what the Justice Department stated to be, in 1973, the meaning of "committee" for purposes of the act. Note particularly the last two paragraphs in this quotation and the two extremes that seem to bound what the act probably means with respect to a committee. As of the date of this text, this 1973 memo is still considered to be the proper interpretation by most government legal counsel offices:

a. The meaning of "committee"
Under 3(2) of the Act, one requisite for coverage is that the group be a "committee, board, commission, conference, panel, task force, or other similar group, or . . . (a) subcommittee or other subgroup thereof." The OMB-Justice guidelines state that the Act was intended to cover "advisory committees or similar groups in the ordinary sense" and then describe characteristics usually possessed by such bodies. Pertinent to the meaning of "committee" are the following characteristics: fixed membership, defined purpose, organizational structure and a staff, and regular or periodic meetings.

Application of the above criteria excludes from the Act's coverage several types of situations. For example, a federal official may, without regard to the Act, "utilize" an individual private citizen as a source of advice.

Also implicit in the present criteria is the fact that the Act may not be applicable when an official informally convenes a group of individuals to obtain their views. If such a group meets only once or twice, has no continuing function, does not as a group take positions, has no organization and does not involve substantial, special preparation it would not seem to be a "committee." (Such a group would be neither "established" nor "utilized" as an advisory committee.)

A Government request to an association, a labor union or a similar organization for advice may be outside the use of the Act, even though in formulating its position the organization relies on one of its own committees. The basis for asserting non-coverage would be the distinction between an association and a "committee." Such a distinction may in general be determinative. However, when in fact an agency is using a committee of an association for advice, the Act applies, even though the association serves as a conduit between the agency and the committee.

Participation by federal officials in conventions or conferences of private organizations would not ordinarily bring the Act into play. Still, in some circumstances, the Act might be applicable, e.g., where the conference was arranged by the organization at the suggestion of the Government for the specific purpose of providing advice to a federal official.

To summarize, there are a number of situations which involve Government requests for advice from non-federal sources, but which, due to the absence of a "committee," are outside the scope of the Act.

So much for the first part of the matter and the definition of a committee. Now, assuming that we know exactly what a committee is under the act, we need only determine whether that committee is *utilized* under the act. We may have thought the former definition to be a little iffy, but matters get worse when we start on the next question. Here is the introduction contained in the same Justice Department memo:

b. *The meaning of "utilized" to provide advice*

The need to determine "utilization" arises when a federal agency deals with a committee established by private persons or by state or local officials. The question turns upon the nature and duration of those dealings.

Advisory committees established by the Government are subject to the Act throughout their existence, but this is not necessarily true of "utilized" committees. Under the OMB-Justice guidelines, the latter are covered only during the time of and to the extent of their use by federal officials as sources of advice.

Under an extremely narrow interpretation of "utilized," a group not established by the Government would be subject to the Act only if it had official status, either express or implied. Under this view, such status might be inferred if the group were to use federal funds, facilities or personnel; perform at Government request a specific function on a regular basis reflecting a continuity of relationship with the agency; and exercise special privileges (e.g., access to confidential information) which are customarily accorded only to other parts of the Government.

At the other extreme, it could be asserted that the Act applies wherever a federal official has regular dealings, including an exchange of opinions, with a private group. This would mean applying the Act to a vast number of professional, trade, labor and public interest organizations. There are no express indications in the legislative history that such a far-reaching result was intended. Accordingly, a middle-ground approach seems appropriate, one which would in general limit the coverage of "utilized" groups to situations involving a "committee" which has a definite advisory role, continuing or substantial in nature. The suggested approach seems consistent with the view that Congress relied upon the executive orders and intended to incorporate a similar concept of "utilized" committees.

Now that we have learned the Justice Department definitions of "committee" and "utilized," perhaps we know everything there is to know. But the Justice Department seems a trifle uncertain when it attempts a summary of "factors":

> c. Factors to be considered
> Determining whether a "committee" is a "utilized" advisory committee requires consideration of the particular facts. A list of pertinent factors or areas of inquiry is set forth below. It should be noted at the outset that no single factor is crucial. All pertinent facts, including those listed below, must be analyzed. The absence of one indication of coverage may be counter-balanced by the strong presence of other indicia.

The memo then presents considerable discussion on each of seven factors that should be considered in attempting to determine whether a committee is utilized under the act. I shall not quote the entire memo, because it discusses many intricate relationships on how the organization was formed; whether the initiative for the advice originated with the government or with the outside group or even whether the agency "expected" such advice; what the purpose of the governmental interest was in the group; what specific dealings took place and how often; what the agency had considered the role of the group to be before the act was made law; and whether the agency has given recognition to the group as an advisory committee. At best, it can be quite a guessing game to determine whether a specific activity of a specific body is providing advice to a government agency and may, therefore, be subject to the act.

Effects of the Act on Private Organizations

Now that I have you worried over whether your favorite organization might end up in court over some violation of a federal law (perhaps a law you have never been aware of) if you have so much as looked at some government man who might be interested in the activity of your organization, I should try to put you at ease again by a pacifier statement that will clear you of any possible involvement with this indefinite Federal Advisory Committee Act.

I cannot do that. But I can point out that your organization can never be taken to court for violating this act, although a government agency and individual *can*. You may not be liable, but your counterpart in the government can be. Although I may not be able to shed much light on any clear set of rules that will keep your organization from causing embarrassment to some government agency, we can find much documented in the literature that points us in the proper direction for avoiding the problem that caused the act to be established in the first place. In reading the history of the act, we might be inclined to interpret the real reason for the enactment to be the saving of money on government advisory committees. Certainly there is much written material that can imply that this was an important reason. But this is only one reason; the key reason is clearly stated in the foregoing Justice Department memo. Let me quote the final paragraph of that memo as my authority:

> *d. Applying the suggested standards*
> The result in a particular case of possible "utilization" will depend upon analysis of all pertinent facts. In determining whether a particular committee is utilized in such manner that it is subject to the Act, the policies underlying the Act must be considered. Certain of the Congressional purposes—i.e., insuring effective use of federal resources expended on advisory committees; limiting the number of Government-created advisory committees—have little bearing upon this inquiry. The policies which are pertinent are (1) openness of committee operations, and (2) guarding against undue influence, through advisory committees, on the part of special interests, particularly, business interests. See, e.g., House report, p. 6; Senate report, p. 2.

The Federal Advisory Committee Act is better known around Washington by its other name, the Government-in-the-Sunshine Act, because that name explains its purpose better than any other. To confirm this, we need only note the statements contained in the court case (Civil Action No. 74-215) previously quoted to show with what vehemence the court seems to apply the principles of openness (as stated in the last paragraph of the Justice Department memo) to the Bureau of Alcohol, Tobacco, and Firearms, as it chastises the Bureau for keeping the meetings private. Here are the words the court employed:

> The purpose of the Federal Advisory Committee Act to control the advisory committee process and to open to public scrutiny the manner in which government agencies obtain advice from private individuals is furthered by the Court's action herein. Indeed, Congressional concern for informal meetings such as those in the case at bar contributed to the statute's enactment:

The lack of public scrutiny of the activities of advisory committees was found to pose the danger that subjective influences not in the public interest could be exerted on the Federal decision-makers." S. Rep. 92-1098, 92nd Cong. 1st Sess. 6 (Sept. 7, 1972).

Once we see what the fundamental abuse was that the Federal Advisory Committee Act was addressing, we should also see what our best defense is against the imposition of that act upon our favorite organization and some government agency which is trying to do what seems to be in the best public interest. Certainly, we cannot believe that the intention of Congress was simply to establish a highly complex set of paperwork procedures to charter and manage more and more government advisory committees. Certainly not. Neither can we conceive of all that paperwork simply as a deterrent to government committees in order to save government funds; the effect would seem to be the opposite, with all the cost of that paperwork. Instead, it must be obvious that the major purpose was, as stated in the several quotations above, to bring the actions of advisory committees, or even those of any committee which could conceivably become the source of some private advice to a government agency, out into the open so that the public could see what was happening. The highly complex adminstrative procedures for advisory committees are designed for the express purpose of keeping the operations public and of ensuring that bodies which provide such advice now, but are not chartered under the act, will have quite a difficult time in surviving *in private* without being chartered.

From the foregoing, it should be evident that I need not, in this text, enter into any detailed discussion of all the complex series of procedures that the act and its current interpretation apply to bodies that find it necessary to be chartered by a government agency under the act. I postulate that the great majority of present industry bodies that operate today without giving any thought to the requirements under the act may quite properly continue to operate in their present mode with only one proviso. That proviso is that if the body is doing a job that conceivably could serve as advice to some government agency (and just about everything done by industry has some connection to some government agency activity), it is well advised to study carefully the basis on which the act was established and then to ascertain that it is not continuing the abuses which caused the act. If you have been reading this text in the order in which the chapters are numbered, you should, long before now, have become aware that my most important message is that there are advantages to an organization engaging in *public* Goldfish Bowl deliberations as the proper means of making the whole process of industry communications work correctly and effectively. Not only does public action avoid most of the problems with the antitrust laws, but it makes the whole decision-making process much smoother. Specifically, it is in the interest of industry to operate in a public Goldfish Bowl. With this conclusion, I shall dispense with further details and analyses of the Federal Advisory Committee Act.

I described in Appendix 1 the almost four decades of experience in one part of the airline industry as it slowly and ponderously crept out from under the bushel into the lamplight and eventually into the sunlight. Every step of the way was difficult for that major industry, but the most recent decade of the four has proved, over and over, the advantages of the mode of operation I have chosen to call the Goldfish Bowl deliberative conference.

In Chapter 19, I presented the rudimentary beginnings of what Washington lawyers call the Government-in-the-Sunshine Act, and I postulated a trend toward more of the going-public process that we see everywhere within the federal government. In this chapter I shall take the postulate further and extend the discussion to other fields that show promise of going public to an even greater degree. The trend seems to be in the direction of more and more public exposure of previously private activities that are of real significance to the public.

Public Debate in the Senate

It was Thursday, April 6, 1978, and another long day of the U.S. Senate debates over the Panama Canal treaties was drawing to a dreary close. After a short interruption of the treaty debate for some early-morning business, as the Senate calls routine items that must be taken care of, the session was about ready to return to the grueling task of debating another amendment in the long series that opponents to the treaty under consideration were laboriously presenting, each destined to be laid on the table by the majority vote of the ever-present Democratic leadership. Senator Robert Byrd, leader of the majority, gained the floor and started what seemed at first to be only a polite expression of graciousness to the opposition for having been so polite and helpful and tolerant in what he knew to be a difficult time for the minority opposition.

20

The Process of Going Public

But it soon became evident that this was not to be his major point; he called the attention of those few senators who were still on the floor at this late hour to the gavel-to-gavel coverage of the debate by National Public Radio as the first time in history when the public, throughout the world and particularly in Panama, might hear every word uttered in the U.S. Senate. He extended his compliments, first, to National Public Radio for providing the radio coverage and, second, to Mrs. Linda Wertheimer, who had been commentator for all the broadcasts and had done such an "extraordinary" (Senator Byrd's word, given with an *extraordinary* rhetorical emphasis) job in the actual broadcasts and in a 1-hour summary broadcast later each evening.

In presenting these rhetorical bouquets to the radio people, Senator Byrd was making an important point, not only to the millions of radio listeners who surveys had indicated were in the audience, but to the members of the Senate themselves (who, he said, not only would read of the debate in the *Congresssional Record* but could hear it, including every inflection of voice, in their offices, cars, or homes or while traveling). His point was that the U.S. Senate had previously been isolated from the nation's public, and although the galleries were open to visitors, the general public had never before had the opportunity to hear, in real time, what actually transpired in the Senate chamber. He emphasized that, far more than just the treaty matter, the Senate *process* was being presented for the very first time to the public.

He reminded the audience that the U.S. Senate actually met behind closed doors for the first 5 years of its life after it had held its first session in 1789. It was 5 years, he said, before it was willing to open the meetings. It was another 184 years before the Senate would permit live radio coverage. Now, he was saying, he was convinced that the stature of the Senate had been raised by this presentation of the debate of the radio audience; he was quite sure of it and believed that all the senators, majority and minority alike, would concur.

Senator Byrd was interrupted by another and then by another senator to give their concurrence. Experiences were recounted of speaking engagements in other cities where a visiting senator found his audience fully informed on what had been happening that very day in the U.S. Senate debate. Large numbers of constituents reported regular listening. Senator James Allen, recognized as the most prolific author of proposed amendments to the treaties, gained the floor to note the first thing upon which he and Senator Byrd had agreed since the debates started. He affirmed his own belief that the coverage by radio *had* improved the stature of the Senate, as his good friend Senator Byrd had stated; he also affirmed the belief that the views of the opposition had been given a better hearing because of the radio coverage. He expressed the view that more special events such as the treaty debate should be covered by radio in the future.

I must conclude that the U.S. Senate is satisfied that opening this treaty debate to the public was worthwhile. A change was made after 184 years. It is true that the Senate did not suggest an open meeting, such as I described in Chapter I, in which even the casual visitor is offered the floor if he believes he can contribute to the debate. Certainly not in our halls of Congress. But my reference in Chapter 14 to the extensive debate in the Senate over the role that a constituency has or should have in influencing the actions of a senator shows the point of view of many senators that a constituency is better informed today than ever before.

Previously, a view had sometimes been expressed within Congress that the public could never know the whole story on any particular issue facing Congress and, therefore, that expressions from an uninformed public could never take precedence over the informed debate that the legislators held. In the past, as I related with respect to the Bristol constituency renouncing Edmund Burke in 1780, a constituency at odds with its representative had little recourse except to vote the representative out of office at the next regular election.

During these months of Senate debate over the treaties, that same point was brought up many times by many senators. The emphasis on responsibility to their constituencies reached a peak in the discussion of what was known as the Hatch amendment, which was designed to bring the House of Representatives into the treaty approval process. Numerous senators opposing the treaties stated that the 2-year term of a representative in the House always served to make the House of Representatives more responsive to its constituencies than a senator who need run for reelection only every 6 years. Although this amendment was later rejected by the leadership of the Senate, its discussion gave an opportunity for considerable airing of the age-old question of whether a member of Congress should trust his constituency or his own feelings on a matter of national interest.

Certainly, the degree to which a constituency can be current in its knowledge and understanding of national issues will be a major factor in setting the level of influence that a representative will accept from his constituency. Undoubtedly, if the constituency is listening to every debate in *real time*, rather than depending upon other media for second-party interpretations of debates, the currency must be greater, and therefore the constituency influence must be greater and more immediate.

In the light of these extensive Senate debates over the currentness of constituencies and of the expressed Senate satisfaction with the radio broadcast of those debates, are we not seeing something that portends a trend toward even more openness in congressional action? In the years to come, the headlines of 1978 on the Panama Canal treaties may be of no more interest than yesterday's newspaper to the constituencies that listened so fervently to the debates of 1978. Yet I suspect that the projections of Senator Byrd regarding the desirability of future congressional radio coverage will be an important matter for future observers to ponder. Certainly this trend toward better public awareness of national issues in Congress, combined with the pressures within Congress itself to bring all government processes into the open as one of many consequential happenings following the long, distasteful period of Watergate, must relate in some way to other trends that we see for industry itself to open its activities to public view.

Trends in Government and Industry

Was the experience of the airlines in the Goldfish Bowl (Appendix 1) simply an isolated case of stumbling upon a methodology that seemed to work better than any other methodology? Or could it be that it was simply a fortunate progenitor of things to come elsewhere? In Chapter 15 and again in Appendix 1, I have taken a quick look at the trends in the Office of Federal Procurement Policy and the fallout effect that has already started within the Department of Defense (DOD) in its "going commercial" in what I have described as the Commercial Commodity Acquisition Program (C-CAP). I have described the earliest beginnings of C-CAP and the public conference activity of early 1978 that was intended to develop into a full-blown public discussion of what, how, when, and why the DOD should buy commercially.

I have briefly described a parallel effort started early in 1978 by the U.S. Air Force (USAF) to do essentially the same thing, but with particular emphasis upon USAF avionics equipment. But still the same effort has been made to bring the public into the activity to aid the USAF in its work. Everywhere we look, we can see the same trend; other laws are being formulated in Congress to open the government regulatory agencies to even more public scrutiny; an attempt has even been made by one congressional committee to introduce legislation to open up the work of existing standardization organizations that are not a part of the federal government.

Although many people in Congress and outside agree with my view that government control of industry standards is going much too far, the handwriting on the wall from all these trends should be very clear:

we are now entering an Age of Disclosure, an Age of Public Kibitzing, an Age of Review, an Age of Contemplation. Certainly a glimmer of sunshine through an open window on federal government processes is welcome; would it not also be welcome and mutually beneficial for industry to follow this lead and bring its deliberations out into the Goldfish Bowl?

Throughout the previous chapters, I have urged an emphasis on informality as a major aid in developing a consensus in the large Goldfish Bowl deliberative conference. The reason is not particularly profound: educators point out the close relationship between discussion and debate, in which transition back and forth from one to the other depends upon whether participants become protagonists for a particular viewpoint or shift into the pure discussion mode as they seek an answer rather than press for acceptance of their particular view.

Preferred Seating Arrangement

With discussion a prelude to debate, the conversational mode is the preferred form, all participants being seated, preferably in a circle, so that everyone can see everyone else, and all being on essentially an equal basis. This is the preferred arrangement for small groups, and it fails only when the circle becomes so large that individuals lose the face-to-face feeling they have in a small group. Yet if a group will start with a small discussion circle and gradually expand the circle, keeping everyone within a pseudocircle, we find that the principles long recognized as the good attributes of a round-table discussion have been carried essentially intact to a much larger discussion group of hundreds of people. Although a single circle is no longer practicable, a series of concentric circles will be the best of all arrangements for a larger group. Because neither the conference hall nor the furniture is round, we substitute squares or rectangles for the circles. It is the concentric-square configuration that we should strive for as a means of maintaining the round-table feeling among participants even though they number in the hundreds.

It is to make the concentric configuration effective that Chapter 3 set forth the *first three points* in the basic methodology. In any properly arranged conference room selected for a Goldfish Bowl deliberative conference, you will certainly want to optimize the seating for the best

21

Aids in Developing a Consensus

possible round-table discussion so that everyone can see and hear everyone else to the maximum possible extent. How the optimum seating arrangement of the Goldfish Bowl originated is explained in Appendix 1.

The first reason for such a seating arrangement is obviously to facilitiate the chairman's maintaining close contact with all participants as an aid in selecting the proper sequence of speakers. Even more important is the fact that the "circle" maintains the air of informality and encourages the conversational mode, which is a prerequisite to success in a small as well as in a large round-table discussion. Each participant will feel less compulsion to recite a long and gory history of an activity with rhetoric that needs much time to expound. No longer does a participant feel compelled to make a speech in order to answer "Yes" or "No" to a simple question. The size of the meeting would ordinarily dictate the magnitude of an oration, in accord with a square-law relationship; but this relationship need not apply if the proper mood is established by the chairman with the help of these environmental ploys. Neither should the chairman be seated high on a stage, aloof intellectually as well as physically from the discussion going on down below. Move the chairman's table down among the participants, maintaining only sufficient altitude to permit him to scan the meeting for a raised hand or even a facial expression that says "I would like to say something helpful." Make the chairman the equivalent of a discussion leader in a small round-table discussion.

Consensus through Debate

With this environment established, it will help the meeting to set the proper round-table discussion mood. This proper mood can permeate the meeting to the extent that when the meeting begins the necessary shift into the debating form, as protagonists materialize for the various proposals, the informal discussion mood may be kept intact to counter the natural tendency for an argumentative spirit to emerge.

Debate is contention. But debate is also one of the oldest forms of education. Professors McBurney and Mills, in their book *Argumentation and Debate*, start off their Chapter 19 with these words:

Debate as an Educational Method

Its origin and development. Debate and its predecessor, disputation, were among the earliest known teaching devices. Protagoras, who taught in Athens approximately 2,400 years ago, is referred to as the "father of debate." He is said to have been the first to encourage regular discussions on set subjects and to organize argumentative contests among pupils. Aristotle, who taught a century later in Greece, commented on debate as a school exercise in his Rhetoric. Historically, the teaching and the practice of debate have flourished and declined concomitantly with democracy. Tyrants have had no use for debaters and their teachers.[1]

We must never thwart the argumentative spirit, but we can make argumentation a better stepping-stone to eventual consensus development if we can successfully employ the informality and nonpompous potential of the small round-table discussion mood as we progress into the debate. We encourage the informal environment and an informal mood in the interest of avoiding the tediousness of senatorial oratory when it is neither necessary nor appropriate.

In the heading for this chapter, you may have noted my use of the word "developing" rather than "finding," with respect to how we get a consensus. I contend that a consensus seldom exists for the finding; if we sometimes find it where it already exists, that exercise is not a difficult one. The real challenge is in developing a consensus when no consensus already exists. As I have pointed out in previous chapters, we are never interested in a consensus that will not survive; we do not covet a consensus as simply the outcome of warriors fighting to the death. Our satisfaction lies only in developing all the necessary arguments in a public forum to the point at which the protagonists of various views have determined the best possible accommodation of all parties. True, this requires the development of a consensus, because consensus does not usually come automatically, but it must come properly, *with the minority disposed to accept the accommodation that the majority adopts.*

Motivation

Apart from a proper environment, other factors contribute to the consensus-forming process. One that would seem obvious is a motivation to proceed toward a resolution of some problem. Sometimes a group simply *assumes* that a decision is necessary, but there may be no real motivation for action. Sometimes the leader of a group is so enthralled with his committee that he fails to analyze the issues or nonissues to see what should be attempted now and what should *not* be attempted now. Perhaps the activity is proper, but the time is wrong. From Arthur Bloch's book *Murphy's Law—and Other Reasons Why Things Go Wrong!*[2]

[1]James H. McBurney and Glen E. Mills, *Argumentation and Debate: Techniques of a Free Society,* Macmillan Publishing Company, New York, copyright 1964.

[2] Price/Stern/Sloan, Los Angeles, copyright 1977.

we learn of Lord Falkland's seventeenth-century rule, which states it this way, "When it is not necessary to make a decision, it is necessary not to make a decision."

If motivation is not adequate, it can cause several troubles. First is the tendency for participants to consider the matter only superficially, if at all, each one believing that someone else has an urgent need for a decision now, and consequently no one has a real *involvement* in the debate except as an exercise. A decision may be easy to find, but it is unreal, worthless, and likely to undermine the credibility of the group when it must be changed after the parties involved in or affected by the matter discover the bad mistake. Second is the possibility that affected parties may refuse to accept *any* solution on the basis that *they are affected* and they have not resolved all the problems, with the result that no decision is possible and the organization appears to have failed miserably in resolving what looks like a simple matter. In either of the two cases, the result is not good, simply because an activity has been attempted without ensuring that sufficient motivation exists.

Identification of Adversaries

Even when the enviroment is satisfactory and motivation exists, the effort may still become thoroughly snarled because of the impossibility of identifying adversaries. This may seem to be a silly problem, but it is a real problem. In past history, generals always have wanted uniforms of contrasting colors on the opposing sides, with one side arrayed in battle formation on one side of some natural boundary, like a river, a valley, or even an entrenchment as in World War I, and the other side properly separated on the other side of that boundary. Generals seem to like to shoot at a well-defined enemy whom they can see and identify. In the Spanish Civil War, the generals complained that they could no longer identify the ones they were attacking; they sometimes found that in these circumstances they had been shooting at their own side. In Congress, the seating arrangement keeps the usual combatants separated by a boundary so that everyone knows to which side the epithets are directed. Imagine a football game with no contrasting colors of uniforms. Even a college debate establishes in advance who will be on which side of which argument. Yet time after time participants in deliberative conferences will refuse to disclose their sympathies as they argue both sides of an issue, claiming a dispassionate search for the truth. There can never be a law requiring disclosure of protagonists' inner thinking; what they want must always be their secret, at least up to the time when an open vote (if legitimate under proper parliamentary procedures) will ultimately disclose their views. Yet it is often in the best interest of protagonists to state their views early in the debate; this has the same beneficial effect found by the generals in other forms of adversary combat. We have postulated for industry conferences that industry has a greater need for *some* decision to be made than for its own preferences to be adopted. Thus, there is little to be gained by secrecy of viewpoints. Instead, the total will of the industry will be best served by divulging, explicitly and immediately, the dispositions of any and all participants as each develops a view.

Unfortunately, getting the adversaries to acknowledge their leanings is not an easy undertaking. Sometimes it is simply poor rhetoric that leaves the listener at a loss, as I pointed out in Chapter 12. There seems to be some hidden force that causes speakers to obfuscate rather than to clarify whatever they are trying to explain in a deliberative conference. As I have urged throughout this text, it is either the chairman or *nobody* who will help the meeting translate the gibberish of a speaker into the "for" or "agin" arguments. If speakers think that they are making particularly important points but fail to get the points across, it is up to the chairman to help them communicate with the audience.

Opinion Sampling

In Chapter 4, I urged opinion sampling and noted the many advantages it offers for consensus development. Yet opinion sampling is so often a major bugaboo that chairmen shy away from it or attempt to make it so formal that it serves no more of a purpose than an ordinary formal vote. Opinion sampling properly done is *not easy* to institute, but thereafter it is quite easy to continue. It is easy to *plan* to do but difficult to accomplish effectively. Let us look at some of the pitfalls that inhibit simple opinion sampling. The first problem is that a burning issue always divides a deliberative body into at least two parts, the fors and againsts. Before opinion sampling has taken place, everyone believes and hopes, but is not quite sure, that he is on the winning side, the side that is right, and is also in the majority. If he is sure that he is in the majority, he will want to close debate and vote quickly. If he is sure that he is in the minority, he will insist upon delaying any vote and any opinion sampling until he has been allowed to give all his arguments (over and over) and those other stupid people have seen how right he is. If he suspects that he might be in the minority, he certainly does not want the majority to find that out, because it would then press him mercilessly for a quick vote.

All this sounds so obvious and even so childish that I should hardly mention it. Yet it is the characteristic of people that a knowledgeable chairman must understand if he is to expedite the long, dreary process of letting a developing consensus finally, eventually, become evident. Conferences often debate a point for hours without realizing that only a small, noisy minority has been objecting. When the chairman or a member of the other side finally can stand the arguing no longer and will press for closing the debate (move, vote for, and order the previous question), it may come as quite a surprise that there is far more than the required two-thirds majority vote to close the debate. Then, everyone is equally surprised when the proposal is found to be supported by almost everyone except a small, noisy minority.

How can a meeting find out who is on which side of an issue? A request to the group will usually produce nothing if everyone thinks *he* is in the minority. If he is, he doesn't want it divulged; he wants to debate the issue further before tipping his hand. The participants may attempt to electioneer by making speeches that do not exactly disclose how they feel and are therefore weasel-worded, so that the debate is pretty confusing. I have seen many a debate in which a simple suggestion to the chairman that he might wish to take an opinion sample causes the most awful uproar among the participants on both sides of the question. It is not like Congress, in which the debating time remaining is often rationed equally to the two sides. In Congress, with good party issues, it is pretty obvious who is on which side and which side controls the majority vote—not always, but more often than in industry debates. When the majority begins to detect its own strength and the minority begins to suspect the worst, we can be absolutely certain of the next happening. The majority will start to exert pressure on the chairman for an opinion sampling, and the minority will resist it so firmly that it will scream "unfair" and insist that *it* has been persecuted by the others and should be allowed to present its important arguments (again).

At this point in my story it will be argued by formal-parliamentary-procedures purists that the meeting would never have gotten into that bad situation if correct parliamentary procedures had been followed from the beginning. The argument will be that the chairman should have exactly allocated time for debate (probably by unanimous consent) to each speaker, giving each his prescribed 10 minutes, with another 10 minutes for later rebuttal, and allowing no one to speak more than the prescribed 2 times on any one item during a day. Such general restrictions may be appropriate for some legislative bodies. Yet in the real world of commerce, in 30 years of attending all kinds of meetings and deliberative sessions and board meetings, I have never seen the rule applied, *not even once*, in its entirety. The closest that it has been followed has been to limit repeated speaking by the same individual when the chairman observes others wishing to speak who have not spoken. Ignoring the 10 times 2 rule is the real-life experience with parliamentary procedures rather than the schoolbook approach, which works well in theory.

Can we imagine a thirty-member deliberative body following these rules and therefore requiring 10 hours of debate (maximum) just to get to a vote on one single question? A 2-day deliberative Goldfish Bowl conference contains little more than 10 hours of deliberative time; could we conceive of frittering all this away on a single question, no matter how awfully important that one question might be? Certainly not. Neither the 10 times 2 rule nor the lesser 5 times 1 rule, often mentioned as an alternative, can afford the best use of time in a deliberative conference in the real commercial world. Instead, I postulate that there should be a careful assessment of the needs by the chairman, aided by repeated and early opinion samplings to determine the needs and to measure progress. Let's take a look at the proper means of instituting opinion sampling in a deliberative conference.

As a start, we can see that a group will tend to resist suggestions for opinion sampling simply because the group is afraid of it. Yet experience of many years with opinion sampling shows that a group can learn to apply it carefully and properly without difficulties. The foregoing experiences show the importance of a thorough understanding of one important rule:

ELLISON'S FIRST RULE OF OPINION SAMPLING

If it isn't spontaneous, instantaneous, and continuous, it won't work.

The first rule suggests what *won't* work. What *will* work? This leads to:

ELLISON'S SECOND RULE OF OPINION SAMPLING

Sneak up on it.

Tom Ellison, of United Airlines, chairman of a number of industry avionic activities, for whom the rules are named, has conquered the usual fears of a group by making opinion sampling so natural and so sensible that no one can find any problem with it. He carries the informal mood of the round-table discussion into the larger meeting and urges people to express their views on a matter in such an offhand manner that they find themselves presenting the various arguments for and against a possibility just as they would in a three-man informal conversation. Conversation is always a pleasure rather than a chore.

Conversational Mode

It was the Rev. Sydney Smith who wrote (*Essays,* 1877), "One of the greatest pleasures of life is conversation." If we can keep a large deliberative conference in the true conversational mode, we have solved most of our problems. But sometimes the problem is one of getting the group started in the conversational mode in the first place. Tom Ellison has reported that in the beginning of some of his meetings it has been difficult to get the participants going; they seem willing to lean on the chairman, to the extent that he has worried that they might depend upon him for discussion, guidance, and perhaps even decision proposals. This dependence he knows would ruin any subsequent group discussion, decision, and eventual commitment to implementation. Tom notes the value of silence: it can be very useful if the chairman simply outlines the immediate problem and then stops talking. The tension that builds during the ensuing loud silence usually gets the group going again in its proper role if the chairman can stand the tension and stay silent.

Think back for a moment. How many times can you remember a chairman who seemed to keep talking endlessly, always promising to ask for opinions but never really giving time for the group to start the conversational mode of expression that the chairman was seeking? He was probably an overly cautious chairman, deadly afraid of loud silence. He may have done what was necessary to start the conversational mode, but he never really allowed that mode to develop.

Sampling Guidelines

Let us assume that you will apply Tom's suggestion to get your group *into* the conversational mode; now, if you can keep the group in that conversational mode, the consensus development will soon start. The consensus development will be helped by the chairman's simply inquiring, in a highly informal way, "Who feels we should do it as George suggests?" and then looking around the room for some sign of "Yes, we like it." After the chairman has started early to find out what the group feels about nonessential matters, members of the group discover that they are announcing their views on highly complex issues and not minding it at all. To get the best utility from the opinion-sampling process, you should watch several points that are important:

1.   Don't wait for a major issue to start the opinion sampling.

2.   On simple questions, don't make a particular point of the majority opinion being settled upon as the conference decision, but let the group ponder the distribution of votes for a while and form its own opinion on the significance of those first opinion samplings.

3.   Use the answers obtained from one question to formulate additional questions that will help to focus the attention of the group on even better questions to be tried next.

4. Keep an informal tally (*not* a formal record), perhaps in your head, at the beginning of opinion sampling until the group is convinced that the opinion sampling is a tool rather than formal and *final* decision making. Later, ask the secretary to make some kind of tally, preferably on the blackboard, and be sure the group knows that it can change its views from time to time as new arguments come out and individuals begin to formulate better reasons for possible action.

5. Keep it clear to everyone that you have no fixed views on how the debate should come out and that you, the chairman, are formulating *your* opinions as you see how others express theirs. Show some surprise at some of the findings from the exercise, even if you have known all along where the dicussion is leading the group.

6. Keep your distance. Ask the group for suggestions on what questions should be asked next. Be sure that everyone is a part of the extended informal round-table discussion.

7. Try to formulate opinion-sampling questions with only *two* choices; not three or more. If opinions have already been expressed for more than two different things, make the questions simple with only two alternatives. For example, if the group is selecting the desired day of the week, ask first whether the day should be in the first four or the last three days. When that shows a definite trend, say, for the first four days, ask whether the group prefers the first half or the last half of that first four. This procedure may seem clumsy, but it is far better than explaining to the group how to go about expressing an opinion for one out of five possible choices. Try it and see. Remember that if you are to apply Ellison's second rule effectively, you must have simple questions rather than complex questions for which it would take a long time to explain the sampling process.

8. If you play the game carefully (and it is a game, as everyone will finally discover and accept), you will find that the whole logical discussion process, just as in textbooks on logical discussion, will open up before your very eyes. You will find that you have no protagonists who are ready to fight to the death for an issue; instead, they will jointly search for the proper accommodation. You will find a solid consensus emerging, and in a very short total time.

9. If you have tackled the less complex issues first, you will discover that the difficult ones come easily too.

10. Be on guard for issues that are not yet ripe. Some questions should be dropped rather than forced into deliberation. One sign of unripeness is a lesser interest in one question than in previous questions. When this loss of interest develops, be prepared to ask whether a decision is really necessary on that question just now. Remember Lord Falkland's rule: the time may not be right for a decision now. Perhaps some other

questions should be taken first; or perhaps the new question, or that whole area of discusssion, should be deferred to the next meeting, when additional information will be available or motivation for a lasting decision will be greater.

11.   Be prepared to turn any consensus opinion obtained through the sampling process into an *actual* decision when the group is *ready* for it: for this decision, your best signal will come from the minority on that question. The minority will tell you and the rest of the meeting when it is time to write down the opinion as a decision of the group. Watch for signals.

12.   The meeting report need not necessarily record opinion-sampling conclusions as decisions of the group. Sometimes, if your group is still a little jumpy about opinion sampling, there can be a long-term advantage in simply tabulating a list of the questions asked and the preferences for and against without drawing any conclusion. If the arguments are sound and the preference is strong for one side, the simple record of what has happened will speak for itself; this procedure avoids the possibility of a member of the minority complaining that everyone was really in support of his logical arguments and that the report was in error in failing to admit that the minority had many other arguments not yet presented which would overturn the premature decision of the group at the next meeting.

Don't underestimate the value of repeated opinion sampling on a highly complex, controversial question. Although some purists will argue that no opinion sampling should ever be allowed until people have had an opportunity to be given the true facts, inasmuch as people cannot make intelligent decisions when they are still unknowledgeable, this is just a ploy to keep members of the majority from discovering that they *are* the majority. If you have started out with opinion sampling on the question before any argument has been given, you will discover a surprising thing: few people having an original fixation on a question will ever change it after debate. If you have the figures on the original straw vote and discover that the majority and minority have not changed at all after 20 minutes of intense debate, you have an important piece of information. A running count of who is for and who is against will soon show up the minority as espousing a lost cause. If you await the end of debate to determine the balance of opinion, you will have wasted a considerable amount of time on debate that hasn't served the purpose. The purpose of debate is not generally to convince a group; it is generally to convince members of the minority that further debate is producing nothing for them and only more tediousness for

the majority. This is an important rule in real-life commercial deliberative conferences, as opposed to theory:

ELLISON'S THIRD RULE OF OPINION SAMPLING

When repeated opinion sampling shows no further change,
write it on the blackboard with a large star, as you may have succeeded in getting a reasonably firm decision.

A Firm Decision?

A problem often faced in a deliberative meeting is to answer a question
that people will ask: "When is a decision firm?" If we study the texts on
parliamentary procedure, we shall find a ready answer to that question
in the parliamentary rule that, except for the process of reconsideration
and rescinding, a decision is final after it has been duly made in accordance with proper parliamentary procedures, with proper notification
in advance, with a proper quorum, and with a proper vote under
proper conditions as spelled out in the book. But I am sorry to report
that things don't always happen that way in the real world of commercial deliberative conferences. Even though a proper final action may
have been taken, a conference may still change its mind; if that happens, the conference is going to change its decision whether proper
procedures allow it to do so or not. And it may chooose to change its
decision back again. An argument could be presented that if this situation develops, it is a consequence of violating some other part of the
parliamentary procedures along the way, and that this should never
have happened. Yet it does happen, and it will continue to happen
despite the best and most proper precautions. I can recall one action in
our group many years ago that was reconsidered three times in one
day. Each time both majority and minority argued that some new facts
were now available. Each time the decision came out the same way as
the first time, but it required those three events to convince the group,
majority and minority alike, that it really had the best decision. True,
the chairman could have attempted to hide behind parliamentary rules
and refuse such multiple reconsideration, but his refusal would only
have left the question still up in the air in the minds of many people,
notwithstanding the parliamentary rule that the decision was really
final.

In the real world we must work with people rather than follow
blindly some arbitrary rules. As I have stated throughout this text, the
test of a decision is whether it is *really accepted* by the industry or community to the extent that private commercial monetary investments
predicated upon that decision will be made. All the paper decisions in

the world will never equal one *real* decision on which industry gambles its own money. Commercial decisions should be more than simple majority votes on a question; they should be a true consensus of majority and minority alike as the best possible accommodation of an important industry or community.

Thus, we can give only one real answer to the question "When is a decision firm?" The only answer is that a decision can undergo change right up to the time of an implementation deadline. This is right and proper; premature decisions are not likely to last. But when some particular expenditure is imminent and this expenditure can go one of several ways, depending upon the decision or preference of the industry, the time is now proper for the decision to get locked into place. When I am asked this question with regard to a particular arbitrary question having to do with some hardware spec being developed, I always have to answer that *a decision never really does become final.* What happens is that the assurance of no further change becomes increasingly better with the passage of time.

I shall explain that statement further. Suppose that a subcommittee or a working group debates the physical dimensions of a proposed device and gradually works the possibilities down to two choices, which we shall call "A size" and "B size." Gradually, the majority finds that the A size is preferred by about 2 to 1, and it decides to write that preference into the draft spec. It knows that once the majority of manufacturers get that size engineered, it will be almost impossible to obtain any further shift back to the B size. Thus, the subcommittee concludes: "The decision has been made." So everyone goes home, and the manufacturers start the engineering designs to tie down the A size.

A month goes by. There are no complaints from anybody. A meeting of the parent committee is soon to take place to act on the complete spec on behalf of everybody. But before that there is a frantic phone call from one customer stating that supplier X has determined that the length of the standard A size is insufficient to allow the whoofizzel to fit; one more inch or a shift to the B size would be necessary. Certainly, costs will be involved in talking the manufacturers into a change from the A size to the B size at this late date, when everyone has seemed happy with the earlier choice and has started the engineering. There will be costs to change; there will be costs *not* to change. Which are worse?

Let us assume that the costs to change are far less and that everybody seems willing to make the change. Then we receive a further challenge from the manufacturers: "If we make the change, can we be assured that there will be no further changes and that the decision is final?" The chairman has been burned before, so there will be no such rash promise. But everybody seems to accept the change anyway. A month goes by. No complaints. Everybody has been alerted to the reason for the change, and no formal decision on the change seems necessary, since everybody knows that the change has been inevitable. Then the parent committee meets to act on the draft spec, an action that seems a rubber stamp, since everyone has already accepted the change. Now something new comes out: several suppliers have made a breakthrough. They can make a whoofizzel fit the A size case! Now we can all go back to the A size, which everyone had preferred. But hold everything. Some manufacturers now have a problem; they have changed their designs to accommodate the users, and now they are beyond the point at which a change back can be made.

Now what do we do? Should the customers take advantage of a change in technology that allows something that couldn't be done several months ago to be applied today? Or should the customers reject this advancement in the state of the art (a smaller size) to keep faith with the manufacturers who have spent funds ahead of the final decision by the parent committee? The answer is that the industry or community that is affected by such a decision must work out the best accommodation for all parties irrespective of any parliamentary procedures or rules that might appear to take precedence.

In a *community* endeavor, the community must be a party to the decisions. The customer could pretend to hide behind the usual principle that no final action had yet been taken by the parent body having jurisdiction and, thus, that any decision which that body wished to make would be its privilege and the rest of the world would just have to accept that decision. But parliamentary rules and procedures are far less important than is the necessity of accommodating the best interests of the industry and the community. A quick benefit might be obtained by the customers' deciding the matter independently of the others who would be affected; but the long-term penalty would probably be to lose the cooperation of that segment of the industry—a cooperation that is highly important in most community endeavors.

The question that I started out with still justifies only one answer. *A decision is never final*; it just gradually works its way to the point at which any change from that decision becomes more and more complicated. A change is never impossible, for the reasons explained in the example; in fact, a later refusal to make a change may be almost impossible. No one without a perfect crystal ball can make any pronouncement on when or whether a final decision is firm enough to allow some gambling of funds on it. This is always a gamble, but after a degree of common implementation has occurred, the decision gets *more nearly likely to be less subject to change (maybe)*.

Now, let us back up to the consequences of such a loose decision. It is quite proper and truthful for you to allay the fears of those who think that they will abhor opinion sampling and who, therefore, make quite a fuss when you first attempt to sample opinion. You can properly promise that there can be no final decision but simply a notation that this result of opinion sampling is the preference of a segment of the meeting at *this particular time*. You can state that the preference will stand until factors not previously known to the group might cause it to be changed. You may state authoritatively that it will not likely be changed (because of the cost) after some degree of implementation has taken place; thus, the more exposure the decision receives without further change, the better likelihood there is of no further change. My experience shows that a decision arrived at by opinion sampling at one meeting tends to become stable if it survives the next meeting of the same group.

You may discover that after you have explained the foregoing your critic of opinion sampling will suddenly shift the argument and insist that the group make a final decision *later*, with absolute finality, rather than mush around *now* in "premature" opinion sampling. I have discovered that those who object most strenuously to opinion sampling also object equally to the consultative process I have espoused, mostly because they have neither been involved in it nor had an opportunity to ponder the processes of debate sufficiently to understand the principles of accommodation.

In summary, I postulate that commercial pressures for finding an accommodation can work to the advantage of a whole industry, once the processes of the Goldfish Bowl deliberative conference are understood and observed in action. The natural processes work toward the end of helping the development of a consensus. A consensus may eventually come about without any influence by the chairman, but that generally is a slow, laborious process under pure parliamentary procedures and rules. Under the commercial stimulus for a lasting decision, the chairman can help develop a consensus with the complete endorsement of the conference and with surprisingly successful results for industry.

Sacrilegious? How can a text on conferences suggest that coffee breaks are wonderful? Because they *are*, that's why. Most conference attendees are too cautious to admit that coffee breaks and other similar interruptions of a conference are the most important parts of the whole conference. No, they will not and cannot admit this even though all participants cherish their coffee breaks.

Let me be a little more sacrilegious and state a postulate: the ideal conference would be one long coffee break punctuated by a few short interruptions for short speeches. Now that I have shot darts at some sacred cows, let me explore the subject a bit further. Note that I apply this all-inclusive postulate not only to *deliberative* conferences, but to *all* conferences. The usual industry conference, which will be the subject of more detailed examination in Chapter 24, is a collection of speeches on such highfallutin subjects by such persons of high stature that it will justify the attendance of anybody and everybody with full and complete endorsement and financial support by the attendees' firms or organizations. Once an individual has gotten a trip approved "to attend a most important conference to learn a lot about our business," he arrives and discovers that it is the outside activities that are really the most interesting and also of the most use to him in his business. The best outside activity of all is the coffee break. There he can observe what I quoted the Reverend Mr. Smith as saying (in Chapter 21): "One of the greatest pleasures of life is conversation." But there is more than that. It is during the coffee breaks, for example, that a supplier can meet individually with a customer or a potential customer and compare notes on their most pressing problems. There he can concentrate on his business problems and try to find a solution to them. Conversation is pleasing, and conversation can produce real answers to real problems, as opposed to the previously announced speeches, which will address someone else's general problems rather than *his specific problems*.

22

Those Wonderful Coffee Breaks

You often hear of attendees sneaking out during formal speeches. Have you ever heard of anyone sneaking out of a coffee break? Of course not. That is the most interesting and the most useful part of the conference.

Now that I have praised the coffee break that is a part of the usual conference, what about the utility of a coffee break in a deliberative conference? In answering that question, I should recognize that deliberative conferences are not 100 percent deliberation. Mixed in with pure deliberation will be a lot of preliminaries, including some speeches, even though they are not billed on the advance program as speeches. The coffee break gives the necessary respite from the rigors of explicit argumentation (Chapter 12) and difficult expert listening (Chapter 13). It is the relief valve that makes argumentation tolerable. It is the means of awakening a nodding audience that has failed or refused to get involved despite the urging in Chapters 12 and 13. It is also the means of advancing coordination of views, which is expedited by the process of informal conversation among and between adversaries. It is the means of softening a bristling opposition. It is the ideal way of taking the sharp edge off a complex issue that has divided contemporaries and even friends. Coffee breaks are wonderful for any meeting of any kind.

No-Coffee Breaks

Before anyone gets the mistaken idea that this chapter is a testimonial for the coffee industry, I shall refute that notion right now. When I use the term "coffee break," I am referring to the traditional name that has been applied since conferences were invented to timely breaks in a meeting, whether for coffee, tea, cookies (or biscuits), cake, soft drinks, water, or other refreshments that might be served, sold, or consumed. Such refreshments serve an important purpose, whether they are served or are available to the attendee if he walks to or orders from a central repository. Having refreshments handy to the conference room can encourage the continuation of the discussion and debate that were interrupted by the coffee break when the participants get together outside the conference room. But I must not overestimate the value of refreshments in getting the advantage of a break. Time after time, I have asked participants at our meetings whether they find coffee to be an important part of coffee breaks, and time and time again the participants have said "No, it is *not* essential." Part of the reason for this response has been the rapid rise in the price of coffee as served during a coffee break in the usual hotel. For many years, coffee was available only at the per person or per cup price, with an extra charge for waiter service. In recent years there has been a tendency to offer coffee at the urn price, with do-it-yourself serving permitted at a much lower cost. But even with this pricing concession the cost of coffee is quite high, reducing its utility as the price advances. I might tell the story of a London hotel conference some years ago at which we followed our usual tradition of having what we call "no-coffee breaks." The president of a large firm was amazed at our no-coffee service; he loved coffee. So he offered to pay for our coffee breaks, and I accepted his generous offer, amid the snickering of the other suppliers who knew what he was in for. He grunted when he received the hotel bill. He continued the coffee service throughout that one day, but we discovered the next day that we had returned to the no-coffee breaks. The cost of the coffee had done him in. He concluded exactly what we had previously concluded: "Them who want it can go buy it; them who don't won't miss it."

That is the ultimate conclusion we have repeatedly drawn with respect to coffee at our coffee breaks. But no-coffee breaks are just as good for the purpose anyway. They are wonderful.

How do you organize a coffee break? Yes, it should be organized to a degree, but not quite as you organize a meeting. Organization will consist primarily of fitting the various topics into the program in and around the coffee break so that the break will be of greatest utility in breaking up logjams that may develop in the debate of complex issues. If a highly controversial question is introduced at the proper time before a scheduled coffee break, you can make the break occur just when it is most needed to allow the adversaries to relax for a few minutes and discuss the issues informally before they return to the combat zone. Coffee breaks are wonderful.

How often should you have coffee breaks? Very often would be best for nondeliberative conferences, and quite often is probably best for the deliberative type. "Quite often" means often enough to keep the group awake but not so often that the members skip the meeting because the meeting time is now too short to bother with. If you follow the urging of your people, you will plan (and intend to have) coffee breaks about once an hour; then you will rationalize them into the usual pattern of one in the morning and one in the afternoon. You will have caved in because of your worry that the firms that finance your operation will believe that the conference is really fun and games rather than work if they see a program containing too many coffee breaks.

How long should coffee breaks be? They should be just a bit shorter than the time your people think it would take to get to a distant coffee shop or bar and get back again. The whole benefit of a coffee break for a meeting can collapse if people dart away and get involved in other activities during an extra-long coffee break. If they feel constrained to remain in the area, they will get business done with their business associates, and they will do enough discussion of the item of business that was interrupted by the coffee break to break a logjam in a dispute. But don't let the coffee break turn into an afternoon break, with people deciding spontaneously to leave for the day. ⸴

Where should a coffee break be? Preferably just outside the conference room door, but in a location reasonably well isolated from other hotel lobby activities and not in a spot where interference from other convention groups will give problems. I recall one meeting in which our group drank all the coffee of another convention group which had not yet broken for its coffee break. The other group was pretty mad when it found all its coffee gone; it raised Cain with the hotel, and the hotel was mad at us. It all came out all right the next day, after the hotel moved the other coffee service to a different location and kept a better guard on it. Conventions don't mix well in a too small hotel lobby.

How should people be herded back into the conference room? A difficult problem for the uninitiated? Yes, it is. The how-to-do-it principles are in a later chapter; therefore, all we shall say here is that the utility of a coffee break *to the conference itself* depends upon your success in getting the people involved in the interrupted debate back into the meeting room *on time.* As you will see in our later discussion, the ease with which most techniques can be made to work is a function of where the coffee break is held with respect to the conference room. Keep it close by even though there may be a far nicer place elsewhere to sip coffee or enjoy the conversation.

Lunch Breaks

Are lunch breaks as important as coffee breaks? More so, of course. Lunch breaks are needed for lunch if for no other reason. And they do help to expedite the resolution of complex issues by allowing people to form smaller groups for discussion. Certainly, luncheon breaks are an immense aid to a conference attendee who has important business with his customers or suppliers entirely apart from the conference itself. But such breaks can do wonders for resolving a complex conference issue over a sandwich or a thick steak, depending upon your palate.

To help understand the workings of an attendee's thinking process, I shall describe a happening I call Oscar's syndrome. It occurs over and over and over at such luncheon breaks, yet it seems not to be comprehended by the usual conference attendee. A large conference has debated an issue until everyone is overjoyed at the chance to escape from it for an hour. A batch of people form themselves into a group, and they depart for a nearby restaurant, determined to refrain from discussing that issue until they return to the meeting. They have had enough. They will give their ulcers a rest. They no sooner sit down and place their order than one individual (the leader type) remarks: "It is nice to have a respite from that awful debate. Wasn't it painful when George started up again on the proposal to rewind all the weils backward?" Now the group is deep into the topic again despite anything it can do. The members debate it and debate it and debate it, finding that they have a consensus on the part that was in dispute just before lunch. They finish their lunch and return to the conference. Their leader immediately asks for permission to make a proposal to the conference; it starts out like this: "We got together at lunch, and we worked it all out; we have the answer to all the problems. You guys are all wrong; we know what it takes to get it settled. What we must do is . . . ," and he explains the whole idea just as though he had had the whole large conference at lunch with him and all the participants had concurred.

What this leader has failed to comprehend is that every other table at lunch did the same thing; they all debated the issue, and every group believes that it has the winning answer. But all the answers are different. None of the groups probably have the winning answer, but it may be just as well that they *think* they have, because the luncheon discussions have served to bring some new thinking, or at least some new reasons for the same old thinking, into the debate. Admittedly the debate was getting pretty bad before the luncheon break, and the stultification needed unstultifying. A large dose of Oscar's syndrome is often just what is needed. Thus, our conclusion regarding luncheon breaks: next to coffee breaks, luncheon breaks, with or without Oscar's syndrome, are the most wonderful.

Industry Receptions

How about other breaks? Of course! Any and all breaks are wonderful for any kind of conference. Receptions and cocktail parties serve an admirable purpose by giving extra time for those important other business contacts. The program should never be so thoroughly filled with conference business that no time is allowed for such contacts. Dinner time is free time if the group is not regimented into formal dinners and banquets with business speakers at every possible moment. Too much is too much. In industry conferences, the participants are volunteers who come partly for altruistic reasons to help their industry, partly to help their own business, and perhaps partly to enjoy themselves; but there is seldom much enjoyment. Deliberative conferences are a difficult chore; the participants need some relief from the work. Our industry has found that a single large supplier-sponsored reception is a wonderful aid if it is not carried too far. For a 3-day conference, a single night can be allocated to such a function with beneficial results. Here are the benefits as stated by the suppliers who finance the affair:

1.   It gets all the customers together in one place and allows the suppliers to determine what company problems each of their customers have and how to assign their sales, service, and design people to each customer to help with his problem.

2.   It allows suppliers to get in touch with the customers who should go to dinner with them that evening or on subsequent evenings to discuss their mutual problems.

3.   It is far more economical of money, time, and personnel than having each supplier try to offer a reception for all the customers.

4.   It is the best possible arrangement for both large and small firms to meet common customers without the necessity for smaller firms, with only limited product lines and budgets, to overspend.

It is not only the suppliers who work out an equitable way of arranging and financing such an affair who benefit; customers like the common informal reception because they can move around freely and see a large number of suppliers in a very short time.

It has been the practice in our industry for at least two decades to have such a reception on the evening of the first day of the conference, in a central location in the headquarters hotel, and to limit its duration strictly to the 6:30 P.M.–8:30 P.M. period so that it will not interfere with any dinner arrangements that suppliers wish to work out with customers.

Trade Shows

Trade shows have a considerable influence on deliberative conferences and are an important adjunct to such affairs. They bring the topics under debate more directly to the attention of the participants than would otherwise be possible. There will always be a natural tendency for products under discussion in a conference to be displayed in an associated trade show, simply because suppliers know that the design capability of their firms is best proved by the display of operating models of a similar (or even the same) product. Trade shows may take several forms. The most obvious is the usual hall with exhibits of any and all suppliers who wish to show their products. The costs may be financed cooperatively by the organization, by the suppliers as a group, or by individuals through the sale of exhibit space. It is not the purpose of this text to cover the extensive planning and management of trade shows but only to describe the simple and beneficial relationship that a trade show of some type can have with a deliberative conference.

The other, not-so-obvious form of trade show is held in what many would call a "hospitality suite" in the headquarters hotel; the supplier employs a portion of his suite for the demonstration of his products to potential customers. This form has an advantage over the usual trade show in the exhibit hall in that it can permit a degree of company proprietary control over the products shown. With our industry and the extensive cross-fertilization of suppliers that exists in a friendly though competitive industry, it is somewhat difficult to keep a new product away from a competitor's view. It is not unusual for one supplier to be invited into another's hospitality suite, along with the customers. But the host may have an extra room in the back of the suite where the really proprietary products are kept under wraps and where only customers are permitted.

Trade shows are important. They are a considerable attraction for customers who may not have the opportunity to visit the supplier's plants and wish to make the best use of their time at an industry deliberative conference. If an outside activity helps to attract participants and thereby to obtain a better cross section of industry, the activity is important and should be nurtured. The conference planner is well advised to keep such outside activities going and to provide the best possible environment in which they can flourish.

Never cut off your nose to spite your face; never make it difficult for an important outside activity to survive. Those wonderful coffee breaks and all the rest of the related and similar activities are highly important. Use them to the fullest.

T he study of conference management is a study of *people*. People are funny. Meeting participants and chairmen are, notwithstanding some divergent views, *real, ordinary people*—perhaps a little funnier than *other* real, ordinary people, and for this we should be thankful. Meetings can be dreary without something on the light side to reduce tension among sometimes-antagonistic protagonists of important commercial viewpoints. Without some humorous interruptions, we might see some difficult confrontations.

Mechanical Failures

Some of the humorous interruptions are the consequence of a mechanical failure or an act of God that a conference might just as well laugh about rather than complain about. I recall the hilarious time in the Hôtel Métropole, in Brussels, when the lights went out in the middle of the meeting. The cause was a blown fuse in the temporary wiring that the hotel had installed the previous day after a fire had completely burned out the ballroom just a few days before the conference. The hotel had, painstakingly and beautifully, rebuilt, refurbished, repainted, and rewired the ballroom after the fire so that our conference could take place on schedule. We arrived to find a beautiful new ballroom that had been a burned-out shambles just a few days earlier. When the lights went out, I had a beautiful sight from the head table: cigarette lighters clicked on all over the ballroom and 300 lighthearted, nice people went on with the meeting, enjoying every moment of that several-minute interruption of the incandescent lighting.

Three hundred participants in a meeting at Atlanta's Dinkler Plaza Hotel recall, nostalgically, what may have been the last major convention (and probably the worst ever) held there before the hotel was closed and torn down. Without our knowledge, the hotel had changed

23

The Funny Side: Let's Laugh at Our Foibles; Let's Counteract Our Foibles

management just before our meeting, and the new management had insufficient funding to keep the hotel facilities in proper repair. Before the meeting, we had great difficulty in locating enough conference tables solid enough for a meeting attendee to lean on without his elbow going right through the tabletop. Chairs were the same. On the night of check-in we had more than 100 registrants waiting in the lobby for hours before being assigned rooms. The computer seemed to have forgotten which rooms were occupied already; the small staff had to make a door-to-door check to find available rooms. Eventually, people were matched to rooms, but we had other troubles all week.

Each time the meeting reconvened, the mikes were missing. We learned later from the general manager that they were being stolen faster than the engineer could replace them. Blankets were scarce; pillows were in short supply; the air conditioning kept going off; the hotel staff was having great difficulty in keeping things going, but the staff simply exuded Southern hospitality as it tried to make the best of a very bad situation, doing its very best for our conference. I report these happenings in some detail to illustrate the poor conditions under which we had to run an important deliberative conference. Actually, the conditions were so unbelievably bad for a big-city hotel (we had met there in prior years) that everything became funny. By the second day everyone had quit complaining, and today, many years later, we all just laugh about it, remembering rather fondly our "roughing it" conference in the now-long-gone Dinkler Plaza Hotel, where wonderful Southern hospitality and a sense of humor helped immensely.

We hear many stories of mechanical failures that cause humorous mix-ups in our everyday existence. But when such a mechanical failure interrupts a deliberative conference, the results seem more humorous because there are so many more people all in one place to enjoy the fun. People are always getting stuck in elevators, but the funniest case happened during the AEEC general session in the twelve-story Hilton Hotel in Amsterdam half a decade ago. Just before the break for lunch, the meeting had been in the middle of a debate over an important specification, and the plan had been to take a vote soon after the break. The thirty members of the committee headed for their administrative luncheon in a beautiful spot the hotel had provided at the top of the establishment. The lunch was excellent, and the administrative session was adjourned to give everyone time to get back to the meeting before reconvening time.

I slipped away from the rest, captured a service elevator direct to the ballroom, and reconvened the meeting. The rest piled into the public elevators for the short trip. But alas! Eighteen of our people had crowded into one sixteen-passenger elevator (as I discovered later) and exceeded the load limit. The flight went some 3 feet more than the prescribed twelve stories and stopped. I was wondering what had happened to eighteen perfectly good committee members who had been with me just a moment ago. They were holding their own private conference in the bottom of an elevator shaft. Eighteen important people leave a pretty obvious hole in the middle of a conference.

Twenty minutes went by before the hotel engineer managed to get the elevator back to the proper floor; then I was surprised by a column of sheepish-looking conventioneers trailing into the large ballroom, past the "late bucket," each throwing a large, noisy coin into the brass champagne bucket that was serving the purpose on a chair near the door of the conference room. They were greeted with stony silence until a spokesman for that "ad hoc committee" explained where they had been holding their meeting. He lodged a complaint with the chairman for a larger conference room and better ventilation if they were expected to hold such ad hoc meetings in the future.

The Light Touch

In any group we find natural clowns. They are often the most serious and erudite participants who love to look at the lighter side of any happening. These are the people who provide a break from stodgy, pedantic deliberations and reawaken the meeting to the real issues. Hooray for the clowns! Treat them right by urging the meeting to take a laugh break at appropriate times; such breaks may be even more productive than coffee breaks.

I shall always remember the droll acts of one member. He would pull one of his favorite tricks when I started the introductions of the members. I would announce, "Will the new arrivals please stand and give their names?" Up he would jump, shouting his own name. He would look around, feigning surprise at being alone, and then he would sit down hurriedly, to uproarious laughter. When the room was again quiet, he would look at the chairman and say, "I thought you meant *all at once.*"

The modesty of individuals always inhibits audible self-introductions at a meeting unless the chairman can turn those inhibitions around. I usually let the first one or two individuals give the usual mumbled retorts, and then I do the following:

1. I stand and raise my hands, indicating a measure of displeasure.
2. I smile as I look directly at the two individuals.

3. I say (still smiling): "We have a saying in AEEC that an individual who mumbles his name, organization, and city must be *ashamed* of the organization he works for." (I am still smiling.)

4. I look around the room to be sure that everybody has received the message and that the room is completely quiet.

5. I look back at the two individuals and say, "Everyone is waiting to hear your name and affiliation. Would you please start over now that the room is quiet?"

6. If the conference room is not carpeted, I add the following: "Because of the noise of chairs, would you please stand and let the noise die out *before* you speak?"

7. If an individual has a soft voice and is so inhibited that he will address his name only to the chairman, I interrupt again with the following: "It is perfectly OK to turn your back to the chairman; please project your words back toward the rest of the people; they are all straining to hear who you are and whom you represent."

With only a few interruptions of this kind, you will have turned a useless rigmarole into a highly useful introduction that is well worth the time it takes. The principle I am emphasizing is that of *understanding and counteracting* the foibles that, left to themselves, will stultify any meeting unless the chairman takes immediate and specific action. With a smile and a sense of humor, a chairman can accomplish wonders.

Psychological Tricks

Sometimes, in our smaller meetings, we have played psychological tricks on the participants to get a particular point across. Here is one with an interesting twist.

For informal working meetings of some 50 or 100 people, microphones for everyone are impractical; yet everyone must hear everyone. To make the system work, tables should be close together, the head table should be quite close to the group, and people should fill the front seats first, leaving the rear rows for latecomers. But human nature being what it is, everyone wants to sit in the back ("I don't want to get involved"). So we set up the room with the front row of tables very close to the head table with some extra space left in the back, beyond the back row of tables. When the starting time arrives, I am seated at the head table, and, as expected, *no one* is in the front row. Then:

1. I call the meeting to order, and if some people are still collecting their papers, I go through introductions. Now everyone has settled down.

2.   I stand; so does the secretary, who is also seated at the head table. I announce: "I know why no one ever sits in the front row, and I have a solution to that problem."

3.   I take one end of the first of the front-row tables while the secretary takes the other end, and with great aplomb we carry the table to the back to the space provided.

4.   We return to the front and take the next table in that first row and move it also.

5.   By this time we have gotten some help, and others pick up the remaining tables and the chairs and help us form a new row behind what was the back row.

6.   Then we move the head table and chairs forward to where the empty first row had been, amid raucous laughter, joined in by those who now find themselves seated in the *front row*.

7.   Surprisingly, those now in the new front row will return to the front row in subsequent sessions without any urging. In meetings of the group months later, people will still enter the front row of their own volition; they sheepishly admit that they have been *had*; they react just as I had hoped they would. The meeting has become a closely knit, friendly group, with everyone now involved, and we have a permanently empty back row rather than the usual permanently empty front row.

Later, in Chapter 29, I shall describe several psychological tricks we have successfully used for decades to get people back into the meeting on time. One, the Curious Sheep principle, utilizes the natural curiosity of people to follow, like sheep, others who are rushing someplace to do something. It is the same motivation that causes people to run to get into a line, any line, in times of commodity shortages.

Another psychological trick, the late bucket, started out not as a trick but simply as a means of putting a price tag on being late. Now few people would pay any attention to a 25-cent lateness assessment, yet the late bucket does a fine job in encouraging promptness. We know it is the game motivation that does the job; people feel that it is an interesting game to avoid the assessment, and they will run in through the doors ostensibly just to save a few pennies. Both of these psychological tricks provide a release from the rigor of technical debate, and both are fully accepted by our participants.

One indication of the enthusiasm with which everyone plays the late-bucket game is a letter that the AEEC chairman received after he announced his forthcoming retirement. My correspondent stated that he had waited patiently for years for the chairman to get caught being late and having to put a coin in the late bucket. He said that he would be watching after every break at my last meeting to make sure I *did* contribute. I had to *be* late and plunk a coin into the noisy bucket, as the conference wallowed in delight at finally having caught its chairman in his own trap just on the eve of his retirement.

Such temporary abridgments of polite formality serve admirably as a means of pulling members of the group closer together so that their deliberations on complex technical issues can be more tolerant and understanding of each other's views.

Problems in Scheduling

Sometimes the funny happenings occur before or after rather than during a conference. Anyone planning international conferences will sooner or later have some mix-up that will generate its share of ulcers; there will be more. As long as conferences are held, they will get fouled up. The task of a conference planner is to minimize the consequences of the foul-ups that will take place despite the infinite care and planning of the best conference manager. When they happen, just grit your teeth and profit by the lessons you have learned the hard way.

The unplanned closing of a hotel just before a scheduled conference can turn a convention manager's hair white, but you *can* survive the experience. This happened to me on *two* occasions in Miami Beach. The first was in the spring of 1961. I had been alerted that the Shriners were scheduled for the same city in the same week as our meeting. That, in itself, posed no problem because all conference planners should be familiar with the

Fez-Tassel Law

Despite all advance planning, the Shriners will get to a conference city first.

But the problem got worse; soon the number of Shriners expected had tripled, and all the hotels in the city began to get worried. The Miami Beach Convention Bureau concluded that other conventions should change their dates if at all possible to avoid the onslaught. We *could* change dates, so we did. On May 18, 1961, we released publicity to alert "the world" that the June meeting would be deferred just 4 weeks, so "Please don't come to Miami Beach in June." Fortunately the technical press helped us publicize the new dates.

But we were doomed to encounter more trouble. One British trade newspaper carried a headline spread across four columns: "Airlines get together on electronics in Australia." The rest of the story gave the correct dates, topics, and events but consistently cited Australia, rather than Miami Beach, as the location. We received no rational explanation, just embarrassed apologies from a red-faced editor. But our real troubles hadn't even started. Just 6 weeks before our new dates, the hotel, one of Miami Beach's finest, closed without advance warning to anyone. The next day I was in Miami Beach under the watchful care of the convention bureau. It required only 2 hours to select a new hotel, an even more luxurious one, and I watched the management of the chosen hotel collect the registration records for our people from the now-closed hotel. We had a new home, and my problems should have been over. But that year was a bad year for us. Although we had enjoyed wonderful publicity from everyone for the date and location change, I had not reckoned with

SAXON'S LAW

Despite everything, someone won't get the word.

Sure enough, the day before the original dates for the meeting in the first hotel, I received a phone call from a Washington government office, asking for confirmation that the meeting *actually had been deferred.* I confirmed the change and heard a sheepish "Damn!" on the phone, as my caller explained that two of his staff people had just left for Miami Beach for what they thought was to be our big meeting the following day. He admitted that the new announcement had been circulating all around the government offices and had arrived in his office just after his people had left. I phoned the closed hotel and arranged for it to hang a big sign out front telling Mr. X and Mr. Y that there would be accommodations for them at the other hotel down the street. I arranged with the other hotel to give them free rooms when they arrived amid 75,000 Shriners and an offer to stay as long as they would like.

Their boss told me later that they enjoyed the free rooms for one night and spent the next day on local government business so that the trip wouldn't be a complete loss. Four weeks later, during the real meeting, we presented to them, with great fanfare, certificates of membership in the very exclusive Order of the Chanticleer (only two members). This entire problem for two nice guys was the consequence of Saxon's law, named after the Saxony Hotel conference that never took place.

It is true that hotel closings in Miami Beach are a regular happening, but the hotels are generally lesser-known establishments rather than top-ranking luxury hotels. How can it be that we have been caught in both of the two most highly publicized luxury hotel closings in Miami Beach in recent times? The second case, of course, was the widely publicized problems with the Eden Roc in the summer of 1975. I laughed when I heard of the potential troubles of other conventions scheduled soon after that closing; after all, we were not due at the Eden Roc until December of that year; I would have plenty of time to determine what should be done.

I thought the problem of the peanut seller convention was funny. This group was supposed to meet in the hotel several weeks after the closing date. It lost its peanuts. Its affair was easily moved to another hotel, but not the peanuts that had been shipped in. The whole thing finally came out all right; the group found the peanuts hidden in the Eden Roc, after quite a peanut hunt, but the story shows the fun-and-games problems of a convention manager trying to avoid his hair turning white prematurely. My problems were minor; from past experience with the Order of the Chanticleer and with Saxon's law, I knew better than to change the dates *this time*, so I selected an alternative hotel that could accept our already-announced dates. Everything was satisfactory, and to my knowledge there were no further problems with Saxon's law.

Sometimes a hotel has problems that are unexpected and troublesome to a conference. I recall a time in San Francisco when we had to compete with a circus in the ballroom next door; there was no wall—just a thick curtain for insulation (ha ha). It seems that the hotel was refurnishing the ballrooms and replacing the movable walls of the main ballroom with better ones. The old walls were taken down before the new walls arrived; a delivery delay occurred, and we were caught with no wall in the ballroom. Then the circus next door insisted upon a daytime rehearsal. The hotel had installed the temporary wall hanging in the belief that simultaneous events would not take place; they hadn't counted on the "necessary" rehearsal. We didn't mind the circus itself, but we didn't like the noisy brass band on the other side of the curtain. The management had a mad conference, and then it had a mad circus, when the circus learned that it couldn't complete its rehearsal.

Individual Contretemps

The humorous happenings are not always related to a whole conference; sometimes particularly funny things happen to just one individual or to several individuals during a conference and are not brought to the attention of others. Thus, only the victim of the mistake, happening, or whatever will have the laugh, and he may not find an occasion to share it with another participant in the conference. Here is one experience that happened to this chairman and until now has not been shared with others; although it seems very, very funny these several years later, it didn't seem so funny when it occurred!

I was one of just two Americans attending a formal luncheon in Paris at which many of the participants were my friends from all over Europe. The president of the conference, of which the luncheon was a part, had asked me to sit at the head table with the French Cabinet member who was the luncheon speaker. For practical reasons, the president dispensed with French and English interpretation during the luncheon. He therefore switched repeatedly from English to French and back again, depending upon the purpose of his remarks at the particular time; in this way, the luncheon was being held in both French and English. As he introduced people to the audience, he would select the language most appropriate for each introduction; the British officers of the organization were introduced in English, and the French officers in French. Although my knowledge of French was quite limited, the president knew this very well. But inasmuch as I was only a visitor, I did not expect any introduction and most certainly not an introduction in French.

The first moment I discovered any such attention was the instantaneous outbreak of applause with the audience and the president looking smilingly at me. What did it mean? Had I just been expected to nod graciously and go back to my dessert? The applause continued to an alarming degree. Had I been asked to say a few words on *some particular topic*? Had I been asked a specific question that would demand a specific (short) reply? Had I been introduced to say whatever I would like to say? A very long 2 seconds expired as I pondered the question. I knew that it was an oversight by the president in introducing me in French rather than in English, and I could not risk embarrassing him by admitting that I hadn't the foggiest idea what he had said. What would you have done? Probably exactly what I did. I made an impromptu speech, just like the one I have urged all chairmen and meeting participants to be ready to make at the drop of a hat.

Was the speech appropriate? Did I say what I had been expected to say? Was the president happy with my discourse? I only wish I could provide a suitable answer to that question. Unfortunately, I have never found out what the president really said that day in Paris so many years ago when he introduced me without warning. Everyone clapped uproariously and laughed at my humorous comments, so I can only assume that the speech was not entirely a faux pas. Perhaps sometime, somewhere, somehow, some way, I shall learn the answer to that imponderable conundrum. In any event, the message is: "Laugh, and the world will laugh with you, *probably*." But the overriding rule is to honor M. Promptu's law at all times:

M. Promptu's Law

Yuh better be ready; the orator's opportunity knocks only once.

Taking Advantage of the Unexpected

There will always be times when some event will cause an interruption or a laugh in your important conference. We have been interrupted by presidential parades outside the hotel, famous people being interviewed outside the conference room door, louder oratory next door, and you-name-it-we've-had-it. A cool-headed chairman can find something funny in such interruptions and avoid the clammy effect that would otherwise thoroughly upset an important meeting. If the chairman accepts the interruption calmly and even laughs about it, the conference will laugh and make the best of it, since there is probably nothing that can be done once the situation has developed. You may dispatch an assistant to take such action as might be possible, but usually the upset is temporary, and an early coffee break or a lunch break can counteract almost any interruption that continues for more than a minute or two. While a coffee break is welcome, a laugh break can be even more refreshing in a tense, disputative conference environment.

It was Joseph Addison who told us in his writings almost three centuries ago: "If we may believe our logicians, man is distinguished from all other creatures by the faculty of laughter." More than 100 years later, Thomas Carlyle added: "The man who cannot laugh is not only fit for treasons, stratagems and spoils; but his whole life is already a treason and a stratagem."

To deny humor and refuse to cause laughter when it is so important to the greater end of consensus gathering, on the presumption that it denigrates a formal gathering, is not only foolhardy but absurd. Make the most of any opportunity for lighthearted fun, and discover the improvement in concentration and productivity that follows as a direct consequence. May the saints preserve us from the chairman who believes that pompous formality is the epitome of erudite stature.

Verne Acular's Law

If a burst of laughter would do you in, so also would a gentle wind.

I suggested earlier that not all deliberative conferences turn out to be quite that. Some, or perhaps many, fall short of the aim of the organizer and either don't deliberate at all or are only partially effective for deliberation. The reason probably is mostly the worry of the organizer that the conference will fail to attract the right people to make decisions or that the right people will refuse to speak out and this silence will leave an awkward gap in the proceedings. If confronted with such an analysis in advance, the organizer would reply that the idea is silly. Of course, the deliberative conference will deliberate; the only reason for all those speeches that are scheduled as a part of the conference is to give all the participants the background before they start making decisions. Yet, whatever the explanation that may be offered as an excuse for such speeches in a deliberative conference, I believe the real reason is pretty close to that suggested here: the organizer is running scared.

In Chapter 3, I admonished the organizer never to allow scheduled speeches or presentations as a part of a deliberative conference. I gave only a superficial explanation there, but in this chapter I shall explore the subject further and analyze the consequences of the organizer's running scared because of his worry.

Organizing a Deliberative Conference

To illustrate how this worry can creep up on a meeting organizer, let us note how conferences intended for debate and decision making on a large scale really get organized. Within one 30-day period recently, I had the opportunity to watch the gestation and birth of two such large affairs, each arranged by a different large United States government agency. The first preliminary word on each conference indicated that decisions were to be made, jointly by industry and government, and that these decisions were later to be incorporated into planning and implementation programs of the two agencies. Both agencies hired outside consulting firms to organize and run the conferences, in a manner

24

The Pseudodeliberative Conference: Running Scared

that is quite usual in Washington. The meetings were both organized with the same basic features, right out of the usual pedantic textbook on meetings: first, lots of keynote and other speeches were scheduled for much of the first day; and, second, the deliberative portion of each conference was subdivided into submeetings, and the submeetings were divided into sub-submeetings, with discussion leaders appointed for each of the small entities.

Certainly there is nothing wrong with such an arrangement if the organizer wants to follow the book and will accept results about equivalent to what book deliberative conferences give: not very much. Throughout these two illustrative conferences, the submeetings were further divided because attendance was deemed "too large for a proper deliberative atmosphere where discussion would be inhibited because too many people would be present in one meeting." Have you ever heard of anybody deeming all that? Yet, conferences get deemed to do all that just about every day of the week, not only in Washington but in every other city on the face of the globe. And nobody seems able to do anything about it. Conferences cost money. Is that the way for effective and efficient conferences to be run? Perhaps not, but that is the way conferences always have been run.

Organizing a Technical or Professional Conference

Let us, temporarily, set aside this discussion of deliberative conferences and take a quick look at another general class of conferences that has similar features but is not organized for quite the same purpose. Don't go away; I'll get back to deliberative conferences in a minute or two, but I need to draw an analogy here while I am "in the neighborhood."

Let us put under our microscope the type of conference that must be awfully important to our world, simply because God and man seem to have made so many of them. Yep, I mean the technical or professional conference across an industry, a discipline, a community, or whatever that brings together people of like interests, needs, or affiliation. Such conferences exist everywhere throughout our world, whether for a subscription or a membership organization like the Phoenix Sunday Evening Forum, the Denver Executives Club, Rotary, the International Platform Association, the Association of American Medical Colleges, the Institute of Electrical and Electronic Engineers, and so on. Some organizations may have only a single dinner speaker on an important or timely subject; others may hold international conventions with hundreds of simultaneous conference sessions lasting a week or longer. Some conferences may exist for pure entertainment; others, for education. Some may be just speeches, while others may include some or much discussion and debate; some may even attempt decision making. Some may attract two dozen listeners; others may attract hundreds or thousands of active participants. There are all kinds of conferences, but they all have one thing in common with true deliberative conferences: they aim at some degree of education and some degree of opinion forming. Some may have been organized initially for deliberation, but that aim may have been so eroded with time that nothing is left but the speeches. Let us look more carefully at those conferences as a general class.

Such conferences suffer, uniformly, from the problem noted previously: the organizers run scared. Each time that such an affair is in the planning stage, the people responsible face two almost incompatible needs: first, they must plan an affair which, through its advance billings, will attract a large *paying* audience (to pay the bills); and, second, it must have something more than pure entertainment value to make a name for the planners. The conference should be educational enough to look good on the advance program, but not so educational that it will scare away the paying customers, who might really want entertainment instead. The education must be woven into the affair so that each participant will observe just the proper amount.

The planner faces another age-old dilemma in dealing with an affair with a speaker: he knows that he must give the audience some opportunity for discussion with the speaker, but not so much that it shortens the speaker's time appreciably and not so much that the audience will get carried away with the discussion and debate and want to continue indefinitely. Probably, the planner will do exactly as millions of other planners have done before him and millions more will do in the future: he will announce a "short" discussion period after the speaker finishes. The appointed time will come, and he, like millions of other planners, will wonder why the discussion is so halfhearted.

He will meet with the planning committee afterward and ponder in great depth the reasons why it is so difficult to get anybody to ask questions or to start a lively discussion. He had, as with many others like him, *planted* questions throughout the audience so that the speaker would not be embarrassed by a lack of questions. Why was the meeting so dreary? Why did people look as though they wanted to leave as soon as the speaker finished? And then, like many planners before him, he will draw the obvious but wrong conclusion: people don't really like to engage in discussion.

Perhaps he will be on a planning committee that has some continuity from one year to the next, and the committee will ponder further how to encourage questions and discussion. Someone will suggest a new approach: "Let's have a discussion panel next year; that way there will be lots of discussion." And so the conference gets organized that way; five speakers are selected and asked to sit on the platform and engage in discussion after their speeches. It works a bit better, but the audience still seems intent on leaving, just as it did last year.

Next year a new idea is suggested: "Let's have five speakers, with five different panelists; that should *really* work." It does work, except that each of the panelists has to be introduced (5 minutes each), and each is invited to say a few words; so the preliminaries eat up all the time, and no discussion can take place. Then another new idea is broached: "We will restrict everyone, speakers and panelists alike, from making any speeches so that there *will* be enough time for discussion." This is a wonderful idea except that I'll lay you a little bet that before the affair actually arrives, everyone will get cold feet (run scared) and decide to let the speakers say just a few words. Again, most of the time for discussion will have evaporated, and the audience still looks as if it would like to leave. At this point, a new planning committee takes charge, and the cycle starts over. The planners go back to the drawing board.

What is the basic problem with each and every one of these arrangements? An answer to that was promulgated in 1954 by the former champion meeting attender in our aviation industry. John Varekamp, of KLM, Royal Dutch Airlines, recognized the dilemma and stated it this way:

VAREKAMP'S PRINCIPLE

A conference announced in the usual way (speakers and questions) will seldom attract the type of people with interesting opinions and points of view who could make an open audience discussion interesting or worthwhile.

Corollary 1 When a conference session, previously billed as a series of speeches, is suddenly opened for audience participation, the only thing generated is a large quantity of spontaneous consternation, because the proper people are not present and those present are not prepared for an open discussion.

Corollary 2 When a conference session, previously billed as a discussion or debate, drags on as a series of speeches or panel comments, without an opportunity for audience participation, the only thing generated is a large quantity of smothered spontaneous combustion in the audience, so that if the session is *finally*, much later, opened for discussion, all the fire will have burned out, and any outspoken members will have left the meeting in disgust.

I shall again invoke the words of the Reverend Mr. Smith, quoted in prior chapters ("One of the greatest pleasures of life is conversation"), to remind us why Varekamp's principle is so authoritatively correct. If a passive audience is what the planner wants, that is what he will get by a *passive* announcement. If an active audience is what the planner wants, he must take the initiative in *announcing* it properly, and *then* he must deliver the goods. An audience, even an active audience, must be activated. It is not sufficient just to turn on some switch and expect a flood of light: light bulbs work that way; audiences don't. An active audience must be given a real opportunity, not just a token opening to say a few words and then shut up. People must be convinced that they are being offered an opportunity for an in-depth discussion; otherwise they simply won't start any discussion.

Thus, almost every meeting planner wants his audience to act like an active audience, but planners are seldom willing to give that audience the opportunity and the *time* to engage in the type of discussion that an active audience thrives on, the kind in which enough time is available to get a good free-for-all going and going well without the necessity to shut it off immediately.

Analysis of the Pseudodeliberative Conference

With my short excursion into the arena of most people's usual conferences completed, I return to our careful examination of the pseudodeliberative conference, the conference that was intended to be a true deliberative conference but became vulgarized when the planners started running scared. That vulgarizing starts when we add speeches or presentations to the beginning, perhaps to the whole conference except for a few minutes of discussion time late one afternoon. Then we wonder why the consequences of Varekamp's Corollary 2 seem to stultify our deliberative conference. We rationalize that it would have been even worse if we had not provided those speeches to get it all started, and we may never know that it was the running scared that caused all the trouble. So, what to do about it? The problem is essentially the same as in the deliberative conferences with which I started this chapter, and the same answer applies.

The answer, as I have pointed out as noisily as I am able in Chapter 3 and elsewhere, is that it takes guts to attempt a Goldfish Bowl deliberative conference in the first place, but once you set your mind to the task, you will find that it can be done. It is a rewarding experience as you see the participants begin to take an active part in discussion, then debate, and finally engage in the decision-making process that is so important.

Even though you may be tempted to break your fine deliberative conference up into a lot of little pieces (so you can have small meetings, which everyone thinks are the only meetings that can get anything accomplished), don't fall into a trap. Let us look at the subdivided deliberative conference and see what it does *for* us and *to* us. First, the process of subdividing generates a lot of general confusion. That confusion can do great harm if the participants are knowledgeable people with broad experience in all facets of the problem. The confusion caused by the process of allocating people to meetings to rooms is bad enough to cause many people to leave; then, added to it is the frustration of those who are not detail people and hate the idea of tackling small details before the general philosophy has been settled. These people are your best contributors to the process of decision making, and they will never like the idea of subdividing a complex matter into lots of little issues that are unsolvable when chopped so finely. Usually the particular groups selected are a compromise to fit into the available conference rooms. The groups produced by subdividing seldom bear any significant relationship to the problem needing resolution. Such breakups are usually highly artificial and are motivated by running scared.

If participation is not job-motivated but duty-motivated and if accomplishment is not very important as long as the participants keep working on the problem, the breakup method is quite satisfactory. But that isn't the kind of conference I have postulated as the reason for this text on the Goldfish Bowl deliberative conference. I have postulated an economic need for obtaining quick and lasting solutions rather than just working away on the problem. The breakup form of conference is quite ineffective in many cases, simply because it causes a loss of communication among the people who must be a part of any decision. The usual breakups are decided upon for two reasons, neither of them good: (1) breakups absolve the planner, moderator, or chairman from the responsibility of managing a large, unwieldy deliberative meeting; and (2) they are what the book suggests be done so that you won't have to manage a large, unwieldy deliberative meeting.

Therefore, the frustration is twofold among the more brilliant of your participants: (1) they must sit through a lot of initial speechmaking, with no opportunity to start deliberating on the important issues (see Chapter 3, item 11); and (2) as soon as the speechmaking is finally over, these brilliant participants are chopped into little pieces and made to sit in some small conference room with some others discussing a very little piece of a gigantic jigsaw puzzle. They yearn for the opportunity to get to the big issues and to the big picture, but they have no such opportunity. If they resign themselves to such a small-scale exercise, they must sit through a long session debating what they would do if such and such were to be the case, predicating their every debate and decision on some corollary decision that another splinter group is probably now dealing with in another small conference room somewhere.

And then the final frustration comes to pass: they get together with all the other groups at the end of the conference to put it all together. Then they discover that their basic assumption was completely backward and that all their deliberations were based on false assumptions and therefore are wasted! Back to the drawing board. Such splintered deliberative conferences are usually highly artificial in structure and must go through such mad scrambling over and over, backtracking, starting over, and starting over again.

It is almost as though an architectural firm were to assign the design for each room of a house to a different office of the firm. Every room of that house will benefit from a wonderful design, but will all the rooms fit together to make a house? Never! It is never an easy task to subdivide any complex problem. Either the tasks must be intrinsically unrelated, or there must be a highly organized superdesign body that will keep close tabs on what all the entities are doing so that they do not go their own ways independently of constraints. It is a much more complicated task to subdivide any job than to do it all in one piece; yet we see it attempted in deliberative conferences over and over again without careful planning and with the same awful results.

Let me repeat again: it takes guts to arrange a Goldfish Bowl deliberative conference, particularly the first time, but the results are so much better that it is well worth the initial worry, which will soon leave when results begin to materialize.

Now I must repeat what I have said before (Chapter 3, item 10): there is an explicit purpose of subsidiary working groups, and there is a proper place for them in our real deliberative, rather than pseudodeliberative, conferences. The proper way is to assign the detail work to detail working groups. They are constituted of working people rather than top policy people and are billed in advance as detail working groups. The top policy people will probably not attend such meetings, but you don't need such participation, nor would such people sit through such meetings. The people you need are the people who *will* attend. Everyone will know what is going on and what is expected to be accomplished in such meetings.

The important point is not to mix both types of meeting in a series string. If you recess the parent (policy) body to allow the detail working groups to meet, you should expect all the policy people to go home because they probably will. If you expect them to wait around for your later parent-body meeting, best of luck! If they do wait, they will be a little angrier than you would like them to be for best cooperation. If you simply must break up the parent-body meeting and have a detail meeting, you had better arrange something special for the others. If you have developed the Goldfish Bowl deliberative conference technique to a fine point (as I believe we have in the Airlines Electronic Engineering Committee), you will never allow such a mixture of events in a single conference. Your people have learned to expect better than that. You have learned how to get the best out of all classes of top management, middle management, and working-level people who will attend such Goldfish Bowl deliberative conferences. Treat them right, and they will cooperate by supplying tremendous inputs of expensive time and personnel as a benefit to *your* industry as they do in *our* industry.

The words in the foregoing analysis of pseudodeliberative conferences may seem very obvious in retrospect. Why would anyone do otherwise? Why would any industry waste money and time on conferences that are supposed to be for decision making and yet are stuffed full of nice, but not exactly necessary, speeches? Why would any industry get the working-group meetings mixed up with the policy meetings? The analysis is rudimentary. I shall leave that to you, dear reader, to ponder. If all this text is so obvious, why am I bothering to write it all down (or up, if that is how I write it)? Is it obvious? Are these practices followed faithfully now? Everywhere? Nowhere? Why? Why not? It beats me.

The longer we gather, the greater the palaver.

Everyone should be familiar with the premises of Parkinson's laws and particularly with his first law, relating to the proclivity of "work" to expand to fill the time available. But true as it may be, having been proved time and time again in conference agenda planning, it is surprising how few people admit to its existence in the real world of conference management. While even the most difficult of complex research and development projects can be planned and even accomplished within the time allocated, such is seldom the case with conference decisions.

Time Scheduling

Deliberative conferences form a problem all their own. To guide conference planners who have the task of scheduling the time of deliberative conferences, there are many other laws that may be helpful. These laws suggest the futility of applying the usual principles of management to deliberative conference scheduling. I suggest reading a useful compilation of such natural laws in a book by Arthur Bloch, entitled *Murphy's Law—and Other Reasons Why Things Go Wrong*.[1] Included in that compilation are many laws on scheduling, but probably the most appropriate of all is the Ninety-Ninety Rule of Project Schedules, which states: "The first ninety percent of the task takes ninety percent of the time, and the last ten percent takes the other ninety percent."

In that law lies the terrible truth of agenda scheduling. As time passes in the real world, the perceived deliberative task grows as Parkinson's first law predicts it will grow. Advance planning of time scheduling seems not always to help but sometimes, instead, to hurt.

[1]Price/Stern/Sloan, Los Angeles, copyright 1977.

25

The Art of Program Planning: Prioritization

Certainly the chairman of a conference can state how much time *ought* to be needed to decide a particular matter in deliberation. This is akin to management's deciding how long it *should* take to invent a particular thing. Unfortunately, management doesn't *do* the inventing; neither does a conference chairman *make* the decisions. Management cannot always depend upon the inventor to judge the time needed for invention; neither can a chairman depend upon a conference's knowing how long it will take to decide something. If we knew all those factors and all the stumbling blocks to a consensus on a particular issue, we probably wouldn't need the discussion; that is what the discussion is for.

True, we can read *Robert's Rules* or any other text on parliamentary procedures, and we can decree that we shall employ the 2 times 10-minute rule or the 1 times 5 rule that I discussed in Chapter 21, and from that we can multiply the time by the number of people who will be allowed to debate the issue; from this we can learn the maximum time for each question. But we don't even know in advance how many questions will arise on an issue; certainly we have no idea, in a Goldfish Bowl deliberative conference or in any other kind of conference, exactly how many people will need to participate in the discussion and debate. If we are depending upon getting an essentially unanimous consensus in order to justify substantial private investments in a new standardized product, a new procedure, or a new process, we cannot accept anything less than a *real* consensus. There is no way in which we can tolerate some shoehorn practice of getting the minority to shut up so that the majority can have its way. *No one has yet found a way of forcing a voluntary near-unanimous consensus.* Congress has its way of forcing a consensus, but Congress has a legislative bullwhip to make its decisions stick. Industry is prohibited by the antitrust laws from any such bullwhip tactic even if it wanted to apply such a method.

It is surprising that conference attendees will so often urge time limits for the debate of questions that they themselves have decreed are of the utmost urgency. Obvious as it may seem, I must state the truism that time must not be constrained if true consensus forming is to be accomplished. Stated another way, in mathematical terms, if time is constrained, the quantity of decisions possible must be the dependent variable. We cannot make both of them independent variables, inasmuch as one (either one) is dependent upon the other.

This text urges full and complete use of the Goldfish Bowl deliberative conference for resolving industry questions. It emphasizes the experience of some 30 years in *minimizing* the time and cost for industry decision making. But there must be a limit: I cannot do the infinite and eliminate the time problem entirely, neither can I state any known method that will allow accurate scheduling of *any* decision-making exercise. All that I can do at this stage of human learning is to suggest some methods that have proved helpful in *minimizing* the time to be spent. Let me emphasize again, therefore, that I cannot set forth any reliable means or even a methodology for *predicting* how much time will be needed to get the necessary results. I shall have made some considerable progress, however, if I can get the message across that such a prediction is, to my knowledge, outside human capability at this stage. The situation can be helped if conference chairmen can accept that statement, point out to their conference attendees the real meaning of consensus, and then get everyone to understand the limitations of the human mind and accept a simple postulate: consensus finding is quantitatively *unpredictable* and *impossible to schedule*.

Suggestions for Scheduling

Now that I have said that, let us look at those things which a chairman or even an attendee can do to help the process wend its weary way through the maze of labyrinthian disputation and logical reasoning. Previously in this text I have given many suggestions, but this chapter will concentrate on *scheduling* aids. Here is a list of the major factors:

1. My first suggestion is to recognize the utter futility of accurately fixing decision-making time.

2. We must recognize the futility of gauging progress on a decision-making task. Inasmuch as the *magnitude* of the total task is utterly unknown and unmeasurable, it is useless to find out how much time we have spent on the matter so far and then to calculate the remaining time required from a knowledge of the percentage of the total task now completed. When we have no way of knowing what the total task consists of, we cannot know what percentage of it has been completed at a particular time.

3. We must recognize the nonlinearity of progress on such projects and the nonlinearity of time passage. The Ninety-Ninety Rule previously given is probably the best statement of the absurdity of attempting to assess the situation that exists.

4. Of all the possibilities open to the chairman, one ploy is known to work, after a fashion, as a means of keeping the conference painfully aware at all times that time is passing and lots of other things remain to be done after the question under discussion is finished. The best method I have discovered is for the chairman to keep looking at his watch or at the wall clock, particularly when the speaker strays into vagaries. By proper use of facial motions and a look of intense worry, the chairman has at least a slight chance of keeping speakers on the subject and of getting them to avoid repeating the same arguments over and over. This practice is never condoned by good parliamentary procedures, but those procedures give frightfully little help in this most difficult and trying problem for a chairman.

5. Although the practice of item 4 is not condoned by parliamentary procedures, there are precedents in Congress for the conference itself to control a tedious speaker. *Deschler's Rules of Order*[2] describes the procedure in the words of Thomas Jefferson (*Hinds' Precedents of the House of Representatives,* 5 HP Sec. 5445): "If a member finds that it is not the inclination of the House to hear him, and that by conversation or any other noise they endeavor to drown his voice, it is his most prudent way to submit to the pleasure of the House, and sit down. . . ." Deschler points out that the House of Representatives has other means now to restrict such speeches and that it has generally been unnecessary to resort to Jefferson's method.

If a conference is desirous of minimizing its own discussion and debate time, one or more members should impart that fact to the chairman and urge the chairman to expedite the debate process, perhaps as suggested in item 4. The effort to expedite must be motivated by a mutual desire of all parties, majority and minority alike, to bring out new arguments but to refrain from regurgitating the same old arguments. A conference membership itself can do much to avoid the necessity for the chairman to instigate on his own the practices of item 4. Let the conference, instead, put pressure on its own people to expedite the debate.

6. Although the foregoing educational and mutual-help ploys are probably the most tasteful and tactful methods of encouraging greater attention to the subject and less redundancy in debate, I shall suggest one other means that I have used, usually secretly, to get the same effect. I have taken the view, based on long experience, that it is almost impossible to get the members of *any* organization continuously to apply enough concentration to keep their minds on the time problem. I believe that *only the chairman* will have sufficient pressure upon him to ensure continuous attention to time expedition. Under this premise, it is up to the chairman, if anyone, to expedite time.

Also based upon experience is a further premise that participants will fail to observe the passage of time and the horrendous machinations of the Ninety-Ninety Rule and Parkinson's first law, so that the

---

[2]Written by and copyrighted © 1976 by Lewis Deschler (longtime parliamentarian of the House of Representatives), published by Prentice-Hall, Inc., Englewood Cliffs, N.J. 07632.

conference holds to the Little Orphan Annie misconception that "Everything is always wonderful." This misconception has the effect of everyone's naïvely believing that "only a few more minutes of discussion will settle it all, so what's the worry?" My experience is that even after another 10 of those few more minutes of discussion have expired, the conference *still believes* that "only a few more minutes are needed." After observing this consequence time after time, I am understandably suspicious of such time predictions by the conference itself.

Accordingly, I have used, without telling anyone, what I shall now call Carnes' Secret Weapon of Time Management. It is exactly what the name implies: it is the technique of not letting anyone know how much time I have secretly allocated to a particular question. My reason for not divulging the time I have set is that, at the beginning, the conference believes that it will require only a short time to get the decision rather than the immense amount that the chairman has thought necessary. In such cases, the conference has a tendency to squander time in the belief that plenty is available for the question.

I have long known that the people in our meetings think they need less than I think they will need; my estimates have been getting better and better through the past 30 years, and I believe that mine are better than those of the participants. My experience is that, *if divulged, my time estimates are ruined for all practical purposes.* The only way I have found to utilize those estimates, which are the best I have, is to keep them secret.

If the premise and advice of item 6 are to be applied, the chairman must maintain a degree of secrecy in the administration of a major deliberative conference that he would prefer not to maintain; but he must do so as a matter of necessity in the best interests of the conference itself. So far, this has not been a major problem, and most of our participants seem to sense the secrecy without expressing any objections. They seem to reason that something must be working right because we manage to get through almost all items of a complex agenda in a satisfactory manner. They *like* the end results; they seem quite willing to accept the means to that end. But this poses some problems that a chairman must learn to cope with, the major one being the dilemma of how to publish an advance schedule of agenda material with time estimates. If everything is to be scheduled rigidly in advance with time schedules shown, the schedules would be proved to be completely wrong the very first time; although the chairman's candor would be proved, *so also would his lack of credibility be proved.* My experience shows that credibility is more important than wishful thinking expressed with useless, abundant candor.

A reasonable compromise that has worked quite well for many years is to schedule the intended order of the agenda items, with the announced proviso that changes will be made by mutual consent and announced as soon as they are known and decided. Remember that the premise of parliamentary procedures regarding the order of business is that the deliberative body itself must determine any changes from the previously established sequential order. Yet all bodies have their own practices for accommodating necessary changes without the necessity of submitting every change to a vote. As Congress delegates certain powers of agenda control to the majority and minority leaders, all groups recognize the exigencies of special needs and depend to a considerable degree upon the recommendations of the leader, which in the usual case is the chairman.

Almost any group which meets regularly for deliberative action will look to its chairman for advice, if not actual decisions, on all matters of scheduling. This is a power of the body which has been delegated, by precedent if not by bylaw, to the chairman, and it can be taken back or modified at any time the body so chooses. Thus, the chairman (particularly when he is a hired or appointed professional) should have *and will have* much say in scheduling the matters to come before the group.

By scheduling in advance the sequence of events *but not the times,* a suitable accommodation of the attendees is usually obtained. I have found it possible to go further by scheduling the explicit starting times for certain selected special items in which almost everyone has more than cursory interest. The rule I follow is to take up the items in the order announced and to interrupt the debate at the scheduled times of the special items. This procedure is the best compromise between reality and wishful thinking that I have discovered. When many important items are on the calendar, I have more special items with explicit time schedules than when few action items are on the agenda.

Your organization will undoubtedly find the best possible compromise as your time control improves with increasing experience. Again, I urge chairmen to avoid the pressure to make wild guesses that can only make them look silly. Speculation that is unfounded can drive the conference into a tizzy when, belatedly, it discovers that the time estimates announced are utterly meaningless and misleading. You should experiment with time scheduling (which you will have to do for your own peace of mind) but keep your records of success and failure *private* as you get better at it. Hopefully, you will not need the 30 years of sixty-seven major deliberative conferences and hundreds upon hundreds of smaller deliberative conferences that this chairman has needed to get to the point at which he is now.

Sequence of Events

I cannot complete this chapter on program planning and time control without some mention of a few other pointers regarding the proper sequence of topics on a deliberative conference agenda. Even though time control is far from any exact methodology (or even a good guessing game), a proper sequence of events can be very helpful, if correctly arrived at, in aiding the process of time control. Of course, your organization will suffer, as every organization does, from the ravages of what I have long called

GOINHOM'S LAW

1. The first act of a committee member when he sits down in a meeting is to take out his plane schedule and plan his departure.

2. The second act is to inquire when the chairman "thinks" the meeting will break up. (A naïve chairman will guess; a knowledgeable chairman will refuse an answer.)

3. The committee member will keep asking. When he gets some kind of answer, he will subtract 4 hours and make final plans for departure, based on that corrected anticipated earlier time. If that corrected anticipated time is before 11 A.M., he will arrange to leave the night before; if after 2 P.M., he will leave before lunch.

If you doubt the power of the foregoing law, do a little snooping among participants at your next meeting (any kind of meeting) and note what the chairman has let slip out (about wanting to leave early and the like) and when he does it. Check offhandedly with your friends from time to time and keep notes. Count heads at hour intervals during the meetings and observe who has slipped out early; write down all the excuses people have let slip out on why they have to be in some other city at a particular time on a particular day; note how these excuses develop strength as the meeting progresses; observe that after the chairman makes some comment about the remaining items being difficult to deal with at that particular meeting, many people slip out to make phone calls; follow them and see if they take out a plane schedule as soon as they get outside the door; and have your spouse chat with their spouses about departures and take notes.

Note particularly the pressures that develop on the chairman as the middle of the afternoon approaches. Does he act very worried, as though trying to get everything finished by the end of that day so that he can adjourn the meeting? Particularly watch what happens when Joe mentions casually to Jane that he is now planning to leave after lunch Tuesday because he has learned that George and Harriet are leaving on that flight and that he believes the meeting will not last much beyond that time anyway. See if Jane heads for the telephone booth immediately. But don't let people know you are taking notes for your own personal, private analysis of people motivation under Goinhom's law.

Some professional meeting attenders know most of these syndromes. An experienced chairman will beat everyone in anticipating what the others plan to do; he will also know instinctively what he must do to counteract Goinhom's law. He must anticipate the time when he will lose his most important people. He must carefully, with much forethought, arrange the order of items, particularly the most important action items, to ensure that the right people will still be present for major action near the end of a meeting. He cannot employ subterfuge; he cannot, for example, put the most important items last on the agenda. That would backfire: the deliberative body would simply rearrange the order of the items to *accommodate its best interest;* this *he* should have done in the first place. Neither can he put all the action items at the beginning; if he tries this method, he will discover that a whole bunch of useless items at the end should never have been included on the agenda at all, for all the good their inclusion does, because everyone will leave town before those items come up. Instead, the arrangement of items must be carefully thought out to accommodate the need for handling action items but allow breathing space between controversial items. Try to arrange the order so that one of the complex items will bridge over one of those wonderful coffee breaks described in Chapter 22. Or a really controversial item could come up just 1 hour before the break for the evening reception (see Chapter 22), so that the reception can serve as discussion time for those who want to work out compromises or obtain additional information before action is taken. A luncheon break gives an excellent opportunity to release tensions and settle some problems that have been introduced just prior to the break.

Considerable benefit can be obtained from introducing a complicated item early in the conference when it is known that the item will soon have to be interrupted for a priority special item. By introducing the topic early, the chairman can obtain a preliminary opinion sampling that will indicate what additional debate and discussion are needed and what additional facts are still lacking; sometimes it is possible for an attendee to phone a factory and get special tests run to answer some technical question that a participant has asked. Also, we must never forget the advantage that time gives us in getting a recalcitrant objector to check with the people at home to see whether they would accept "this proffered compromise." Face-saving is important for everyone, though seldom will anyone admit it. An early assessment of where the land lies on a complex issue can allow everyone to get his fences mended and be ready for the compromise that may be inevitable.

Throughout this exercise in deliberation, the chairman is the key to success, whether he is planning the agenda items in advance or pondering what to do during the meeting. He must decide quickly what should be done next when alternative choices present themselves. To rearrange the schedule, the chairman need simply suggest to the group: "We might take up the Gizzelwhop now, if this doesn't give anyone any problem, so that we can get a feel for who likes what on this agenda item before we break for lunch in about 15 minutes." Such a candid explanation will usually convince the conference that it is a good idea; the chairman will have everyone's acceptance of that step, and he will have the attention and complete cooperation of everyone in getting that "reading" from the conference in the few remaining minutes. No one will likely attempt a long speech or filibuster if the chairman has piqued the attendees' curiosity properly. Everyone wants the same answer the chairman wants.

Throughout a meeting, the chairman must be on the watch for such dangerous indications of Goinhom's law as occur when meeting participants ask (sometimes plead) for their favorite agenda items to be taken up early (so they can go home). If a chairman grants such a privilege to *one*, he must be prepared to give equal treatment to *all* who request it; if he starts this process, he probably can neither stop it nor tolerate it. Yet he should not refuse necessary changes which are for the total good of the conference and which will usually be acceptable to everybody if properly explained.

Handling Details

We must mention one other time control factor: how should the chairman handle debate on minor details of one project that should certainly have been settled among the subcommittee members prior to presentation of the paper to the parent body? Not only are details time-consuming, but they often are of such limited general interest that their debate may chase participants out into the halls to conduct more important business until the major issues come up again. No chairman likes to handle such details in a large session, but what can be done when one detail remains unsettled? A chairman has several choices when it becomes evident that a quandary exists on a point which the participants are not interested in or knowledgeable about.

One choice, obviously, is to continue the discussion, recognizing the tendency to aloofness described in Chapter 12, which may cause people to lose interest and leave. Such a discussion will tax the patience and capabilities of even the most expert chairman. A second choice, of course, is to send the whole package back to the subcommittee or working group for resolution, but that course seldom solves any problem. That choice is usually a bad one. A third choice is to let the proponents of action convince the rest of the meeting that the whole paper, spec, proposal, or whatever should be adopted anyway, subject to getting a complete resolution of that one detail before the action is implemented (possibly by a delay in publishing the document until the detail is resolved to the satisfaction of all parties). This *can* be done, and sometimes it is the best of all possible choices. If the group appears willing to compromise, the conference is usually safe with such an action, particularly if only a few people or organizations are really affected by this detail decision.

Another possibility is to suggest that the parties affected get together at a coffee break or lunch break and work out a compromise to present to the body. By deferring further discussion until the parties report back with a consensus, the detail can often be settled in a pretty short time. This is not practicable when the detail needs additional test data or study to answer questions that are a prerequisite to a decision. Another possibility is to ask the subcommittee and anyone else who is interested to hold a meeting concurrently with the general (plenary) session to settle the matter and come back with a consensus. I suggest this choice as the last one because I tend to look with disfavor upon parallel subcommittee meetings during a major deliberative conference. Part of my objection is my knowledge that our airline industry meeting participants have had great difficulty with such rump sessions for a variety of reasons. The most important is that such a meeting can seriously disrupt other company business, which will usually be interspersed with the deliberative conference business.

As I pointed out in Chapter 22, we must never forget that industry deliberative conferences are supported by industry contributions of time and personnel. With parallel meetings, a small organization, with a small staff present and with many business demands on those people, is caught in a dilemma. Thus a decision by the chairman to ask for a parallel meeting that can become a major conference itself is not always in the best interest of the conference or the industry. Evening meetings interfere with business activities that are worth money to the participants. Don't get so carried away with your enthusiasm for a solution that the interests of the meeting are not served. A chairman can usually determine, with a little care, whether such an outside meeting is appropriate or impracticable; he should avoid browbeating a small group into accepting such a meeting.

Often the parties most deeply affected by the decision would rather attempt some discussion first to find out how far apart they are before any meeting is scheduled. A meeting, by its very nature, is bound to be far more ponderous and lengthy than an informal chat of the principals at a reception or over lunch or coffee. Stick to informal methods if at all possible; urge the combatants to report back at regular intervals so that those in the large meeting can be apprised of progress and everyone can know the direction in which they are moving. Regular reporting takes very little time of the large meeting, yet it keeps the curious from having to attend the rump session of the few people who can best work out a compromise.

I have argued in this chapter that time control of deliberation is not compatible with the principles of free debate, and neither is it compatible with the practical realities of consensus development through compromise and careful deliberation. Only by allowing and even encouraging free debate among the parties to be affected by the decision can we ensure a proper decision that will be a lasting one, a decision that makes industry feel comfortable in investing its own funds in the resulting product or process. The chairman must have the wisdom of Solomon or use all the tricks of the trade to make up for the lack of that wisdom.

Where's the use of sighing?
Sorrow as you may,
Time is always flying—
Flying!—and defying
Men to say him nay.[1]

Pick up any book of quotations and discover how many writers have philosophized on time through the centuries. While the philosophers philosophize, the world rushes through the static labyrinths of time. We contemplate time from a fulcrum we perceive to be steady; but perhaps time is steady, and we are moving, as expressed in the words of Austin Dobson in "The Paradox of Time": "Time goes, you say? Ah no!/Alas, time stays, *we* go."[2]

Subjective Nature of Time

In our world of conferences, we have all pondered (or at least, we should have pondered) why time seems to stand still when others are orating and yet goes so very fast when we are speaking so very concisely. Conference managers and chairmen have long pondered that conundrum, and I certainly don't have any scientific or other explanation. And so I come to search for a suitable definition of a "too long meeting." Perhaps the best definition is a paraphrase of another law that we have used in commercial avionics for many years. Named after a now-deceased but well-remembered avionics engineer from Scandinavian Airlines, Svend Bagge, this law defines customer needs for special features in an avionic product in a very subjective manner. The original content of Bagge's law will be readily apparent from my paraphrase, which I shall call:

[1]W. E. Henley, *"Villanelle,"* from *The Pocket Book of Quotations*, Simon & Schuster, Inc., New York, 1942, edited by Henry Davidoff.
[2]Ibid.

26

Long Meetings and What to Do about Them

BAGGE'S LAW OF THE TIME DOMAIN

Your meetings are much too long.
My meetings are just right.

We must recognize the subjective nature of time's passage and cater to the *perceived* problem whether we believe it is a real problem or not. If we inquire whether the participant believes that a particular meeting was too long (he will always say "Yes"), we might ask a second question with a not-so-obvious answer: "Too long *compared with what?*" This is the real question we should ask ourselves and each other when pondering the proper length of a meeting. It, too, is a philosophical question with many philosophical answers; but it does prod each of us into thinking through the problem faced by a meeting planner as he contemplates the work schedule and predicts the time needed to get answers to questions in a deliberative conference.

Experience of Others

We may get some idea of what *should* be necessary from our experience with other people's deliberative conferences. Perhaps we might note that the U.S. Senate required 38 days to settle the 1978 Panama Canal treaties and, therefore, that a 5-day meeting should be quite appropriate for our next deliberative conference. If we chose the time on that basis, we would probably be fired. Or we might recall our most recent deliberative session, in which we didn't quite complete all the work in 2 days; so we should schedule 3 days for the next one. Perhaps this seems a good "Compared with what?" evaluation of real meetings with real people in real time. But that, too, would probably be unacceptable to the conference itself. Why?

The problem, simply stated, is that there is no answer to the question of how much time is *really needed* for that deliberative conference; the time needed has nothing whatever to do with the question and the answer. Certainly, in the U.S. Senate, where the tradition that a senator must never be limited is still upheld, there could be a rational reason for controversial matters, such as the Panama Canal treaties of 1978, to dictate an indefinite deliberation time. But we all know that soon after the beginning of debate on the first treaty, Senator Byrd, the majority leader, announced the exact time and date for the final vote; he did the same for the second treaty, and those times were met exactly. But let us not presume that those debates were true deliberative debates. Note the assessment given by Ward Sinclair, in *The Washington Post Maga-*

zine story of April 23, 1978, entitled "The Closing of the Senate Club."
Here is Sinclair's introduction to the story:

> So it did not begin as a remarkable day. The Senate went into
> session at nine o'clock on March 1, earlier than is its custom, to
> continue a tedious and rambling debate on the Panama Canal
> treaties.
> But first, a thought: This canal issue is more symbol than sub-
> stance. It has little to do with the price of corn or kids in Harlem
> without jobs. The debate is not much of a debate. Most of the 100
> minds that populate the Senate were made up before it began. All
> 100 senators know this. As a consequence, few of them attend, or
> even take part in the debate.

Thus, if we think we should use the world's most prestigious deliberative body as a guide, we are picking the wrong example. At the other
extreme, if we select the Podunk Suburban Civic Club as our example,
we may not have helped our problem when we study the debate over
that mammoth controversy, "Resolved, that we shall write a letter of
protest over the high sewer charges," as a guide to determine how
much time we shall require for *our* next meeting. It is unfortunate but
true that most organizations have a particular acceptable length for their
deliberative sessions, and not much of anything is likely to change it.
By giving a few examples from my own experience, I may bring to your
mind similar examples from your experience.

One federal advisory committee finds that it is quite practicable to
hold morning meetings that extend just barely to, but not beyond, the
lunch hour. Thereafter, we all go to lunch together or in small groups to
discuss other mutual business matters. C. Northcote Parkinson's first
law applies just as explicitly as though Parkinson had had our group in
mind when he formulated the law. Several attempts to extend the meeting into the afternoon when an extra-complicated agenda was scheduled failed. A shorter, less complex agenda has not permitted a shorter
meeting.

A church board meeting held in the evening is traditionally known
to last until about ten o'clock, since that is about the latest that people
will remain and ever come again. One night last year the board meeting, for some reason unexplained to this day, finished its agenda before
nine o'clock. This was such a surprise that I even wrote a musical play
about it. The song that resulted, "Let's Have a Meeting, and We'll All
Be There,"[3] produced the appropriate theme song for this text. No one

---

[3]Copyright, 1978, William T. Carnes.

has yet been able to explain why that particular board meeting finished so early.

National and International Conferences

For deliberative conferences of national or international scope other factors than agenda length or complexity seem to take over control of the time. People seem unwilling to travel across the United States just for a 1-day meeting. In our airline industry, in which transportation is our real business, a 1-day meeting can sometimes be acceptable; but we must then worry about the ravages of Goinhom's law (Chapter 25), which trims that 1-day meeting down to a few useful hours and causes the participants to boycott the next such meeting scheduled for a single day. For national deliberative meetings, 2 days are just about a minimum, with 3 days a better choice when international participation is expected or wanted.

For any deliberative meeting, you should analyze the likely attendance to get some pointers. First, are the attendees people who have numerous opportunities and requirements to travel, or are they people who will welcome an opportunity for a once-a-year business trip to some city—any city a long way from home? If the latter, they will probably stay (if the boss lets them) until the end of your conference even if it is 3 weeks long. I recall the candid explanation of one of my friends from a far-off country serving on a delegation to a United Nations deliberative conference of some 4 weeks' duration. He explained that this conference gave him 4 weeks of good food and gracious living that he could never have except once a year on these assignments and that he could save enough money to give his family some better living when he returned home. That annual trip was the inducement for him to remain in the employ of his nation and do it a service, which he truly wanted to do, rather than accept a high-paying job in the United States, as others had done.

Although an infrequent traveler will accept a long meeting, his management *will not*. You should trim your meeting down to size; don't depend upon the participants to cut down their own meetings in the future. It simply won't happen. You should cut the length before your bosses cut your administrative throat.

If your likely attendees are frequent (too frequent) travelers, they will choose the length to suit their own travel preferences, and the length will most likely be a more reasonable figure than would be the case if it were selected by an infrequent traveler desiring a company-paid vacation. But frequent travelers present other handicaps. For example, a frequent traveler will seldom accept a meeting starting on Monday or finishing on Friday. A frequent traveler insists upon traveling on Monday or Friday rather than on Saturday or Sunday or on holidays. The exception is a meeting on the French Riviera; for that, he will travel on his own time. Inasmuch as you probably will not be scheduling meetings on the French Riviera, or even the Italian Riviera, you will not often be successful in choosing any meeting days except in the middle of the week. This is unfortunate for busy organizations desiring to hold several such meetings of 2- or 3-day duration in a single week, but it is a practical problem that an organization must face.

This is a basic problem with calendars having only 5 working days in any week; thus, 3 days are just about the maximum that can be allocated for any deliberative conference whether your organization likes it or not. Certainly, some organizations have extended this period to include Friday when the sessions are on the East Coast, inasmuch as an individual can get anywhere in the United States with a five-o'clock plane departure. Sometimes an organization starts a conference on a Monday, but that is often an optional, or getting-ready-to-do-something, day. For West Coast conferences, from which nobody can go anywhere after midday (except for those infrequent travelers who will ride the "red-eye" going east), the 3-day limit is very much a real limit.

For your international shindigs, you may be successful in getting people to stay longer (and perhaps work longer) in a European locale, but even there when Friday comes, they start peeling off early, heading back to Fort Lauderdale or Olathe or Cedar Rapids. It may seem surprising that I should state with such abandon that European meetings have so little holding power that participants will flock back to the United States at the slightest indication that the meeting is nearing the end. But that is my experience with meeting after meeting which I have organized or that others have organized and I have attended. I must emphasize that there is much more leeway on the front end of a European meeting than on the back end; experienced travelers going east know that they must have extra time to get caught up on sleep before a major meeting in Europe, and they will arrive a day or so ahead of the starting time just for their own protection. But that does not apply on the hind end of a European meeting; attendees will leave at the first opportunity. Goinhom's law seems to apply for Americans in Europe just as in the United States.

What about United States meetings attracting Europeans? They are different, but the difference is in certain specifics, not in the general desire to go home quickly. I can best illustrate this syndrome by telling the story of John, a Dutchman well known in our airline technical community. John was such a dedicated worker that he would never arrive ahead of time; he would go to his office in Amsterdam in the morning before the day of a meeting in Los Angeles and get so involved that he would almost forget to get on the flight. Usually he would take the very latest flight that would get him in town just shortly after the meeting convened; he felt that he could afford to miss some of the meeting so he could get more work done at home. Invariably, we would be in the middle of a debate as John walked in. While chairing the meeting, I would nod at John as he came in, and John would be in the middle of that debate within 5 minutes. Many of the others in the large meeting would not know when John arrived; some didn't know where he was from and seemed absolutely convinced from seeing him at so many meetings that he was a local representative in that area. They could never quite comprehend that he had just gotten off an international flight, which he had boarded after a quick run from his office in Amsterdam. John would rush to the airport after our meeting and go back to the office for a few more hours before hopping another flight going in the other direction to some other international conference. John would rush home for a weekend and then rush back to Los Angeles for an early-in-the-week meeting there. European travelers are much more used to quick trips over this way than we are used to quick trips over that way. But they like to be home, too.

A Conclusion

So far in this chapter I have carefully sidestepped the question posed in the title; instead of answering that question directly I have chosen to skirt around it and offer only suggestions regarding the factors that will influence the opinions of participants and the people who pay the bills for the meetings on what to do about long meetings. Perhaps you can see that, like beauty which is in the eye of the beholder, a long meeting is long or short only in the eye of the beholder. Our answer to the question can be only one possible piece of advice, and as you have probably already guessed, this suggests that another law will be coming on:

B. HOLDER'S LAW

All meetings are too long.

Unfortunately, you will never be allowed, except in meetings of the naïve, to have enough time to get the matter needing attention thoroughly deliberated and settled without running out of time. And if you are ever lucky enough to be the chairman of a meeting with plenty of time scheduled for all possible deliberations that could conceivably be necessary, you will probably be ravaged by:

THE EGG TIMER PRECEPT

With time on your hands, the sands of time will leak out of the hourglass into the gears of the well-oiled machinery of progress, and it will grind to a halt instead of grinding the sands of time.

Coverage of a topic so immense as this one cannot be completed in a single chapter; it is a topic about which books have been written, and it is a topic, although very important, that is really outside the scope of this text. But it must be covered, in a broad-brush way (as it will have to be), simply to complete the circle of planning, implementation, and reprise of the Goldfish Bowl deliberative conference.

Goldfish Bowl deliberative conferences have a lot of things in common with other conferences and trade shows of industry; yet they are different in at least one respect that must influence advance planning. That difference is in the mood and involvement of the participants. Unlike the usual trade show or technical conference, for which continuity from one session to the next is not so important, the individual and the continuity of his participation are very important in a deliberative conference. You, the chairman, want him to remain for the entire deliberative session, and you want him to be in a good mood and frame of mind and to *maintain the continuity of participation from beginning to end of that deliberative session*. The reason for continuity is evident from the points I have emphasized in prior chapters throughout this text; without continuity the deliberations would be a shambles.

In a trade show, you would be more interested in having a good buyer attendance and sufficient attendance at the technical sessions to make them look successful and to make money through registration fees and continued member dues. Trade shows are generally, though not always, economically motivated; registration fees are substantial for many conferences, and they show signs of rapidly increasing in coming years. As a comparison, we have yet to charge our first registration fee for any Goldfish Bowl deliberative conference in our industry. You must have present the organizations that will be affected by the decisions for a deliberative conference to be effective; it is difficult to set a price figure for admittance and get the right people there.

27

Advance Planning: Arrangements for the Large Goldfish Bowl Conference

As I explained in Chapter 22, our deliberative Goldfish Bowl conferences have a trade show attached, but there is no charge for exhibiting; the hotels do not charge for the space, and the only expense is incurred when an exhibitor wants hot and cold running helium or some other special facility and has to pay the hotel for piping it in. Trade shows are not prohibitively expensive for an exhibitor unless the whole effort is commercially motivated, in which case hotels will suddenly start charging an arm and a leg for exhibit space so that they, too, can get a piece of the action.

Therefore, your major aim in a deliberative conference is to make it easy and profitable for all who are a party to the decisions so that they *will* attend. Thus, the first rule is:

Rule 1

Don't get commercial itching, or everyone else will too, and then *you* will pay through the nose.

To make it profitable for suppliers, whom you will need to help with any decisions that involve products, make certain that you keep the customers nearby and bunched in one place. Suppliers love having their customers handy so that they don't have to spend a lot of time and expense in searching for them all over town. You, too, want them handy for your deliberative sessions, so you don't want them scattered all over town. This leads to the second rule:

Rule 2

Select only cities with a hotel large enough and well equipped enough to accommodate your whole entourage under one roof, complete with conference rooms, trade show, plenty of hospitality suites, and economically priced single rooms.

Despite the obvious advantages, the usual trade conference will seldom make any effort to coordinate such a total arrangement, in the belief that the sponsoring organization should stay out of the housing business and just make money on the trade show, registration, and social events, which it arranges with great gusto (no pun intended). True, the sponsoring organization should stay out of the housing business, but not to the extent that housing costs *everybody* a lot of money. Let's explore that problem a bit more. Hotels of the commercial type have long looked at the *total income* from a convention against the *total cost* of handling that convention, and they are seldom able to give credit to a group for things not used. For example, if you wish to rent all the public space in a hotel without renting sleeping rooms, the hotel will be glad to accommodate you. But with certain exceptions you will probably pay heavily for those public rooms, for the simple reason that most conventions need public rooms and the hotel cannot now sell its sleeping rooms to any other convention needing such space, but only to transient guests not needing conference space.

Hotels almost always prefer a convention group to transients for a variety of reasons that we cannot go into here; just talk to the management of a large chain hotel. If you take all its public space, you will certainly have to pay for it. And you will pay plenty. At the other extreme, if you want a large block of sleeping rooms but intend to hold your conference elsewhere (perhaps in free conference rooms in a local college or factory), the hotel discovers that it will have no sleeping rooms to market to another convention wanting its leftover public space. Thus, in either case the hotel has something to offer you as a balance of public space *and* sleeping rooms that you don't seem to want. You are nuts. Conference space is seldom charged for with a proper balance of sleeping rooms, and hotel conference space is far better and more accessible than anything you can get for any reasonable price elsewhere than in your headquarters hotel. Use the space. You're paying for it anyway. The hotel wants you handy so that it can sell your people some food; the food doesn't have to be served in organized lunches, dinners, and banquets, despite what some salespeople in hotels would like you to think. The hotel gets a lot of the meal income anyway, despite the *intention* of your participants to select a new restaurant at the other end of town every night.

The hotel knows it, you should know it, and you should benefit from it. Furthermore, the real income of any hotel comes from hospitality suites; your suppliers know it, the hotel knows it, and everybody is happy because the suppliers don't have to hunt all over town for their customers in order to entertain them and demonstrate their latest products. Suppliers want to use their own suites (as we explained in Chapter 22), and they don't object to the cost of such entertaining, which is a legitimate business expense. If you and your organization don't get the dickering advantage from that money flow, you are letting a good thing that is convertible into money go right down the drain.

All these trading factors give you, the conference organizer, a leg up on the hotel in making arrangements in advance for a Goldfish Bowl deliberative conference after you have developed a good record of attendance over a period of time. You need not keep the records; the hotel will report the bar profits and everything of importance to the local convention bureau and to other hotels in its own chain; the sales managers of the hotels will be after you for repeat business. This leads to my third rule:

Rule 3

> You have enough leverage on a hotel anyway with a good atten-
> dance at a Goldfish Bowl deliberative conference; so don't browbeat
> the hotel into an agreement that leaves it on the short end of the
> stick, or you will wish you hadn't.

Rule 3 simply recognizes the need for a good commercial arrangement in your dealings with a hotel, as in all other commercial dealings throughout the business world. Unless the arrangement is good for both parties, it is bound to backfire on one of the parties. Those who have worked the conference management circuit long enough to gain experience (and to get burned a few times) know that a binding contract with a hotel will never make up for a bad agreement in the first place. Suppose that you get carried away by your negotiations and demand things that a hotel should never agree to do for the price you are paying. You are happy; the hotel management has not yet discovered what the sales representative agreed to give you, or perhaps it simply felt, at the time, that this was a necessary prerequisite to stay in your good graces for possible future business.

But time will pass before your group arrives at the hotel, and a lot of management changes may have taken place; the new management looks only at cost versus income and is bound to start cutting services. It has no alternative. Your group will hate you, the hotel will hate you, and you will hate yourself when you try to arrange a future conference in any city served by a convention bureau. And the worst part of such a bad arrangement is that the things you negotiated were probably things your people would never have noticed; they were probably the frosting items which look nice when you plan a conference but cost an arm and a leg for a hotel to supply and which are just not worth the trouble or the cost. Unfortunately, this kind of feature is what the naïve convention manager usually sets his heart on; he must learn through my next rule:

Rule 4

> Let the hotel lead you in suggesting the things it can easily do
> for you that are not expensive, rather than insist upon frosting
> items which you think you would like but which it can supply only
> at high cost or at the expense of other, more important features.

As I said earlier, you are the convention manager, not a social secretary, and you should avoid getting in the middle between a man and his hotel reservation. I don't know your participants, but if they are anything like ours (the airline industry and its suppliers, which we call the most sophisticated traveling industry on earth), I can state without question that the last thing you want to do is to make a hotel reservation for anybody. Stay out of that messy loop. But for the reasons related to Rule 2 and explained earlier, you are interested in having your people all under a single roof.

I have found the best compromise is to get a block of rooms set aside as a part of the deal with the hotel, with the rate structure defined and with *you* supplying hotel reservation forms to your likely participants. Don't offer to make reservations for them; wean them. Make it easy for them to make their own reservations, and thus let them make the necessary *changes* in those reservations as they change their arrival dates and type of accommodation many times before they actually get there. This way, they rather than you are responsible for any "no show."

We have successfully (almost) trained the people in our industry to do this for themselves, and you can do it too. Stick to it. It's well worthwhile. This procedure will not give the hotel any problems; it will save it trouble. Only once in many years did we get crosswise with a hotel over such arrangements. It was a European meeting, and the local airline, wanting to be a good host, offered the services of its own travel agency to help everyone get rooms in the large commercial hotel. It convinced the hotel that it could help in the room assignment and record keeping at no charge. The result was pretty bad despite the best intentions. The hotel was oversold, with hundreds of weary travelers arriving in large bunches without any rooms.

A professional hotel organization knows its business; it doesn't need any help. A travel agency knows its business, too, but hotel officials are the best experts on room reservations and assignments *in their own hotel*. No two organizations can simultaneously arrange hotel accommodations for the same rooms as well as a hotel can do it *alone*. This is another rule:

Rule 5

Leave hotel reservations to the experts: the guy who wants them and the guy who has them. Don't get in the middle.

As a convention manager, you will need comfortable and proper conference room facilities, and you (no one else) must select them. Hotels are used to dealing with naïve convention managers who don't know what they need for their conventions. A hotel sales representative will ordinarily react as he is used to reacting with the great majority of conference managers who want facilities: he will promise to provide your group with "suitable" conference facilities. If you were the usual conference manager with whom he is used to dealing every day in the week, you would accept such a proposal; you would now have a deal with the hotel. A year later, when your meeting was coming up, you would get in touch with the hotel, asking "Which conference room are we in?" only to learn that all the conference rooms have been taken by other groups and you will be accommodated in a "suitable" sample room in the third subbasement next to the freight elevator and the truck entrance. Perhaps this is an exaggeration; but even the largest professional societies appear to arrange conference rooms essentially in this way and tolerate meeting rooms just about as inadequate, year after year, even though they run thousands of meetings and major conferences with attendance ranging from a half dozen to thousands of people. In criticizing such organizations for their lackadaisical meeting-room planning, I am criticizing myself right along with them, as I have served in many positions, including membership on the board of directors, in such organizations, and I was unsuccessful in improving the situation. But you need not suffer; the hotel people will quickly recognize an expert when one shows up, insisting upon a specific conference room assignment 3 years before a meeting comes to town and before any agreement has been settled. A hotel representative will welcome such an individual and will make the arrangements on professional terms whenever he discovers that he has a customer who knows the difference. When the conference room is mutually agreed to (I assume you have not pressed the representative for something way beyond your real needs, such as the master ballroom for a 50-participant event), get the agreement in writing from the hotel management for the reasons given in:

Rule 6

> When making final arrangements for a future conference, *assume* that the whole management, including the sales representative, is going to drop dead 1 week after you accept the arrangements. If anything is important to you, get it in writing.

There are exceptions to this rule, and I have learned through the years which hotels justify making an exception. A good commercial hotel, part of an important international chain, will have a reputation to hold up that is far more important to it than any agreement it has with you, no matter how legally binding the agreement may appear to be. This is probably why so few hotels seem to care whether a customer (with stature and a good record of past performance) signs anything more binding than a letter accepting the general terms of the arrangement.

Our legal counsel has never wanted anything more than that from a hotel, and I know of no hotel wanting more than that from us. The arrangements are not legally binding (in the opinions expressed to us by our legal counsel and the hotel managements), and both parties to such arrangements recognize that there may be circumstances in which one party or the other may wish to change the dates, locations, or facilities of a meeting scheduled and agreed to in advance. Fortunately for the conference manager, he usually holds the upper hand and can decide whether a request from the hotel for a change should be honored or rejected.

A piece of advice: if a hotel requests a change of dates or a move to a different conference room or even to a different hotel, I urge you to agree to that request if at all possible. The hotel probably has an important reason that may be to your advantage, too, and it will usually make the change well worth your while. Even if you obtain no other written concessions by accepting its request, you will discover that you are meeting in a very grateful hotel that will treat you much better than you could ever believe possible. You will have a friend for life in an organization where friends are important. Hotel people have memories like those of elephants, for good deeds as well as bad.

I remember a phone call I received not too long before a meeting in a Midwestern city; the hotel had just learned that the city had won a championship high school basketball game and that the finals would be played there in the same week in which we were scheduled to convene. Although the hotel would honor its commitment to us for rooms and public space, it was suggesting that perhaps the thousands of visiting high school people that week would be a problem for us all over the city. We could defer the meeting a week; the hotel could accommodate us the next week (with some careful rearrangement of its other events), and we dodged the high schoolers.

Everybody was happy, and the hotel picked up some high school business, which made it even happier. Such help from a hotel management is mutual help to both parties that benefits the good commercial arrangement I have urged. In all such deals, your credibility and reputation are being formed for many years in the future. This brings us to:

Rule 7

> Your reputation with your constituents and with the hotel industry is being shaped by every conference you negotiate. Keep the proper balance of doing right by both parties and so best serve the future interests of your constituents.

In making a choice of the right conference room for a Goldfish Bowl deliberative conference, you should be aware of several factors that are not usually so important in other conferences but make a difference in the success of a deliberative conference of the Goldfish Bowl type. For one thing, the head table is not the most important piece of furniture, as it is in the usual trade conference. The people seated there are not the principal speakers, as they are in the usual trade conference.

Have you ever watched how the usual trade conference meeting room gets set up? Try this simple exercise: for the next trade conference you attend, arrive early and watch the hotel arrange the setup in the conference room. Watch the attempts by the hotel to guess what the conference management wants; no one from the conference probably will be present—least of all anyone who will be taking part in the conference session in that room. For an early-morning conference, the hotel will usually make the setup around 7 A.M. and get it finished just before the first participants start to arrive about 8:45. First, the hotel people will construct a large raised platform at one end of the room (never in the middle of the long wall, where I would want it located). The platform will be set away from the end wall, wasting good space, and the first row of seats will be placed a long way from the platform, wasting more space and constructing a philosophical barrier that will inhibit informal communication back and forth. The platform will be so high that the king (I mean the chairman) must look down upon his subjects (I mean his participants). The space on the sides of the room will be empty of tables and chairs, wasting much more space, and the chairs will be set so close together that people will occupy only alternate chairs to keep their shoulders from bumping those of their neighbors. The rows will stretch almost to infinity in the far reaches of the back of the room, where no one can see or hear but everyone can sleep quietly.

When the preparations are all set, you will discover that the most convenient entrance door is near the head table, with a less convenient door about halfway back on one side. (Later, you will discover that only one side of the room is full of people, in alternate chairs, with no one on the side without an access door. The back of the room is crowded, but no one is in the first seven rows.) But you watch the setup crew as it carefully arranges the tables and chairs in schoolroom style so that they are in perfect alignment like the crosses in Arlington National Cemetery, row after row after row.

You will discover that the tablecloths are now being put into place with the cloth hanging down to the floor in front of each table just as the setup crew has been trained to do. You wonder how anyone can sit in any of the chairs since the crew has arranged the tablecloths to droop down to the floor behind the tables as well as in front, just as every setup crew has done since the beginning of time. The crew members have never sat in those chairs, all day, during a tiresome conference; they have never tried to figure out what you do with that big wad of tablecloth in your lap. Then you will discover that hard chairs have been used in the setup even though you have seen softer chairs in the hotel before. Why? Are the crew members sadists?

A man in a tuxedo walks in (a tuxedo at 8 A.M.?), and you decide to ask him; he looks like an inspector. His reply: "We knew this would be a tiresome meeting, and we wanted to be sure that no one goes to sleep in the meeting; the chairman will appreciate this." You mutter under your breath; could that really be the thinking that caused such a horrible affront to meeting participants? Yet I have had that explanation from hotel managements time and time again. If you want soft seats, you should make it clear to the management (if it *has* any soft seats) that the responsibility for keeping people awake is yours, not theirs.

Now, as you survey the beautiful but unfunctional conference arrangement, you will observe that the workers have left except for the guy with the water pitchers, who is carefully arranging them on the tables, and the guy with a roll of wire and some mikes, who is busily connecting up the head table microphone, with the podium installed squarely in the middle of the table. Soon the man with the projection screen will arrive; he will survey the room for about 10 microseconds and then move with his heavy load to a spot behind the head table, squarely in back of the podium. He will cuss a bit over the height of the screen supports he needs, but he will get the screen installed on the platform if there is room; if there is not, he will extend the base supports upward so that he will not have to wait for the hotel staff to install a larger platform.

It will never occur to either of these workers that the speaker standing at the podium will obstruct the view of the screen and that the podium light (if they remember to arrange one) will shine on the screen, washing out the picture anyway. (Later, after all this has been discovered when the first speaker asks for the lights to be turned off, they will have to move the screen to one side rather than move the head table and the podium, which they should have set up at the side, simply because the wiring for the microphone isn't long enough to let the podium be moved.)

Now all the carefully arranged cemetery-precision chairs will have to be moved, along with the tables, so that the people in the room can see the screen in the new location and still see the speaker. I have observed this same sequence of events over and over in the conferences of the most prestigious organizations in the best hotels in the world. Just keep your eyes open before, during, and after the next conference you attend, and see for yourself: people *still* do it that way.

And there is one additional act in this play: after you have positioned yourself in the conference room while it is going through its setup exercises, watch to see the reaction of the conference boss when he makes his first entrance. See what kind of facial expression he shows when he sees what they have wrought in his conference. Listen to his mutterings or cusswords under his breath. You might even pretend to be the hotel management and see how he explodes. But don't get too close; he may get violent. You will quickly get a liberal education in hotel-customer dealings if you watch. Here are some typical reactions:

1. The boss looks satisfied. Write him off your list as a naïve conference manager who has not had much experience with any kind of conference management.

2. He looks surprised, but also dejected and resigned. This guy has learned something, and next time (if there is a next time) he may arrive earlier to explain his wishes.

3. He looks mad enough to eat nails. Keep a respectful distance, but inquire whether he had wanted something slightly different. When he lunges for you, back away, explaining that you just happened to be there and observed his displeasure with something (at this point, perhaps he will put away the butcher knife and tell you what he had expected to be arranged and whose fault it is—obviously the hotel's— that the instructions have not been carried out.) This guy is the noisy kind who explains what he wants and then forgets all about his instructions until he discovers that things have been done wrong. (In defense of the hotel people, I have seen some of the screwy drawings that convention managers have given to hotel people. I have to admit that they could never be deciphered.)

In any of the foregoing cases, there is no way that the guesswork of a hotel staff can be corrected at the last minute by a convention manager, even if he does know what he is doing. My experience is that once a hotel staff has made a hotel setup, you had better relax and enjoy it;

ask to have it changed only as a *last resort*. If you *do* insist that the hotel change it, that hotel may be your last resort (pun intended). There is one ideal defense against such happenings, but most people don't want to employ it because it causes a lot of trouble for the convention manager and is hard to insist upon, although hotel staff people will love you afterward when you explain why you have done it that way.

Here is the procedure: tell the hotel management in advance that you have a very special room setup you are very particular about and that you need it done just right. You will have your staff present when the hotel crew does the setup if the hotel will select the day and time. When the hotel people ask for a preliminary drawing, explain that the setup is too complex to be committed to paper and that you have no choice but to await that day and time. Tell them how many tables of which size you will need, how many platform sections of which height you will need, and how many chairs you must have so that they will know that you are not asking for anything they will have to buy or rent. Have *them* select the time (offer to meet them at 3 A.M. if that is when they would like to make the setup). If you absolutely refuse to give them any hints, they will be scared to make any start and therefore will save you and themselves from the embarrassment of having made the wrong setup.

Hotel staff people are great (but usually wrong) guessers; if you give them any hint whatsoever, they will get everything set up, trying to save you trouble and time. They may get the head table and its platform in the worst possible place and have to tear it all out again, with bitter feelings all around. Your next step is to show up *well ahead* of the appointed time so that there is no possible chance of their anticipating your needs; with your staff present, busy yourself in deciding the placement of the platform while you are waiting, so that when they arrive, they will find you hard at work. They will pitch right in and work with your staff in getting the head table and its platform positioned just where you want it. Then start on the rows of tables.

With a good staff and with a hotel crew that knows its business, you can have enough of the total room setup for a meeting of 500 people done in about 30 minutes. Then you can go off to breakfast with absolute assurance that the room will be exactly right long before a nine o'clock starting time. Hotel people sometimes *do* make room setups at 3 A.M. just after a crew has torn down a large setup for a banquet that was just cleared out. But if you offer, graciously, to meet the crew at 3 A.M., the hotel will usually select a more practical time, because hotel people really are very, very friendly, gracious, and helpful from the top right down to the bottom of the staff. If you treat them right, they will jump through hoops for you.

Hotel staff people have great professionalism, entirely apart from any unionization, and it will work *for* you if you help it work. One way to get more work out of a hotel crew than even the hotel management can is to pick up the end of a table and start to drag it to a special place. Ten crew members will rush to get hold of the other end of the table regardless of what any supervisor does or says. Nope! You will not run into any union problems; at least I never have in 30 years' experience all over the United States and Europe. Usually it takes just about two table-end liftings by you or your staff; from then on you simply point, and what you want will be done. I laugh as I recall how many times I have had a hotel vice president on the other end of a table when no crew people were present and I wanted some minor shift made quickly so that I could go to breakfast knowing that the last fix had been made. So we have:

Rule 8

> Hotel people are wonderfully nice. Treat them just as nicely as that, and watch them respond.

With all the concessions that will be yours with a simple expenditure of effort and graciousness, as I have told you, you are probably wondering how the hotel can give such things for free; how can it afford all that service, and who really pays for it all? A good question. Many convention planners are tickled to receive some small discount off the price of the regular sleeping rooms and a little discount off the regular $3000 conference room rental (or whatever the going rate is). Those are the penny savings. One key to success in negotiating with a hotel is to get ahead of everyone else. You do this by planning ahead despite the reluctance of your group to make decisions more than one annual meeting in advance. Most organizations can never seem to get organized well enough to make orderly plans very far in advance, saying, "We don't know whether we will have enough business to justify that future meeting at that time."

If you arrange your annual meeting just 1 year in advance, you must expect to accept the dregs, at noncompetitive prices, and with little, if any, choice of anything. If you make your plans 3 years in advance, that is just about the minimum. A longer period is highly desirable. Get your group to consider the cost savings of getting the best, rather than the least good, hotel in a particular convention city. Consider the saving in having a free choice of almost any date with any conference room in any hotel, rather than being stuck with few choices and no competition for your business. It adds up to help the bottom line, as urged by Rule 9:

Rule 9

Get ahead of your competition for hotels, and make the competition work *for* you rather than *against* you by planning ahead, years ahead.

To optimize competition on your behalf, you should be rather picky in choosing cities and hotels. Unless you are pretty rich or pretty stupid, stay away from cities that everyone else likes and where the few hotels are always full. There most certainly are such cities, many of them, and they can take you to the cleaners. Even though you might get an agreement with a hotel if you start early enough, you may find that when you arrive, the hotel has scheduled back-to-back conventions, with conventioneers tripping over each other. You may have to stand in line in the lobby for half a day for the prior convention to check out; then your people start standing in long lines at the restaurants and waiting for all hotel services, including room service. Then you have pressure from the management to get your people out of their rooms on the final day so early that your conference is discombobulated.

Is that a bargain? Wait a year or two, and watch for new hotels that start digging holes and are looking for business for 3 or 4 years hence. Sign up quickly if you are satisfied that the hotel is a reliable chain hotel with good backing and plenty of time leeway between its announced opening date and your meeting date (at least 1 year) and if you have checked on the hotel with the local convention bureau and it is convinced that there will *be* a hotel rather than just a big hole in the ground. This brings us to Rule 10:

Rule 10

Select a city in which you are very much wanted (rather than a city you very much want), where the good commercial deal is tilted in *your* favor by the pressure of competition for *your* business.

The foregoing ten rules hit only the high points of a very complex business, that of selecting and negotiating with a hotel for a large conference. Most of these rules apply to almost all conferences, whether deliberative or not and whether large or small. For the most part, the exceptions have been explained or are obvious.

Yet there are other aspects of conference arrangements that really are different for the large Goldfish Bowl. These will be touched on here to supplement the commentary of prior chapters.

Special Requirements

One specific difference that I have referred to previously is the seating requirements. For the success of the Goldfish Bowl deliberative conference, it is very important that no artificial barriers be introduced between the chairman, at the head table, and the participants. Hotels will invariably space the head table from the rest of the meeting as though some sort of stage show were anticipated, with the attendees in the role of a passive, settled audience that has paid an admission fee and is expecting all kinds of wondrous things to happen on the stage. The hotel staff seems always to be upset when the conference manager attempts to shove the head table down into the vicinity of the audience. Yet the proper mood must be established: the mood is to be simply an extension of conversation, a larger-than-usual round-table discussion with everybody in the circle. This arrangement is hard to explain to a hotel management and hard to get set up unless you and your staff help the crew make the setup for the first time.

In planning the room arrangements, you should select a conference room with a proper ratio of length to width; about 1½ to 1 is a good ratio. You should *never* accept a long and narrow room, typical of the rooms of which old hotels have so many and which are usually a string of small sample rooms with their end walls opened up. Neither should you accept any room with posts unless the room is very large and you can accommodate your whole shindig in the area free from posts.

When the room is decided upon, select the best possible configuration, with the head table (raised slightly so that the chairman can see everybody in the room—1 foot or 18 inches is sufficient) serving as one end of an open square. Do *not* raise the other three sides of the square, for that would obstruct the view across the room. If you have a finite number of official members, as suggested in items 1 and 2 of Chapter 3, choose the dimensions of the square so that there are exactly enough seats around it to accommodate those official members.

Space the seats properly so that the members can sit comfortably for the duration of your meeting. Arrange another 100 or more seats at tables (of the 18-inch-wide variety) around this central square to obtain the best possible visibility and ease of hearing for every seat from every other seat. If the kitchen, air conditioning, and lobby noises are low enough, if the sound system is adequate, and if the room is large enough, you can add more tables to accommodate another 100 or 200 seats close to the others and so get as many as 400 or 500 people accommodated at tables. To do this sensibly, you must help the hotel staff place the tables. Hotel people will always space table rows so far apart that without your insistence the third 100 attendees will be in the next county.

Put numerous aisles at strategic places, but *don't* go overboard in spacing, or all the attendees in the back will be so far away that they will miss all the action. When you have chosen the maximum practicable number of seats at tables, have the hotel add seats without tables behind and close to the back tables. There will always be the "Don't get me involved" people whom we described in Chapters 12 and 13 and who will love to occupy those back seats.

Tables are not an absolute necessity for a deliberative conference, but they are a big help if the attendees have lots of papers; also they are wonderful for leaning on and, therefore, can be a big comfort to those who arrive early and are willing to make a commitment to get involved, which is what you do when you select a seat at a table. But the number of tables must be a compromise with the characteristics of the conference room. If, for example, you have been sold a conference hall in which every word and every rumble of a chair starts a never-ending roar that echoes from floor to ceiling and wall to wall, you had better get rid of all tables and bunch all the chairs together in one corner if you still want a meeting.

The seating arrangement you arrive at will bear no relationship to that which you have seen time and time again in the usual trade conference. A stage at one end of your ballroom is just so much waste space; a podium at your head table is excessively pompous and utterly useless. Large, wide aisles between table rows are a poor substitute for closer participants. But don't skimp on side-to-side spacing of chairs; hotels assume that the chair manufacturer designed them in the proper width to accommodate people, and the crews will place them touching each other if you don't intervene. As I have said before, you will then discover that your 400-participant conference room will accommodate only 200 people of the standard size who attend industry conferences. Have you ever measured the shoulder width of a "standard man"? But you have watched two standard men try to sit in adjacent seats in a hotel conference room. Watch how many participants try very hard to find a seat on the end of a row; then watch what happens after the conference has been going on for a while: the end seats have somehow slithered out into the aisle, and the next seats themselves will soon start slithering outward too. After a whole day, participants will have carried chairs out into open areas in the back, each with a *second* chair on which he can lean. Observe the facial expressions on two men spaced one empty seat apart when a latecomer sits down between them. Keep your eyes open, and you will observe much more than you will find written down in most textbooks on conference management.

Remember that in Chapter 2 we emphasized the importance of a chairman's solicitous concern for the comfort of his audience. Item 4 under "Responsibilities of the Chairman of a Goldfish Bowl Deliberative Conference" stated that comfort is a prerequisite to a successful deliberative conference. Careful attention to arrangements with the hotel in advance, during the conference room setup, and during the conference itself can pay immense dividends. Perhaps, with this insight into people comfort, you will see why some of the laws of conferences we have laughed about through the years are no laughing matter to the poor, bedraggled, uncomfortable meeting attender. I presented some of those people characteristics near the end of Chapter 12. Here are those characteristics with others added:

CLARITY'S SPECIFICATIONS FOR CONFERENCE SEATING

1. All seats on ends of rows and separated from adjacent seats
2. All seats very near to door
3. No front-row seats, even if on ends of rows and next to door
4. All seats on last row or next-to-last row
5. All seats allowing an unobstructed view of the head table and of all other seats and not facing the backs of any other seats
6. All seats next to an open window
7. All seats in locations impervious to noise from outside or inside even with an open door or window
8. All seats well removed from drafts from windows, doors, or air-conditioning ducts
9. All seats in locations where light, sound, and temperature are just right

And after you have planned and checked and double-checked and worried and worn yourself ragged to get everything just right so that no one could possibly have any complaint about your highly professional job of organizing, you discover that something *did* go wrong from the perspective of some participant. It may or may not have been anything that you could have done anything about, but nevertheless it did happen. Sadly, you turn to the paper you have pasted to your office wall and add another item to those already there, each of which has happened at one of your meetings. I don't know what is on *your* list, but here is what is on *mine*:

CARNES' CONFERENCE CALAMITIES

1. The relative importance of all items on the agenda will change the day before the meeting. Usually but not always, the least important item will become the most important item, and vice versa.

2. The importance of any item on the agenda at the time of the meeting is an inverse function of the amount of advance preparation on that item by the participants.

3. The greater the consensus and the better the justification for a course of action in a meeting, the more likely that a basic flaw will be found at the next meeting so that the decision will have to be reversed.

4. Despite advance planning something will foul up everything. If the hotel doesn't burn down and all airlines don't go on strike, there will be a snowstorm, a hurricane, a garbage collectors' strike, or a parade outdoors (or at least a circus rehearsal in the adjacent conference room), or a larger convention will take over the town, or the hotel will close for refurbishing.

5. If you have an interest in only one item on the agenda, this item will always be covered at the very instant when you leave the meeting to make a quick phone call.

6. Advance documentation on items of only little interest to you will always arrive early, but eagerly awaited material will be delayed—probably burned in a railway mail-car fire in Daggett, California.

7. Important data or correspondence handed to the staff for reproduction and distribution will invariably get lost and necessitate resubmission. But nobody made a copy.

8. The hotel reservation confirmation will usually arrive 2 weeks after your return from the meeting.

9. Even if confirmation of the hotel reservation is received in advance, the hotel will *always* be out of rooms when you arrive at the desk. Then the only available rooms are in a small but expensive hotel on the other side of town.

10. The meeting which was missed turns out to be the most important meeting of all time.

Joe's Name

In Chapter 5 not only did I urge the beginning conference chairman to be informal in the use of first names, but I urged concentration on remembering names. In Chapter 13 I carried the discussion a little further and gave some suggestions for chairmen and meeting participants who claim to have difficulty in remembering names. It would seem highly redundant and unnecessary to state here the trite old adage about *your* name being music in your ears; therefore, I shall not state it, but I shall say that it is so very important that we should all remember it, stated or not.

In industry meetings, an individual receives too few accolades for what he does. I described, in Chapter 8, the glory battery and how it can be used to fuel the ego power from which most volunteer committees get their continuing motivation. Remembering a volunteer's name is another way of fueling ego power, and it can be a very worthwhile, as well as proper and polite, thing to do. Joe cannot change his name to a more esoteric, euphonious handle, and thus you will have to remember "just plain Joe" whether he is rich or poor, boss or worker, leader or follower. Maybe he will have some kind of title such as Professor, Admiral, or Doctor. Maybe he will be just plain Mister. Whatever it is, plain or with a fancy title, it is his very own name, and he will cherish the sound of it. Use it. Save the "Hey you, . . ." for flagging down a taxi.

The Committee's Name

In Chapter 8 I explained the ego power of a committee and *its* desire, expressed through its members, for recognition. Unlike Joe, a committee can try to raise its stature by changing its name to a more highfalutin one. To a committee, the name "commission" sounds much more important; to a commission that name may seem of lowly stature, and it may scout around for a better name, such as "board." Whatever the

28

Publicity: What's in a Name?

name, the pasture will seem greener over there, and the group will covet the name of another entity. What I called the pecking order of the unctuous in Chapter 8 will never be stable or constant.

Only people seem happy with a name. Joe Smith cherishes his name and keeps it all his life, while the Hammer Handle Advisory Task Force wants to rid itself of that name. The bootstrap stature building starts with the Hammer Handleers first wanting to drop the "advisory" part of the name and become a policy group instead of an advisory group. Also, the work is too specialized, so they want to become the Whole-Hammer Task Force. None of their members like the name "task force" because it sounds temporary; they would love to become a committee. When someone of higher authority refuses that request and offers them the name Whole-Hammer Ad Hoc Subcommittee, they all reject it and eventually settle for a "more accurate" name that "properly reflects our expanded responsibilities." The new name: Whole-Hammer and Meat-Cleaver-Handle Special Subcommittee for Advisory Recommendations and Specification Drafting. Surprisingly, the members actually live with this awful name for several months until they merge with the group standardizing tack hammers; now they simply give up and rename the group once more: Pounding-Tool Subcommittee.

At some time in its life, every group goes through such a cycle; sometimes the debate lasts the whole lifetime of the group. The name-changing gambit takes a lot out of the glory battery and inhibits the group's ability to do useful things and get the glory battery charged up for more useful life. If the group ever gets time between name changes to do anything useful, the credit is usually wasted because the group changes its name from that under which the accomplishment was made. Glory and publicity are cumulative only when that glory can be credited to someone or to some organization. If the name keeps changing, all the previous reputation goes right down the anonymous drain. Joe Smith may have a ho-hum name, but he has an identity that stays with him all his life, an identity to which all his accomplishments, large or small, can be attached. In the lifetime even of a committee many accomplishments can be tacked up under a single name to build the stature of the committee. With repeated name changes, the group will have to work a lot harder just to hold its own. Is it really worth that great a penalty just to gain a fancier name?

Around Washington, an observer can almost always judge the year in which a particular group was formed by noting whether it is a working group, a task force, a subcommittee, or whatever. The fashion changes from year to year; I have never learned who establishes the fashion, but it is certainly true that groups scurry around to get their names changed to match the fashion of a particular time. Government entities seem to influence that fashion in names, but I don't know what it is that makes a task force more powerful than a working group at some particular time; all I know is that the weaker groups around town change with the breeze from one to the other and then back again, as though a new name would give them greater power and higher stature. Through all this long, mad skirmishing, our own entities have remained with the same old outdated names: AEEC is still just a committee, and it still spawns only subcommittees, nothing more fanciful. Maybe we are missing something.

Publicity for Someone or Something

Those organizations which have *not* changed their names with the changing times or changing tides can look back at the publicity they have received in the last year, the previous year, and even the previous decade for things they have done and are continuing to do. As Lord Byron said 170 years ago, "'Tis pleasant, sure, to see one's name in print," and even though he was referring to the writing of a book, the quotation expresses the value of publicity for encouraging accomplishments. With a volunteer organization, the value of publicity is just that much more important than with paid workers. Every little bit of glory helps with that glory battery; it can always use a greater charge, as I emphasized in Chapter 8. The group runs on love, not remuneration. While there will be benefits to each and every participant and his organization, some of those benefits will be long-term and will go to the whole industry rather than just to the volunteers who did the work; therefore, accolades and names in the paper are about all the immediate pay that comes for certain tasks.

Assume that your group *has* a name, and a name that has been around for quite a while, and that your people are working hard on some activity. How can some publicity get shoved their way? Unfortunately, it is not within the power of a committee to dictate what publicity it will obtain. It can certainly toot its own horn through its own horn-tooting paraphernalia by issuing press releases and pronouncements to its own people and to the press, but that is not the most coveted type of publicity. You might issue dozens of press releases before the group ever got mentioned in print. You might make friends with every member of your particular trade press and still not get your name in the paper. You might invite important people (and even pay them to come to your meetings as speakers) and still get no coverage.

But whether or not you are successful in the beginning, keep after it. Publicity *is* important, and it will come at the proper time when your group *does something* that is newsworthy. Your idea of what is newsworthy may not coincide with that of an editor unless you have experience in the news field. To define "news," we run into some odd incompatibilities. One news bureau definition goes like this: "News is the opposite of what is going on." Another definition states it this way: "News is what is going on that no one knows is." If these definitions fail to enlighten you on what is or is not news, I am sorry, but they are the best I know of. Probably the best indication of whether the activities of your group are newsworthy is whether the trade press prints anything.

Having the press attend your meeting has little to do with anything; it may be there just to wait in case something happens. I recall a recent committee meeting of the House of Representatives at which three television networks spent several days setting up and operating their cameras but without any coverage on any of the networks and hardly a word in the newspapers. Later I learned that someone had sent the networks a tip that some very important news was to be broken in those hearings. The networks were there until they satisfied themselves that no such news was likely; then they left simultaneously and instantaneously. You can have press coverage even when the press is not present, although it is facilitated and improved if members of the press are actually present. But tips only backfire on the organization; don't try them. They won't get you press *coverage*—just press attendance and a very bad reputation with the press.

But even though the trade press may follow much of what you do and the technical editors attend your meetings, you should not automatically assume that what you do is newsworthy as they would define it. Possibly the writers are using your meetings as background for other writing on related subjects. Or, quite likely, they are simply using the occasion of your meeting to interview people attending the meeting. When you first discover this happening, it may make you hopping mad. Imagine! They are using our meeting to benefit their own purposes and save travel costs. And when you see the write-up, you will be even madder when you discover that they haven't even mentioned your meeting or your organization. But you may not understand that the writer probably tried to sneak a mention of your activity into the story, but his editor snuck it right out again, simply because it wasn't news.

There just isn't any way to make nonnews into news. True, a good, highly paid publicist can do wonders for gaining publicity when news isn't really there, but sometimes the publicity gained through such cavorting isn't worthwhile. Is it worth the cost? The advice of professionals is to keep on sending out press releases anyway and to wait patiently for someone to latch onto something your group does that is newsworthy. Don't make a big hullabaloo over picayune items; state your activities carefully and accurately and treat the press properly if you want it to keep tuned in on your wavelength. Keep in mind that you are doing your part to help your volunteers feel appreciated; even though their accomplishments don't rate national news coverage, you are saying "Thank you" to many hardworking volunteers by announcing what they are doing. It may be only an internal publicity loop that goes round and round inside your own organization, but it can be mighty pretty music to some ears that are straining for faint sounds of praise. Someday, something will hit home with an editor somewhere, and your people will read those same words in a trade magazine. Those words sound so different when someone else, outside your own community, echoes them; the editor may even write some new words, and these sound better yet.

While you may not get coverage in the *Washington Post* unless you are the U.S. Senate debating the solution to the energy crisis, you may get some good coverage in the *Podunk Observer* when your national organization meets for the first time in beautiful downtown Podunk. You may prefer *The Wall Street Journal* for your news coverage, but you might as well take what you can get. The old saw that any press coverage is good as long as your name is spelled correctly is very good advice; don't get too worried about the intimate details that an editor seems to have gotten a little mixed up: all publicity is worthwhile as your organization starts the slow and laborious task of developing a good reputation as a group that gets things done. Even though what you get done may not hit the front pages, keep at it; concentrate on work rather than publicity, and the publicity will come at the proper time, when it is justified.

Good Reporting on a Meeting

So far in this chapter we have looked at individuals' names, organizations' names, and the processes of publicity for individuals and organizations. But we should give further attention to the *prerequisite* to good publicity: good reporting of what takes place in a meeting.

Entirely separately from press releases on the activities of your group, I must emphasize again, as in prior chapters, how important are regular, complete, and accurate reports of what happened. While some of your press people will get their information from direct contact with your people, from attending your meetings, or from reading your press releases, that is only the superficial information transfer route and not the route that will be of greatest long-term benefit to your organization. If you are following the precepts of this text and are making good use of the Goldfish Bowl, you will have no reason for not sending the trade press the report material you send to the participants in your meetings. Even some of the material that is almost of an executive or administrative nature and is not permitted to be released for publication can be very useful to certain selected members of the trade press for background material. If it is useful to *them,* your organization can benefit by your making it available.

When something finally happens that *is* newsworthy, one of these writers will be sure to catch it, and you will have some outstanding publicity just because you have kept the writer up to date all along on the progress of the activity. Most writers will treat such material properly and not use it in any manner that would hurt your organization; they want to keep in your good graces rather than blow their reputation for some sleazy story that wouldn't be worth anything newswise anyway.

So, if you do a good job of reporting promptly and expertly what your organization *does,* as I urged in Chapter 11, that material should be circulated to the trade press for the benefit it will give you in keeping the press up to date. You may be surprised how the cumulative effect of such regular publication distribution to the press can work in your favor. Here are some examples that happen regularly in our business:

1.   A technical writer is doing a story on some very elaborate military research and development (Yep, that's newsworthy), and he phones to ask about parallel development work in our group. He had seen some reference to the activity in one of our papers and wanted the latest word so that he could round out the story with the related commercial work. Although our commercial work would not, in itself, justify a story, we get some excellent coverage in a military story.

2.   A writer who has to cover a technical development for a government agency hates to admit to that agency that he hasn't understood what it is referring to because his own background isn't highly technical, so he asks us for a technical explanation of the technique. We can explain it to him, and he now owes us a favor and bends over backward to get a better news story for us over the objections of other writers who want the space for their stories.

3.   A government study suggests to a writer that the commercial people have done similar studies in the past, and he checks with us to find what he should say about *our* conclusions on such a study to make his story more thorough; so we get our name in the papers, too.

4.   We just happen to be planning a meeting on a subject on which a government agency is about to release some regulatory findings. This upcoming meeting gives the writer an excellent justification to do a

story on the subject even though there is nothing yet available from the regulatory agency. By this technique, the writer gets the jump on his competitor publications by finding news in a not-yet-quite-released government pronouncement. When the release comes out, he can do a second story, referring to his prior story.

All the above are just examples of how continued expeditious reporting of your ordinary activities can turn into a cumulative source of material for eventual continuous news coverage of an activity that, in itself, is not particularly (if at all) newsworthy. Still, you get your name in the papers.

Who Are You? What Are You?

In my previous admonitions to keep your organization name intact, I gave as my reason the need for a handle for any publicity that comes your way so that it can build upon previous publicity and produce a cumulative benefit that will far outweigh any tiny advantage from a better, more fashionable, or more timely name. Yet you may have an opportunity sometime to form a new organization to engage in some new activity, and then your organization will have the freedom to take flights of fancy and speculate on the heights of fame to which your new organization will someday rise. You will want a name that is appropriate for such a grand organization.

In starting an organization that is motivated by an urgent commercial need (rather than a social group motivated to engage in noncommercial activities), little if any attention will usually be given to such unimportant matters as an organization name. If we take the fictitious example given in Chapter 9, the group was the outgrowth of a former entity known as the Poofduffel Standardization Committee, but that did not cover its new needs. I suspect that the group might likely be known by some unimaginative handle such as "that bunch of people working on ruband definitive standards."

If no further thought is given to a name, the group would probably be assigned a numerical designation by the parent organization and thenceforth be identified as APA Working Group 45—Rubands. This is quite satisfactory if its only work is of internal interest and the activity is of an ad hoc nature that will soon be done so that the group can fold up its tent and disband. Yet almost all important activities, as well as the ho-hum variety, get their start in almost this same way, with a rudimentary name that means nothing outside the parent organization and even means very little inside the organization.

Perhaps my hypothetical ruband gang would have been better if it had used the informal handle: at least this could make an acronym, Bopwords, which is at least a conversation piece. But no thought goes into naming groups that are destined to become important at a later date for the exact reason I gave in Chapter 8: only the unctuous committee with nothing of much importance to *do* spends time on folderol such as naming itself. Committees destined to become worth remembering are busy *doing* the things that will make them, at a later date, sufficiently memorable to warrant a proper identity. So there seems to be no good answer to this problem. I would never suggest spending much time on developing a proper name in the beginning; even that much effort could be sufficient to run down the glory battery, as Chapter 8 suggests, leaving your group with its first accomplishment delayed by just a little too long a time to be useful. Instead, let us look at "good old WG-45," as this group will undoubtedly become known, and see what this odd handle does to the prestige of a budding organization: not much, I suspect.

In one organization with which I have been affiliated in Washington, such a development actually occurred when good old SC-31 became a nationally recognized institution despite its odd handle. That was the name of the committee formed in 1947 by the Radio Technical Commission for Aeronautics (itself better known as good old RTCA), which is not a governmental body but a cooperative group of all kinds of organizations interested in electronics in aviation. SC-31 was a cooperative effort of industry and government people to decide upon a single system of air navigation and traffic control to be recommended for the United States to replace the burgeoning multiple systems left from the recent war. The group completed a report in February 1948; 2 weeks later the Congressional Aviation Policy Board released its report urging adoption of that SC-31 report by the federal government; 8 months later, the Secretaries of Defense and Commerce announced the creation of a joint Air Navigation Development Board to supervise the implementation of that common system of air traffic control and navigation; the following year President Truman personally presented the Collier Trophy for 1948 to RTCA for the SC-31 effort, which had led to the congressional appropriations and federal program of implementation of the common system.

Good old SC-31 has been well known by that name for 30 years so far, and its fame will extend for generations to come, although it was only an ad hoc special committee that was formed, operated, and disbanded in the short period of 9 months over 30 years ago. Names that are fashionable may be nice to have, but it is far better to be known as good old SC-31 for something that is memorable than to be identified fancifully as the Board of Reconstruction and Management for Poofduffel Facilities and probably be referred to informally and stodgily by the trade press as "the what . . . ?"

House Organs and All That

My urging that your group keep the trade press aware of your work through meeting reports and other papers must be qualified to a degree: if your work is highly technical, highly detailed, or even heavily institutionalized, it will get little if any attention by the busy editor. One of my friends, a busy editor, tells how he peruses incoming material: it arrives in his in-box on his desk, and he transfers it slowly from that box to the wastebasket. He says, "Unless something on the first page grabs me as I shift the packet across my desk, it goes out." He explained (for my benefit) that he had a special pile for "some" of our material that he felt might be of use to him later in connection with other stories he might be doing. He knows that when some special issue of the magazine is in the planning stage, he may find an interest in something for a particular story, but he can always phone us (or you) for the latest on that topic. He will seldom keep all the material on file "just in case."

Knowing how the trade press works can help you organize your publication material to meet the editor's needs and, incidentally, to meet your constituents' needs even better. If your work is detailed, technical, or in depth, as it should be for the several uses of meeting reports I identified in Chapter 11, you should put yourself in the position of your constituents and determine what their *needs* for documentation are and how those needs should be met. While you may have been publishing working papers, meeting reports, and all other documentation in immense quantities, you may never have determined just who needs what. Although a good public relations staff would know what to do about such documentation, a technical organization or a committee staff may not have the publication expertise to know what should be done.

Here is one suggestion: establish one single publication, perhaps a house organ, that will give your constituents everywhere an overview (to use a well-worn Washington buzz word) of your activities without getting them involved in the details. Undoubtedly, you will have a large following of workers who want to know all the details of the meetings they have missed and who will need even the handouts that industry people undoubtedly always pass out in your meetings to make up for the advance documentation they didn't get around to submitting early enough. But those workers have bosses who aren't much interested in details but would like to keep an administrative eye on the meetings their staff people attend. Those bosses, in turn, have upper management to explain their travel budgets to, and that upper management is certainly not going to read much of the material that even the bosses will wade through. And upper management has top management; top management has a further upper echelon of people in its ivory tower; and even the ivory tower has people above it, and so on and so on.

When you get high enough, you find a turnover: a guy at the top has a hobby which somehow meshes in with something that some worker way down at the bottom is attending meetings to standardize. Maybe that hobby is ham radio; maybe it is instrumentation for power boats or racing cars; maybe it is a personal computer that runs a home workshop turning out wooden dolls; maybe it is windmills running a farm energy source, astrological computations, space studies, or hi-fi tinkering; or Masonic workshops on the Goldfish Bowl deliberative conference methodology. You name it: it becomes a hobby rather than a profession when the profession gets far enough removed from the natural interests of people.

My message: a properly designed house organ may serve many public relations purposes that you would never dream of. And every little bit of public relations helps immensely when dealing with any trade association activity that seems mundane and low in publicity value. If you can capture the interest of just one top executive in the firm of one of your constituents which has contributed working people to your committee, you will benefit greatly. Chapter 31 of this text gets to the final, ultimate determination of what good your whole effort is doing for your constituents by way of the bottom line, where decisions are made to cancel support or add support for your little committee of your little trade association. Watch for public relations opportunities.

So you decide to institute a top-management house organ. Now what? Where do you aim it, since you can't conceive of any particular individual up there whom you can identify? What do you call it? A newsletter? Published how often? How thick? How expensive? How individualized? I cannot give answers to all these questions in a text that would find such a topic way outside its scope. All I can do is encourage some thought and perhaps some outside help and advice and possibly offer some suggestions of pitfalls to watch out for. Here we go:

Pitfalls and Chuckholes for House Organs

1. Get the best quality of *writing* and *editing* that you can muster or afford. Even the best will be none too good if you are aiming, as you should, at the busiest people at the top. If you end up writing it yourself (if you can't afford any better), put your best effort on that task and make sure your whole staff knows that you consider it *that important.* Don't *tell* the staff that; make it obvious by your actions.

2. Select a length (one page, two pages, four pages, or more) as the maximum length any issue will ever have, and stick to it consistently. Never let the length be flexible to expand and contract as you have more or less material to fill it, or you will have the world's most extensive and lavish wastebasket. Make the length always a delimiter on your writing so that you will have to select the most important topics and the most important words to fit the small space available. Write and rewrite.

3. Don't name the house organ *Poofduffel Newsletter* unless you are seeking anonymity or the mundane; instead, seek a short, succinct, descriptive, and distinctive term that is probably registrable as a trademark. Assume that the publication will someday become publicly important and that you will then need a name more munificently endowed than "bulletin" or its many synonymic equivalents. Think ahead to the day when the name of your house organ has finally become better known that that of your most important trade magazine and the *real* owner of the registered trademark that is your magazine's name insists that you must change the name to avoid mix-ups with *his* magazine, which has also grown in importance. It's a great feeling if you *know* that you have the right to the use of that name.

4. Add the trade press to the mailing list; check with it from time to time to see whether the press yet refers to the publication by its name rather than by the words "that newsletter of yours—what do you call it?" If members of the press use the latter, don't worry; just tell them the correct name, and keep using the name in your contacts with the press. But keep up this exercise, for years if necessary, until the trade press people refer to your publication by its proper name without your coaching. This may take years, but it is worthwhile pursuing. The great day will eventually come: you will see a reference to *your* publication in some quotation from it in another magazine, and the name of your house organ will stand out just as though it were *Time, The Atlantic,* or *The Guardian.* Then it will all have been proved worthwhile.

5. But *for* this to happen, your publication must have been doing a service, first to your constituents, then to the community or the industry, and also to the other members of the press. Your publication must have already established an important reputation and consistently maintained a level of quality for a long period of time. A reputation is not established instantaneously even with a large expenditure of time and money and with an outstanding staff. It takes time.

6. Evaluate initially and reevaluate regularly the level of reader you are aiming for. Don't shoot so high that your workers are left out; don't direct the publication to the level of the workers' details and make it miss the upper echelons.

7.   In avoiding details, don't fall into the trap of *saying nothing*. A story need not tell what was decided in a technical meeting, but it must succinctly give the *consequence* (the big picture) of the action in general terms, suitable for an executive to identify "what it does for *us*." The executive may not care whether the part is to be fastened on with lots of little bolts or with a few big bolts; but if the decision will save him some big dollars, tell him that. If the poofduffels now will run more smoothly than ever before and more cheaply, too, now you have a story that will attract some interest. Search for the big-picture view of what happened and tell it quickly, preferably in the first few words of the story. Don't start with the usual meeting-report format of who was invited, who was there, who went home early, what was supposed to be talked about, what was actually talked about, why they talked about that and not about something else, how long it took, who said what, why they did, what happened, what didn't happen, why it didn't, why all this background and stuff has to be told in the meeting report chronologically rather than sensibly, and so on. Put yourself in the position of my real-life editor in the trade press who must have something to grab him during the passage of the first page across his desk from in-basket to wastebasket.

8.   Don't make the mistake of avoiding contention. If everything is sweetness and light in your meetings (I don't believe it), it just ain't going to be news, either to the press or to any executive. If there ain't no contention, you'd better keep it mum. That meeting was unnecessary. No one will keep on paying the bills for meetings to rubber-stamp something that isn't controversial.

9.   Go back and read item 1 in this list. If you don't pay any attention to that admonition, the others aren't important anyway.

If the reader got as far as the first page of Chapter 5 and discovered that I had no intention *then* of presenting any advice on how to get a meeting started *on time*, he may have surmised that the problem was even more difficult than I stated it to be, for the simple reason that I hardly even alluded to it in the next two dozen chapters.

Yes, it *is* a difficult problem; no, it is not impossible; yes, I know exactly how to do it; yes, I have a worldwide reputation for having started large and unwieldy meetings exactly on time (sometimes a few minutes early); yes, I have regularly moderated sessions in other people's conferences, and I have consistently started those meetings on time, too; yes, any member of our technical staff can, and does, do an exactly equivalent job of it; yes, I have to be pretty demanding with people to make it work; yes, it can sometimes make some people mad; yes, it certainly makes a lot of people glad; yes, it takes some careful advance preparation; yes, it *may* require some advance training of an audience (if it has been used to late starting over a long period); yes, it can give a chairman ulcers until he gets used to it; and, last of all, it separates the men from the boys in conference management.

If the foregoing has already started giving *you* ulcers, I suggest that you return to the first page of Chapter 5 and read my reference to what *Robert's Rules* suggests for a first meeting. Then, you should relax and pretend that this text says nothing else about starting on time. Just do the rest in this text, and leave well enough alone. I will never tell.

But if you just can't stand it until you find out what tricks I have for solving all those problems with speakers, you will probably read further. What about speakers who won't even show up on time, or audiences that are still having coffee in the dining room when the starting time rolls around, or gourmets who explore luncheon restaurants on the other side of town, taking many of the meeting participants with them? Those are just a few of the problems.

Then, when I answer the related question of how I go about stopping speakers who drone on and on, there is the other half of that problem

29

Starting on Time; Stopping on Time

of time control. Neither of these time control questions was addressed in the Chapter 25 discussion of scheduling or in the Chapter 26 discussion of long meetings. These are very specific problems needing treatment in a separate chapter, and I shall address them right here. Let's take the worst possible problem first and get it over with.

Muzzling the Long-Winded Speaker

To make the problem the absolute worst it can possibly be, let us assume that you have been invited to guest-moderate someone else's conference with a string of speakers and a time limit problem due to an important luncheon immediately following. I recall that several years ago I was on a discussion panel at the Washington annual convention of the very prestigious International Platform Association. I told the audience that *this* was the worst possible problem that a moderator faces. At the end of the discussion, one woman in the audience stated, "You haven't told us how to cope with that problem." She was right. I had no time for the solution to the problem; I could only tabulate problems for coverage at a later time; now is that later time. Here is the quickie answer I gave at that time which still applies to the question today: if you haven't made careful arrangements in advance for dealing with that problem, my only advice is to do nothing and relax and float with the tide, as most moderators do anyway when caught in such a situation. Simply accept the sharp criticisms that you will receive from the mad luncheon speaker who now misses his flight, from the indignant chef who has to keep the pot boiling, from the other panelists who don't get as much time as the long-winded guy does, and from the conference management which has to accept the barbs of all the attendees. That, my friends, is just about all that can be done without careful planning ahead.

So, what *should* you have done instead? Rather than answer this question just yet, let us look at some factors that should be considered in planning for such a problem.

Trouble Areas with Potential Long-Winded Speakers

1. *All* speakers are *potentially* long-winded. Chapters 12 and 13 explain why. The ones to look out for, particularly, are the ones who tell you beforehand that they have a very short presentation and intend to make it brief. Everyone intends to be brief. Such a statement marks the speaker as an amateur who has little concept of time management; *that* is the guy you should watch out for.

2.   Telling the speakers that you will control their time is like a ship's captain telling passengers that he will make the sea calm. Every moderator has always said this to every speaker; so, what's new? Why should any speaker pay any attention to such admonitions? If a speaker shows signs of hearing these words (whether you drone them or not), he is one to watch out for.

3.   If you do not yet have a reputation with those speakers for having consistently controlled time at previous conferences, you are already in trouble.

4.   If you have, for example, 3 hours of which you plan to allocate 2 hours to four speakers and 1 hour for discussion, with each speaker being given 20 minutes for speaking (the usual amount) and with the rest of the time for questions, you are getting into real trouble. Do you know that even speakers who have Ph.D.'s in math cannot do simple short division like that and get the right answer? Do you know that speakers all rationalize that the others will not need much time, so "There will be plenty for me because my talk is very important." Speakers never *say* this; but just watch them and listen to them.

5.   If the time allocation is as in item 4 and your first speaker has to keep another appointment and uses only 15 minutes, you are in awful trouble. Each of the other speakers now believes that he has the right to the time that was saved *plus some more time*. It never occurs to any speaker that only 15 minutes were saved. Even if you have threatened all the speakers in advance, this happening can void all the control you might have had. The only protection I have found is to anticipate this happening in advance and announce to the audience that any time saved reverts to the audience by courtesy of that particular speaker. So the meeting might adjourn early. This works.

6.   If the time allocation is as in item 4 and one of your speakers cancels his talk at the last minute, you are in even worse trouble, particularly with Ph.D.'s in math. They know how to do this arithmetic: this adds up to more time for the remaining speakers, and (you've guessed it) each believes he deserves that additional time. You can hardly believe how long each of your three speakers can make those 20-minute speeches.

7.   Have you ever timed an opening introduction by a moderator, including the time to trip over the mike cord, get the hall quiet, find the switch to get the piped-in music turned off (that's a doozy), get the mike turned on, find notes, find the lost speakers, tell all those stale jokes, rationalize why the moderator and the speakers are all there, get the introduction complete for the first speaker, let the applause (if any) die out, and get the neck microphone disentangled from his neck onto that of the first speaker? Time the next one you hear.

8.   Assume that you have 3 hours to divide equally between six speakers (for you nonmathematical types, this gives each speaker 30 minutes) and you are to moderate the session. There is a disturbance out in the lobby, and that delays the arrival of your first speaker and most of the audience for 10 minutes. Then you read, verbatim, the biographical material the first speaker provided and you use up 5 minutes more. The first speaker takes 35 minutes (the extra time is to tell a story the disturbance in the lobby reminded him of). The second speaker's introduction and speech have to be given equal time, and you do it before you figure out what is happening to the time.

While the second speaker is winding up his speech, you do some simple arithmetic (which no speaker is ever able to do, however), and you discover that you are one-third through and you have already used up half the time. If you give the *next two speakers* treatment equal to that for the first two, you will have to chop off both the last two speakers or run into the luncheon. (The fact that you are only one-third of the way through and have done some arithmetic puts you considerably ahead of most moderators in initiative.) Next time you may plan things a little better *in advance* and get the whole thing under control. At least you have worried instead of blaming the whole problem on an act of God (the disturbance in the lobby). That first 10-minute delay in starting has already multiplied into an hour and will be blamed for all future troubles in your session and in *all the subsequent sessions for the 3-day conference.*

9.   If you successfully run conferences on schedule, you will probably make somebody a little peeved. Not to run them on schedule will make a lot of people mad. To decide, at the last minute, to run a conference on schedule and then actually to do it will really make everyone mad. To run a conference properly on schedule, you must plan ahead, publicize your plan beforehand, be fair and equitable, and stick to your plan.

Item 9 suggests the only possible solution: the most difficult part of the exercise is convincing your speakers *ahead of time* that you really know what you are doing, that they believe you *will* cut them off before they exceed your announced-in-advance time limit, that their time must include whatever time it takes to introduce them, plus incidental time required for mikes, applause, and so on, and (this is the hardest to get across) that their time limit will be determined after the first introduction has been started, on the basis of an equal division of the available time among the several speakers. This means that you will divide up the time *equally* just as soon as you, the moderator, can determine the actual time available, *after* the session has actually started and *before* the first speaker has appropriated any time.

To get this point across will require more than simple verbal instructions and promises. I know of no means except a rather firm and threatening letter, containing examples of how each speaker should do his own arithmetic after the session has gotten under way. Nowadays, speakers could even be alerted to bring their own pocket calculators so that they will not have to know how to do short division manually, as we had to make speakers do back in the olden days.

Apart from the math problems, this moderator prefers telling speakers that he will read whatever biographical words they wish him to read. This helps to get across the point that speakers are welcome to use up all their speaking time on an introduction if they prefer it that way. This usually causes speakers to be pretty austere in their biographies when they become convinced that the *total* time, rather than just *their* speaking time, is being limited.

I strongly urge that in preparing such a letter you make the words strong but add a smile to them, exactly as you will do when you stop a speaker's too long speech. It always helps to put into words what speakers seldom anticipate: that delays due to any acts of God during the session will be subtracted equally from all speakers' time; this means that *all* speakers should be prepared to cut their speeches on the spur of the moment, preferably in places that are preplanned rather than at the end of the speeches, as would be necessary otherwise. I have reminded speakers for decades that their respective tales, unlike the tail of the cat on the railroad track, would be better if trimmed in the middle than at the tail end. Planning in advance by each speaker can help each choose the proper place for each tale to be trimmed.

My experience shows that if you give sufficient care *in advance* to alerting the speakers to the limiting facts as explained above and if you put enough heat into the letter, you will seldom have any trouble; speakers will go right up to the limit and stop just 30 seconds under the deadline. True, you may, with the first speaker, have to stand when the time limit is approaching, you may have to walk up to the podium and stand alongside him, and you may have to move up really close, possibly even reaching for the mike, smiling all the time just before he finishes his last sentence. Never assume that the speaker is just finishing his last sentence; stop him when the time is up. Last sentences have a way of running on for hours. Your first speaker is the testing ground for the whole session; if he can get a few more minutes out of you, they all should be given the same extra amount. Your budget will be shot. Your budding reputation is shot. You, too, are a gutless wonder; you would have been better off if you had followed my suggestion in paragraph 3 of this chapter.

Although you may have gotten the idea that all you need do is exert firm control in the beginning and depend upon a good bluff to make everyone cower from intimidation, here is our advice: forget it! If you are not prepared to prove to a speaker your capability even to turn off the public address system, if necessary, by actually doing it, you are in no condition to make a lot of noise. You would have to back down on your promise. As I said in the beginning, all moderators threaten and bluff the speakers; few do more than that.

Now that I have thrown down the gauntlet to you and have stated enough of the real problem of speaker muzzling, the cure is self-evident: you need only add appropriate armor, defend yourself with a large sword, and develop a solid footing on the platform from which to fight those who have not heeded your advance written-in-blood warnings. Be sure that your hospitalization is paid up, along with your liability insurance. Your only solace will lie in the possibility that the speaker who has been angered by your advance warning will have had several weeks or months to ponder his alternatives. He will have discovered, once he has pondered the question, that *there are no alternatives* except compliance with your rules. He will realize that the conference attendees will be on your side; he cannot complain of any unfairness on your part since everyone seems to be receiving the same threatening letters; and he can find no rational reason to object except one: he can claim that *he* always controls his time and you are being very unreasonable to intimate that he doesn't. Fine. If that is his reaction, you now have him committed; his reputation is on the line. You may apologize profusely for mistrusting him, but I advise you to watch him most closely and sharpen your sword a bit more just for him. By the time of the conference, your speakers will fit into one of two categories, those who took you seriously and planned their presentations accordingly and those who ignored you completely. It's that first speaker who tells the tale (no pun intended): if you control him, you are in; if you fail, you are out.

An Illustrative Example of Time Control

Here is a true story of real problems in the real world of conference speaking, taken from original notes prepared at the time of the occurrence. This was a single session of a 3-day conference held in the spring of 1976 by a major United States government agency. This particular session was organized and moderated by Jim, a former head of that agency. Jim announced to the audience at the beginning that there were to be four speakers with 15 minutes each. He would rap the first gavel when 5 minutes remained and the second gavel at the 2-minute point; the third gavel would mean that the time was over.

Fred was the first speaker; he presently worked for that government agency and kept his time well within the prescribed limit. So far, so good. Jim was lucky.

The second speaker was a congressman who spoke for 26 minutes, (without any gavels). With the delay in starting and the time required for transition, this left the session just 21 minutes late when it recessed at the time prescribed by the conference for the coffee break. As Chairman Jim rushed past me on the way to the rest room, he seemed a little apologetic for the lateness and told me, "I won't have any trouble with the next speaker, the general, because he works for me." Off he went and then came back to the podium to get the conference reconvened. He got the session started.

After Jim introduced the general, the general announced that *he* would tell Jim when 5 minutes remained, and again at the 2-minute time, and when the time was over. But Jim had to tell the general when 5 minutes remained; the general did a quick double take and stated that he would cut out some; he finished right at the deadline and then told Jim, "Rap three times."

Jim introduced George, the fourth and last speaker. At the 5-minute point, Jim tried to get George's attention and finally succeeded. George stopped his speech, turned to Jim, and asked, "Am I through or at the 5-minute point?" Jim said, "Five minutes." George had now interrupted his own speech, but he went on, "There could be a third answer, that you don't like what I'm saying." Jim and George laughed about that one, and George went on with his speech. Jim didn't bother him again, and George went 3 minutes over his time.

We should observe from this true-life case that bluffing *never will work*. Also, observe how everyone seems to have missed the point that time control must control *all* time, not just the time that a speaker takes. The miscellaneous time between speakers and the time taken by a moderator must all be accounted for if the session is to fit into the prescribed slot without slopping over on the back end. Moreover, we must observe the pickle a moderator finds himself in when a first speaker has obeyed the rules and an important speaker then takes all the time he wants, with no interference from the moderator. Now, how can the moderator catch up by browbeating a subsequent, less important speaker into taking less than the announced-in-advance time?

In the above example, I have no certain knowledge that Jim, the moderator, failed to state the conditions in writing in advance to all four speakers; but I suspect that the first warning was the one announced by Jim when he introduced the first speaker. My guess is that Jim figured the agency man, as the first speaker, would conform, but Jim did not believe it would be proper to browbeat the congressman into exact conformance and therefore tried to rely on the power of positive suggestion and depend upon his gavel-warning announcement and the hope that the first speaker would conform, making a good example for the congressman. But if this was his plan, it didn't work, as we have seen.

Training an Audience to Start on Time

Audiences and conference participants most certainly can be trained. If the group has been used to a lackadaisical manner of operation, it may take a while to get a bad practice corrected, but it certainly can be done. But before we study methods of improving an existing organization, we should ask ourselves what we hope to accomplish by changing something that obviously must have been that way for quite a while. Do you recall my suggestion in the second paragraph of Chapter 5 for determining which parliamentary procedures should be followed in an organization in order to maintain proper discipline? I suggested the obvious: ask the group.

Do you recall, also, the first question I postulated for such an inquiry? Start on time? If a group couldn't care less whether its meetings start on time or not, why waste a lot of energy on a very difficult endeavor which would not be appreciated? Yet, as I intimated in Chapter 5, if you *know* you are up to it and ask your group what *they* would like you, as chairman, to do, I believe it is pretty certain what they will say unless they don't believe you can do it. Even though you may know that they will want your meetings to start on time, it is good practice to ask the question, explain the consequences, and get their directive, which you will keep in your pocket in case of any future challenge of your authority.

Getting a directive is one thing; starting the meeting actually on time is still another thing. Unlike the guest moderator role I described earlier, your own action as a chairman of your own meeting is a lot easier to manage.

You are responsible for advance publicity; you are the one who can take rather firm action over those acts of God used as excuses by others when they think they need an excuse. You can plan the whole conference to avoid such acts of God (not entirely as explained in Chapter 27, but nearly so). You can alert your membership to the change that will be instituted. (I hope you can think up a good reason that would explain why, at this late date, you have decided to start on time meetings that were never on time before. Are you intending to tell the members that you read in a book how to do it, really, truly?) You can arrange the program or agenda to emphasize the importance of having the meetings run on schedule and by this means alert your people to the impending change. You have many advantages over a guest moderator operating in somebody else's territory and under somebody else's rules or lack of rules. Now, everything is in your favor. All you have to do is do it. The solution is not particularly profound: all you need is (1) guts, (2) advance planning, and (3) advance publicity.

I have already talked about the guts part; now for part 2. It is in the advance planning area that you need to do some careful thinking. What are the trade-offs between starting on time and delaying the start a few minutes? What would be the consequences if your whole committee were unavoidably delayed in arriving? Half of your committee? One-tenth of your committee? In Chapter 23 I described an example in which *half* of our committee was stuck in the hotel elevator for quite a few minutes. In that case, I convened the meeting on schedule anyway, even though objections could have been raised (there were none) if action had been taken with so many people absent. Everything is a trade-off with everything else. That particular meeting was costing our industry about $300 per minute; should I let those highly paid people sit there for half an hour doing nothing? Of course not, from one point of view. Should I convene the meeting with those highly paid people now captive and with no attempt to decide anything because the decision makers were not yet present (I didn't know at the time that they were stuck in an elevator, so I didn't know how long they would be delayed)?

We have had occasions on which an administrative luncheon meeting has delayed all the decision makers so that we were all some 2 minutes late in getting back into the room; on those occasions, the reputation of the chairman was saved by a candid contribution to the late bucket described in Chapter 23. As I stated there, the late bucket is a psychological trick that I shall tell you more about later in this chapter. It serves an important purpose. The late bucket establishes an either-or set of alternatives for the meeting attendee so that he is never faced with any ultimatum requiring him to arrive on time (even if it were possible to apply such a thing). By giving him an acceptable alternative, he is allowed to be late if he will contribute to a worthy charity; thus neither the chairman nor the honorary sergeant at arms is responsible for insisting upon attendance on schedule. But that little inducement is the best medicine for lateness I have ever discovered; it is publicly accepted; everyone feels an obligation to be present on time, and it really works.

But that is only one reason why people arrive on time; the real reason must always be that something of importance *to them* will be missed if they are late. If you prioritize, as I suggested in Chapter 25, and concentrate on the showmanship angle of making the meeting the most effective from the participants' point of view, as I urged in item 3 of Chapter 5, and if you constantly strive for reports that are effectively presented as in Chapter 16 and with proper debating, listening, and consensus developing, as urged in Chapters 12, 13, and 21, and with empathy for the funny side, as described in Chapter 23, you will have a conference that will attract the people you need, and they will arrive on time, give you their best, and even compliment you for running a good, effective meeting. Most certainly, an audience can be trained to operate on a schedule. But just be sure that you do your part.

One last point to remember: a reputation for starting on time can never develop through a proclamation; it can come about only after a long record of having done it consistently and fearlessly. A reputation for not starting on time is easy to attain; almost everyone already has that, and you need do nothing to attain it again at any time.

The Late Bucket and Other Psychological Tricks

Earlier in this chapter and previously in Chapter 23, I told about the many advantages of the late bucket. As I have stated repeatedly, it is quite desirable to avoid any ultimatums to a conference; thus an alternative should always be stated for anything that seems like a rule. For example, rather than insist that a whisperer cease his whispering when he is bothering many others, it is far better to give him the alternative of moving in and out of the conference room at any time he wishes, so that he can conduct other business outside rather than inside the room. Similarly, the late bucket gives the participant a legitimate alternative to being on time: he may contribute a noisy coin or quiet folding money to the late bucket immediately after a much-too-short coffee break.

Here are the words we have used to publicize the late bucket in the program for AEEC general sessions for almost three decades:

THE LATE BUCKET

You can be as late as you wish, if you get in before the meeting starts. Many meetings ago we started lateness fines, with a bucket to collect them near the door of the conference room. We then donated the money to a local charity. This worked so well that we have continued it ever since.

Of course, you all know that the chairman reserves the right to change the bucket rules (even retroactively) without notice, but we will remind you of one particularly effective rule: approximately 1 minute after the chairman calls the meeting to order after each break, the bell will be rung. Anyone left *standing* in the room continuing a private conversation thereafter owes the bucket fund two bits [NOTE: Overseas we substitute 2 guilders, 2 francs, and so on] and is expected to pay up at the next break. If necessary, the second ring will add one buck. Keep your ears open for new bucket rules.

[Person's name] of [firm] is our honorary sergeant at arms, and he will accost you first with the bucket following the Wednesday morning break. If you are not back in the room by reconvening time, you will be expected to make a *voluntary* contribution when you enter.

The administration of the bucket is quite simple. Its success depends upon the chairman's playing the game as the meeting is called to order after a break, calling everyone's attention to the particular charity (usually a local children's hospital) and entreating everyone to be a little bit late for the benefit of the children. It is our practice to employ an oven timer with a loud bell at the head table to keep track of the time during our breaks. After the bell rings, the chairman must threaten to raise the ante with the second bell as everyone rushes to his seat. And they *do* run. And they love to get caught with a penalty so they can throw a noisy coin into the bucket. We have learned that the best and noisiest bucket is a hotel champagne bucket; it will ring beautifully from a small coin, and this calls everyone's attention to the late arrival. In a 2- or 3-day meeting of several hundred people, we can collect $150. The hospitals are always surprised at the novel way of collecting the money and write us beautiful letters which we reproduce in the meeting reports. We make no claim for having invented the strategy of the late bucket; fining people for being late is a practice going back to antiquity. Neither can we take any credit for rediscovering and reapplying it to conferences; I know that the Radio Technical Commission for Aeronautics started applying it to their committee meetings over three decades ago; we copied it from them. You may copy it from us.

The Curious Sheep Principle: A Psychological Suction Pump

Another psychological trick that I *did* discover myself is known as the Curious Sheep principle. As I mentioned in Chapter 23, it depends for its operation on the natural tendency of people to act like sheep and follow each other in groups, without knowing or caring exactly where they are going or why. To make this trick work properly, the coffee breaks must be held in an area close to the meeting room but separated from it by a number of large doors. An outside foyer to the main ball-room works fine. Here is the way to make it work:

1.   During the coffee break, be sure that all doors from the coffee area to the conference room are wide open. Alert your staff people and assign one to each major door or pair of doors, but have them move away from the assigned doors during the coffee break.

2.   Ensure that your staff people are aware of the exact time and are ready to run to their assigned doors the very instant that the timer bell at the head table rings. (The chairman should be at the head table and immediately ring the bell several more times directly into the micro-phone so that everyone can hear the bell.) The staff people should make a lot of commotion as they unhook the doors from their holders and close them as quickly and ostentatiously as possible. As people rush to get through the doors before they get closed, let them through but con-tinue the closing process as noisily as possible.

3.   If this is done with proper fanfare, almost everyone in the foyer (even hotel guests not a part of the meeting) will get bundled through the doors and into the conference room in nothing flat. The Curious Sheep principle works like a gigantic suction pump.

Now that you have the Curious Sheep principle to get the partici-pants into the conference room and the late bucket to get them seated, what else is left? Unfortunately, there will be times when the private business of the participants will simply drown out the public address system so that, with a friendly group, it is quite difficult to get the attendees quieted down so they can hear what you are saying. Now you need to apply nonsensical chatter to get their attention.

Nonsensical Chatter as a Quieting Method

Not only is banging on the table or employing a noisy gavel bad parlia-mentary procedure, but it is bad manners as well, and it won't serve any useful purpose except to generate more noise and confusion. But a chairman can employ the same curiosity syndrome that makes the Curious Sheep principle work so well by starting to talk on any subject that comes into his head. Usually the best source of talk is publicity put out by the local convention bureau on the city.

Using San Francisco as an example (because it has one of the best convention bureaus of any city anywhere for publicity), you can start by telling about the history of the hit song "I Left My Heart in San Francisco" and how it was first written with different words from the ones we all know. You can tell them that the original lyrics are available for view in a special exhibition on Market Street along with more of that history. I can practically guarantee that by this time the whole conference room will have stopped its own talk and will be listening with great interest to what you are saying.

You will find, after one sentence or two, that you must drop your story (promising to tell the rest of it after the next break) and move into the meeting, now that all the attendees are quiet and you have their undivided attention. Don't get so carried away with your story that you hold up the start of the meeting to finish your anecdote. *Always keep your priorities correct,* remembering that a typical meeting may be costing your group hundreds of dollars per minute.

NATIONAL POLITICAL CONVENTION GAVEL SYNDROME

And don't ever make the horrible mistake that so many chairmen make, which we shall call the National Political Convention Gavel syndrome because United States national political convention chairmen seem always to fall into this trap. A chairman has labored diligently to get an audience quieted down enough so that he can speak to them and have them hear him. He finally succeeds in getting the noise level down to a small din, and what does he do? He walks over to an associate and engages in some conversation with him, leaving the audience to resume its conversations and yelling again. Thus, here is the rule: don't waste your time and that of the audience in trying to get it in the mood for a meeting *unless you are ready for the meeting.*

Let's back up to the nonsensical-chatter method and see what variations of it can be applied. There are many variations on this theme, but watch carefully that you do not present legitimate announcements during that time, so that only a small portion of the group hears the announcements. Stick to subjects that are of interest but are not vital; tell some stories that relate to previous meetings, future meetings, or that particular meeting, but stay away from the usual jokes; once *you* have taken time to tell a joke, you will have no basis for keeping other speakers on the subject of business. But you can tell of prior visits of the group to that city or to that hotel, or you can tell of happenings that bear some specific relation to the meeting but not necessarily to the *subject* of the meeting. You might recall the time the group got stuck in the elevator on a previous visit or the special luncheon it held the previous time for George, or remember the garbage strike. Watch the group to determine when the meeting is ready to convene, and don't drag out the nostalgia. And, most of all, be ready to shift right into the next agenda topic before anyone can return to a private conversation. Don't allow any gaps to develop. Once you have that group quiet, don't lose it. Keep tight control.

Anticipating the Starting Time

Is it possible to start early? Certainly it is. It is quite practicable and a good idea to start the nonsensical chatter several minutes before the scheduled starting time so that the room can be quieted down before the scheduled time arrives. Then, when that time arrives, you can announce with assurance that it is now time to start, and you will immediately move into the first item on the agenda. With the beginning session of a long conference, you can expect more confusion as people try to get registered and then select suitable seats and get all their papers ready for the meeting. It may take 2 or 3 minutes even with a trained audience and an experienced chairman. An early start is quite helpful in getting the businesslike mood properly established.

Who Starts a Meeting?

In our business, the meetings are so expensive that we must ensure proper operation regardless of what might happen. Thus, all our staff people know that they are expected to get that meeting started and business conducted no matter what. If the chairman were to trip and break his neck, the meeting would certainly start on schedule and accomplish the business. The vice-chairman knows it is his responsibility as next in line, and if he is unavailable, one of the other staff people would start the meeting. Once you establish a work pattern that indicates how important you consider the meeting to be, everyone will fit right into that pattern. I postulated in the beginning of this chapter that really, truly, repeatedly, and consistently starting meetings on time is difficult, but it most certainly can be done. I claim nothing more than perseverance in having a whole staff of people who can do such a job. You and your group can succeed in this, too. Just stick to it until all the principles come easily and you feel reasonably certain of your capabilities.

How to End a Meeting on Time

Early in this chapter I started with the most difficult problem of all: muzzling the long-winded speaker. In a deliberative conference, if the chairman follows the precepts of earlier chapters and maintains tight control over the deliberations, the chairman will not face the problem of muzzling, which is most applicable to the pseudodeliberative conferences of Chapter 24. Instead, the chairman must worry over the timing of deliberation, described as futile in Chapter 26. Futile or not, the conference will expect accomplishments and will want adjournment at the proper time, and it will want recesses at appropriate times. The problem of final adjournment is different from the problem of recessing. Let's take them separately.

How to Have a Recess: The Last-Word Syndrome

Having a recess *should* be simple: just have it. But it isn't so terribly simple because of the Last-Word syndrome. No one is unaffected by this syndrome: chairmen, participants, everyone. Nothing will generate greater motivation to talk than a suggestion by the chairman that now is the time for the break. While it might be thought that coffee time would attract everyone's attention and interest, such is not always the case when a technical meeting gets deeply engaged in a complex debate. Everyone wants to have the last word in order to leave his argument fresh in the minds of the participants while they are at coffee. The individual who is speaking will finish his words, but then another participant wants to refute those words before coffee. I have seen coffee breaks delayed for half an hour while the debate continues, with the chairman always expecting that the next word is the last on that topic and that the meeting can recess with it completed, but this never happens.

The cure: use the oven timer set to chime at the coffee break time; then follow scrupulously the principle that the whole meeting must stop in the middle of a word at the sound of the bell. To get the message across to the participants, keep an eye on the timer and make sure that you, the chairman, are speaking when the bell rings. Stop in the middle of a word and stand; leave the room, and everyone will get the message and enjoy it immensely. After you have followed this practice for quite a few meetings, you will be ready to modify it slightly by allowing a sentence to be finished before recessing. But when you sense that the old dillydallying pressure is developing, go back to sentence interruption for a while. Now that you are able to break for coffee on schedule (the easy job), you are ready to consider the adjournment process.

How to Adjourn

The method: plan it in advance. Determine what will have to give in accordance with the precepts of Chapter 25. If your group wants a specific finishing time, you will have to finish at that time and hope to get as much accomplished as possible. If your group has a flexible closing time (don't count on it), you will have more leeway in planning, so that more can be accomplished. If your group has a firm adjournment time and is quite insistent that certain matters be settled too (the usual case), you have a problem of the kind described in Chapter 25. Although you cannot schedule deliberation to finish at a certain time, you can follow the suggestions in Chapter 25 and prioritize (there's that Washington buzz word again) your action items in the order that best fits the time available, with the most important items early in the meeting so that you will have the best chance of completing them, even though this must be done at the expense of certain other lesser items.

You can be reasonably successful with that technique unless you run into the situation, described in Chapter 17, known as the Nice Little Old Lady and Gentlemen syndrome. In that case, just forget the whole matter of scheduling and wait for some researcher to discover a cure for that syndrome. Fortunately, your group will usually be tolerant if you apply some effort to the scheduling process and succeed in getting some important accomplishments before adjournment. The rule is: if your group establishes an adjournment time, use the oven timer and quit when the bell rings. Don't set the clock back repeatedly, as has been known to happen in certain legislative sessions. Stick to the time established.

Can You Teach an Old Conference New Tricks?

I observed, at the beginning of this chapter, that it will always be a lot more difficult to institute time control in an established organization than in a new organization. Recall that I described the most difficult problem of all as that of a guest moderator in someone else's conference when the audience has never been trained to expect good time control. Almost as difficult is a decision to introduce time control into an established organization which has very infrequent meetings (perhaps once each year) and a long history of slow starting and late finishing. Let me tell you about one such organization's successful implementation of such a time control system.

I shall tell you about the International Platform Association (IPA), the modern-day version of the Chautauquas, founded as educational lectures in 1874, which themselves were an outgrowth of the lecturing started under the American Lyceum Association founded by Daniel Webster in 1831. In recent years, the IPA had become less careful over time control, and something had to be done. My first visit to its annual convention in the early 1970s gave me the impression of a beautiful mansion filled with works of art and with termites eating away in the woodwork. I was horrified to discover that although the IPA attracted the nation's greatest and most expensive entertainers and lecturers, the program was left pretty much to manage itself.

I remember one nationally known speaker who was scheduled to open the session one morning sitting there and fidgeting because there was no one to introduce him. He waited a few minutes, moved to the podium, introduced himself, and went on with his speech. To this day, I don't believe anyone on the IPA staff knows that this happened. In one VIP evening session, national columnist Jack Anderson was left sitting on a table against the wall of the ballroom waiting for a feminist speaker to finish. She went considerably over her time and refused the moderator's polite requests to stop. When the audience finally shouted her down after she asked it whether it would tolerate the complaint of the moderator, she decided to quit. That was the only time in many years that an IPA audience showed intolerance for a tedious, long-winded speaker; it was almost as though the attendees had all read about Thomas Jefferson's procedure for the House of Representatives (see Chapter 25, suggestion 5).

Harry Weber's Program Control Committee

This was the environment that had come into existence and caused the director general of IPA to search for a means of instituting time control. He put the bee on Harry Byrd Kline, the boss of one of the most prestigious speaker bureaus, to fix things. The culmination of this effort was Dr. Harry Weber's Program Control Committee. Harry Weber had been teaching public speaking for years and knew the subject; he also was cognizant of the problems that would face his committee as it started the task of educating an audience and a group of rugged-individualist speakers simultaneously. Harry developed a set of rules and some guidelines for the speakers; he trained his volunteers in the art and science of time control. For example, one instruction to his committee reads: "See that the speaker begins on time and stops on time, even if it requires being aggressive on your part. Remind speakers of the signal system."

The signal system referred to was developed by Tim Letchworth, one of Harry's committee members, so that the timing of speakers could be given an air of impersonal control. People can be blamed for calling time on a speaker; a machine is so impersonal that it cannot be blamed when it calls the time. This machine consists of an electric light box placed on the podium facing the speaker and controlled by the program session manager (*not* the moderator). Being impersonal, it gets the message across to the speaker in no uncertain terms that it is time for the first warning or time to stop. This avoids the necessity of selecting moderators having enough guts to turn off a famous man. Harry lets the machine do it. But the machine is backed up by the program session manager on duty for that particular session, who is duty-bound to guard the time with his trusty sword. Under Harry's capable prodding, the IPA Program Control Committee succeeded in eliminating the long-established laxity and getting the sessions back on time. It wasn't all accomplished the first year, however; ingrown practices take a while to get changed.

I made my own check of the starting and stopping of the various sessions the first year the system was in effect and found the improvement from preceding years almost unbelievable. For example, the first speaker at the 1975 IPA Convention was Ralph Nader, who started *exactly* on time and finished 40 minutes later exactly at the prescribed time. To my knowledge this had never happened before. The rest of that day ran just as well, with the head of the Central Intelligence Agency (CIA) speaking that evening on a program that included the Israeli Ambassador. That year the program had not made provision for the time gaps needed to get the important personalities out of the hall and away from the newspaper people crowding around the podium.

Thus, the CIA head got started 8 minutes late; yet he finished 10 minutes early, so the session was still on schedule. He was followed by one more speaker, and the final count showed that the evening session closed some 6 minutes early. Quite an accomplishment for the first year of program control. On subsequent days, there were some mix-ups due to improper time allocations in the published program, but the results showed what can be accomplished when someone—in this case, Dr. Harry Weber—sets out to make a basic change under a firm directive from management.

How to Introduce a Speaker

But that was not all that Harry's committee was expected to do. He gave the members training and strict rules to be followed by the moderator in introducing speakers. Controlling a speaker in time is useless if the moderator is allowed to drone on and on in making a windy introduction. Harry insisted upon a 1-minute limit for introductions, and he made it work.

How to Handle Time Control of Questions and Answers

And that still isn't all. Harry decided that one of the major problems in program control was the question-and-answer session after an important speaker. How do you turn off the questioners? How do you keep them from making speeches instead of asking questions? This had always been a particularly nasty problem with political speakers. With a senator, congressman, mayor, governor, or especially the President or Vice President of the United States, all the protagonists of various political theories and philosophies will rush to interrogate the speakers. Each has a speech he wants to make; each wants to debate some elusive point that is of little general interest; each has an ax to grind.

Harry solved this problem admirably by taking a sheet from Ted Mack's demonstration of how to do it at an IPA panel session several years earlier. Ted Mack, well known for his many years on TV's "Original Amateur Hour," showed us all how the experts control question-and-answer sessions. He took up his position out in the audience at the microphone and introduced each questioner by name and city; he would then hold the mike so the questioner could ask his question. If the question turned into a speech, he would withdraw the mike and remind the person to get directly to the question, again holding the mike so the questioner could be heard.

The real expertise came when time was getting short and questioners were building up in a long line. Now Ted anticipated just how many more speakers could be accommodated with the time remaining, and he would tell the others that the time was running out. Never did a questioner find himself in the line after time had run out; thus there was no embarrassment for anybody. The procedure was handled as only a professional like Ted Mack could handle it. Ted died several years ago, and it was IPA's loss; but many will remember the teaching Ted provided so graciously by his example and the experience that had done so much for Harry Weber's IPA Program Control Committee a few years later.

Though an important TV personality, Ted Mack helped everyone share the rudimentary and the advanced principles of program control in a modest and unassuming manner. Ted knew what I suggested earlier in this chapter, that many people and many organizations don't know good time control from bad time control; many people seem simply to accept bad time control as inevitable and naturally to be expected. Even after improvements have been instituted, some people will never know the difference or even care whether meetings start and stop on time.

Fortunately, most people *do* notice an improvement when things have been fixed; but though they may not thank you for your part in that improvement, they appreciate the saving of *their* time. Commercial conferences *will* observe the difference; commercial firms have to pay for any wasted time, and they want and *demand* effectiveness. Whether you get compliments or not, time control is important. Probably the unfortunate truth is that, appreciated or not, time saving in conferences *is* most awfully important; don't expect solicitous praise; take it as expected by your constituents that time will be saved.

Ted Mack realized that this lack of praise for good time control was inevitable. I shall always remember Ted's comment when I observed the expertise of his handling those sessions at the IPA so many years ago, and I expressed my thanks to him for what I knew was a thankless job. His reply: "I'm afraid that only you and my wife understand the significance of that compliment—no one else." Ted was right then, but changes have been made in the decades-old bad practices of time control in the International Platform Association. He would be pleased today to see what Dr. Harry Weber has accomplished, building on that wonderful example of the late Ted Mack.

Shall We Run on Time?

Perhaps, as I suggested in the beginning of this chapter, some readers are reading this chapter only to find out what tricks I have up my sleeve, never intending to attempt what I told you in the beginning is a very difficult task: starting and stopping sessions on schedule. You will have discovered what I suggested in the beginning: I have no magic elixir for solving the time control problem. Time control *is* difficult. If you are not ready for it, just revert to what *Robert's Rules* suggests for the first meeting of an organization and let a few minutes go by before attempting to start the meeting. Later, you may find that the audience gets so interested in the meetings you are conducting that you feel sufficiently encouraged to ask your group the first question posed in item 1 of Chapter 5. When you are ready to apply time control, you should ask the question, *not before.* Maybe you will find that doing it comes more easily than you had thought.

Based on the advice I have given in Chapter 27, you may be convinced of the desirability of utilizing a hotel for your deliberative conference rather than some convention hall or conference center. If your meeting will be larger than about 500 people, you may have greater difficulty in finding a hotel that can accommodate all your people for sleeping rooms; but you can still run a very large conference wholly within a single hotel except for some spillover of sleeping rooms into an adjacent hotel. Thus, your major dealings can still be with a single hotel. Yet you may have received some brochures from a convention center, and you may wish to compare rates between that place and nearby hotels to see whether you can save some money by utilizing the convention center for the conference space and the adjacent hotel for the sleeping-room space. Although the arguments given in Chapter 27 will usually apply, there can sometimes be mitigating circumstances that will make such a comparison desirable.

I can recall only one case in which such a combination of hotel and conference center was practical and the rates were comparable for a conference of several hundred people. This was in a European city where one major-chain hotel was built as a part of a central municipal convention center. In our first negotiations, we were told that we would have to negotiate the sleeping rooms with the hotel and then the conference space with the convention center (the usual case), but after other cities began to show strong competitive interest in our conference, the hotel made an arrangement that I have never seen done for such a small conference. The director of sales for that hotel worked out an arrangement with the conference center to rent for us whatever conference space we would need. He made an offer that was the best of all combinations for us by absorbing the conference room cost whether we chose his hotel conference rooms or the separate conference center. Never has this combination been offered to us elsewhere, even in the United States, where competition is usually far better than in Europe. Our preference was for the conference space in the hotel simply because it was a lot

30

How to Negotiate with a Hotel

closer for our people, even though the conference center was in the same building as the hotel and was beautifully appointed. It turned out that the city and the hotel could not compete on rates with another city in that country, and we chose a different city.

Making Arrangements

Although selecting a hotel and completing the arrangements in major commercial cities of the United States is rather simple, it may not be so simple in other not-so-commercial cities of the United States. When a city has gone through what I shall call the Hilton-Sheraton metamorphosis, things get better in a hurry for the convention planner trying to deal with a hotel. To illustrate this syndrome, let me take San Francisco as an example. (The people at the San Francisco Convention Bureau will not likely get very upset over my telling this story because they have heard it from me many times, and they understand what happened very well as they ponder the olden days before competition in San Francisco.)

Once upon a time, conventions all wanted to go to San Francisco. The people of America's favorite city knew San Francisco was well liked as a convention town, and they wanted to keep it that way. They didn't want to get so many hotels in town that prices would get watered down. Those hotels that were there didn't want any interlopers sopping up the convention income. Business was good; the Nob Hill hotels were always full. Why should there be any more hotels? Then business would be bad for all hotels, and the city would get run-down, with no income and no fixing up of the hotels, and conventions would shun San Francisco. That would be terrible.

Back in those olden days we held a small conference in the city, in a small, not very good hotel in the cheap district; later, our group became larger and needed a larger, better hotel, but our people couldn't afford the going Nob Hill rates; so we held our meeting elsewhere in town, but still with high prices and still in the wrong-side-of-the-tracks location. Our group wanted so much to go back to San Francisco again, but it also wanted better accommodations and lower rates. I snooped around San Francisco but unhappily discovered that the rates were getting higher, the hotels were getting snootier, and the convention bureau was finding less and less interest by the hotels in new convention groups unless they were rich.

Those were the golden olden days of San Francisco. I lowered the boom and told the convention bureau that we would not set foot in San Francisco again until the hotels, the convention bureau, and the city decided they wanted our business. I told them to call me when some new, big, competitive hotels were built. I could anticipate what was likely to happen because I had watched other cities change their tune when some new, competitive hotels came into them. I had watched one Texas city as first Hilton and then Sheraton managed to get approval from the city fathers to build hotels there. The change had been unbelievable. Instead of stuffy (yes, stuffy) old hotels that hadn't been modernized in years and still charged high rates, we were treated to beautiful new facilities in hotels that wanted us and proved that point over and over by the way they treated us. The Hilton-Sheraton metamorphosis had occurred in Texas.

I had seen it happen elsewhere, and it finally happened in San Francisco. It was slow coming in San Francisco; I got the first inkling of the change when the local Hilton people called to tell me that their approval to build had been held up on technicalities by the local people for far too long and that they were just about to get it pried loose from all the red tape. Approval took years. But the city's foot dragging finally was overcome, and the Hilton people were quoting actual opening dates and quite satisfactory rates for everybody's second hometown. Still, the old-line hotels on Nob Hill were just as snooty as ever, just as expensive as before, and just as full. The convention bureau was as happy as could be; now it had a lot more rooms to sell.

To make a long story not too much shorter, I shall soon get to the point after a suitably long period of suspense for you, my readers. Although I had long been able to view drawings of the conference room layout and could even sleep in the hotel, I could not accept final arrangements until I had a specific named conference room in the letter of agreement, along with actual costs for everything. We were expecting to use a large conference space that had not yet been completed, and I insisted upon seeing the final layout before acceptance. It finally happened, and I settled the arrangements; time went by fast, and our group showed up for the conference. We were the first convention group to use that new space; the hotel was pleased to have us and showed it in its attitude and in its handling of our affair. Our people were happy; the hotel was happy; it wanted us back; our people wanted to go back. That was more than 20 years ago; our group has been back many times to Frank Karliner's establishment, our fond name for the San Francisco Hilton, called after the genial, efficient assistant general manager who got us to come in the first place and has been making our arrangements there so effectively for the last 20 years.

You may ask what happened to the original hotels after the Hilton and then others came into the city. Competition was good for the city, for all the hotels, and certainly for many convention groups that otherwise could never have held a convention in San Francisco. The Hilton has expanded its facilities several times, the older hotels have built large additions, and there seems to be plenty of business for every new hotel that comes to town. The convention bureau is proud of the city and cites statistics to show the phenomenal growth of convention business in that beautiful city by the sea. Needless to say (but I will, anyway), all the hotels in that city have been after our group for years, hoping to woo us away from the Hilton. Our group may change hotels some day, but not until there is a good commercial reason to leave Frank's place.

I wish I could say that all cities by now have passed through the Hilton-Sheraton metamorphosis and that arrangements are easy everywhere. Not so, although most commercial cities in the United States have done so. In Europe, however, it is an entirely different story. Convention groups must go through that agony all over again, as they decide to try their luck in European capitals or, even worse, in the resort cities of Europe. Because European conferences can be quite trying for the neophyte conference planner, let me take the European big city as an example to show how to go about arranging conferences in problem cities. While you might safely relax some of the rules for hotels with which you have had good success in the United States, you would not do so for European meetings, at least until you have had experience with a hotel and a city.

In Chapter 27, my Rule 6 is most important in urging advance documentation of *everything* before accepting any arrangements with a hotel. How should you do this? Should you write up what you want agreed to? Should you have the hotel write up the items? Most experts concur that it is the responsibility of the hotel to make the *complete* proposal so that you need only accept it by a simple letter. Easier said than done. You are in for disillusionment when you visit a hotel and find that you and the management can agree upon just about everything; the questionable items are still to be checked with top management, so you head for home, expecting a letter soon. But it doesn't come. Months go by; you have phoned the hotel and received promises of "Letter next week; everything settled." But nothing comes until so much time has gone by that you can't remember any of the things you talked about (next time you will take better notes, or you will find a better place to file them so that you can reconstruct the agreements when the letter finally does come).

More time goes by; you phone and learn that the sales representative has left that hotel and the new director of sales has never heard of you. Back to the drawing board; back to that city, to visit the hotels all over again and start from scratch. This time you are lucky. You get a letter within 4 months, but hold everything; all it says is, "We shall be glad to host your fine group and will accommodate your every need with suitable conference space and appropriate sleeping rooms at very fine rates for the dates of ———." What do you do when you receive that kind of letter? Welcome to the club! After you have received a few such letters, you will learn that it isn't easy to get much of anything tied down by a hotel, even one that really wants your business.

As a neophyte, you will probably contribute to this bad situation by repeatedly visiting the hotel, each time coming away convinced that the letter will be on your desk before you get home. But it doesn't arrive. True, most major United States hotels catering to the convention trade don't procrastinate like that, but wait until you try to get details tied down by a major European hotel. You will find yourself back in the middle ages of conventions. If the hotel is a major American chain hotel in a large European city, you will receive numerous phone calls from your local representative, inquiring whether anything has come from "them" yet. He will tell you that he will be in that city next week: "Would you like me to jog them for the letter again?" Of course you would, but the letter still may not get pried loose.

SIX SUGGESTIONS

Another year can go by. You thought that you had everything agreed. Why can't you get a letter tying things down? Why can't the head office of the chain get something done in *its* hotel overseas? (It really isn't its hotel; the chain just provides some reservations service, international publicity, and some management expertise, but the ownership is probably local in that city, and the owners, with the money, don't pay an awful lot of attention to "those Americans.") This brings me to one means of expediting the letter from a hotel. It doesn't solve all the problems, but it will save you a lot of travel money back and forth, and it will force some early thought from a hotel about what it can offer you. Here is my

Suggestion No. 1

Refuse to set foot in a hotel until you have received in writing a proposal that makes at least a little sense and addresses almost all your needs, with specific conference rooms, on specific days and at specific rates (or free), and with specific quantities of sleeping rooms for certain dates at stated rate structures.

Once you have received such a proposal, you know that somebody read your letter or talked to the chain's local representative from your city about your needs and obtained at least a rudimentary understanding of what you want and thinks he can supply it. You may not like the first proposal, but it can be modified by mail a lot more cheaply than by personal visit to a far-off country. Even if a European hotel offers to pay your expenses to visit it, don't fall for the offer; it may expect you to come and sign up on the basis of mutual trust. If you do, you ought to have your head examined. Stay home. Write a letter if you have to. Get the local chain people to be your messenger to that faraway place. Get the competition lined up in that city and in other possible European cities. Hold your horses. Your constituents will not be happy if you traipse off to foreign shores and come back empty-handed. Neither would they condone an agreement of hope. It may be difficult to move mountains, but eventually, with sufficient patience, the mountain will come to Mohammed. Staying away is your only leverage. Stay away.

I recall the difficult time we had in selecting a city and hotel for our 1976 European affair. That particular meeting was to be held in conjunction with a European airline conference, and the host airline for that meeting was to be Deutsche Lufthansa (DLH). Its people would have liked the conference to be held in Hamburg, where its maintenance base was situated; thus they and I started dickering with Hamburg hotels. The arrangements were not the best, with rates rather high, so DLH expressed willingness to consider other German cities as well. I provided some documentation on the needs for our conference (to be held in the same hotel the week prior to the European conference) and asked my DLH friends to dig up as many specific proposals in writing as they could. The proposals were pretty sparse, but I got lots of invitations to "come visit our fine establishment." I insisted upon commitments in advance on what the hotels could offer, and after I had prodded local chain representatives for many a month, the hotels finally realized that I meant "No proposal, no visit."

After many months I had received sufficient proposals to warrant a trip. My DLH friend Peter Reichow was quite new to conference facility hunting and arranged to be gone from his office with me for a whole week to help me check out hotels. Armed with those proposals, I met Peter at the first hotel, in Hamburg, bright and early on a Monday morning for what he thought would be a week-long trip around Germany. By Tuesday afternoon, I said goodbye to Peter in Berlin after having covered seven hotels in Hamburg, Frankfurt, Munich, and Berlin in a total time of 30 hours. Soon after I returned home, I agreed with Peter that the Sheraton Munich was the best hotel for our affair, and I had it settled in writing. That was several years before the meeting; the time came, everything came off beautifully in Munich, and neither of us had again set foot in the hotel since that rush trip in and out of it several years previously. Munich is a better bargain than most European cities simply because of the expanded housing for the 1972 Olympics; thus the city is better equipped with large, fine hotels than most other cities of Europe.

You may ask why you shouldn't visit many hotels in advance, as the occasion permits, so that you can make a first approximation of which hotels in which cities might be suitable in case you eventually get a proper proposal. Yes, visits to hotels are important if you make those visits *business* visits rather than just fun visits. Site inspection without proper notes is generally useless. Within a month, the variety of hotels you have observed casually becomes just a blur in your memory. To make such visits useful later, I offer:

Suggestion No. 2

Take copious notes. Keep a potential hotel and site file. When you visit any hotel, either as a paying guest, a guest of the hotel sales department, or a drop-in visitor unannounced, have a notebook handy for conference room notes and layout sketches and details that would never appear in the regular official hotel brochures (such as the location of rest rooms near the conference room, obstructions like corner bars in conference rooms, types of lighting, firmness and acoustic characteristics of partitions and moving walls, and hours of operation of the coffee shop or lunch counters, as well as restaurants, telephone service, room service, bellman service, and so on).

As you travel, you may do much of your snooping as you pass through hotels and cities en route to other conferences. A good record of possible sites and hotels can be extremely helpful when your organization develops a spontaneous desire to meet in South Podunk next April. If you have a checklist on South Podunk (or even central Podunk), you may know that the town has certain facilities but that they are not particularly modern, they are always crowded, and April would be just about impossible. You should talk the organization out of it by suggesting North Squeedunk as a better location with *three* fine hotels.

Hotel inspections, although necessary, can be fraught with problems. Many experts tell horror stories of their visits to hotels under special conditions, under which they were invited by the hotel management and squired around the facilities, observing all the good things the management wanted them to see, with beautifully appointed suites, lavish food, outstanding service, and accommodations leaving nothing to be desired. But these facilities were not what the conference attendees found when the conference arrived; somehow, things were different and rather austere. Those experts learned that it is better to make an inspection of your own beforehand, so that you can ask the proper questions of the management when you arrive for your official inspection. This procedure is particularly desirable for neophytes who may truly believe that *all* conference attendees will receive the same treatment as the convention manager does on an inspection trip.

Hotel inspections can sometimes produce other problems. I recall some snooping I did, unannounced one evening, at a West Coast hotel which I was expecting to use for a future conference if things worked out properly (which they did). It was around 8 P.M., and I was checking the various ballrooms in a rather quiet and deserted convention area of the hotel, which is my usual practice. I was surprised to discover that our ballroom was directly adjacent to another ballroom with a less-than-solid door between the two. Would the sound from one ballroom interfere with our meeting?

To my great delight, I discovered that some shindig was going on in that adjacent ballroom; I could hear faint sounds from a public address system entering "our" ballroom. I moved closer to the door to check the sound level. I decided that it would be no problem. As I started away from that door, I was grabbed by the hotel security people. What was I doing there? I kidded the staff about how I always wandered around in hotel lobbies as a part of my inspection for future meetings, but my explanation didn't go over very well. Never before had I been bothered by any hotel staff as I made my rounds in and out of dark conference rooms all over the world. Why this time?

It all came out OK when I did a little name dropping of people in the sales department whom I knew well, even though those people didn't know I was there. The hotel people accepted my explanation and then told me what had caused them concern: the speaker in that ballroom was Governor Reagan. Only then did I remember that just a year earlier Sen. Robert F. Kennedy had been assassinated in that same hotel, the Ambassador, in Los Angeles. A frightening memory! Thus, it is wise to have your credentials with you when you make such inspections if you wish to avoid mix-ups.

Even when you visit a hotel as the guest of the management to inspect the property, you will find it especially helpful to make your own inspection privately the night before the hotel people are to receive you officially. Then you can quietly wander around the hotel, get a feel for the layout of the conference space, and be prepared with your questions (such as whether the adjacent ballroom *will* or *will not* be rented to another group during your meetings and, if so, what restrictions the hotel will make on the class of group in the adjacent ballroom. Recall the example, given in Chapter 23, of the circus next door and nothing but a curtain to absorb the sound of the circus band. The next day, when you meet with representatives of the management for an official tour, they will be mightily surprised at how much you already know about their hotel. You will receive the treatment of a professional rather than the treatment they give the usual rank amateur.

You may be surprised to hear that the majority of convention managers with whom the usual hotel must deal are really quite rank amateurs rather than the sophisticated experts you might expect. After you have developed some experience in negotiating *successfully* over a period of many years, you will know this as a fact yourself. If you have any doubts about its truth, ask your best friend in the hotel business for a candid answer and see what he says. I know what he will tell you. Most of the people with whom the hotels must deal seem to make up for their lack of experience by a sense of bravado, apparently to cover up their inexperience. Hotels end up by giving amateur reception to amateur visitors, because they give the convention manager about what he wants whether it is what he really needs or should have. "The customer is always right," and the customer gets what he requests (for a price) if he insists upon it, in violation of my Chapter 27 Rules 4, 5, 7, and 8.

My first awakening to the inexperience of convention managers came abruptly during a seminar for conference planners conducted some years ago by the staff of *Successful Meetings Magazine*. During numerous workshops on how to arrange a conference, I was amazed by the questions of the many convention managers from big business. In chatting with those people, I discovered that big business generally appoints some individual or a whole department to manage and arrange almost all their corporate meetings and conferences. Management was quite happy to send its people to such seminars as the one I was attending, because it believed that this was the best route to a crash course to make them experts overnight. I learned from many of these people that they had been in their jobs only a week, or several months, or possibly a year. They were all anxious to learn, but it was obvious that they, too, would move up the ladder in a few months and no longer have any need for the expertise with which they were being crammed. Conference management in many organizations is a part-time task, to be learned quickly and then forgotten as the convention manager shifts around in the corporate bureaucracy. Even though such convention managers generally report to some high-level executive (perhaps the president or the chairman of the board), they do not stay in that convention-managing job very long.

Lack of longevity in conference management does not always extend to trade associations or professional organizations, in which a career in conference management may cover quite a span of time. But many trade associations seem to be amateurs at the conference management gambit, because top management has more important things to do (it thinks) than to organize conferences. I may lament this lack of experience in the business, but my purpose is not to criticize managements for doing what they think is best with their time but only to document here what I believe to be the true situation and the lack of experience in *average* (I don't say *all*) convention managers. If you recognize that hotel people will therefore, in the *average case*, be confronted by amateurs, is it any wonder that an experienced convention manager may have some difficulty in locating a sales representative in a hotel who knows a professional when he meets one? In major United States hotels (unfortunately, this is not true in Europe), salespeople will be utterly delighted and will fall all over you when they discover someone who can discuss hotel capabilities and user needs in a professional manner. This is why I added, in Chapter 27, my Rule 8. The hotel people would all like to help you; if you treat them properly and help them help you, they will be tickled pink. I make this next offering for neophyte convention managers in the hope that it will point such individuals in the right direction:

Suggestion No. 3

If you are attempting to negotiate with a major hotel (with a good reputation) something (or everything) that you do not understand, be candid and tell the hotel people that you need help and advice on what to negotiate for. Let them lead you through the negotiations, and you will gain a remarkable insight into the hotel business and the convention business.

I cannot treat the subject of hotel negotiations without at least some mention of the proper means of dealing with sleeping-room rates. This topic has upset many a convention manager, and it has confused many a hotel man. Years ago, it was quite proper to expect that a hotel would commit itself to specific sleeping-room rates before you signed up for a conference there. Then, you may have read in Chapter 27, Rule 9, that you should arrange your conferences many years in advance, as smart convention planners all do now. Now what do you do? Ever hear of inflation? Only the little hotels will commit themselves to rates in advance, even 1 year in advance, and the major hotels simply state, "Our rates are X dollars for singles and Y dollars for doubles. We will set aside 300 rooms for your fine group and will let you know when the rates are established for that year."

You will say, "Why do the little hotels quote rates?" I can only suggest that you read the fine print written between the lines of the handwriting on the wall in such letters of acceptance. Even if you do get a commitment to specific rates at a future date, I wish you the best of luck when the conference date rolls around. I have a whole drawer full of such letters and follow-up letters, with sad tales of inflation, and how the rate structure has "gone higher than anticipated," and how I must certainly understand that their fine hotel cannot accommodate us without a small increase (about 250 percent) in the rates. All those letters you have in the file of several years ago are just so much paper.

If you protest the increase, you should expect the next typical letter with the words: "Surely you didn't really believe, back in 1954 [or whenever it was you made the initial arrangements], that those 1954 rates would still apply in 1998 [or whenever you are complaining], as you have been in the convention business long enough to know that inflation is horrible and cannot be predicted in advance. Besides, we have wholly new management since your arrangements were negotiated back in 1954 and new policies [we fired that sales manager many years ago for making silly agreements like the one you arranged], and today we have a *responsible* management that offers a fine property second to none and with a rate structure that is competitive with other fine hotels in our class. You are an expert in conference management, and you would not want to take your fine group to a hotel with facilities today commensurate with the rates you had in mind back in 1954, would you?"

Halfway through this missive you realize that you have been had and that you have deserved it. You do know about inflation, and you certainly do recognize the implications of Chapter 27, Rule 3, as every convention manager worth his salt must recognize them.

So, what should you have done? Here is one subject on which you will seldom, if ever, get any useful suggestions from hotel representatives, simply because they still have not become accustomed to coping with inflation, or even admitting to it, and they never want to call attention to the *fact* that their rates will be higher next year or maybe even next week. Thus, they avoid this question as carefully as they can. There is a glimmer of hope, however, in a recognition by other writers that there most certainly is a solution to this dilemma that does work for a convention manager and for a hotel so that both parties will have an express agreement and consensus on what the rates will be when their 3-years-away conference date rolls around. This is the procedure which I have been touting for many years and which I have employed successfully *even in dealing with European hotels* for over a decade.

Before I delve into that procedure, I should provide some help to the neophyte on how rate structures are developed, publicized, and administered in the major international chain hotels. Smaller hotels use procedures similar to, if not explicitly the same as, the procedures of the large chains. Using Hilton as an example, suppose that you, as an individual, want to go to the Chattanooga Choo Choo Hilton Inn. Assume that it is 1979; so you look in the Hilton *1979 Guaranteed Range of Rates Plan,* and you find that singles are priced in six steps from $28 to $38, and doubles or twins are priced just $8 higher. Generally, you can request a $28 single and have it confirmed, thereby *guaranteeing* that price when you arrive, even though nothing but more expensive rooms may now exist.

If the time of year, heavy advance bookings, special events, or whatever get in the way, the hotel (through Hilton Reservations Service or direct) may have to confirm the price for the rooms of which they have the most, which is shown in the book as $34 for Chattanooga. If conditions are really jammed up, the hotel may have to confirm $36 or $38 for a room; but you know in advance what the tariff will be through the guaranteed-rate program that Hilton has used for many years. There are other published rate schedules that Hilton makes available for groups and for special business travelers, but the principle is still the same.

Published rates give the public a range of prices to accommodate, at one extreme, the individual who wants a small, perhaps slightly austere, sleeping room and, at the other end of the range, a businessman wanting a better-than-average room for stature, better comfort, or whatever. Suites are not usually priced on these rate structures but should be arranged separately. Unlike the rooms of older hotels of a bygone era, the lower-priced rooms are not that bad; they may be on lower floors, with a back view, or possibly adjacent to the service elevator, but these are not problems for most travelers or conventioneers preferring economy rather than show.

For trade conferences, the customers may prefer the lower-priced rooms, while the purveyors will want either the top regular rooms or fancy suites for entertaining clients and potential customers. American commercial hotels have capitalized for years on the American class system by offering exactly what the customer wants and needs. This is not so in either American resort hotels or European hotels. American resort hotels are willing to construct rate structures for a convention group that wants them, so that rooms with an ocean-front view, high in the sky, will be priced higher than the same-size room, down low, overlooking the front street; the European hotel seems unwilling to concede that one room is more desirable than another room, even if one room looks out over the Mediterranean and another fronts on the garbage dump.

These are the procedures used for pricing sleeping rooms in the United States. Now, how do you apply them to conference planning when rates are escalating every 10 minutes? Here's the answer: you meet with the sales representative of the Chattanooga Choo Choo Hilton Inn (or work the planning out through your local Hilton national sales representative) with the rate structure in front of you. The representative already knows that you are working on a September 1982 time period, with arrivals to be on Tuesday and departures to be on Friday, in a week that you have already settled upon with him when no holidays will interfere and that you have both checked to satisfy yourselves that no major public event now known will present any conflict.

You ask him what the rate would be if you came in the same equivalent week in 1979. He will give you some set of rates, based upon the current rate schedules for 1979. You then convert those dollar figures into percentage variances from the 1979 rate structures, right off the sheets. Let's suppose that he tells you that he can give you a 5 percent reduction from the across-the-board rates, that the same percentage reduction will apply in 1982, and that he will put this in writing now and let you know the actual dollar values when the rate structure for September 1982 is established. Or perhaps he suspects that you may want all minimum-priced rooms and that he needs to be more careful in his offer. Perhaps he may offer you the rates in the accompanying table.

Quantity of rooms	Rate bracket	Discount (percent)
Not to exceed 25	Bottom doubles	0
Not to exceed 15	Bottom singles	0
Not to exceed 40	Second singles or doubles	5
100	Third, fourth, or fifth singles or doubles	10
Not to exceed 30	Top singles or doubles	15

The reason for the limit on top-bracket rooms is that hotels don't have many more of these higher-priced rooms than they do rooms in the lower-priced category. Most modern hotels have the greatest number of rooms in the middle (third or fourth) bracket. Although the quantities in each bracket can be shifted to accommodate a particularly important conference, don't expect to get a commitment for all low-priced rooms.

From the above example, it is obvious that both parties can now have a clear understanding and a documented agreement on what the rate structure will be in 1982 despite the vagaries of inflation. This leads us to:

Suggestion No. 4

If a hotel man makes you a firm dollar quotation of room rates for a period off in the future, be mighty suspicious. You may wonder why, if Hilton and other major-chain hotels quote rates in five brackets (six for some hotels), so many conventions announce run-of-the-house rates for their accommodations? My answer is that many hotel salespeople know that a lot of convention managers *think* they are getting real bargains by negotiating run-of-the-house rates with a hotel, so they cater to that demand and offer such rates even without a convention manager's requesting them.

When you analyze such rates, you usually discover that they are somewhat *above* the median, or most usual, rates, so the hotel isn't giving you much of a bargain, particularly since it is much easier and cheaper for them to administer run-of-the-house rates. This is particularly true for the large corporate sales meeting or other corporate conference for which individuals will not pay their own bills but the hotel will obtain rooming lists from the corporation and bill the corporation directly. In that case, it is quite proper to arrange run-of-the-house rates, and the discount should be a lot better than with each individual making his own reservations.

For a classless convention or conference (*not* suppliers and customers but merely people), run-of-the-house rates may be satisfactory, but they generally are no great bargain to either the hotel or the group unless almost all the hotel space is used up by the convention and the hotel will accommodate few if any other guests. But that situation doesn't exist much anymore; it used to be the case in Miami Beach many, many years ago, when the season finished on a particular day, and not so many years ago in Puerto Rico, when everybody left at the end of one particular week in the late spring. In those days, the hotels could be kept open 1 more week if they could book a large convention into the hotel on the day on which everyone else left.

With the demise of the season in a particular city, the rate structures became better equalized throughout the year, so that hotel people in most cities today will accept a convention group at any time in preference to rich denizens of the season. Times have changed, and conventions are in. That is the reason for Chapter 27's Rule 3.

When a convention develops a hankering to go overseas, particularly to Europe, the convention manager has real problems. He is no longer working with salespeople who deal with conventions of all kinds daily;

he discovers that attitudes are quite typical of the olden days in the United States, when trade conferences were not courted by even the major hotels and you were darned lucky if you could get a resort hotel even to speak to you kindly.

In the European hotels of the American chains, the directors of sales have often received their training in the large commercial facilities in the United States. One such director of sales, regretting his inability to offer commercial deals, as he could in the United States, showed me his one big ballroom, noting sadly how he was used to hotels of the same size in the United States offering a dozen ballrooms that large. A hotel in Europe can quote a conference price of thousands of dollars per day without batting an eye; social events alone can keep those ballrooms filled every night with a lavish formal dinner that must be set up early that morning.

Here is one illustration of the problems facing a hotel man in a major city of Europe just a few short years ago (new hotels are being built that may eventually alleviate such problems). We were holding a major conference in a large, new, modern hotel in that city, and we employed the only ballroom for our affair. As I was packing up to leave after a successful week of meetings, the management told me about a shindig that was taking place in several weeks' time in that same ballroom. It seems that at this major affair being held there all the crowned heads of Europe would be present for the daytime conference. Belatedly, the planners decided that they should feed those kings and queens, but there was no other ballroom for the middle-of-the-day repast, and time would not permit transporting them elsewhere. What did they do? You would never guess. The hotel arranged box lunches, with everyone, including their hostess, Queen Elizabeth, eating in the foyer of the ballroom, where we had held a large manufacturers' reception during our week. For us, the foyer was no problem; but we'll bet it was a mess for the kings and queens. For receptions, no one expects to sit down; for managing a box lunch and a cup of coffee, a chair would be much appreciated.

Many a time I have spent hours measuring and remeasuring a too small conference room in a large hotel in Europe to see whether our small group of a few hundred could squeeze itself in. Usually we managed satisfactorily, but not always. With only a single small ballroom, it should be evident why those particular hotels have to charge an arm and a leg for space rental. Fortunately, the newer conference hotels are much improved, and the competitive situation is getting better. With American chain hotels everywhere and with American representatives for most of the large European chain hotels, it is so much easier now than it was just a few years ago. I even boast that I have arranged small conferences (approximately 100 participants) in many of the large cities of Europe on short notice, with acceptable arrangements and with only one local telephone call. Yes, it can be done in cities where you know the hotels and the people and the convention bureaus and where the hotels have knowledgeable local representatives, as we do in Washington, D.C. But still it can be quite a challenge for cities and hotels where you have not met before and where you have difficulty in cultivating the competitive spirit that is found almost everywhere in the United States.

The foregoing lack of interest in *you*, a convention manager with a good reputation in the United States, courted by every hotel and convention bureau there for your business, is another important reason why I offered Suggestion No. 1 earlier in this chapter. If you wander into a European hotel unannounced, you will be lucky if you can get anyone to talk to you. Even if you write in advance, the hotel people still will shuttle you around as though you were a liability. Only if the local representative for that hotel has started and waged a drumming campaign on your behalf and supplied all the United States convention bureau reports on your meetings for the past 10 years, will you get any reception. Sometimes you can work through the local convention bureau in the European city with better results, but its people seem to have very little influence on the status quo of the European hotel community. Even the big-chain representatives in the United States have little influence on their own properties in Europe, as I pointed out earlier in this chapter. This gives you:

Suggestion No. 5

If your group *really* wants to meet in Europe and you have to arrange the facilities for the first time, (1) be quite rich; (2) be very patient; (3) get yourself armed with all information you can collect; (4) procrastinate as long as you can, hoping that the hotel and convention bureau people will learn something about your organization's past record and decide to want you or a new hotel will arise in that city; (5) plan to write lots of letters, containing lots of detail on what you must have in a proposal; (6) apply follow-up that you would never have believed necessary to make simple arrangements; (7) visit for an inspection only after things are nearly settled with several alternative locations; (8) tie everything down in writing even if you have to write the proposal yourself and wait for the hotel's acceptance in writing of your terms; and (9) be very, very tolerant of the conditions under which those hotel people must operate.

Whew! Still want to go to Europe? It's worth all the trouble and worth all the extra expense when your group finally arrives and you discover that mixed in the group are hundreds of people who have never visited Europe before and you get to watch them enjoy their first visit *at your convention*. Even in our group, which I repeatedly have referred to as the most sophisticated traveling industry on earth, manufacturers who go to Europe at least twice a month tell me they plan years in advance for our conferences; they expect to take their families along and have a really happy time. The airline people, who spend much of their time in Europe, express the same comments. European conventions and conferences and meetings are well liked by Americans and thoroughly enjoyed by our (and your) European hosts, who will love showing off the old cities and rare art treasures, museums, castles, or whatever. I remember well our shindig in Munich, where the Deutsches Museum was inundated with our engineers at the very hour our meeting adjourned on Friday. I recall running into all my friends, American, European, and others, in the Amsterdam art galleries, the Tower of London, the Bavarian Alps, the Leningrad Ballet, and the Roman Forum, just as I would meet them all at the wharf in San Francisco.

Negotiations with a hotel or a city may be difficult in some parts of the world. But they eventually come out all right with patience and tolerance, leaving me to conclude this Chapter with one more suggestion:

Suggestion No. 6

Please read Rule 8 of Chapter 27 once more; it really is quite true.

Fasten your seat belt. *Now* I shall talk about money. Get ready for a rough ride. There is no such thing as a free lunch; as I stated several times, your constituents don't attend your commercial deliberative conferences just for fun and games. Whether or not your constituents can identify the costs they pay for your meetings, they still contribute a lot in personnel and time. Meetings are expensive; they must fill the bill and satisfy the constituents' needs, and they must not be *too* expensive compared with the benefits.

Comparative Costs

Too expensive *compared with what?* How can anyone gauge the too high costs in the real world of competitive services? If you don't like the standardization service of your friendly neighborhood association or if the costs levied upon your firm seem too high for the benefits, you can just take your business away and go down the street to another store and buy your standardization service there. You can shop around for the best service at the lowest price. Ha, ha, ha!

If you ponder the eight epochs that I described in Appendix 1, you will ask yourself the question, "How do we *know* we are holding efficient meetings when we cannot compare one group holding our meetings with another group doing the same chore for our industry?" This may be a ponderous philosophical question and no more than that, or it may be a real question to which we should give more than the usual thought. If Appendix 1 shows the power of competition in standardization for a major industry, why should you not shop around in the conference management field for the organization that can give you your greatest money's worth. Maybe it would be a good idea. But I have seldom seen indications that this shopping around is done or even contemplated seriously. It is something akin to urging the U.S. Navy to shop around for the best available aircraft carrier. A nice idea, but how can you shop for aircraft carriers in someone's warehouse or showroom? How can you shop for a meeting in a warehouse or showroom?

31

Costs and Budgeting: The Bottom Line

You could only set up another organization in the business and try that one for a few years or decades to see if it outperformed the other outfit; if it didn't, you could, in a decade or so, return to the original purveyor of services.

I remember the business which a friend set up for himself many years ago and which proved to be quite a remunerative activity: he contracted with nonprofit organizations to show them what they were doing wrong, in wasting money and in not recouping the costs of doing business. Apparently there were enough nonprofit firms losing too much money to stay in business. He explained that the lack of competition for a nonprofit organization makes the management and all the activity very sluggish and nonresponsive to means of reducing costs that other organizations (ordinary corporations) would adopt immediately when costs got too high compared with income. He described the lethargy of such organizations and how an outsider was needed to tell them what they should have known and *done* for themselves.

This *lack* of competition and lack of a good measure for comparison of one meeting with another meeting or with some absolute standard of goodness may be a major millstone for trade associations. Always suspect but never exonerated, a trade association—or, in fact, any organization attempting to accommodate and placate a wide variety of interests making up an industry or a consortium of firms—must always be searching for ways to save money. Though such an organization may have been established by top management in the particular industry, it will eventually be accused by its originators of empire building, lackadaisical accounting practices, or poor control of costs.

Although this chapter should be prime and be placed at the beginning, it can only be near the end. It is as your organization is nearing the end of an important endeavor and successful accomplishment for your constituents that, when least expected, the ax will fall. Austerity in your industry will hit trade associations even harder; no matter the benefit, costs must be cut. This will happen over and over without any pattern except irregularity. And there is probably good reason for all this happening. When you work for a variety of bosses, firms, or interests, you must think economy first, last, and always, continuously and devilishly. Although this chapter may be at the end, that bottom line will trip you up even if there may be no comparison with any absolute measure of performance, quality of service, or cost of doing business.

Growth of Costs

In this matter of cost, we finally come to one of the small disadvantages of the Goldfish Bowl deliberative conference: by their very nature Goldfish Bowl conferences not only are large but are visible for miles, even across oceans and continents. The very strength of such conferences is a disadvantage when it comes to paying for them. Unless you watch everything you do, you will be accused of developing the largest-budgeted boondoggle in your industry. You may start small and austere, just as I have suggested, but you will grow in size and stature, and then in opulence, as the expansion continues. Your people will try to continue the activities you started as a small (invisible) group; perhaps verbatim recording of meetings, perhaps social affairs that were economical while they were invisible, perhaps banquets, perhaps simple coffee breaks with coffee.

Whatever the activities were, the costs will start upward when the size of the conference grows. A small (invisible) coffee break grows into a monster of a hotel bill, as I pointed out in Chapter 22. Although you can arrange a small social get-together in the evening, it can turn into a large cocktail party bash that not only costs a fortune but now needs some professional organization hired by you to organize it with the hotel. All these simple things grow in cost. Perhaps it was fortunate for me that I was raised in an industry that had many austere periods and few good times; I was weaned on economy and even the appearance of economy.

I have watched many a conference in our industry and in others expand out of all bounds into a major activity, seemingly fulfilling a need for a larger affair. I have seen those conferences turned off overnight by the people who had to pay the bills. Despite the lack of competition and the lack of a measuring stick for economy and efficiency, the turnoff in each case was quick and final, and something was now left undone for that community or industry. Some triggering mechanism seems to act to wreak havoc in a stable activity that has seemed to be doing a fine job for its constituents. And I am not talking about the effects of preoccupation with folderol, as described in Chapter 8, when the stultification of a group can justify its demise from Foil's law. I am recalling many fine groups that simply hit the fan, almost instantaneously, after a long and useful life.

I know of only one protection against such a happening: continued alertness to costs; continued overpreoccupation with any increases in costs; continued vigilance to find ways of doing more for less each succeeding month and each succeeding year; and relentless watching to eliminate unnecessary activities, particularly highly visible activities that could be *considered* to be unnecessary by your constituents.

Questions to Ask

This chapter cannot delve into all the things you should watch out for, nor can it give any advice that is guaranteed to keep your conferences from being scuttled; it can only suggest alertness to all things. Here is a tabulation of some conference expenses and the syndromes which cause them that can be dangerous.

1. *Is this meeting really necessary?* I suggest that you review again the words of the song that is the theme of this text, "Let's Have a Meeting, and We'll All Be There!" as a constant reminder that, necessary or not, the meeting will *appear* unnecessary to some of your people. If it appears that way, it is subject to scrutiny by others trying to save money or to avoid having to attend a meeting for which they feel they have neither the time nor the need. I suggest that you take the initiative, from time to time, in urging a reduction in numbers of meetings by asking critical questions on whether the time is right, the data needed is available, the people needed will be present, and so on. If you can cut out some meetings, you will get the edge on your detractors, and every conference manager has some people who are just waiting to catch him in some activity that is inappropriate or unnecessary. Beat them at their own game.

2. *Is this resort location proper?* The members of the group probably selected Las Vegas themselves, knowing that costs for the meeting itself can be lower there. But have they actually gone on record in endorsing that location, or will you take the blame when someone raises a question later over the propriety of selecting that site? Test them by suggesting that they look again. If they mean it, make sure the record is clear that you raised a question over the wisdom of that choice. Try suggesting another city where you know the environment is less likely to generate criticism from the bosses back home. Have your people asked their bosses back home for a company reaction to Las Vegas? (Some organizations have had great success with Las Vegas conferences; others have had some horrible aftermath problems. I take no sides but simply leave it to your discretion to decide for your organization. Neither have I ever held a conference in Las Vegas, although I have planned one on several occasions and have checked the city out thoroughly as a conference site, and I have attended conferences there and in similar locations around the world.)

3. *Does this annual meeting really need to be held in Paris?* You probably have a good reason for Paris; there are many good reasons now that better convention facilities and hotels have started to sprout there. It is still probably the preferred city of Americans who have never been to Europe and a favorite for old-timers as well. Today Paris may not be so overly expensive as it was some years ago, because other cities of Europe have seen the inflation that started in Paris decades ago. Yet there is still an aura about Paris that suggests expense and justifies your asking the question, "Is there some other city in Europe for our first meeting abroad that will make it easier for us to explain our need for contact with European industry, without taking a chance on Paris just now?" You should ask this question before you go; others might not before but may afterward.

4. *Do you really need a banquet and all those large luncheons?* Costs for social events can be high, and they are difficult to predict accurately in advance. Who will pay for them? Will there be extra costs that you cannot recoup from the participants? Will your bosses back home object because of the fringe costs to their company people who are expected to attend the social events? Does the social activity add more than it penalizes the meeting. (See Chapter 22 for a discussion of the pros and cons of spending money for coffee or organized receptions or other social affairs, noting that if you can get the costs completely out of your budget, so that industry groups that want such events can plan them, manage them, and *pay for them*, you will not have such expenses to explain later.)

5. *Is this hotel too elegant for your group?* A plush hotel can bring criticism back home for some groups. How high in the corporation pecking order are your people? Are they the presidents of the corporations or the maintenance foremen? With the former, elegance is acceptable because there is no one to complain; with the latter, you may get some criticism from the presidents. Even though the costs may be low in the best of Miami Beach hotels if you have selected the proper season and arranged the affair far enough in advance (Chapters 27 and 30), the *appearance* of excess elegance may hurt your record of accomplishment and austerity.

6. *Does the meeting have to last all week?* I suggest that you shorten your meeting when you go to Miami Beach or other sites where the appearance of opulence and fun and games may hurt you. Chapters 25 and 26 suggest ways to help out what may seem to be a fun-and-games meeting (to the bosses who stayed home).

7. *How large a staff do you need at the conference?* Do you pick up all your stenographers and secretaries and copy machine runners and public address system and tape recorder runners and errand runners and ship them all off to a fancy resort hotel on the other side of the world for 3 weeks for a 3-day conference? Probably not, but some organizations do. We like to think that we get our documentation done in advance rather than after the meeting starts; we like to utilize local convention bureau registration people (highly experienced) at a piddling small or zero cost instead of tying up our own people; we can use local services for almost everything a conference needs without elaborate equipment being shipped from place to place, and the costs are quite low.

There were times, in prior decades, when conference tables would have to be locally manufactured, reproducing machines would have to be rented from 2000 miles away, registration clerks would have to be imported, and staff would have to arrive weeks in advance to get everything ready. But that was years ago; today you select a hotel in the part of the world you want to utilize that *has* those facilities, and you arrive the night before your conference opens with a staff just large enough to conduct the meeting itself; all the ancillary matters are handled as needed by the same staff that has to be there to run the meeting itself. A conference chairman can arrange things in a hotel effectively and easily; it is his job to know how to get things done without tripping over his own feet or his staff people.

8.   *Do you need all those other small subcommittee meetings?* This is a question that an empire builder running a trade association would never ask. But it is a question that *you* should ask. Who will attend such a meeting on whifflestick testing? Can the people who are affected justify another meeting so soon, or will they find reasons why it will not be well attended? Does it have to be held now, or can you postpone it until fall? If you have to have it now, why does it have to be held in Podunk, where it will be convenient to the chairman, who lives there (no one *else* does)? Hold it at your headquarters, where your staff transportation costs will be zero and facilities are available.

9.   *Do you really have to make all the reservations for the group?* That is quite a chore, and it can tie up your staff on things that others can do better (Chapter 27, Rule 5).

10.   *Do you have to have shrimp for lunch?* This is a facetious question to illustrate a point. I have suggested (Chapter 21) that you can help the development of a consensus by meetings at lunch. I urged (Chapter 3, item 9) that you arrange administrative meetings to preplan discussion strategy in the larger meetings; such administrative meetings can take place at a captive luncheon, which you arrange and finance. This saves the time of the group members so that they can get their business out of the way while they are eating, which they have to do anyway. I described this process in Chapter 17, noting the difficulties in running a small business meeting of this kind.

You may wonder why, if we are so austere in our conference costs, we pay the costs for a luncheon of some thirty people out of our meager conference budget. The answer is that people will be quite conscious of the cost of the luncheon whether they are paying for it or you are. If they are to pay for it, they will decide (just as with the coffee breaks of Chapter 22) that it is an unnecessary expense and they will prefer the corner drugstore for a simpler lunch. You cannot have cheap luncheons in a hotel room suitable for a meeting. No way!

Thus, in our experience, our buying the luncheons and their attending the business meeting is the best arrangement. They all know the luncheons cannot be cheap, but they never complain about the economical menus that we select for them. We usually arrange for a meat dish (such as roast beef) the first day or two and then end up with salads or lighter dishes later in the week. Typical costs for a 2- or 3-day conference luncheon bill will be several hundred dollars, and that is money well spent. To answer my own question: "No, *we* don't have to have shrimp for lunch, and we don't usually, except in salads."

Cost Guidelines

Now that I have set forth some danger signals to watch out for with your conferences, perhaps I should give you some guidelines that can help you evaluate the typical costs for your usual needs around the world if you hold Goldfish Bowl deliberative conferences of about the size, shape, and style of ours.

Conference costs will depend upon what you include in the costs and what you exclude and charge to something else. As an example, if you work on documentation for months before a major conference, as we and most other deliberative conferences do, you can make a sizable difference in the cost of that conference depending upon whether the costs of preparing all that documentation, printing it in quantity, mailing it in advance to many people, and shipping extra quantities to the conference all are included in or excluded from the costs of the conference. For how long in advance should you include such costs? A month, a year, a decade? It is difficult to decide that question because it is fraught with so many variables. Also, most of that documentation (perhaps even more) would have to be prepared anyway for distribution to the same people if the same job were to be attempted *without* such a conference, using only correspondence. Thus, we include only the direct costs of the conference. Although our records are pretty good for budgeting purposes each year, I kept some better-than-average records one particular year which I shall use as illustrative. That year was 1970, and although inflation has changed things quite a bit since then, other factors have made some meetings more economical in later years as accommodations have improved and competition has increased for convention business.

During 1970 we held two major general sessions, one in Denver and one in London, England. The London meeting was better attended, with some 400 plus (not including wives and other family members) registered. The distribution of this group was approximately 17 percent airline people (customers) and 83 percent manufacturers (suppliers). Approximately half of the people were from the United Kingdom, and the other half were split 38 percent from the United States and 12 percent from continental Europe and elsewhere.

Now are you ready for the costs? The big costs were staff travel and airfare, which added up to almost $4000 for six people for the week. Even in the airline industry, there wasn't much to be done to reduce that expense for an overseas conference. Next, I find a charge for the three days of administrative luncheons of $480, and that completes the big expenses. We paid out some $70 for receptionist charges for the week (for this meeting we got a lot of help from the local airline people, who supplied staff people; the costs were out-of-pocket expenses). We spent $60 on projector rental and $10.50 for group photographs. That is the complete total for the week-long affair.

Earlier that year we held a similar general session in Denver with a total registration 15 percent less than in London. Our staff travel (the same people as in London) was about half of the London costs; the administrative luncheons were slightly smaller and 20 percent cheaper; the registration people (this time from the local convention bureau) were $4 cheaper; and the photos were about 3 times as expensive. Remember that, as I have noted previously, these conferences cost our industry some $500 per minute of meeting time; they are not cheap in total cost. But our costs are minimum, and we make sure that we keep them that way. Yet we meet in the best hotels, with wonderful accommodations and never a complaint of too much austerity. Conferences don't have to cost the sponsoring organization an arm and a leg.

Before I close this chapter with the impression that you will never have conference costs other than those few items tabulated above, I shall tell all. Earlier that year, we had held a much smaller subcommittee meeting in London, at the same hotel where the large affair was held later, and we did have to pay conference room charges of $360 for that 3-day meeting, utilizing a much smaller conference room, with a total registration of just forty-two people! In this particular affair, there were no offsetting events which would bring other income to the hotel; we were aware of this situation in advance, and we accepted the charge graciously.

I started this chapter with the admonition to fasten your seat belt, as it was to be a rough ride. Cost cutting is never an easy chore, but it is a necessity, particularly under the conditions I have described in which the whole name of the game in our commercial world is competition. Even though we can never have any exact yardstick for determining what a conference or a standardization activity should cost, it is probably that lack of a qualitative and quantitative yardstick for comparison that makes costing such a difficult endeavor.

In this chapter I have emphasized the parts of the costs, particularly conference-related costs, that are hard to relate to such (nonexistent) yardsticks. I have not delved into the many areas of cost in which you can make competition work for you in buying services. Chapters 27 and 30 offered help in arranging hotel facilities, but there are many other costs that need regular watching. As an example, every group needs printing (perhaps, like us, large quantities of it) for conducting the standardization process in a worldwide arena. What can you do to keep printing costs down? Perhaps your organization, like most organizations, has its own internal printing facility. Is it cost-effective? Is it really cheaper (or just more convenient) than having printing done outside? Printing is just one example that history shows an organization may be inclined to forget about, as it espouses competition for others while it does its own printing in house because this is so much simpler though more expensive than having it done outside.

To illustrate how this situation can creep up on even a strongly competitive organization, I shall report what the top management of one Washington-based major magazine told me some years ago. This firm printed its own magazine for many years and also sold printing service to others. One day, the boss decided to check competitive costs of outside publishing of the firm's own magazine (its business was publishing). Was he surprised! The decision was made to have the magazine printed outside by another equally large publishing house despite screams of "Unfair" from the internal operation. The boss explained that this decision caused a general uproar in the corporation, but it stuck for many years. He said that eventually he introduced an entirely new method of pricing for publishing, so that his magazine would now get a fair price from his own publishing house. Apparently, without eternal vigilance and price comparisons that publishing house was simply not competitive for internal publishing even though it had to be competitive for its other business if it was to remain viable as a publisher. When the pricing became competitive with the outside world, the boss gave the magazine-publishing job back to his own publishing house.

If a huge publishing house can have that problem, we can be pretty certain that almost all internal publishing operations have fallen prey to empire building and now have less than the best service. We have tried the same practices in our internal publishing with somewhat the same results. One time, I was approached by a major publisher in a city hundreds of miles away. The salesman agreed to accept our master copy and meet a better delivery schedule than that of our own shop, with better quality, and with a lower price. We had a logjam in our own print shop at that time, and I gave him the job; he delivered the goods. The quality was better, the price was much lower, and he did get the copy to his plant and the finished material back to us on a schedule that beat our own shop. In that case, I didn't give him our business *in toto* but made good use of that competition to improve the quality and cost effectiveness of our own facilities.

We espouse competition. Commerce needs it and thrives on it. Why should we ignore the potential for saving money through its benefits in our own backyard?

As I said before, it's a rough ride. Cost cutting is better initiated by you than by your bosses or your constituents' bosses after the fact. The bottom line is the name of the game in industry; don't let a lack of awareness or a sense of isolation from its ravages keep you from success in the one matter that can change you from a winner to a loser: the bottom line.

It was just after the War of 1812, when tourism was again developing, that it all started. Joe Harrigan was a tourist; sightseeing was strenuous for a small-town boy (from Hastings, Nebraska), and he was relaxing in the Hollywood Hotel bar. It was there that he met Jim Hamilton from Hempstead, Long Island. "It's a small world," Joe declared. " We both have names starting with *H,* and we are both from towns beginning with *H.*" Together they ran in and out of the bar and coffee shop searching for and finally locating a third out-of-towner who met their hastily developed specifications: a guy from Halifax who was a heater salesman by the name of Halstead.

Then and there, right in the middle of Hollywood, Jim and Joe invented what came to be known as a convention. With only three members it was not difficult to select a name; they selected the H Society (international, of course) and immediately elected officers and planned their next annual meeting.

The next year it was held in Holyoke, then in Hoboken, and so around the country. But the members soon tired of towns starting with *H* as convention sites, and they accepted such alphabetically adjacent towns as Great Neck and Islip. They were branching out. They even allowed the Gilberts and the Irelands to join the H Society, but not the Jacksons or the Fosters. The society was extremely large but highly exclusive, as would have been predicted by the Country Club syndrome described in Chapter 7.

The influence of that syndrome caused even further changes in the H Society. Joe was in the hammer business and longed for some friends at the conventions with whom he could talk shop. Soon he organized the Hammer Division of the society, but that soon was broadened into the Hardware Superdivision; thus the first trade show was invented. The hardware business spawned the Hydraulics Technical Society (still tenuously connected through the letter *H*); this eventually embraced Hydroelectrics and finally just plain H-electrics. Then the Hamerican

32

Apocalypse: The Past and the Future of the Conference

(pronounced with a silent *H* like the *Q* in "cucumber") Hinstitute of Helectrical Hengineers soon evolved as a part of the society.

The mechanical engineers, the chemical engineers, and many others were excluded; they had to form their own societies. But the Hradio Hengineers were included, and this was particularly significant to our important history of conventions. The Hradio group was a small, almost outcast part of the giant Helectricals, but it didn't stay that way when Helectronics later became important. First a merger between the Helectrical and the Helectronic Societies became necessary; then both discovered that they no longer needed their parent H Society, as they no longer had anything in common with those *H* people. Now they were even letting the Webers and the Andersons join the Institute of Electrical and Electronics Engineers (IEEE). But such largess was soon to be replaced by specialty divisions, groups, and subgroups in the world's largest engineering society that the IEEE soon became. Today the 180,000 members, worldwide, function in some three dozen individual societies that are loosely bound together by the giant parent IEEE.

Human Gregariousness and the Conference

Our partially tongue-in-cheek and partially factual history of conventions and trade shows emphasizes the vibrant and alternating expansion and contraction that are destined to take place as groups search for a common basis for existence and then alternately broaden and compress their scopes of activity. Man is a gregarious individual and is never content unless he is forever to apply his Country Club syndrome—like nature to form or simply to join an exclusive club.

In the play *1776*[1], we recall the words of John Adams before the curtain rises: "I have come to the conclusion that one useless man is called a disgrace, that two are called a law firm, and that three or more become a congress." When a convention (or a congress) is organized, there must have been something to justify that gregariousness; there must be something in common to bind the people together. Whether it is the Citizen's Band Club craze of the early 1970s, or the growing Computer Club craze, or the Camping Van craze of the later 1970s, there will always be a new group to attract and exclude gregarious people.

Although it is common knowledge that meetings need a common stimulus to get started in the first place, there is considerable doubt as

[1]Text copyright © 1964 by Sherman Edwards; copyright © 1969 by Peter Stone; lyrics copyright © 1964, 1968, 1969 by Sherman Edwards; first published by The Viking Press, Inc., New York, 1970.

to the percentage of such meetings that continue under that stimulus. We might note:

HENDRICKSON'S LAW

If a problem causes many meetings, the meetings eventually become more important than the problem.[2]

The foregoing philosophy explains why so many conference activities seem so difficult to kill off after the original task has been completed; this philosophy also underlies my prognostication for the future of conferences. Now that I have reviewed the historical basis for conference activity and have looked at the factors that influence the gregarious tendencies of human beings, I may make some guesses (and that is all they can be) about the future. So here we go.

Developments in Communications

Anyone who has read any recent scientific predictions for communication will observe more and more similarity to the science fiction stories of past decades. Jules Verne, H. G. Wells, and Sax Rohmer, to name a few, gave us wonderful stories, a generation or two ago, about how people's thoughts would be transmitted through the "ether" directly into the minds of others. They showed us the marvelous machines that we would use to transport people instantaneously into a different area of the world. Some of these things have come to pass in a less-than-perfect manifestation of modern science. Modern transportation, although not quite instantaneous, has given much momentum to the expansion of the conference business. The transportation industry, while generating a much greater need for deliberative conferences just to solve *its own* industry problems, also has facilitated the solving of those problems by providing the improved transportation to get people to *its own meetings*. Other industry follows along, not too much behind the transportation industry, in traveling to conferences and meetings.

But we have one advantage over you, perhaps, because we have been a part of the air transport industry's communications company. And though our original destiny was to aid the airlines in communications, we are in a part of the airline industry that should, more than any other part, see the relationship and even the equivalence that has always existed between transportation and communications. Philo-

---

[2]Arthur Bloch, *Murphy's Law—and Other Reasons Why Things Go Wrong!* Price/Stern/Sloan, Los Angeles, copyright 1977.

sophically, one can be traded for the other: if we can communicate sufficiently well, we need not travel; conversely, if we can travel sufficiently well, we need not communicate so well. To illustrate that
relationship, we might look at the early postwar history of air transportation in Europe. Communication in some areas was so bad (slow) that
messages could be sent via an airplane faster than by telephone or wire.
The ordinary airline dispatch messages relating to an airplane departure or estimated time of arrival would get there faster if carried on the
aircraft itself. Of course, that situation didn't last very long, because an
airline couldn't run passenger service without communications that
were at least faster than the subjects of the communications.

The science pundits have long predicted that communications would
soon become so good that travel would seldom be required; not only
would communication be much faster than transportation, but it would
now be better and far cheaper than travel. These predictions are usually
related to meetings and conferences as well as to such subsidiary functions as remote viewing of things and people. Communication companies have made these predictions for the future and have demonstrated
the televiewing capabilities of their firms' developments for many
years, with a big display at the 1939 New York World's Fair and subsequent reviews at intervals ever since.

Every time that some cost or technological breakthrough occurs in
long-distance communication, we see the predictions again. With the
developments in fiber-optic transmission lines in recent years, the predictions came again. This time, the press stories reported the elaborate
facilities in trial operation by the telephone companies, predicated
upon market surveys that indicated teleconferencing to be the coming
thing. One very thorough survey article on the technological status was
in a story by Howard Falk in the May 1975 issue of *Spectrum*, a major
publication of the Institute of Electrical and Electronic Engineers. After
reviewing the many new developments and their likely applications to
the conference business, Falk commented on the other-than-technical
aspects of equating communications to transportation with a note of
caution:

> Some observers believe that formal conference sessions and pre-
> sentations serve mainly as a mechanism to bring together people
> with common interests and concerns. The truly valuable and mean-
> ingful conference exchanges, according to this view, take place
> across the hotel breakfast or lunch table in brief personal contacts
> outside conference rooms and en route to an evening's entertain-
> ment. Mutual confidence developed through these personal con-
> tacts make the most useful flow of information possible, both at the

conference and afterward. The key question may not be whether clear voices and images can flow between conferees, but whether trust, and just plain liking each other, can be built by remote control.

As we ponder Howard Falk's question, it may seem ironic that only a threat to substitute communication for transportation can make us seriously ponder what meetings and conferences are *for* and how best to utilize them for our needs in industry. In the world of tomorrow, the speeches could easily be sent by video (in fact, that can be done today), but how do we expect to videoencapsulate a coffee break? We may have retained the watermelon seeds but lost the melon.

What part of your conference or my conference could be videoencapsulated? What part would be acceptable if it were sent by video so that the conference attendee could stay at home or remain in his office without any need for travel to the conference site? Probably the most likely candidate portions are the nondeliberative, or possibly the pseudodeliberative of Chapter 24, in which the audience is just that, a passive audience which does nothing but listen or sleep while speakers high on some platform at a remote podium drone on and on and on. If we have very much of this sort of meeting, we are becoming candidates for videoencapsulation, in which the purpose is to make a record for posterity, not for real people to waste time on. I have my doubts that a good, lively deliberative meeting can ever be teleconferenced without a lot being lost in transmission. Those wonderful coffee breaks (Chapter 22) are exceedingly important, with or without coffee, and I would hate to see them discarded simply because no one knows how to send them over a telephone line.

But perhaps there will be new ways in the future. Perhaps the nature of the deliberative process will change so that it will become unrecognizable by today's standards. Perhaps the time will come when we shall sit at home and take an active part in deliberations, using our telescreen, and we shall all be able to disseminate our thinking to everyone else without doing it as we do today. Today's technology can speed up ordinary speech so that speeches can be listened to much faster. That little feature alone could shorten all speeches today by 80 percent. Naturally, a small problem is posed when an individual can listen to you 4 times as fast as you can speak, but that is a minor problem easily overcome with our simple technology.

The major problem is twofold. First, no one or no organization seems to be doing anything about the horrendous redundancy in ordinary speech in any language; orators are even more redundant. Second, no one seems to have any technological or physiological means by which multiple orations can be heard and comprehended simultaneously. While a group of people in a cocktail party can sometimes listen to multiple conversations simultaneously, it is not easy to do, and it is very upsetting and uncomfortable for the listener who feels he has to hear even two people at once.

If we were to let our science fiction thoughts run wild, we would want to see listening machines developed that would hear, comprehend, and abstract all the useful information in a speech, encapsulating that information into a small glob which could be fed, orally or visually (or otherwise), directly to an individual listener. Now each participant in a deliberative conference could orate to his heart's content into a microphone and have his speech summarized and disseminated, almost instantaneously, to everyone needing or wanting that information. He might even, with some practice, develop a facility for listening *while* he is orating, so that his orations could accept or reject the views of others coming to him in his headphones. It is just as practicable (if we can do all the foregoing with our wonderful technology of the future) for a machine to sense any common consensus that may develop among the multiple simultaneous orators. It would seem that this process would produce through the automatic processes of computer analysis the same results that this whole text advocates now by manual means. Can we imagine the benefits to the United Nations of such a development? If the technological trend were to move as we have suggested, the time required for even the most complex decision making by deliberative means would be so short as to allow plenty of time for the conference attendee to travel after the deliberative conference is over, to visit all the thousands of people who took part in the teleconference and whom he knows so well. In fact, it might be desirable to hold coffee breaks at the central site, just as we do today, for the social and business benefit they offer, allowing the participant to travel back to his home or office for the short teleconference sessions that would be held between the coffee breaks.

As I prognosticate these wondrous things for the deliberative conference of tomorrow, or at least the day after, I faintly recall having heard all this before. My mind goes back to a story I read in *The New Yorker* over three decades ago, describing a wonderful new contraption known as a reading machine.[3] The author told of its potential for reading anything and everything at an exceedingly fast pace: it could go through novels, newspapers, or technical articles at such a rate that with a machine of his own an individual would never again have difficulties

---

[3]Morris Gilbert Bishop, "The Reading Machine," *The New Yorker*, March 8, 1947.

in keeping up on his reading. After expounding on the speed and remarkable intellect of this machine, the author mentioned, in a rather low key, the printer attachment so that the machine could make copies of everything it read. Undoubtedly, it was later equipped with a headphone attachment so that you could listen to everything it read.

There is more, much more, to be included in this important chapter, but I have to stop now. It's time for our coffee break.

How can this dissertation put such a heavy emphasis upon the chairman of a meeting without equal emphasis upon the participant? Surely the participant carries a lot of the responsibility for a poor meeting, does he not? His attitude, if not his behavior, must influence the chairman and thereby establish the mood for the conduct of the session. Why, therefore, must the first specific mention of the participant and his etiquette be deferred to the last chapter of the book? Why should not the participant take equal blame or equal responsibility with the chairman for the conduct of the session?

I could claim that the final chapter in the book is the most important: *that* is where the casual reader looks first; that is where the outcome will be. I could argue that everyone knows that the reader always turns to the last chapter to find out whether the butler did it. But no, my premise is that the chairman must be the one upon whom we concentrate almost all our attention. We must understand the problems of a chairman, whether he has a sympathetic group or not. He is the key to success. He is the cause of any failure to fulfill the desires of anyone attending the meeting; he must take the blame or get any small credit, if there is any. In no way can the group itself be blamed for what transpires, good or bad, in any meeting. This chapter is not describing a suitable alternative to a good chairman, it is simply suggesting ways for meeting participants to make a bad meeting less bad and a good meeting better. Knowledgeable and conscientious participants can help a bad chairman but cannot make a good meeting. Thus, in this chapter, let us keep in proper perspective the limitations of *any* chairman, good, better, or even best. Then we can see better how a chairman can be helped by his meeting to run an even better affair.

33

Reprise: Etiquette for Meeting Participants, or How to Run a Meeting from the Back Row of the Audience

Reaction to the Chairman

I have explained how important it is for a chairman to maintain good, close, fast communication with the meeting. Once the chairman has demonstrated to the meeting that he does want its reaction to any proposal made before the group, the participants can help the chairman and help themselves by giving him that reaction quickly, regularly, and spontaneously. *If* the chairman asks for a "Yes" or "No" reaction to a question, and *if* he has previously told the group that he will watch for vertical and horizontal nodding to signify such a reaction, and *if* he is capable of *seeing* a "Yes" or "No" reaction from his group, it behooves everyone to give this kind of response to the chairman even when he has not explicitly asked for it.

Remember that I have postulated meetings for a commercial purpose, in which the participants are present for their own commercial benefit. Thus, if a participant *reacts* to a quick question (giving a "Yes" or "No" answer), not only is he expediting the meeting, saving both time and money, but he is getting his own commercial point of view across. He may, incidentally, be helping the chairman to run a better meeting; but, most important, he is profiting his own organization: this is what he came for. Although most of such participant responses will be utterly wasted in the usual meeting of a large group chaired by a not-so-knowledgeable individual, there can be some good effects upon even the most miserable chairman who notices no one and cares not what people think. The usual poker-faced meeting participants do not aid the chairman in understanding the desires of the meeting, and it is only through proper but lengthy parliamentary maneuvering that such a chairman can be reached. But if just a few participants, particularly those in the front rows, will start reacting to a chairman's words, even densest individuals will eventually get the idea. This takes some guts by the participants, but it most certainly can work. Here is how it has been done in conferences.

Let us hypothesize a proposal by Mr. A in the third row to adopt one meeting per year as the standard. Mr. A starts to drone on and on about the advantages, so Mrs. B, in the first row, turns around and starts slowly to shake her head horizontally at each of the fallacious arguments, while smiling in the most friendly manner at Mr. A. Soon Mr. C, also in the front row, does the same, and Mr. A can't help but observe that he is generating doubts. Only a hardened, impractical diehard can avoid reacting to such obvious dissent. At worst, the chairman will observe the effect and feel obligated to call upon Mrs. B or Mr. C to explain their differences of opinion with Mr. A. At best, Mr. A, knowing that Mrs. B is being objective in dissenting, will shift his presentation to answer what he knows are the obvious fallacies in his argument; perhaps he will cite some real advantages that will cause Mrs. B to stop shaking her head and possibly even to nod vertically in giving in to Mr. A.

This chairman has seen such participant reaction time and time again, sometimes with a somewhat different outcome. Mr. A, seeing that he is generating dissent, will stop his presentation and ask Mrs. B what she proposes instead. Usually Mrs. B suggests only a minor variation of what Mr. A has proposed, but a change that would allow unanimous support for the proposal. Parenthetically, it is well to remind ourselves that the U.S. Congress has evolved some procedures that are strikingly similar to this hypothesized situation. Within all the formality of senators addressing other senators in highly formal, impersonal terms, it is quite proper for a senator to interrupt another almost in midsentence with a request to make a point or ask a question. The "good senator" will often yield the floor temporarily while another colleague (usually of the same view) will suggest a modification of a statement, or a reason, or a proposal which the first senator may find acceptable and espouse. Remember that I have urged informality, candor, and friendliness in Goldfish Bowl deliberative conferences; without friendliness, it is difficult for one individual to sway another to his views, and it is even more difficult to shortcut the ponderous parliamentary procedures without that friendliness. And this leads us to:

CARNES' LAW

Poker faces are for poker playing, not for Goldfish Bowl deliberative conferences.

Once a chairman has shown a willingness to communicate with a group through such informal means, there is much that a participant can do to make the meeting better in other ways as well. Chairmen with tunnel vision need all the help they can get, and a knowledgeable participant can help immensely. Everyone, whether wearing eyeglasses or not, suffers from a tendency to watch only what is happening straight ahead. But participants sit at the sides, too. Even with a reasonably well-arranged conference room, some of the participants at the sides may attempt, with little success, to be recognized by the chairman. Here a helpful, knowledgeable participant has a duty to aid the chairman realize his oversight before a meeting disintegrates with people at the sides speaking without being recognized.

Perhaps the chairman does not yet have enough confidence in himself to employ anything but the triggered Ping-Pong mode (see Chapter 2), and he insists upon recognizing all participants before allowing them to speak. A simple word to the chairman that "George has his hand up" will do the job, and you will be thanked by the chairman for your consideration. You have helped that chairman run a better meeting; you have avoided a serious frustration complex in George, who didn't know for sure whether the chairman saw his hand or not and, therefore, didn't want to speak out. At times, you may not see the whole room, and thus you may fail to see someone hold up a hand when the chairman misses it too. The meeting may shift almost instantaneously into the precarious Ping-Pong mode and soon into the impossible random-splatter mode (see Chapter 2). Here, if *you* are the most knowledgeable person in the room, it is your duty to speak out: "Mr. Chairman, too many people are speaking at once; we can't hear them. Who *has* the floor?" You have become the equivalent of the *deus ex machina* of Chapter 9. If *you* fail to interrupt immediately, the situation will quickly get worse, establishing a very bad precedent for the chairman. If the chairman is unable to keep the meeting from degenerating repeatedly into that mode, he is unlikely to know how, or have the ability, to extricate it from that mode without some help from a participant who is more knowledgeable than he is.

Even some interference with the meeting (noise perhaps) can be cured by an outspoken participant when the chairman is too preoccupied to observe what is happening. A word to the chairman will cause even the most stolid chairman to react.

Helping the Chairman

But the problems that prove most irksome to meeting participants who are present for an important purpose are simply the result of oversight by a chairman who is mightily trying but is simply not sufficiently experienced to run the most effective meeting. Such a chairman will respond to proper stimulus and appreciate quiet encouragement from the back row of the meeting. Perhaps the meeting is hung up over sticky parliamentary procedure, with everyone groping for a legal way out of the dilemma. A quiet suggestion from the back of the room, along the lines of the examples of Chapter 6, can often solve the problem by suggesting a solution that is acceptable to everyone but has not occurred to anyone else. Sometimes a procedural suggestion can reverse the order of doing certain things so that they are handled in a more logical order and are easier to administer. Remember that a naïve or inexperienced chairman may be unwilling or unable to suggest to the meeting the best way of doing business. If *you* have that experience and can make such a suggestion, it can be helpful. The chairman and the meeting may be waiting for it.

If *you* are experienced in predicting what will happen logically as the outcome of a complex debate with few real options open to the group, you may know what is likely finally to happen when all the debating is finished. But it may not be easy to impart this information to anyone else. Remember my admonition in Chapter 4 to a chairman who has this capability: " . . . the experienced chairman knows what the eventual outcome is bound to be but can do little, if anything, about it except to provide a suitable climate for someone eventually to offer it as the *only ultimate solution.*" Although *your* hands are not tied in the same way that a chairman's hands are often tied, you may find even less acceptance to the suggestion than the chairman finds when *he* suggests it. The reason, of course, is that the chairman is usually assumed to be impartial, while the participants are assumed to be partial to their own interests rather than to those of the body itself. It is this role playing or assumed role playing that makes it extremely difficult for even an experienced nonchairman to suggest an eventual solution that will be accepted by a group.

Fortunately for a meeting, those in the room who have had long experience as chairmen will often tend to search for answers that are acceptable to the meeting rather than answers that benefit just a few organizations. But unfortunately the meeting can seldom see or understand such motives. A meeting expects everyone to push for his own interest rather than for a common interest, and it is simply incomprehensible to a group that an individual would propose a solution which he himself does not favor in order to get an acceptable solution. It is only with lots of exposure to commonality of thinking that a group develops a community interest and can comprehend a common solution to a complex problem even when it is proposed *as that.* While the chairman *may* have some success in making such a solicitous suggestion, the meeting may find it highly suspect if a member offers the same suggestion. Thus, like the chairman who discovers a shortcut route to an obvious ultimate solution, the experienced participant may have to bite his tongue and wait for the mood of the group to change from one of "me first" to "we together." This change will eventually come with any group, but it can be frustrating to an experienced participant who feels that he can do nothing just yet but must sit and stew over the wasted time until a ringleader in some harebrained scheme discovers that it can't fly and finally sees what must be done to get a solution. *You* could have suggested it hours ago.

Perhaps now, if *you* have been reading this chapter in its proper order (rather than reading it ahead of the rest to find out whether the butler did it), you may have discovered a pattern. Perhaps you have found that this author chose to preach first to chairmen and potential chairmen for a specific reason. Perhaps you have now suspected that if this chapter were to be written in its entirety (rather than simply abbreviated), the content would have to be as great as all the rest of this treatise put together. Everything I have touted as advice to prospective chairmen of Goldfish Bowl conferences would also have to be touted herein as advice to meeting participants. Everything applies equally (or almost equally) to meeting participants as the mirror image of the chairman. I have given enough examples to show that when the chairman is slightly imperfect (everyone is), the knowledgeable meeting participant probably has, or should have, a commercial reason for helping him out. A good chairman will certainly rub off on a meeting of inexperienced people; a group of experienced participants who have worked with a good chairman in other meetings can do a lot to get a meeting onto the right track and keep it there despite a poor chairman.

Even just one truly experienced participant can run a meeting all by himself from the back row of the audience up to a point. He may be misunderstood; he may be accused of all kinds of conniving. But if he keeps an absolutely altruistic motive that all can see and if he behaves with solicitous concern for the feelings of the inexperienced chairman and the other participants, he *can* succeed, though not as well as with an experienced chairman too. And there is no comparison with what can be accomplished with an experienced chairman and *all* experienced participants. But still there will be quite an improvement over what might have happened.

So we are back to the purpose of this treatise. Ostensibly, it may aim at giving the participant in any meeting a free ticket to cause as much trouble as he wishes, while heaping all the blame for a bad meeting upon the shoulders of the poor, naïve, unpracticed chairman. Yes, outwardly that is the impression, and I must, for the record, still put the blame on a poor chairman. But people come to Goldfish Bowl deliberative conferences to accomplish something that is worth something to each of them. If the chairman, for whatever reason, is not the best, the participants cannot just pass the meeting off as useless; someone must do the things that the chairman cannot do. If *you* are not the chairman but have become knowledgeable on what makes a good or bad chairman, you may just decide to take over some of the responsibility that is traditionally for the chairman only. If others like you are also knowledgeable on what makes a good chairman, you will have a lot of encouragement from them. Furthermore, they will understand what you are facing in potential criticism and misunderstanding when you attempt to help the chairman.

But someone should do it. It is better that one who has studied the problem should do it than one who has never taken the trouble to gain experience or learn through personal hands-on experience. Much can be learned through personal observation of chairmen, good and bad, and by watching other participants in meetings—good meetings and bad meetings. Practice by watching others if you can't get an opportunity to perform as chairman yourself.

Just think. If you *hadn't* read this book, the next meeting could have been a catastrophe. You could have found yourself up there at the head table with everyone in the meeting having read this book except you.

But I feel like a trained seal in a one-ring circus" was Pete's description of his feelings at that first open meeting of ARINC's Airlines Electronic Engineering Committee. "All these manufacturers of radios and airplanes are sitting around the room while we try to decide what we want our new radios to do and what we want in those new airplanes." That was a very real concern for Pete and the dozen other airline technical people who were attempting to decide their next move in the development cycle of new avionics equipment for new fleets of airline aircraft. How could Pete avoid showing a lack of knowledge on some technical points when all the knowledgeable equipment designers were kibitzing on his every move? How could Pete and his counterparts throughout the airline industry discuss their internal differences and problems in front of "all those outsiders"? "We really ought to kick them out of the room before we start discussing details, and we should do the decision making privately among ourselves" was heard repeatedly from the airline members of that small committee.

But that outmoded private way was the way the airlines had done it for some 14 years; that was the way all industries and all organizations had always done it. Get rid of the people who are trying to market something to you before you start discussing the merits of the market product. Could a new method be employed? Could we dare to let the marketeers be a party to decisions that would influence their own fate?

All the foregoing debate took place following the February 5, 1953, date when the Airlines Electronic Engineering Committee (AEEC), after a long period of soul-searching, held its first general session with man-

A.1

The Evolutionary Development of the Goldfish Bowl Deliberative Conference for Airline Avionics Standardization

ufacturers (only a few, by invitation) in the meeting. Thereafter, the general sessions *were* continued, though pretty shakily at first. Today no one questions whether decisions *can* be made in the presence of suppliers; no one questions letting *any* visitor get up and say what he wants to in an AEEC general session; sixty-odd large general sessions plus hundreds and hundreds of smaller working meetings have proved, over and over, the utility of this practice for the airline industry. In a typical week-long combination of avionics trade show, deliberative meeting of the AEEC, and associated seminars, the thirty official members of the AEEC are joined in their deliberations by another three dozen airlines and hundreds of manufacturers, government people, and others from a dozen-odd countries. Yes, it is an established fact that such cooperative decision making on spec writing *can* and *does* work for a whole industry worldwide.

But let me shift gears for a comparison of avionics cooperative development in the world's airlines with avionics acquisition in that large organization, the U.S. Air Force. It was on October 5, 1972, that the "number three man in the Pentagon," Dr. John Foster, announced in a public speech a changed Department of Defense (DOD) policy on research and development: affordable, interchangeable, competitive, and serviceable equipment. Dr. Foster went on to elaborate, suggesting that the DOD might attain this end by emulating the ARINC/AEEC techniques of interface standardization and industry consultation over spec features. That was in 1972; there have been several changes in Pentagon management since then, but the intent still persists after countless committee studies, board pronouncements, and personnel shifts up and down the line. In 1977 the Air Force started in earnest to adapt the AEEC practices and Goldfish Bowl technique to its own avionics acquisition with a spec development known as the USAF Standard Inertial Navigation System, or simply Standard INS for short.

The Air Force has had many problems, but its intent and its need are still abundantly clear. It covets the free and open communication the airlines have with their avionics suppliers; it yearns for avionics that has good serviceability; it drools over the manufacturer competition that the airlines generate for their new avionics after an ARINC spec has been completed by AEEC; it wants the low, low prices and the high standard of quality attainable by the AEEC process. The USAF has now recognized that better specs alone won't solve its problem, nor will any amount of urging of manufacturers generate the continuing competition that is the key to lower prices and a more acceptable product. The USAF has concluded that it must go the whole way that AEEC has traveled if it is to reap the benefits which the airlines have obtained from AEEC. Thus, the new DOD policy pronouncement of 1972 was supplemented, early in 1978, by the first regular Air Force Goldfish Bowl conference on avionics, patterned after AEEC practice. Later in 1978 the USAF held its second avionics conference and scheduled its 1979 conference; now it is prescribed by Air Force regulations.

Although the foregoing story of success would suggest that the Goldfish Bowl deliberative conference must have been a simple evolutionary step from the early beginnings, such was not the case. It didn't come easily in the airline industry; neither did it come quickly. Our only solace is in the knowledge that in most, if not all, other industries it hasn't come at all. Therefore, I shall back up to the beginning and describe the whole history—the entire eight epochs—that it required for us to learn a few things. Those eight epochs took half a century, the whole lifetime of the airline industry's telecommunications company, Aeronautical Radio, Incorporated, which celebrates its fiftieth anniversary in December 1979. Although the Airlines Electronic Engineering Committee (the entity of Aeronautical Radio which developed the practices of the Goldfish Bowl and on which the continuing U.S. Air Force efforts on avionics standardization are based) celebrates only its thirtieth anniversary in 1979, the efforts of predecessor committees date back to the beginning of Aeronautical Radio, Incorporated.

So, how did it all start?

Genesis Epoch I of 1929–1935

Perhaps it was a fluke of circumstance that caused one part of airline aviation, the electronics and radio in the aircraft, to get standardization treatment to a greater extent than any other aspect of aviation. It probably also was a fluke of circumstance that caused that standardization effort to get started in the United States, in a firm owned by the airline industry. That effort was spawned and has been nurtured for just about a half century, the lifetime of scheduled airline operation in the United States. It all started because some of our predecessors in this industry had a belief that commercial aviation could not operate efficiently and safely without good and reliable communications. At the inception of commercial airline operation in the United States in the late 1920s, radio was the only alternative to a long telephone extension cord. But radio frequencies were in a mess even after the Radio Act of 1927 created the Federal Radio Commission.

Simultaneously with the introduction of the first regular passenger schedules in 1928, the first aeronautical radio license was issued. The Commission held its first hearing on aviation radio in early 1929 and recognized the immense problem of licensing such a radio service. The consequence of the series of hearings that year was a request from the

Commission for the airlines to get together and police their use of the radio spectrum in some way. Thus, the airlines' own organization, Aeronautical Radio, Incorporated, was formed on December 2, 1929. It served as the corporate entity which could hold the licenses issued by the Commission for all the airlines in the United States.

This rather odd fluke of a licensing need served to get the radio people of the industry working together through the regular meetings of ARINC, as the new corporate entity was called. This organization provided a means of communication with the various government entities in addition to the government radio-licensing people, and it initiated cooperation on navigation aids and communications hardware.

In retrospect, with our excellent 20-20 hindsight, we can see the first beginnings of standardization even in that early period almost a half century ago, in what we can now designate Genesis Epoch I of 1929–1935. It was the period that saw the early beginnings of instrument flying on the commercial airways, using navigation aids developed by the Bureau of Lighthouses in the Department of Commerce and employing radio communication from the airline aircraft to ground radio stations licensed to ARINC and operated by the various airlines at the proper places across the country.

Government Epoch II of 1936–1938

Soon the industry found itself in Government Epoch II, with the federal government entering into hardware development to make airborne navigation equipment available for the airlines as a part of the new program of instrument landing. A new agency, the Civil Aeronautics Administration (CAA), prepared the specifications, and thereby the standards, and the airlines began to purchase airborne hardware to those government specs. But there were some problems: we had a rather rugged individualistic industry that didn't like the government telling it what to buy with its own money, and that epoch was rather short-lived.

Coop Epoch III of 1939–1946

This epoch saw a great innovation which was built upon the spec-writing effort that the CAA had already started and upon the ARINC effort toward coordination that had been under way for almost a decade. The board of directors of ARINC decided in 1939 that the airlines together should do the spec writing for airline aircraft hardware. It established an office of a chief engineer in ARINC to coordinate the needs of all the airlines and procure the necessary hardware for all the airlines that chose to take advantage of that cooperative mass buying. The arguments for this effort were the same that are used to this day in some industries in which cooperative buying is practiced: central procurement of a large quantity will be more economical than individual procurements spread over a longer time.

This was not a particularly new idea. Government procurements to this day are predicated on the same concept that George Washington is supposed to have first employed for defense buying when the country bought its first cannon. In the days of Coop Epoch III, the airlines thought this was the most cost-effective way of buying, and perhaps it was, for we were only in Epoch III. We had a lot to learn in subsequent years. But the system was a success. ARINC's operation started out with a bang, writing specs faster than the CAA could ever have done and placing orders for large quantities of radio hardware built to those new specs.

We shall never know just where that first effort might have led, for it was short-lived because of the impact of World War II, with the impossibility of buying anything new for commercial aviation for quite a period of years. As the war neared its end, the airlines were allowed to buy war surplus electronics, leaving the industry with a mammoth unfulfilled market in the early postwar years of 1945–1946. Then the same mode of operation that had been dropped previously was reinstituted, with ARINC again serving as the buyer for everything. ARINC started the first postwar spec activity, but although everyone had intended the effort to introduce competition into the marketplace, that couldn't happen in that epoch. We all thought we would have competition, but the plan fell apart, and we found that we were using the same old concepts of prewar spec coordination and common purchase.

It is interesting to note in passing that at about the same time the British government was trying the same experiments with its industry, but without any attempt to introduce competition on a particular avionic product. The British government parceled out the various hardware projects among the supplier firms and supplied development funding to get the hardware into production. Although many large firms were engaged in British hardware development, there was no competition simply because no two firms developed the same product. In England the lack of competition was deliberate, in the belief that the market for a single product was insufficient to warrant more than a single supplier.

In the United States the lack of competition was inadvertent. Although suppliers were competing with one another for the same product, only one of the suppliers for each product managed to get the business. But it was this Coop Epoch III which proved that the airline industry was a sufficiently large market to attract competitive suppliers for almost any product if we could just figure out a way to get it working.

Gaslight Epoch IV of 1947–1951

Then came Gaslight Epoch IV, which introduced some important changes that started the move toward true competition for avionics. First, ARINC consolidated purchasing, which had built up to a mad frenzy in 1946 as war surplus avionics became procurable, was closed down in 1947 by decision of the ARINC board of directors. The airlines were now mature, and even separately they represented a large market for avionics. The suppliers, which had been constrained by war production, descended like vultures upon the airlines, looking for new business. The airlines had all the ingredients of a new order of competition if they could just figure out how to introduce it.

Just a year earlier, the airlines had made an important change in their ARINC committees: all ARINC industry committees were henceforth to be chaired by ARINC professional staff people and supported by a professional secretariat. That was probably the most important and far-reaching decision of the decade. With a full-time staff, small but effective, industry standardization of avionics could move ahead rapidly if we could just figure out how to do it properly. We did what came naturally, with a hungry supplier industry watching our every move and wanting to market new products. The suppliers were not very well organized either, and they didn't want to wait for standardization and for industry specs. They wanted airline avionics business. Thus, everyone was designing and selling despite the standardization attempts of the ARINC staff and the predecessor committee of AEEC. The committee tried to concentrate on just a few projects, but the standardization was not very good. The customers couldn't wait for complete standardization, and they bought various products without the benefit of much standardization.

It was many years later that we learned what we had been doing wrong: we had refused to take the suppliers into our confidence and let them give us their help in the spec-writing process. As they were not a party to the standardization process, they had little understanding of *what* the airlines wanted and *why* they wanted it; the specs never contained such information, and no one took the time to explain them to the suppliers. Yet the key to the success that was to come later was the mushing around in the standardization process. This caused a concentration of customers to appear at ARINC meetings, which took place at regular intervals, usually in Washington, D.C.

We discovered a great truth of marketing: where the customers are, there also will be the suppliers. True, the suppliers had been chasing the customers in and out of ARINC meetings for some two decades, but no one had thought to do anything about it before. Even as early as 1945, the airlines had invited selected suppliers to make presentations to them on a new product on which a spec was being developed, but the customers had refused to discuss collectively with any suppliers the details of what the airline consensus was on any of the presentations. Suppliers were destined to be kept at arm's length in industry meetings at least until 1952, when AEEC tried the difficult experiment, described at the beginning of this appendix, of letting a few carefully chosen suppliers into the meetings.

Awakening Epoch V of 1952–1954

This epoch saw the beginning of the true learning process on how to make friends with and influence the suppliers. As I explained earlier, the airline reaction to those first open meetings was pretty bad. Some people wanted to stop the whole process immediately; others were willing to try it a while longer and see if we could make it work. Of course, the suppliers loved it; they could watch their favorite customers' every move and every reaction to a proposal. I was chairing those meetings, and I had a different kind of problem: I couldn't *find* the official committee members in that melee of faces. I found it rather difficult, to put it mildly, to ask the committee what it thought about something. I was certainly not going to ask the whole meeting to decide a matter which was really the airline customers' prerogative. Together, we came up with the winning idea that is still a winner and with the real solution of the original problems of the Goldfish Bowl deliberative conference.

That this idea has survived for a quarter century since it was invented back in the first really open AEEC general session of February 5, 1953, in the Whitcomb Hotel in San Francisco, proves that we really solved the problem. Of course, the winning idea is that stated in items 1, 2, and 3 of Chapter 3, under which the customers are given decision authority on matters of spec content, with official members seated in a central area where the chairman can easily locate them for his opinion sampling and for any formal decision making that the customers wish to do. Although the vast majority of all decisions now made in AEEC general sessions are made by the whole meeting (and then perhaps confirmed in a formal vote for the record by the voting members of AEEC), there is an immense psychological advantage in the customers reserving for themselves the right to decide a matter if a difference of opinion exists. But in the real world AEEC and the whole airline industry have learned, slowly and ponderously, that it is far better to find a consensus that the supplier community can accept, too, than to attempt arbitrary decisions, as we used to do in Gaslight Epoch IV and earlier. Arbitrary decisions tend to leave the supplier community in a bad quandary over what it should do.

It was during this Awakening Epoch V that the airline industry really discovered the middlemen in commercial avionics. In our business, the middleman is the airframe manufacturer, who may, on behalf of an airline customer, purchase the avionics for installation in a fleet of new aircraft on order by that customer. With some types of avionic equipment, the airframe manufacturer selects the supplier; with other equipment, the airline customer for the aircraft makes that decision, although the airframe manufacturer will install the equipment. In either case, the airframe manufacturer is directly involved in the procurement and installation process and thus has a considerable stake in spec writing and hardware development, at least for new aircraft.

In the early 1950s, the airline community first took the airframe manufacturers into its confidence and invited them to join the industry meetings as full partners with the airline customers. It was later that suppliers were welcomed into that partnership. Inasmuch as the airframe manufacturers always risk a considerable amount of their own capital in the development of a new aircraft type, they have an important stake in hardware development. Yet they must weigh customer preferences quite carefully because the investment that a customer already has in spare avionics can be a major factor in deciding upon a certain product for another new aircraft type.

Now, at this point I must explain a principal tenet of the airline avionics standardization process, a tenet that has been a major forcing function in causing the high order of standardization in airline avionics. This tenet comes from the desire of an airline to save money in logistics support cost for a fleet of aircraft flying over vast distances. The airline knows that avionics can be serviced much more easily and economically in some central overhaul shop than in the confines of a companionway or baggage compartment. To accomplish this central overhaul, each avionic box must be quickly and easily replaceable at any place on the route with another box that needs no adjustments or fiddling to make it work. This permits the use of nontechnical people at an outlying way point on the route to make the replacements. For this to be possible, the airline must have exact standardization of the box size, mounting, wiring, connectors, power circuits, and controls. That part is reasonably easy as long as all boxes are procured from a single supplier and sufficient spare boxes are procured for distribution along the route system. This much was understood even back in Genesis

Epoch I, and almost every airline had achieved that degree of standardization by at least the middle of Government Epoch II.

To accomplish such standardization during that early period when the government wrote the specs required some coordination, but coordination was relatively easy because each airline needed only a standard within itself. It was not entirely necessary then that the standards apply between and among the airlines. It was during Coop Epoch III that the suppliers themselves began to see a light in the dark tunnel. When the market began to grow and a second potential supplier wished to enter the business, he discovered the cost penalty of an airline's having to replace a large quantity of spare avionic boxes spread across an airline route. To avoid that replacement, the customer insisted that the new radio exactly fit the installation he now had in his aircraft; that demand caused the new potential supplier to copy the physical configuration of the existing product. The propriety of copying another product aroused mixed emotions in the supplier. But the customer made it pretty clear that he couldn't afford to change his fleet of aircraft just to be able to buy a newer and possibly better model from a different supplier.

Thus, it was squarely in the middle of Awakening Epoch V that the airline industry discovered that its failure to have *exact* interchangeability standards for a particular device was keeping it from some rather large monetary savings. The industry was precluding use of the newer technology that the new suppliers were offering. The airline avionics community had discovered the wonderful *potential* benefits of competition, but it couldn't *get* any of it. The apple on the tree of knowledge looked good enough to eat, but the industry couldn't quite reach it. By the end of that epoch it had done some patching up of old specs to gain some interchangeability, but the real potential had not yet been discovered.

It was during this period that another trend developed that was to broaden even more the scope of the United States airline community and point it toward the international standardization that was destined to come later. In the early 1950s a few European airline people started to visit the AEEC meetings. These people carefully avoided getting involved in the work of AEEC but simply were observing to see what was going on. It must be remembered that the European airlines had been operating over expansive world routes before World War II, and some had been in operation for at least a decade longer than United States airlines. They had pioneered civil aviation in Europe, and yet their organizations had been decimated by World War II. Thus, it was almost a decade after the war before they were fully organized and able to look around at the rest of the industry. Now they were showing interest in AEEC and that vast domestic United States airline community which dominated the AEEC in those early postwar years.

No wonder the Europeans found at first that they had very little in common with the United States domestic airlines, which were engaged in a kind of airline operation different from any that the Europeans had ever observed. Yet avionic hardware development was blossoming in the United States. The Europeans wanted to see what was going on. At first they kept a respectable distance from AEEC decision making; then they found enough mutual interest with United States domestic airlines to join up in the common effort to develop standards. But there was still a long conflict of emotions for some European airlines that had been able to command considerable attention from their own manufacturers; these manufacturers wanted to enlarge their market potential.

Working with AEEC could disrupt the rugged individualism of a European airline, but it seemed necessary to work together for a common good. AEEC was friendly; the European airlines were friendly, if not completely free from standoffishness; and the suppliers were looking to broader markets. The process continued to improve. More and more European airlines were attending the meetings regularly by 1954 despite the immense distances they had to travel to attend quite frequent meetings. It was this rapidly expanding international marketplace and the ever-broadening scope of AEEC activity that led to the next epoch.

Boundless Epoch VI of 1955–1960

This epoch bounded into reality with suppliers coming out of the woodwork and airlines expanding their fleets and their avionic contraptions. AEEC had now discovered competition, and it was just about to discover the real money-saver as a consequence of that competition and the newfound interchangeability of hardware across the lines of several suppliers. For the first time ever, the airlines could use a bevy of ARINC specs on a variety of avionic systems, and by then they had defined product interchangeability so well that several suppliers' products were actually interchangeable. The industry had discovered that it no longer had to copy a competitor's product now that ARINC specs were sufficiently definitive to tie down form, fit, and function features. This solved the suppliers' conflict-of-emotions problems.

And then the great change happened. The airlines pounced on the airframe manufacturers and insisted that the installation in the new aircraft conform exactly with the ARINC form, fit, and function specs rather than just with installation drawings supplied by a single supplier. Now the airlines had a bonanza: they no longer had to select and buy the product of their choice some 3 years prior to the delivery of a new aircraft type. For the first time ever, they could enjoy watching competing suppliers parade the new products through their offices for another several years, knowing that any product made to the ARINC specs would fit the installation that the airframe manufacturer was supplying in those new aircraft on the production line. The airframe manufacturers were happy; they, too, liked the idea of getting for installation a late-model avionic unit instead of a first, early design that was quickly made obsolescent in the wake of busy competitors' redesigning the product feverishly to get the jump on a competitor with an old model. It was a new game; buying the latest become the fashion, and the customers never had it so good.

Form, fit, and function specs were *in*. Everyone was benefiting; even the suppliers liked the idea because they could count mounting holes in real aircraft on real production lines for real orders by real airlines. Market surveys were easy when every hole in an aircraft was an unsatisfied market. Development funds were easier to come by now that management could count holes. It was still a game, but it was the kind of game that American industry just loves to play: a real market just waiting for the best product at the best price with the best delivery. It couldn't be better. Boundless Epoch VI was thundering forth. Now, too, European airlines were bypassing European suppliers in favor of the standardized products of the United States suppliers. Even those Australian and Canadian airlines and others of the British Commonwealth that were buying British aircraft were insisting upon United States–made avionics. A few British suppliers of avionics and aircraft had attended the AEEC meetings sporadically, but soon the supplier community of England descended upon the AEEC meetings en masse; then other suppliers from other countries began to develop an interest.

European airlines were coming in droves, so the suppliers from those countries simply followed their potential customers wherever they took them, despite the mammoth dents these trips made in their limited travel budgets. AEEC was in. The airline industry was in. AEEC became the focal point for commercial avionics. Things were going so well that it may not have been evident that a change was soon to happen and that a new epoch was starting with the beginning of the turbulent 1960s. But it was, as we now see with our 20-20 hindsight.

Turgescent Epoch VII of 1961–1970

This was the period in which jumbo jets ushered in a turbulent expansion of airline operation and caused increased buying of expansive aircraft with expensive avionics. No one had much opportunity to ponder what was happening as the technology was blossoming and the avionics state of the art was obsoleting on Tuesday what had been current as of Monday. This was the age which we called the Age of Proliferavionicism, leading to a state of confusion in which developments came so fast that true standardization was difficult. Standardization must always be imposed at the expense of initiative. But previously it had been practicable to maintain a standard long enough for the user to gain a considerable advantage before that standard was outmoded. In Turgescent Epoch VII this compromise with the technological onslaught was impossible; a standard lasted only a moment, then to be as out of date as last year's Easter bonnet. This was a long decade; it eventually came to a proliferavioniclasmic ending with the austerity forced by a declining airline passenger market at the end of the decade. Proliferavionicism was over, at least for the moment.

Ruminative Epoch VIII of 1971 Onward

This was the start of austerity and of reflective, introspective pondering of what should be done to attain better stability in the standardization that had not been possible during the prior epoch. It was at the beginning of this epoch that retrospection of the AEEC Goldfish Bowl deliberative process was induced by a new forcing function that had never before been present: now the DOD was going through a similar period of austerity, with Congress beginning to apply mammoth pressure to save money. Several governmental advisers began to take some hard looks at DOD expenditures for avionics (avionics was now a large part of the new military aircraft costs, and thus its cost stood out). Everyone was comparing the quality, performance, and cost of U.S. Air Force avionics with that of the commercial airlines. Studies by several advisory committees to DOD, particularly the Defense Science Board, focused on what the airlines were accomplishing through the ARINC/AEEC endeavor. It seemed evident that USAF and the rest of DOD ought to have some of these accomplishments.

By 1972 the top management of DOD had decided that it should do it as AEEC did, and it made some important pronouncements that echoed throughout the industry that supplied DOD with its aircraft and avionics. By 1973 DOD's Institute for Defense Analyses (IDA) was deeply engaged in the question, and the AEEC chairman was asked to serve on the IDA Advisory Committee to help it understand what it was that AEEC did and how AEEC and its suppliers managed to accomplish so much for the airline community. It was that activity that convinced the AEEC chairman that we all needed a better understanding of *just what had happened* in the airlines during this quarter century that the AEEC/ARINC process had been under way. How *had* it all come about? What were the causative factors that had made the process so successful for the airlines worldwide while the DOD and other government agencies had been spending far more money than the airlines had on development, but with far less satisfactory results? It also became evident that DOD seemed intent upon applying the AEEC practices across the board to all kinds of odd procurements rather than just to avionics, for which I knew it would be successful. I had a problem. If DOD got carried away with its enthusiasm and tried the AEEC processes everywhere, it could flop horribly, and I would get the blame. Worse than that, DOD would probably forfeit the potential for improvement in some procurements for which the process most certainly could help immensely.

It was that worry that caused the AEEC chairman to start the ruminative process, with much of the conclusion documented in editorials and other articles. I began to discern the logical steps in what was now evident as a slow, ponderous, experimental process of finding *what should be done* and *how* it should be done, extending over a quarter of a century. Fortunately, I had a lot of records, and I had a long memory of the history inasmuch as I had been a part of most of it since the middle of Government Epoch II. This involvement in itself did not produce answers; I and almost everyone else who had been involved in the effort had always been too busy to philosophize over the consequences of what we were doing. It was the pressure of having to explain it to our DOD friends in the early and mid-1970s that caused the ruminative process. Eventually I had a better understanding of the process that we had gone through as an entire industry.

That is the story of an industry's experience of some 38 years of experimenting in avionics development. The first several decades were spent mostly in experimenting without fully tapping the gold mine that lay in wait. Then the AEEC discovered the technique of the Goldfish Bowl and spent the last decade in fine-tuning the process and publicizing its success as an iterative step in getting even more benefits from it. Today, no one need spend decades hunting for the goldmine in the quicksands of futility; anyone who wants some improvement in this kind of product standardization and in the better decision-making processes that are a prerequisite and were a fallout of the experimentation can study a real-life example that is a known success. ARINC's AEEC is that example. The decision-making "how to do it" is a thirty-three-chapter book that points out the quagmires to watch out for and the methodology that is known to work for AEEC. Though chairing such a

Goldfish Bowl industry conference is not for amateurs, or beginning parliamentarians, or the weak in heart, it is something that can be learned and developed and improved with care and thought and study.

The short Chapter 15 in this text cannot do justice to the total findings on product standardization that were the consequence of that introspection. Further details of the process would be applicable primarily to the technical aspects of the standardization process, and those matters are outside the scope of this text. In this appendix I can only recount the epochs that I can identify clearly in our own industry. Whether the total process, as AEEC has discovered it, can be applicable to product standardization in all other industries or to other forms of standardization I cannot state exactly. Still, there are some important precepts that I am quite certain do apply to almost any kind of product standardization, and these are given briefly in Chapter 15 to outline the proper place to start.

Here I shall examine the historical origin of the term "Goldfish Bowl", as defined in the Author's Preface, and its application to a procedural methodology for consensus development in a deliberative-conference environment.

It was some years ago that lawyers with several of the large manufacturers began to ask me questions about the meetings I arranged that their people were attending, meetings where decisions were being made in the presence of other manufacturers and many customers. Back in the olden days the meetings of the Airlines Electronic Engineering Committee had been so small and so unimportant that nobody was concerned. But times had changed; now the whole avionics community was meeting *together*, searching for a common consensus, and finding it. Although the specs that resulted had no teeth in them (nobody was required to conform to them, and the specs even used words like "should" and "ought to" rather than "shall" and "must"), the mere fact of so many organizations getting together under one roof caused some eyebrow raising. The consequence was that our corporate legal counsel, Charles R. Cutler of Kirkland & Ellis, decided to be present at every major meeting so that he could answer any questions that might arise from other lawyers on what transpired at a particular meeting. It was after his participation in the meetings that Charles Cutler used the term "Goldfish Bowl" to describe what he believed to be an important attribute of such an activity: an operation carefully and properly conducted out in the open so that all could see that competition was being enhanced rather than being restrained and that decisions were being made in the best interest of customers and suppliers. A coordination activity is better if it is open, and this applies both to industry and to government. Chapters 19 and 20 emphasize the new look in the United States government now that it also has discovered the word "open." If

A.2

Historical Origin of the Term "Goldfish Bowl" as Applied to Deliberative Conferences

your trade association meetings are still closed as tight as a drum, perhaps you should take a new look; perhaps you need a little sunlight to improve your effectivity as we improved ours.

For the record, the first documented reference to the term "Goldfish Bowl" occurred on the occasion of announcing the twentieth-anniversary general session of the Airlines Electronic Engineering Committee in the May 14, 1969, issue of the AEEC house organ, *Aero Line* ®. The "Chairman's Corner" column in that issue contained the following explanation of the term:

> Even though AEEC obtains boundless assistance from the avionics and airframe manufacturers and from airlines and other industry organizations, the responsibility for final decisions remains with the fifteen voting members [number increased later]. Their deliberations are subject to the observation, comment, and criticism of some three hundred spectators who have almost complete freedom of speech! This method of conducting AEEC business at the General Session is known as the "Goldfish Bowl" mode of operation. Its evolution from the original method of generating specs (as done about thirty years ago) makes an interesting story in itself and appears elsewhere in this issue.

The foregoing was supplemented by a short summary of AEEC history (see Chapter 1) elsewhere in that issue of *Aero Line* ®. It started out this way:

> The Chairman, from his front-page corner, proclaims and designates AEEC's mode of operation as "Goldfish Bowl." The term refers to the open and unrestrained manner of conducting the business of the Sessions, wherein the principal participants, the airline representatives and other AEEC members, state their views and opinions from their stations at a central group of tables. They are surrounded by manufacturers, government representatives (U.S. and foreign), press representatives, and interested observers.

That article gave some early history and concluded with these words:

> The final chapter in this epic was not written by directive, but was the result of natural evolution. Manufacturers and their customers were given the unparalleled opportunity to state their needs. Thus, since about 1953, the principles of free enterprise, unrestricted competition, and wholesome cooperation have made AEEC's General Sessions deserving of the "Goldfish Bowl" title they carry today.

Index